PERFORMATIVE CIRCUMSTANCES FROM THE AVANT GARDE TO RAMLILA

PERFORMATIVE CIRCUMSTANCES

CIRCUMSTANCES

FROM THE AVANT GARDE
TO RAMLILA

RICHARD SCHECHNER

SEAGULL BOOKS

CALCUTTA 1983

Sponsored by

DUNCANS AGRO INDUSTRIES LTD.

SEAGULL BOOKS
A Publishing Programme for the
arts and media scene in India

Cover design by Ashit Paul
Ramlila mask from the
collection of Natya Shodh Sansthan
(Theatre Research Archives), Calcutta

Published by Naveen Kishore, Seagull Books
26 Circus Avenue, Calcutta 700017

Printed in India by P. K. Ghosh at Eastend Printers
3 Dr Suresh Sarkar Road, Calcutta 700014

Welcome to India, Carol

Contents

Thanking People

A book like this which mixes styles, years, subjects, and experiences owes so much to so many people and institutions. I can't really thank everyone because I don't know everyone who deserves thanks. I want to mention a few though: Porter McCray and the JDR 3rd Fund (now the Asian Cultural Council) who made my first trip to India, and other parts of Asia, possible; the John Simon Guggenheim Memorial Foundation which supported my work in 1976; the Fulbright program which sent me to India in 1976 and 1982–3; the Indo-American Fellowship program who supported my research into Ramlila in 1978; the Social Science Research Council who supported my Ramlila work in 1982; the members of The Performance Group who went with me to India in 1976.

I want to thank David Oppenheim, Dean of NYU's Tisch School of the Arts, where I have taught since 1967: my home base.

Special thanks to Carol Martin who helped me with several writings.

Special thanks to Victor and Edie Turner with whom I have had many good talks concerning anthropology and performance.

Special thanks to Lita Osmundsen and the Wenner-Gren Foundation for Anthropological Research whose conferences in 1977 and 1982 on performance have so strongly affected my thinking.

And thanks to many Indian colleagues who have been my teachers, hosts, and guides—especially to Suresh Awasthi, Shyamanand Jalan, E. Alkazi, and Kedar Nath Sahoo.

Acknowledgements

These writings appeared in various journals and books over the years. As they appear some have been slightly revised. I wish to acknowledge the following with whose permission the material published here appears: 'Environmental Theatre: Space', from *Environmental Theatre*, New York: Hawthorn Books, 1973; 'Performers and Spectators Transported and Transformed', *Kenyon Review*, 1981; 'From Ritual to

Theatre and Back', from *Essays on Performance Theory*, New York: Drama Book Specialists, Publishers, 1976; 'Restoration of Behaviour', *Studies in Visual Communication*, 1981; 'Letter from Calcutta', *Salmagundi*, 1974; 'The Performance Group in India' and 'Ramlila: An Introduction', *Quarterly Journal* of the National Centre for the Performing Arts, Bombay, 1976, 1982; 'Performance Spaces: Ramlila and Yaqui Easter', Wenner-Gren Foundation for Anthropological Research, unpublished; 'The Crash of Performative Circumstances', *TriQuarterly*, 1981.

I also wish to acknowledge that several of the essays first appeared in *The Drama Review* and were later incorporated into *Environmental Theatre* and *Essays on Performance Theory*. Several of the essays included in this volume will also appear in collections of mine to be published by the University of Pennsylvania Press and by Performing Arts Journal Press whose permission to include these essays here I gratefully acknowledge.

Briefly, as an Introduction

Right now, 28 July 1982, New York City is a lot like Calcutta. Outside my window a thunderstorm is booming. The streets are flooded, traffic wallowing and bellowing. Heat, humidity, noise, lassitude: the monsoon as I remember it from July 1976 when I lived in Calcutta. New York, like the Indian metropolis, pushes the very poor up against the very rich, sometimes with violent results. New York, these days, has thousands of 'street people' whose only residence is a railway station, a subway train, a doorway, a strip of sidewalk. Yet at the same time I feel New York disintegrating I also see her being rebuilt. On the block that I live alone two buildings are being reconstructed. Everywhere new shops open, restaurants are crowded.

Today or tomorrow I'll mail the last of this book to Calcutta where it will be published. I am happy about having my work come out in India. India is my second home, my 'culture of choice'. Since 1971 I've been to India three times, and by the time this book appears I will be back again. I expect that my sojourns to India will never cease. I've seen many kinds of Indian performance—Ramlila, Raslila, Kathakali, Chhau, Jatra, Kutiattam, Teyyam, Yakshagana, Bharata-natyam, Kathak, Odissi. I've heard different kinds of Indian music, seen the modern theatre, the circus, street performers . . . and the trains, the temples, the chawks. Often India has offered herself to me as a special kind of performance. Performance, not just theatre. Performance is a wide range of activities—from theatre and dance to sports, from entertainment to ritual and healing, from children playing make-believe to the *swarupas* of Ramlila incorporating in their very bodies the steadfast beliefs of millions who are both spectators and worshippers. Thus, among other things, this book is a response to India's varieties of performance.

Not only India, of course. I look for performances wherever they occur—and I like to travel and observe. This book includes writings of mine that go back about ten years. Some stuff is very recent. Much of it is restless and happily inconclusive. The material can be divided into three categories: essays written for theatre workers, essays written about 'performance theory', and essays dealing with particular events. The concerns in each of these categories overlap each other. I have long argued that scholars ought to be doers, doers ought to know history and theory, and theorists ought to experiment in the actual theatre. At bottom, I am a man who works in theatre; sometimes this work eventuates as productions, sometimes as theory, sometimes as description.

As far as the particular ideas expressed in this book, I prefer not to summarize them. Let my writings speak for themselves. I want to advance, and renew, the dialogue I have enjoyed with so many Indian colleagues. Nothing I have said is the last word. May there not be a last word now.

R.S.

I

A Letter from Calcutta

First Day

Our airplane is late from New Delhi. Before taking off at 10:15 p.m.
our luggage is thoroughly searched and we are bodyfrisked. Tension
along the borders with Pakistan is high. I fantasy being attacked in
the air. On board we have a choice between regular and vegetarian
supper. Dum Dum Airport is beyond the north side of town. The
domestic arrivals building is a one storey green and white wood shed.
The air is moist, heavy, hot. I can't avoid thinking of film versions of
British colonial types—and spies like Sidney Greenstreet sweating in
the midnight heat. Joan convinces me that we should not wait for the
Indian Airlines bus but taxi to town. As usual I am torn between
wishing to be 'just like the others' and feeling the need to be treated
like a tourist. I am humiliated by our Calcutta address: the Oberoi
Grand, a 'hotel in the old tradition at the centre of town'. Our cabbie
charges us Rs 14 and we check in. I brush my teeth with bottled water.
Before coming to Calcutta I'd read about cholera here. Our doctor in
New York told us that Dacca in East Pakistan (soon to become Bangla
Desh in my developing geography) is 'the only place in the world
where cholera has never been gotten under control'. We are not
satisfied with our room, which is on the second floor and looks like a
rehearsal set for a Bette Davis movie—replete with curtained dividers
between rooms and cold marble floor. Just after we unpack, the desk
calls and tells us another, 'more satisfactory' room is available. We
move. The second room is identical to the first.

Second Day

On the way to the street I look out the Grand's window onto its
courtyard. A big, gleaming pool surrounded by palms and deck
chairs. Empty except for one European stretched out in a chair,
wearing bathing trunks, reading. 'European' is the word here for
whites. In a way it is a very comfortable word for me. It avoids
identifying me as an American. Although it is true that Americans are
more popular in India than the American Government, our govern-

ment's support of Pakistan is incomprehensible to those Indians who concern themselves with international politics. There are many of these, even among the very poor. We leave the hotel for the first time around noon. We go out into Chowringhee, the Main Street. It is crowded. I have not gone five steps when a young man sidles up to me and says, 'Change money? Marijuana? Acid? Hashish?' He is very persistent, following Joan and me for more than two blocks, whispering into my ear like a tempting angel. He wants me to come to his shop. I demur. Finally, at the edge of his territory, he gives me his card. 'You come, yes?' I mumble something like an agreement. It is stupid being foreign.

Coming in last night from Dum Dum there were thousands of people sleeping by the side of the road. Sacks and piles of people. The 'luxury' Grand is coming apart—faded paint, leaky bathtub, rooms of abysmal colonial architecture and design. But soon it is clear that the hotel is doing what it can to keep itself together. When Joan and I dine on eggs and toast, juice and coffee we are alone in the dining room. Later friends tell us that tourists no longer come to Calcutta. 'At best it is a transit stop.' In New Delhi a couple of British hippies taunted us for going to Calcutta. 'You want to step on corpses, huh?' They suggested Benares. 'It's beautiful, man, all the pilgrims bathing in the river.'

The streets left us curious and in shock. Everyone who was asleep is awake. More people than I can hope to describe. People everywhere: shoving through the sidewalks, in the streets, in shops, in stalls and lean-tos lining the streets. Calcutta is an outdoors city, just as New York is an indoors city. In the streets of Calcutta every kind of living, and dying, goes on. The beggars, the hungry, the con-men, the rickshaws, the cabbies, the hucksters, the stall-keepers selling thousands of items like pens, candies, clothes of all kinds, sandals, nuts, rice, pots, dishes, wire—an endless inventory of things that in themselves contribute little to the sustenance of life. That is a strong impression: the business of irrelevant things which clog the streets, eyes, ears, and spirits of those going to and fro in Calcutta. One toy among hundreds impressed me with its allegorical precision. It is a toy in two figures—usually wrestlers but sometimes lovers. Through the use of magnets these figures struggle with each other—approach, flee, somersault, embrace, release—never resting.

The most pathetic sight are not children begging. There is even some humour in that. The children pursue you, tag your clothes, keep their deep eyes focused on you, smile incessantly, call you 'aunty' or 'uncle' or 'mama'. They follow to the limits of some defined territory and then suddenly turn back with or without their reward of a few paise. We gave and withheld arbitrarily, always embarrassed by our wealth which was obvious in our clothes (blue jeans, shirts, shoes) and our apparent well-fedness. We never found the proper solution to the Viridiana dilemma: how to discharge our obligations to hungry fellow humans by distributing a few pennies. Such street charities are hopeless, and more substantial contributions beyond our means. 'Yes,' one of our Indian hostesses said, 'the time comes quickly when we just step over the dying.' The most pathetic sight are those nearly dead. Lumps of burlap collapsed in the fierce sun. Unmoving. These people are ignored by everyone. They have gone over the line separating the living and the dead. They make no demands.

Thus we made our way during our first Calcutta day, stepping over the dying in fact as one does in consciousness of them, relegating these people to empty places where they perish in the void. But despite all that the strongest initial impression of Calcutta is of life, of indomitable, endless, deep, insistent, surging life. With that sense as support we went to see a much-praised local adaptation of Brecht's *Threepenny Opera*. We were late and saw only the last act-and-a-half. That was more than enough. After the streets the theatre was dry and shallow. After the final curtain we were taken to meet the play's director. He told me that his next production was *Arsenic and Old Lace*. 'We need some comic relief,' he said. Of course.

Third Day

Someone just stole my Cross Pen—12 carat gold-filled. Joan gave it to me for my birthday. We were approaching the hotel and I was thinking that while I was in Calcutta I should get a cheap pen. A beggar with twisted legs walking on wooden cups fitted over his knees came by. Joan said, as she saw him, 'Oh, Richard,' and grabbed my arm. As I turned to see the man I felt the 'click' of my pen being taken from my shirt pocket. I turned immediately but there were only a sea of people. I caught the glance of one man, and he returned my look, but I'm not sure whether or not he was the thief. I think that maybe the pickpocket and the beggar were working together, shades of *Threepenny*. It was a brazen and skilful job of pickpocketing. The hand getting the pen without touching me, just a 'click' and a twitch on my shirt like a small fish biting. I moralize that maybe the pen will keep someone eating. I am angry at losing a gold thing I cherish.

Around 2 p.m. I am sitting next to a sleeping Indian street person in the Lalbazar section. This is a section of north-central Calcutta devoted to small shops and made of many narrow streets. We have been walking here since noon. I am writing with my new Rs 2 pen. The streets in Lalbazar are not as medieval, crooked, and narrow as in Old Delhi. Calcutta is a new city, invented by the British to facilitate the East India trade. It has recently been inundated by three gigantic waves of immigrant-refugees. The first from the partition of the sub-continent into India and Pakistan (part of Britain's colonial habit of divide and control), the second during the Indo-Pak war of 1965 and the subsequent disturbances, and the third—and largest—since the 25 March 1971 assault by West Pak troops on Bangla Desh. This last genocidal attack—whose fury has hardly abated since it began—has squeezed more than 10 million persons into West Bengal, many of them into Calcutta and the camps surrounding. 10 million people— the world's second most populous city—added to the nearly 5 million refugees from earlier disturbances. Lalbazar streets are crowded, then, not because they were made small but because no street system in the world can handle the overfeed forced into Calcutta. Lalbazar is teeming with life. The insect analogy forces itself on me. The speed with which people move, scurrying through the streets, surging into alleys, trotting, walking, carrying bundles on their heads, on balance poles across the shoulders, pulling large barrows loaded with grain sacks, or iron bars, or anything, pushing carts, pedalling bicycle barrows—the means of locomotion and bearing-of-goods has reached ultimate development here. We wonder—who buys all these things? A whole street of shops selling and repairing watches, another of spoons, and another of wicker baskets. The thousands of shops mostly sell small items at a cheap price. Scattered among these shops are some medium industries like welding, gasoline and diesel motors, scrap iron, and so on.

The strongest impressions are on the nose and ears. The music of Calcutta's streets delights me. Everyone who has a horn or a bell sounds it. The traffic weaves like a perpetual dance. In the centre are the motor vehicles sounding their horns like cow calls. Then the motor bikes and three-wheeled cars. Then lanes of bicycles, rickshaws, pedal carts, cows and pedestrians. Each with bells, calls, screams, talk. All the shops open onto the street, and most of the business is transacted there. We found few open markets as in Mexico. In Calcutta the markets stretch along the streets with few open places. The sounds crescendo and descrescendo according to the intensity of the traffic. The slightest argument gathers a crowd. Every gesture is public and the larger the audience the more articulate and histrionic the show. The smells come from cowdung, piss, spices, exhaust fumes, vegetables, oils and perfumes (the Calcuttans love these), and simply the great density of people.

Surprisingly in Lalbazar the poverty is actual but it no longer disturbs me. Truly there are so many people it is hard to focus on the plight of this or that individual. If it were not for my fear of cholera and dysentery I would eat—the piles of nuts, oranges, mangoes, and coconuts look delicious. As it is we stop only for coca-cola, the *lingua franca* of 'safe' beverages.

Near me in a small alcove two persons are having an argument. A barber with a straight razor is shaving a client and shouting at him too. A third man, standing over the others, joins loudly in the dispute. The barber gestures with his razor. The client, his face half covered with shaving cream, rises. The man standing, sensing the gathering audience, speaks more forcefully, almost singing as his voice changes from tenor to soprano with streaks of coloratura. His eyes flash and he speaks directly to the spectators. As he approaches them they fall back. This is not to be a participation piece. A second crowd begins to accumulate around Joan and me. We are writing in our notebooks and we are European. These two facts are enough to make of us a spectacle.

I look out into the street and see a woman who seems incapable of maintaining her own life so thin are her bones and flesh nursing an infant. An old man dozes, sucking in on what appears to be an opium pipe. Two young men come in and join us on our ledge in the alcove, shoving a third man who is sleeping on the ledge back against the wall. Thus there are five of us together in this niche, and around us maybe fifteen people, mostly children, watching. Whenever a crowd gathers around me I feel uneasy. I believe this collecting of people-energy is the prelude to attack. We have heard so many stories of Calcutta violence, of the terrorism of the Naxalites who are extreme Leftists devoted to ritual murder, advocates of 'instant revolution'. They have been suppressed recently, but the memory of 4,000 murders in little more than a year is present all around. Our friends assure us that we are safe. 'The Naxalites are after Indians, not Americans.'

Scant comfort. I put away my pen and break through the small crowd into the streets of Lalbazar.

An hour later, quite by accident, we are drifting, we find ourselves on an incredible street. I do not know its proper name. We dubbed it Meat Street. It was the smallest, poorest street we have seen in Calcutta. Here animals—primarily goats but cows too—are slaughtered and their meat displayed and sold. Along the sides of the narrow roadway goat and cow hides are piled for transport elsewhere. Gunny sacks loaded with goat heads stripped of flesh so that through the holes in the sacks wild grins appear and from the open sack-ends tumble grimacing goat heads and bloody skulls. Displayed on butcher stands are some of these heads, with faces turned away from the street so that customers see only the severed spinal column, some coagulated gore, and the skin rising to the ears. Large slabs and sides of meat hang from hooks. The meat is covered with flies. Customers squeeze and stroke the flesh, testing it as our ladies squeeze tomatoes at the Grand Union. Squatting in the roadway are old women, their haunches tucked so far under them that they seem to have tails between their legs. In front of these old, silent women are some bare cupfuls of rice. No more than a few spoons worth. And next to the women a few young boys displaying ten peanuts or so for sale. On this street no one approaches us for alms. In the alleys, lying in mud, are many people. The houses of Meat Street are typical Calcutta houses, but in a late stage of decay. Yellow stucco two and three storey structures with alcoves and terraces and interior courtyards. The street is not paved and the alleys are thick with gooey, gray mud made from dirt, excrement, rain, and urine mixed with the blood of the slaughtered animals of Meat Street.

The smells are overwhelming. They claw at my nostrils. Clearly dominant is the smell of decaying flesh. I have infrequently smelled that stink. Once when a rat died in my New Orleans apartment and I found its partially decomposed carcass. This sharp smell fills the air, and joins with that of human and cow piss and the smell of wood, charcoal, and burning dung. There are many small fires on Meat Street. These burn in the gutter, in the alleys, in pails over which people boil rice and stew. In Calcutta the air smells cooked.

The sight of so much meat is strange. More than half the population, we are told, are vegetarians. But cows are slaughtered and most restaurants serve at least lamb. The cows themselves wander everywhere. They slowly cross the busiest streets or languidly sleep in intersections. They raise their tails and drop their dung plops which are then sometimes gathered and dried and used for fertilizer or fuel. There are brown cows and white cows, black bullocks and brahmin bulls with huge humps. The cow is not sacred. She is ever present, patient, slow, gentle, enduring. She gives milk and people take care not to harm her. One of our hosts told us of an accident between auto and cow. 'Luckily the cow was not injured. The driver swerved to avoid her and smashed into a lightpost. He was hurt and his car was demolished.' I asked if the cow was 'sacred', an incarnation of the gods. 'Oh, yes, maybe, but that is not important. The cow gives milk. The cow is an animal, a thing of life.' Among 6 million persons of Calcutta there must be 200,000 cows at least. These 'things of life' are cherished. They eat refuse such as coconuts emptied of their water, leaves, discarded bananas, and grass. Most of the cows are owned by someone, although without brands or collars I did not know how ownership was tracked. In the midst of the hurry of Calcutta the cows are an element of slowness. Nothing, neither police nor truck, nor screaming cowherder, nor vast crowds, seems to hurry the cows. They move one step at a time. They keep their own rhythms.

Fourth Day

I will go back towards the beginning and tell of some people we met. They were very kind to us. Without them we would have either sunk into Calcutta hopelessly, or remained chained to our hotel. We did not come to Calcutta anonymously or without preparation. We were armed with letters of introduction to theatre people from Mr E. Alkazi, director of the National Theatre School in New Delhi. Mr A. J. Gunawardana—the editor of the TDR special issue on Asian Theatre, himself a professor of theatre in Ceylon—wrote of our arrival to some of his friends in Calcutta, particularly Mr Amiya Dev, a teacher of English literature. On our first day in Calcutta we walked from the Grand through central Calcutta to the office of Shyamanand Jalan, solicitor and theatre director. We presented ourselves and the letter from Alkazi.

Jalan is a big man with an addiction to betel nuts. 'I used to smoke 50 cigarettes a day. This is better.' His teeth are stained red from the mixture of nuts and tobacco. Chewing betel slightly narcotized my tongue and made me feel warm in my belly. The nuts taste sweet, especially when mixed with essence of lime and tobacco. Jalan sat us in his office and spoke with us in English. 'I will arrange your stay here, yes?' Then he introduced us to his nephews and assistants. He made some phone calls. We wanted to get out of the Grand and Jalan found us lodging at the pleasant (and less expensive) New Kenilworth Hotel. He phoned a Mrs Agrawal. 'She is expecting you anytime today. She will arrange everything.' We had not yet got the knack of understanding Indian English. I trusted to my basic impulse of going where the currents took us. 'Fine, very good,' I said. We set out for Mrs Agrawal's in a car driven by Pramod Shroff. 'My uncle Jalan is training me to be an advocate so that he can put all his time into theatre,' Pramod told us.

We came to Mrs Agrawal's apartment house. The tallest one on Lower Circular Road. We went up the lift to the seventh floor where Mrs Agrawal—a spacious and charming woman—welcomed us into her house. We took off our shoes. She ordered a servant to bring us tea and sandwiches. This was very different from Meat Street. Out from Mrs Agrawal's apartment windows one could see three spectacular views of Calcutta. The city is not crowded with skyscrapers. There are four or five buildings over 15 storeys. So from Mrs Agrawal's seven storey vantage we could see to the Howrah Bridge spanning the Ganges and to the Kalighat Temple in the south. Mrs Agrawal's husband owned 'several factories'. She herself was an actress and also was finishing a book on the relationship between idioms in Bengali and English. 'Do you know that "you're pulling my leg" means the same thing in Bengali as it does in English?'

We sat and talked for maybe 75 minutes. I began to appreciate the structure of Bengali theatre. There were the commercial theatres, 'just like Broadway', Mrs Agrawal said. There were the folk theatres, the traditional theatres such as Jatra. And there was the 'serious' theatre of involved groups like Jalan's and Agrawal's Anamika Theatre. These were amateur or semi-professional groups of 'modern theatres' that traced their style back to the drama introduced to India 200 years ago by the British. This 'serious theatre' held the commercial players in contempt and felt no real connection to the folk theatre. 'Folk forms are in the rural areas. We are from Calcutta. We have done Ibsen and Chekhov and have our own playwrights.' Mrs Agrawal made us a list of what she felt we should see. The 'serious theatre' rehearses for a couple of hours each night and performs mostly on weekends. Its audience—as its producers and actors—are exclusively middle class. Its theatres are almost all proscenium theatres. Its repertory—both Bengali and Western—derives from a 'good Eng-

lish public school' set of values. No question here of 'cultural colon-
ialism'. The Calcutta bourgeoisie originated with the British and are
proud of their 'modernism'. They are not eager to make contact
with Indian traditional theatre. 'Those forms have not changed
in 1000 years. What have they to say to me?' We agreed to Mrs
Agrawal's schedule which had us booked into 5 plays on Sunday. 'No
need to see all of each play,' she said. 'You won't understand the
language anyway.' And for Friday night we planned to travel about
25 miles to Ranaghat to see a 'modern Jatra' written and directed
by Utpal Dutt for a professional Jatra company.

Before that we went with Mrs Agrawal and Jalan to hear a lecture
by Dr Suresh Awasthi on Indian traditional theatre. A certain formidable argument was developing, one that is to be decisive to the future
of Indian theatre. Dr Awasthi—a fanatic of the best kind—is at the
centre of this argument because he believes that only through incorporating India's many and rich traditional theatres will the
'modern theatre' have a chance for survival here. Awasthi is a small,
birdlike man. He cocks his head to the side as he speaks. He turns
every conversation into a description of this or that traditional performance. He laughs loudly and is a good man for a joke, being warm
and attentive to others. He knows his subject—he spends much of his
time away from his office as Secretary of the National Academy of
Theatre in New Delhi. We caught him in Calcutta by accident as he
had just come from observing theatre in Orissa and was on his way
to Assam. He was glad to meet us—he knew of TDR. (Everywhere
I went it was as if the last three years of my life did not matter. I
was 'editor of TDR', no matter what I said. It was a bit like real-life
No Exit.)

We first saw Awasthi at a club on the second floor of a building off
Chowringhee where Awasthi was to give a talk. The whole floor was
covered with a huge white sheet. About 30 men and 5 women were
there—all in traditional Bengali dress. The men all in white, and
the women in saris of different colours. In Calcutta—as elsewhere—
men frequently wear western clothes during business hours and Indian
dress in the evenings. Jalan doffed his trousers and sports shirt for a
long white blouse and pajama pants. The gathering of men in white
flowing robes and shirts reminded me of nothing so much as a San-
hedrin of rabbis.

Dr Awasthi's lecture is in Hindustani, with brief summaries in
English for our benefit. It concerns elements of the Ramayana story

as it is acted in Assam. Later Awasthi told me that the same story is acted in variations from northern India down into Burma, Thailand, Indonesia, and Bali. It figures as a key motif in dance, drama, puppet and shadow plays. Awasthi kept regretting that we had not told him of our visit. 'I could have given you a calendar of ritual performances in every part of India. You could have travelled with me.' He left the next morning for Assam, but planned to return on Sunday to accompany us to the theatres.

After Awasthi's lecture, on the night of our fourth day, Amiya Dev takes us to the house of Joti and Mimi Datta. They live in South Calcutta. They are as different from Mrs Agrawal and Jalan as these are from the street people. Joti had, at one time, been a fiery radical, a journalist. He described the leader of the Naxalites as 'a poet, a visionary, and a madman—and a great master of the Bengali language.' With Dev, Joti edits a small literary journal. He speaks peculiar but flawless and highly imagistic English. He is a small man, and when, later, I embraced him I could feel his ribs sharply beneath his shirt. He took to me and wished to lecture me. We entered his house at about nine p.m. and left after midnight. Before our arrival the company there had been drinking brandy and talking.

Joti reviews for me the violent immediate history of Calcutta. He describes a Naxalite ritual murder. 'Four young boys surround their victim—perhaps a school teacher or a petty official. Two of the assassins have not killed before. They are to be initiated into the mysteries of blood. Two are experienced in this business. The victim is a "class enemy" of one kind or another. The assassins have nothing against him personally. The killing ceremony is an adaptation of ancient Bengali Tantras. It combines our deepest religious convictions with the immediacy of the "revolution". Chanting litanies the assassins slit the throat of their victim. The initiates are made to dip their hands in the blood. Revolutionary slogans are proclaimed. Much is made of the similarity between the vermilion of the Tantras and the red of blood and the Red of revolution. It is so easy,' Joti says, 'to believe in the immediacy of the revolution. If class warfare means the liquidation of the class enemies then why wait until the revolutionary party is in power? Why not begin at once, now, here on my own doorstep, by murdering my neighbour who is a bourgeois, or a government clerk?' Joti takes a deep breath. He is explaining the conversion of revolutionary rhetoric into direct action. I associate events of the Weathermen in America. It is a story of the children of the bourgeoisie intoxicated by their own bloody rhetoric and frustrated by a lack of party organization. Suddenly, it seems, their 'integrity' is on the line. The time for manifestoes is passed. The slogans demand immediate translation into action. Terrorism begins. But it is not tied to a party or a programme. It is, as Joti has it, 'the revolution of persons'. He says there were 4,000 such murders in less than two years. 'Among some of us a revulsion set in. Was this what revolution is about? Did these killings foster a new social order? Can such violence be justified for any end? I believe that the end is only as just as the means.' I sit across the bed from a man who has come around to Gandhi's views. He fixes me in his glance. He attacks me for being a 'politically active' man. I insist that I am not politically active. 'The intention is there,' Joti replies. He takes me to the roof of his house. He points out the stars. 'Two weeks ago Allen Ginsburg was here and we sat looking at the stars until dawn.'

As we walk towards the centre of Calcutta after leaving Joti's, Amiya tells me that Joti underwent a transformation during the Naxalite terror. 'He used to be cantankerous, sharp-tongued, and as radical in his demands as anyone. Now he has become guru-like, a proponent of "tend your own garden".' We agree, however, that much is unsettled in Joti. In him the contradictions of a certain wing of Calcutta intellectuals is focused. And I see in these contradictions a forecast of an American dilemma. The violence of intellectuals, students, poets, and the children of the bourgeoisie is inauthentic. It takes on a literary and pretty shape, like the Naxalite rituals. It strikes out at the leaves of oppression and leaves untouched the roots. I am troubled that Joti scornfully names me 'commissar'. I know I will see him again.

Fifth Day

I found my Cross pen but lacked the Rs 95 to ransom it from the display case of a stall keeper in New Market behind the Grand Hotel. When I tell Jalan the story he laughs at me. 'I know a man who gave the box office at a cinema a 100 Rupee note and asked for five 2-Rupee tickets. He got the tickets and waited for his change. He waited and waited and finally asked, "Where is my change?" The ticket seller said, "You have not paid for your tickets." Without hesitation, my friend reached into his pocket and gave the seller 10 more Rupees.' Jalan wanted me to go to the police. He instructed his nephew Ashok to fetch the police for me. I did not want to make a fuss. I said that I could not prove that the pen on display was mine—but that because of a special point I had put in I was reasonably certain that it was mine. (While buying a new ball point pen I had inspected the Cross.) I agreed to the plans made for recovering my pen. But Ashok was suddenly called from Calcutta to business 150 km away. For all I know my pen remains at New Market.

At night Jalan invites Joan and me to his room next to the offices of the Anamika. 'These are my vacation weeks,' he tells us. 'Instead of leaving Calcutta I leave home. I come here. I direct a play.' He explains how his family is a joint family—his father, his brothers and their wives and children, his nephews' wives and children. In all 18 family members, 5 servants, 2 maids, 2 drivers, and a cook in an 8 room house in north central Calcutta. 'My family is unusual for a joint family,' Jalan says. 'We are not merchants as most of them are. We are professionals, advocates and doctors.' Jalan asks me about the American theatre, especially the avant-garde. He has been to Europe and is extremely curious about America. Also he wants to know about Grotowski. We drink Johnny Walker Red Label, eat some food sent up, chew betel. Finally Jalan comes to the question pressing most heavily on him. 'How can a theatre be made by people who do not give their whole lives to it? No one in Calcutta is ready to give his whole life to theatre! Here theatre is from the amateurs!' I listen as Jalan talks for about an hour. He wants to give up his profession, but cannot afford it. He wants professional actors, but doesn't know where to find them. He wants to work with new forms but doesn't know how to learn them. He invites The Performance Group to come to India soon. 'I know a lot of businessmen from all over India. Our people have been in business for hundreds of years. We are the Jews of India. You come here and rehearse for 6 weeks and then you will tour India —not only the big centres but the villages too. You can do your own plays and a play with Bengali actors. Language is no problem. People know English. And with our actors I will work with you and we will produce plays in both languages!' Jalan gets excited and happy. And he is a convincing negotiator. He is confident when he manipulates money. He throws figures at me. I accept what he says—but I have no way of judging whether he is offering too little or too much. We agree that he will put it all in writing, at once, tomorrow.

Sixth Day

We leave the Grand and move into the New Kenilworth. Also at this hotel are headquarters of OXFAM and the Save the Children Fund, two

groups most active with the Bangla Desh refugees. The time has come
for a trip to the camps. My first request to Jalan upon meeting him
was that he help me arrange a trip to the Bangla Desh refugee camps.
These encircle Calcutta on two sides, forming a crescent from the
south-west to the north-east. Not all the refugees are in camps. At
least 3 million people live along the roads, or in villages, or with
friends and relations. (East Pakistan is linguistically and culturally
contiguous with Bengal. It is another of those 'divided' areas so
popular after World War II—a kind of 'slice the pie' approach to
international tension.) As of the 25th of September 1971 there were
935 camps holding an *official* total of 8,986,000 persons. Everyone
agrees that the unofficial or actual number of people in the camps is
closer to 10 millions. Estimates are that by March 1972 there will be
13 million people in camps. Westerners are accustomed to think such
figures only when appropriating money. To conceive of a refugee
population 30 per cent greater than all of New York City . . . how?

Each day Jalan promised to get me to some of the camps. But
nothing happened. I detected a reluctance on his part, and on the
part of everyone else I spoke to. The situation was too immense. 'To
go there? It would paralyse me. I would not find living possible
any longer,' a theatre director told me. 'As for the theatre? How could
I continue to do my work?' It is not a question of guilt as some
Germans may have felt when they discovered concentration camps in
their midst. The Indians are sympathetic to the refugees, and officials
and volunteers make life as tolerable as it can be under such circumstances. But the mass of humans there . . . it is simply too large to
be contemplated. (A week later, in Madras, I asked the daughter of
our host why she did not swim in the ocean. Fear of sharks? 'Oh, no,'
Shashi replied, 'the sea, it is too vast.') Nothing was done to get me to
the camps.

Seventh Day

It is Sunday. We are going to see theatre all day. What a grind!
Dr Awasthi is back from Assam and he picks us up in a car supplied
by a wealthy industrialist, Bishu Sureka. (Later I got to think of him
as a 'nice rich man'.) The first play is by Badal Sircar. It concerns the
labour movement which is controlled by the middle class. What is
interesting about the play are its elements of song, Jatra, and audience
contact.

Next we speed across town to north Calcutta, the working class
sector, to lunch with the director of *Threepenny Opera*. First he takes us

on a tour of his theatre. It seems to be a very old and dilapidated theatre. I think that maybe it has been converted from movies to stage. Behind a cyclorama are stacks of stock flats. Above us is a fly space. It is a conventional theatre, and not a very good one. But the director is very proud of it. He is one of the few 'serious' people who have rented a theatre for the season. The owner of the building confides in me that he is losing money, but is glad to do it. He tells me that the building is barely three years old. After lunch we see most of the first act of *Threepenny*, which is much better than the last act which we saw several days back. The audience in north Calcutta is good. It is raining out and the audience reminds me of Sunday afternoon at the movies back home. Kids, mothers, men from the street. Tickets are cheap—from 1 to 10 rupees, and most of the cheap seats are filled. I do not understand why the portrayals of the beggars are so inadequate with so many actual examples on the streets to copy from. It is the same problem as the refugee camps. There are some things that cannot bear scrutiny. Remember *Uncle Tom's Cabin*? (Or *Guess Who's Coming to Dinner* for that matter.)

Dr Awasthi suggests that we be late for the second play. But it is not possible to be late enough. It is staged at a new private high school. The audience is richly middle class. I am in turn restless and sleepy. This audience and the play—about differing versions of a murder larded with banal observations concerning violence—are exactly what I want to destroy in the USA. The staging is routine textbook blocking and the acting is suited to the high school. I lean back and snooze. Joan nudges me each time I begin to snore. The next play is directed by Mrs Agrawal and our appearance there is a command performance. At that we are one act late. But two acts are plenty. The play is well done of its kind. Its kind is Ibsenite drama of personal anguish and murder. The play's title, *The Steel Frame*, refers to the privileged bureaucrat class that have perpetuated themselves since independence. This class was established by the British and they are British in every detail of their behaviour. The play concerns a medium-high official who has gotten his maidservant pregnant. He is not up to acknowledging his liaison and, in a rage, he strangles the girl. His co-bureaucrats cover up the case and convene a tribunal of their own. At the final curtain the culprit is left with a gun and told 'you know what you must do.' I knew what I had to do—find supper.

Instead Mrs Agrawal prevailed on Joan and me to stand on stage, along with Dr Awasthi and a dozen others in commemoration of the play's twenty-fifth performance. We were displayed and introduced to the audience who couldn't care less. I felt particularly uneasy because this kind of ceremony is so familiar to me from my own childhood. At no other time did I feel so keenly the amateur basis of 'serious theatre' in Calcutta. From *The Steel Frame* we zipped off in Sureka's car to see the final 20 minutes of a one-lady show tailored for Tripti Mitra, Calcutta's leading actress. She is superb, reminding me of Zoe Caldwell by the way she trills her voice, masters the tiny gesture, and brings her toes into the play—curling them and tucking them and dancing them. The play was pure vehicle—about an actress who can't decide what to do with her life and monologues her various crises. Ultimately she is offered a chance to perform again. She hesitates. (All the 'dialogue' is over the phone.) Then, when she wants to accept, she cannot remember the critical phone number. The curtain falls. We go backstage and I give Tripti Mitra the phone number. She laughs. She is much smaller than I thought her to be. Awasthi tells me she is nearly 50 years old. That knocks me out. She seems 30 on stage and 35 off.

'The Mitras are the closest thing the "serious theatre" has to professionals,' Dr Awasthi tells me as we drive to Sureka's for supper.

The after dinner talk is good. Dr Awasthi explains a folk theatre festival he saw in Assam. 'The whole thing takes place in a meadow 100 yards square. There are 21 groups each performing the same play simultaneously. The stages and audience are so arranged that the field looks like a giant lotus flower with 21 petals. The petals are the places for the performances and the space between the petals are where the audience stands.' I explain how The Performance Group stages its plays. Joan and Badal talk earnestly and she arranges a meeting with him. He is at the end of a certain phase of his life. He feels he must speak with us. 'It is important. No, it is necessary,' he says.

Eighth Day

Amiya told me that he had a friend who would take us to the camps. But when I got home from Sureka's there was a note from Amiya saying that his friend was not going. Amiya felt I would have no trouble getting to the camps. After all, two of the relief agencies were headquartered in our hotel. 'I believe in such coincidences,' Amiya's note signalled. I got up at 8 a.m. and visited OXFAM, the group from Oxford. Joan's stomach was a mess and she decided not to go. The OXFAM people told me that they could not possibly take me to the camps. They showed me a recent government announcement banning all foreigners from border areas except with permits. I knew it was hopeless to apply for a permit with only 3 days left in Calcutta. I cursed myself and thought that I too had fallen prey to the 'don't look' syndrome. I met a man from Save the Children but their truck had just left and he did not know when or if another was going. In despair I spilled my story to a French photographer in the New Kenilworth lobby. 'Oh, go see Father Fernandez at Caritas,' the Frenchman told me. 'They go out often. They will take you.' I had not heard of Caritas. But I rushed upstairs to Joan. 'I'm going to Caritas,' I said. 'If I'm not back in an hour I'll be on my way! See you this afternoon—at around three, I guess. Or if it's later I'll meet you here and we can go to the demonstration together.' We'd agreed to show our basic exercises to the actors at Anamika. The lecture-demonstration was scheduled for 6:30. After that we were invited to Joti Datta's for supper.

There is an undeniable excitement to catastrophe. A social adrenalin roughly equivalent to the private doses of that stimulating drug the body administers to itself in times of physical danger. I sat forward in the cab to Caritas. The headquarters at 4C Orient Road were unimposing. Several jeeps, a couple of trucks, an office of five ground-floor rooms. But Caritas was an impressive organization for medical help and food. At Salt Lakes—the largest camp—Caritas fed several thousand undernourished children daily, and distributed high protein bread to 36,000 people, and ran a hospital of several wards— TB, children's, obstetrics, general. Plans were under way for expanding their programme to feed 10,000 more children. Emphasis was always on the children—those precious organic bundles of future.

Father Fernandez greeted me. I told him I was a journalist. He said he would arrange for me to get to the Salt Lakes, but that I would have to wait. 'It is necessary here to travel on refugee time.' While sitting in the lounge reading the newspaper I reviewed my guilt feelings, my utter inadequacy, and prepared myself for I don't know what. TV has offered too many images of starvation and death. I came armed with preconceptions. I held Auschwitz and Biafra in my head. I pondered the statistics of Bangla Desh.

The Salt Lakes are out past north Calcutta. An extension of the city is planned for this area. Streets have been laid out, some central sewage installed, and much dumping of trash to fill in the salt marshes. Driving out the place looks funny because there are no houses, no street signs. Drivers get lost making their way to the camps. The only sure arrow is a line of people stretching 4 miles from north Calcutta to the camps. These are like a line of ants, or the picture of the people from Eisenstein's *Ivan the Terrible*, Part One. They go to and from Calcutta endlessly, day and night, bearing bundles, or nothing but themselves. There is no regulation keeping people in or out of the Salt Lakes camp. Each time our jeep lost its way we headed back towards that human string tying Calcutta to its sister metropolis.

Arriving at the camp trailing dozens of children. Something like stock footage of liberating Paris. Where are our Hershey bars? The camp is in a miserable setting. The ground is sand. There are no trees. The place stinks like Meat Street multiplied. The people live in hastily constructed bamboo and thatch barns. And there are so many people —300,000 at the very least in an area of 30 or so square city blocks. We force our way with honks through the crowds, forge a stream of sewage swelled by 3 days of cyclonic rain. (That storm killed about 10,000 persons in Orissa. Disaster here is as regular as rain. 'If it's not one thing it's another,' our Madras hostess said smiling. She is a good woman, with no touch of cynicism.) The Caritas headquarters in the field is a well scrubbed tent. At one end a table and several stools. Inside the tent about 20 blankets covered with plastic, each with a mother (or elder sibling) and child. The babies are being fed high protein gruel. 'It is hard to make them eat,' a Dutch sister and nurse tells me. 'They are not used to this kind of food. We have to bribe them to come at all with an orange or a banana.' A discussion immediately unfolds among an Indian doctor, the nurse, a German lady doctor, and the Indian chief administrator of the Caritas food programme. I am given a seat at the table, and some tea. I dare not drink the tea.

Later it turns out the people thought I was a doctor. Then a male nurse who would stay for a few weeks. Finally they understood I was an observer, a journalist, a more or less useless person. Still later they took me around to see what I could see. 'We need publicity,' a doctor told me. 'We need our story told in America.' An argument develops about bribing the children with fruit. 'Who is to pay for it?' the nurse asks. 'I have given my money. I have not been paid back. I have no more.' Shyly I slip her 100 rupees for bananas.

A refugee now working for Caritas takes me on a quick tour. 'I used to be a school teacher. The Paks came and shot up my village.' I peek inside a people barn. Each barn is divided into 12 × 24 foot sections. Usually there are about 5 families to each section—that is, about

2

25 people. Here they eat, sleep, and entertain themselves. The barns are smoky because fires are built inside to cook with and to keep warm at night. (To my New York ways the weather here is hot, but to the refugees it is near winter and cold at night.) It is not possible to convey the feeling of crowdedness. People are literally lying on top of each other. Some are playing cards, some dozing. Most are coughing. There is no sound of children's laughter. The children are mostly quiet. Outside the barns conditions are no better. The camp is pitched in a sandy, salt marsh. It is dank, fetid.

I go with the Caritas people to a place where new tents are being put up to feed 10,000 children. Sand. No trees. Hot. I sit on a bench to write. Children gather around and watch. I wonder what gesture of mine could transmit the feelings I have for them. I am uneasy when I look at them. But maybe I should not be. They look at me with very wide eyes. They stare and eat me up with their eyes. Their eyes are deep—as deep and black and bottomless as eyes can be. But warm also. A little girl with an ivory necklace, maybe 8 years old she is, takes me in and smiles. Then she turns shyly and seductively away. I begin a flirtation with her. She looks back, we smile at each other. She fingers her necklace. I notice that none of the other children are wearing jewelry. This is important evidence because these people love jewelry of ivory and gold. It is their family wealth. When they left East Pakistan they left naked. I look at a teenage boy who stares suspiciously at me. I say 'hello.' He does not reply.

The smell here is of decaying flesh. It is a probing smell that would make me vomit if I concentrated on it. The steadiest sound in camp is of coughing. 'Lots of pneumonia,' says a doctor. 'You see people have sent blankets but no cots. The refugees put the blankets on the wet ground. It is as if they had nothing. The pneumonia takes the old and the young. We need cots. Cots. Cots. Cots!' Out in the swamps people make their toilet, squatting and bathing in the same places. There is no choice. The Bengalis are fastidious people. But here there is no alternative to bathing in one's own excrement.

About 25 children press close to me. The girl with the ivory necklace is less shy. She flirts openly now. Some others smile. A boy says 'America'. Most stand and watch and cough into their hands. These people appear gentle. Rahman, an ex-engineer, and now an organizer for the Mukti Bahini rebels, tells me: 'These are the children of Bangla Desh. Why are they in camp?' He does not wait for my answer. 'How long did you fight for your independence?' I do not understand.

'How long! 7 years!' I compute the time from 1776 to 1783. 'On the night of 26 March the Pak soldiers shelled my town with 80 lb. shells. If we had air cover we could have struck back. We would be independent now. We had nothing but knives and sticks. What do you think?' I am silent. Rahman walks away. The children remain. I have nothing to say to them. I sit and write and look up at them. Now I have nothing to give them by my awareness.

The German doctor calls me to come back with her to the main Caritas tent. Then the Dutch nurse takes me on a tour of the children's ward. Rahman goes with us. 'We asked for independence and this is what we got.' The ward contains about 30 children, most suffering from acute malnutrition. The children of the concentration camps. The pictures we have become familiar with these past 25 years. The triangular, huge faces of bone with vast eyes, no longer expressing fear or hunger or sadness or anything except limitless distance. Eyes that move but neither smile nor weep. No expression on the face. We bend over a small boy, maybe 2 years old. He is no larger than 18 inches and weighs I don't know how little. His legs and arms are thinner than my Calcutta-made imitation Parker Ball Point. His stomach is bloated. His head is proportionately huge. Only his eyes and the tips of his fingers and toes move. His skin is yellowing and like old paper, the skin of the very oldest man this planet contains.

I recognize how much I have been trained by the movies and TV. Hearing the phrase 'children's hospital' I expect a place white and scrubbed, with toys, and beds made up with sheets, charts at the foot of the bed, some kids getting fed intravenously, and so on. Or, if I'm feeling perverse, I expect a kiddies version of *M*A*S*H*. This place beyond north Calcutta is neither. The little starving child could be saved with intravenous feeding, but there is no equipment available. There are only a few cots in the ward, and no sheets. Each child, usually with his or her mother, lays sprawled on a cot covered by a blanket covered with a clear plastic sheet. The plastic sheet is 'washed' when a child leaves. It is gone over with a damp cloth. But of course there is a water purification problem here. Missing from the ward are the usual sounds of children, even sick children. There is no talking or laughing. Not even much crying. What there is is lots of silence underlined by muffled coughing. Silence, wet, and the smell of life ending.

The Dutch nurse pinches the skin of the dying baby. 'This is a case of severe malnutrition. Carbohydrate and protein deficiency,' she says. (I wonder if she still thinks that I am a doctor.) She goes over to another child, nearly as gaunt. She picks up the child's foot. 'See how puffy and swollen the top of the foot is? That is a sign of protein deficiency. We can treat a case like this.' I ask about the little boy. 'When they get like that they won't eat, they won't take medicine. They just wait. I find children like that hard to treat.' Then she sees the mother of the child. Her tone changes. 'Yes, of course,' the nurse says to the mother, 'your boy will be all right.' We go away.

A doctor tells me that mortality in the Caritas children's hospital has been reduced greatly. There is some disagreement on the figures however. The doctor says that it is down to 3 or 4 a month. The nurse says it is down to 2 or 3 a day. But everyone agrees that the mortality outside the hospital—in the camp itself—is many times what it is in the hospital. 'How many doctors are there?' I ask. 'For our part of the camp there are four. We have a 260 "bed" hospital. We need 6 more doctors for a workable total of ten.' Caritas is responsible for around 15,000 children—which means a total population of around 25,000. I don't know how many doctors there are for the 300,000 at the Salt Lakes—but Caritas is very well organized. I would guess that the over-all doctor population ratio is about 1 to 50,000. In a community that is overcrowded, starving, and sick—almost to epidemic proportions, that is not an encouraging statistic. At the same time it is difficult to describe how hard it is to work at the camps. A tour of 6 weeks is about the limit.

The experience here is different than among the poor of Calcutta. Calcutta's poor have a place in the city—even if that place is just a rag on the sidewalk and the bare awareness of passersby. (Badal told how hooligans make a living by charging rent for sidewalk space— shades of Mafia 'insurance'.) Also, despite the poverty of Calcutta, malnutrition of the concentration camp kind is neither so widespread nor advanced as it is at the camps. Among the refugees *no one* is well fed. No question of 'balanced diet', but of survival. Everywhere one confronts the concentration camp look. The effect of this on relief morale is hard to calculate. Most volunteers work at the camps during the day and return to Calcutta at night. At first the camps were thought to be temporary. Now they are developing structures of permanence—schools, shops, social organization. One of the peculiarities of human life—one of its glories—is the persistence of life at whatever level and rhythm it finds itself. In the children's ward of the Caritas hospital there is no laughter. But in the roadways and people barns, swamp marshes and 'playgrounds' (barren lots marked off by barbed wire) children play tag, laugh, seem to enjoy themselves. Their parents are more glum, but not without some gaiety.

Rahman reminded me that there were two refugee problems—and you had to be careful about confusing them. The first is the camps—of making them livable, providing food, shelter, medicine, schooling, entertainment, and ultimately work for 10 million, maybe 15 million people. As of now there is little to do. People visit, walk back and forth to Calcutta, play cards, or, mostly, stand, squat, lay, or doze hours away. The Jesuit observed that 'idleness is dangerous'. I saw the camps as a very sullen circumstance, and explosive. The other problem is Bangla Desh and the Mukti Bahini. There is little evidence of political agitation and organization. Once, seeing a crowd, I expected some radical action. It was a bread line stirred to confusion and anger by delay. However, Rahman assured me that politics were active in the camps. 'We recruit for the Mukti Bahini here. We educate people.' Indian political groups are also agitating in the camps. Had I more time Rahman could have arranged a meeting with some Mukti Bahini at a cafe in Calcutta.

Around 2 p.m. a truck is leaving for another camp around 20 miles away. I jump aboard. Before getting to the camp we stop at a Mission School and Jesuit Seminary, which is the warehouse for the Caritas operation. We load the truck with sugar. Or rather workmen load the truck while the driver, two passengers, the German doctor, and I sit and talk. Next to us are around 300 cases of condensed milk. Each case has forty-eight 14 ounce cans of milk. The German lady doctor shrugs her shoulders in dismay. 'They won't drink it. Too thick. They don't like the way it tastes.' I ask why it isn't diluted in water. There is no answer. I ask again and then drop the question. A few moments later the doctor holds out a bottle of Beech-Nut Chicken Hi-Protein baby food. 'They won't eat this either. Afraid there is cow meat in it.' She is clearly angry. I can understand her side, but I can understand the refugees too. Cultural habits do not break easily. And in times of trouble religion is strengthened.

'There is problem with the bread too,' someone says. 'You see, these people are rice eaters. They do not like bread, they are not used to it. They don't appreciate the flavour of wheat. They take the loaves and break off pieces and roll it up into hard balls. Often they choke on the bread. They don't know how to eat it. So a large black market has grown up. People take their ration and sell it for a fraction's worth of rice, which is not high in protein. Or, even worse, they take the bread to Calcutta and sell it for a few paise and buy betel or tobacco with the money.' Also tensions have risen sharply in villages near the camps, and in Calcutta. The refugees work for less than half the going rate, which is barely subsistence. Villagers grow excited and there have been many beatings of refugees. The whole economy, which was just getting off the ground, has been upset. This is, of course, a national problem with so much hard money being spent on refugee relief, money that India could well use elsewhere. But the impact of the physical presence of the refugees is confined to the border areas. Here the traditional hospitality of the Indians has been strained to the breaking point.

'What if war?' I asked Rahman. 'It is inevitable, it is necessary.' 'What will happen to the refugees? They are on the border. They will be caught in a cross-fire.' 'Yes,' said Rahman, 'they will suffer. But there is no alternative to a free Bangla Desh.' A young Jesuit seminarian—an Indian—riding with us atop the 100 lb. sacks of sugar chimes in. 'War will help no one. In the camps there will be massacre.' Rahman asks the Jesuit where he is from. 'Bombay.' 'Of course,' replies Rahman. Then he turns to me. 'In the night of 26 March the Pak Army shells my village. I am separated from my wife and two daughters and my son. The next day I look but do not find them. Are they dead or alive?' We ride for a few minutes in silence. The seminarian says, 'These people have suffered incredibly. Remember the 1970 cyclone? That took nearly 500,000 lives. They do not smile, these people, though the Bengalis are generally a happy people. At the camp a woman will invite you to her hut and then weep because she has nothing to offer you except a few grains of rice.'

At Nilganj camp there are around 7500 people in an area of 4 or 5 city blocks. The people barns are roofed with black plastic stretched over thatch. It looks weird. Conditions here are worse than at Salt Lakes, but the place looks more like a village. In fact, it is an extension of a village—a packed crowd of people barns set just off the road. We arrive during distribution of bread. One medium sized loaf—less than a pound—is food for 5 people for a day. There is also some milk-sugar mix, but not much. Everyone must have a pink ration card to get food. There are many who don't have the card. Atop a hill of rubble is the special thatch hut of the camp Commander. We have been in camp five minutes when word is sent down for us to report. News of a foreigner spreads fast. On the hill we go through several cubicles before getting to the Commander. Sitting behind a desk, a few papers in front of him, he salutes me, half in greeting, half as a military gesture. 'Yes?' he asks. I tell him I am 'a friend of Caritas'. He confers in Bengali with Rahman. Then the Commander says, 'OK, fella.' Outside Rahman tells me that it is better if we leave quickly. As we haul onto our sugar truck someone points out two corpses by the side of the road—a woman and a child. 'Awaiting collection,' Rahman says.

On the way back to Salt Lakes we pass many open trucks filled with workers. These are amused to see a European riding in the back of a truck. I give them the Hindu salute (hands pressed together against the chest as in prayer) and they laugh loudly, returning the greeting. At Salt Lakes word has spread that I am writing a story. Volunteers crowd around me. They want their names mentioned. They want copies of what I write. There is Vernel Pereira and Piren Drosingh, Prosun Das and Benjamin Gomes. They pass my notebook around. 'Are you writing about me?' 'Not yet.' 'He's writing about you, uncle,' one of them says to an old man, one of my sugar truck companions. All day he has led me by my shirt sleeve, beckoned, always smiling, offering me cup after cup of scalding tea. He doesn't understand when I refuse. 'It is hot, hot, sweet!' The old man takes the notebook and laboriously enters his name. 'Send it care of my brother, the address is here!' He points. 'I am F. Saldanhe of Bombay and I am 72 years old.' He runs his biography—this is his moment on camera. '. . . retired now, I am with the Bread Distribution Centre, Caritas.' I ask him why a 72 year old man has come so many miles to help. 'I am still hale and strong enough, thank you!'

The truck broke down in the middle of north Calcutta. I was late for the lecture-demonstration at Anamika. I hopped from the truck, hailed a car that appeared to contain some upper-class folk, and asked them for a ride into town. After the camps north Calcutta seemed a placid suburb. The men who agreed to ride me to Anamika were businessmen. They had heard of Jalan and Mrs Agrawal. They took me straight to the theatre. People were already assembled. It was ten-past-six. 'Where's Joan?' Mrs Agrawal asked. I phoned her at the New Kenilworth. My temper was short. My head was muddled. 'I'll be right over,' Joan said. I went into the rehearsal room and faced around 25 theatre people. I began talking about our work. I felt empty and confused. I wanted to cry, to spill tears. Even as I spoke of 'association exercises,' and the need for 'whole body contact' I wondered what on earth this stuff had to do with what I'd seen at Salt Lakes.

After a while Joan arrived. Slowly I sank into the reality of our work together. It was something we *did*, it was concrete, and I loved doing it. I let myself go into it and passed through the waves of doubt and guilt. Joan began moving her body and singing. The Anamika people were enraptured. I was proud for Joan and admired her skills and artistry. I began to feel better as I watched her. Through her movements and sounds I started my way back. At the end of the demonstration I lay down next to my wife. I whispered 'thanks' into her ear. Then I said, 'I am not going to kiss you or touch you. I haven't washed.' At the end of the demonstration—after about 20 minutes of discussion relating our exercises to yoga, dramatic texts, and the 'serious' Calcutta theatre—Amiya arrived to conduct us to Joti Datta's for dinner. As we were leaving Badal approached us. 'Can I see you on Wednesday?'

Riding out to Joti's I tried to put the day's events together in my head. Waking up at the New Kenilworth and drinking coffee and orange juice, eating toast and marmalade. The Salt Lakes camp and the Nilganj camp. Showing the work of The Performance Group. What were the connections? All these things happened to me within the space of 10 hours. All were closely joined in physical distance. But I couldn't get it together.

Joti embraced me at his door. In his living room his father-in-law, whose name I forget but who I was told was one of India's best known poets, was holding forth. An eloquent man with eagle sharp features, long straight hair, a crooked set of teeth that made his consonants hiss urgently. A man in his fifties, or maybe sixty, who looked like no one so much as Antonin Artaud during his last years. This poet spoke of the Bengali language, and of English. 'I wish with all my might to see English perish from this continent,' he said. 'We have our own languages. Yet, I use English, I *enjoy* English.' Sitting around him in a courtly circle were an American couple (he works at the USIS) and Mimi's brother and some other Bengalis. Amiya kept going into the kitchen to work with Joti on dinner. This was the first, and only, house in India where we visited and there were no servants.

Dinner was of many courses, both meat and vegetables and a sweet yoghurt dessert. I ate but did not speak much. About half-an-hour after dinner I challenged the Old Man on some point about grammar.

He had been holding for a strict adherence to grammatical rules. 'But grammar is only an axis, a wick,' I said. 'Language forms itself around that wick, bends it, takes it in new directions.' Suddenly Joti exclaimed, 'That's it, Richard! Go after him! Give it to him, left and right!' Joti laughed very hard, and announced that there would be a swell argument soon. But the Old Man got up and said he had to leave. I was embarrassed and fell back into silence. The usis man announced that his car and driver would return in a half-hour and give everyone a ride home. I no longer felt a need to contest the Old Man. And he obviously wasn't looking for a fight. Joti was disappointed.

We slept late on Tuesday. Even after we got up I didn't want to go into the streets. I couldn't spill what I felt about the camps to Joan. It was locked inside me—kept in some kind of psychic spore to explode I don't know when. At around 11 o'clock Badal phoned. 'I am so happy you didn't go to Bolpur,' he said. 'Would it be too much to ask that I visit with you today?' His shyness and gentle politeness ineffectively concealed his urgency. 'Yes, yes, come as soon as you like.'

Of all the people we met in Calcutta, Badal Sircar is the most difficult for me to describe. That is because of the love I feel for him. I do not want to reduce him to a literary artifact. I see his large, nearly bald, bony head—a gaunt man in a society where few who can afford fatness scorn it. I see his mouth and smile, sudden, shy, hardly offered when it is threatened and suddenly guarded. I see his small but tightly-built, thin and excitable body. And then I don't see these things. Badal's physicality metamorphosized during our afternoon's talk. Replacing the come-and-go of a city-wise cat was something incredibly childlike and trusting, soft, vulnerable, and wishing to begin again, and again.

Badal is in a bind. He knows that the 'serious theatre' is derivative. 'But it is my tradition,' he says. 'It is wrong to think of Bengali folk tradition as belonging to those of us who live in the cities. We were brought up on the "modern theatre"—that theatre has been ours for nearly 200 years! We do not think of it as foreign. The folk theatre, that we think of as foreign.' But Badal knew that the 'modern theatre' of psychology, drama, the spoken word, the proscenium stage, the box set, and the separate audience was dead. Worse, it was rotting. 'But I cannot just reach into the Indian folk culture. You probably know more about that culture than I do. We were taught to despise it as old-fashioned and reactionary.' Tangled with these problems of the profession were Badal's personal crises as a man, as a writer. His plays had made him famous throughout India. They were translated into several of the 'mother tongues'. Formerly the City Planner of Calcutta, Badal gave up that career to accept a Nehru Fellowship. 'That will keep me eating for a while,' he said. 'After that, I don't know what.' In his early forties, he can no longer write and produce plays in the old style.

Like us he was unhinged, artistically adrift. Last year he went to East Europe, saw Grotowski's *Apocalypsis Cum Figuris*. 'I began writing a new play this Friday. Then I met the two of you. I stopped writing.' Badal turned to Joan. 'You have come here at the right moment for me,' he told her. I told him that we had come to India because we had also come to the end of a certain phase of our living. 'Don't feel that you are being selfish about us,' I said. 'We are just as selfish about you.'

The dark had come. It was past six. Amiya knocked. He had come to take us to Shambhu Mitra's *Oedipus Rex*. 'Come with us, Badal.' 'No, no. Tonight I meet with my group—it is called Satabdi, that means Century—and I will talk about Joan's demonstration at Anamika.' Suddenly Joan and I flashed the same idea. 'Let us do a demonstration for Satabdi! Can we?' 'Yes, yes. Will you really?' 'Tomorrow night. And first we can meet—just the three of us, and talk some more.' Badal was very pleased, as were we. 'We are friends,' Joan said.

Ninth Day

The rendezvous with Badal was set for 3 o'clock at the New Kenilworth. In the morning Joan and I set out for the South Side to see the Ganges and Kalighat Temple. Calcutta is named for Kali, it is the City of Kali. We took a tram marked Kalighat, but had no idea how to find the Temple. We got out at the end of the line and walked south and then west. Soon we were in a very poor neighbourhood. I grew frightened as people crowded round. Children shouted and teased. Teenagers made cat-calls. We started down one street and then turned back as it got narrower and more crowded with the poor. Then we walked through an ornate gate into a weed-filled garden. At the end of a pathway was a building which I thought was the Temple.

The building stood aside the Ganges. In an alcove an old man with long, tangled gray and black hair squatted. His eyes were very bright as they followed our approach. Squatting behind him was an old woman, toothless, very thin. With deft, bony fingers she plucked lice from his hair. Beyond them, in the river itself, a lone boy, maybe nine years old, naked, with a small beach pail. He waded into the river, filled his pail, came back to the Temple steps, poured the water over his head, laughed, and repeated the cycle. Around us the raspy racket of big crows. To my right was a small temple building. I took off my shoes and socks and went up on the porch. As I turned the corner facing the Ganges two men came up. They spoke in Bengali. They wanted money. I was afraid that they were going to rob me. I asked 'What for?' and they continued to press me for cash. I gave one of the men a rupee. He smiled and saluted and withdrew. The other man asked for money. I said no and fled. I was trembling.

Back in the streets we saw many people grooming each other. Nowhere else did we see people picking lice from each other's hair. We turned down a crowded street to the river again. Along both sides were many shops selling religious items. This must be the Temple, I thought. At the river there were maybe 40 people bathing, mostly children. A young girl cautiously descended the steps to the water. She held a bouquet consisting of flower petals. She walked into the river and threw the bouquet onto the water. Red and white petals made a meek S on the water and drifted first one way and then another. Across the river—maybe 60 feet—a raft was leaving dock, being punted across to a landing close by us. A pedlar offered us some religious artifacts. I declined. I turned to leave the river and saw the Temple rooftop, gracefully onion shaped, about 1/3 of a mile away. 'You know,' I said wonderingly to Joan, 'if we hadn't come to the river we wouldn't have found the Temple.'

The Temple is in two parts. A colonnaded porch open to air on three sides elevated 8 feet above the street, and the Temple proper: a small deep chamber filled with the enormous red-dyed statue of Kali. Only her shoulders and head peer above the deep alcove in which she sits, her sword bloody with the blood of a decapitated devil. I sat in the alcove, thought of Greece, looked at the men and women sitting cross-legged around me. Some of the men were reading old texts, I suppose in Sanskrit, and quietly chanting. Then I thought of synagogues, and the old Prague synagogue I visited in June, with its thick walls and handful of remnant, store-window Jews.

I feel uncomfortable among so many believers and I decide not to go through a brief ceremony that would bring me face to face with Kali. I leave the prayer porch, shoe up, and gesture to Joan that we are going when a young man says, 'This way, this way.' I take off my shoes as the man ushers me into a line culminating in a swift baptism. A priest pours a spoonful of water on my head. I wonder if I'll get cholera. I observe others and drop 50 paise into a tin plate. A man in English explains that Kali has cut off the devil's head. Then he asks, 'You've been Benares?' I remember the kids in Delhi and envision the Hippy Tour of Spiritual India.

Badal is early and we get to the university district of north Calcutta around 3:15. Marxist slogans—in English and Bengali—adorn the walls of all buildings. We turn down a side street, go up a flight of stairs, and enter a very noisy, very big coffee house. 'One of two coffee houses in Calcutta,' says Badal. The place is about 100 feet square with a 40 foot ceiling. Around all four walls at a height of about 20 feet is a balcony. Big fans slowly circulate the hot air. As we enter there is a wave of interest and many heads turn. Once again I am impressed with the swiftness and finality of the information system here. We have encountered few radios and TVs. This is still an oral culture. Badal tells us that 'this is a place where we can be quite alone. So many people, so much noise, it makes it private.'

It was dark when we began walking to Badal's home. He lives on Peary Row in a house built by his father some years ago. Calcutta streets in the early evening are like thousands of small naturalist stage sets clustered together. Many of the shops are lit by kerosene lanterns, and some by gasoline. The first light is soft, yellow, and fluttering. The basic colour of the shops is deep dry-thatch brown. Shopkeepers often live in their shops so there is an air of home as well as business. People relax on mattresses covered with white linen. (On entering every building it is custom to remove shoes or sandals. This habit pays sanitary as well as social dividends.) Business is combined with visiting, talking and dozing. But it is serious and there are frequent flare ups and incessant bargaining. Each of the small shops fronts around 8 feet and is about 7 feet deep. These proportions add to the feel of a stage with the fourth wall removed. And when closing time comes— between 8 and 10 p.m.—wooden or metal doors close or descend. The fourth wall is locked in place until the next morning.

Peary Row sounds English, as do many of Calcutta's streets, but it is pure Bengali. A small, crooked lane slanting inward from one of north Calcutta's main drags, Peary Row is jammed with people, cars, cattle, and bicycles. Badal's house is one of the better places. Here there is a difficulty of cross-cultural references. By American standards Badal lives in a 'lower-middle class' house of the kind found in 'ethnic neighbourhoods'. There are four rooms, a toilet (hole-in-the-floor variety) and a kitchen. On the walls of the living-room are pictures of Badal's father who built the house. The rooms are small, poorly lit, and there are cracks in the plaster. The furniture is too solid for comfort and more often than not the family sits on straw mats on the floor. Street noises pour into the house through closed shutters. Overhead fans make the air stir comfortably. The over-all impression is of homeyness without show. An old-fashioned house, utterly unlike Sureka's American Mod Town House.

By the time we get home there are around 15 people gathered in the living room, which is also the rehearsal room. (Badal lives with his wife, three children, mother, and unmarried sister.) Badal's group are mostly young men between 18 and 25. There are a few older, and about 5 women. Joan goes into the next room to change into her leotards. Meanwhile people pour in until the small room is jammed with 30 some. Amiya arrives. I am very happy that he is here. Badal opens the door to the dining room and all the living room furniture is carried out. A few more people sit in the dining room and peer through the door jamb. Joan returns and we begin our demonstration.

I explain how the theatre uses at least four languages—verbal, body, musical, and contact. That our demonstration will illustrate body language and contact language, with some reference to music. This is all a set patter on my part. One of the reasons I came away from America was to write this patter out, and be finished with it. I look around the room at these Bengali actors. Most of them are not going to give their lives to the theatre. I recall Jalan's complaint. 'How can I make a theatre when no one will give themselves to it!' Jalan got an important phone call on Sunday night at Sureka's and he dropped out of sight, suddenly and with finality. An illustration of the dilemma he felt so sharply. Badal is up against the same thing. Going one step further than Jalan, Badal gave up his career as city planner. Now he is struggling almost alone. I stopped talking and asked Joan to begin what we do.

Tenth Day

We're due at Indian Airlines at 8:45 a.m. Our flight leaves Dum Dum for Madras at 10:45. We will take the free bus out. This awkward time of farewell. Amiya says, 'As soon as you see Madras you will hurry to return to Calcutta.' He pronounces the name of his city precisely, hitting the "Cs" and "Ts" very sharply. Badal says that he will visit us in Madras in December. 'My troupe goes to Hyderabad and from there I will come to Madras.' Amiya likewise. Now the people move to the bus. I embrace Amiya and embrace Badal. Suddenly I kiss Badal, not on the mouth but on the side of his neck. I realize that embracing is not very common among Bengalis. These people who live so close do not touch each other much. Joan and I climb aboard the bus.

2

The Performance Group in India
February-April 1976

There is a life rhythm to any group that presumes to the status of ensemble. At intervals it re-creates itself, or ends. The Performance Group (TPG) began in 1967, re-created itself in 1970, again in 1972, and again at this moment (summer–fall 1976). Re-creation isn't simply about people coming and going: people leave for reasons and join because they feel their careers and the Group's trajectory are moving in the same direction. In the winter of 1975 Timothy Shelton who played Eilif left TPG because he wanted to test himself in commercial theatre and because TPG didn't offer him the range of roles or the position within the Group that he needed. At the end of the India tour James Griffiths (the Cook) left because he wanted to work in a 'directorless' group in San Francisco. But even more basic shifts are taking place as long-time members of TPG create their own works separate from me, and we all re-construct relationships to each other. There is a long history of working together: MacIntosh and I have been at TPG since 1967; Borst joined in 1969 summer and Gray later that year; LeCompte and Griffiths joined in 1970, Clayburgh in 1972, Sack in 1973, and Vawter in 1974. Rayvid has worked with TPG since 1973 but became a 'provisional member' in 1975. Charney was taken on specifically for the India tour when Alexandra Ivanoff said she didn't want to make the trip.

The changes within TPG reached a critical stage during our India tour. Two rhythms interacted: (*i*) as individuals and as a theatre we met audiences, sponsors, and the multiplicity called India, itself undergoing stress and change during the Emergency; (*ii*) within each of us and as TPG we began to work through—by means of two sets of talks, one in Calcutta in March and one at Juhu Beach near Bombay right after the tour's end in April—our past relationships, present circumstances, future arrangements. There's no doubt that the high of the tour—we were praised even when our work fell short—mixed with its difficulties to bring on the crisis within TPG. It's hard to adjust to a strange culture when you're running around the country on a breakneck schedule needing to perform artistically and socially at every stop. More so when, as we wanted, we didn't get transplanted from one Western style hotel to another—but lived with families, in Indian style tourist bungalows and, as much as time allowed, interacted through workshops and meetings with Indian theatre people. So I'm writing not only a travel journal but an exposition of the group-making process as I see it manifesting itself under stress. I'll probe as deeply as I can how the tour worked on TPG: I'll make suggestions for future tours. But first I must review how *Mother Courage (MC)* was developed in New York, and how its preparation relates to TPG's over-all work.

Work on MC in New York

We began in April 1974, the same time we decided to come to India. All roles are cast from inside TPG. This in-looking leads to 'role clusters,' a chorus-like effect as different characters are played by the same performers and costumes carry over from one role to another. For examples, Borst and Griffiths play Recruiter and Sergeant in scene 1 and Lieutenant and Sergeant in scene 11; Gray and LeCompte play the peasants in scenes 5, 10, 11, 12; Gray and Shelton play Swiss Cheese and Eilif and the two soldiers in scene 6. The blue officer's coat is worn by Recruiter Poldi in scene 3, Clerk in scene 6, and Lieutenant; the khaki soldier's coat is worn by Sergeant in scene 1, Soldier in scenes 3 and 6, and Sergeant in scene 11. But necessity and chance also operate: only the Chaplain and Cook aren't in scene 1; when Shelton left TPG, Rayvid took the roles of soldier and peasant son, while Clayburgh took Eilif. Desire also counts: LeCompte wanted to play the General in scene 2—and this meshed with my wanting to show a woman in a role traditionally linked to male power. In costume she looked like South Vietnamese dictator Ki; this added parody to the role. Also everyone was musician, stagehand, supper-server, and reader of the introductions to scenes. Seeing the performer playing Eilif adjust the ropes, hearing the one playing (mute) Kattrin read the introduction to scene 2, or getting supper served by the person playing the Chaplain all help open conceptual spaces between performers and roles, dramatic narrative and theatrical environment. These methods, long a part of TPG's work, agree well with Brecht's *verfrumsdungeffekt*.

From April through June 1974 we worked upstairs at the Performing Garage in a space 40' by 25'. Our main theatre was full of the environment for Sam Shepard's *The Tooth of Crime* which we were performing four times a week. We worked on *MC* about 5 hours a day, four days a week. *Tooth* closed in June and we began teaching days at NYU—rehearsals of *MC* shifted to the 50′ by 35′ by 18′ (height) main theatre, and we worked four nights a week from 7 to 11 during July and half of August. Then we left on a tour of Europe with *Tooth*. (The summer was very full: part of the NYU work was developing the script of David Gaard's *The Marilyn Project* which opened 18 months later in December 1975.) During the six weeks' work on *MC*, Clayburgh and Jerry Rojo set up the basic environment: a 'wagon-store' area against the west wall, a bridge across the centre of the room (later demolished), galleries at two levels all around (adapted from *Tooth*), an open pit 6′ by 25′ by 8′ deep along the north wall. We decided to play several scenes outdoors on Wooster Street which runs along the east side of our theatre building. It wasn't until November 1974 that we rehearsed *MC* full time, five days a week, six or seven hours a day. It opened in February 1975.

After one read-through the performers were on their feet wrestling with the physical problems: what should the wagon be? how does Courage move? what props were essential? what sounds does Kattrin make? etc. etc. I don't believe in 'work around the table' or talk-analysis of characters: it all happens up against the problems of staging, and in constructing not just characterization but the entire world of the performance, including the roles of the spectators. I get the performers moving around, with someone feeding lines so the words are learned through the ear, as speech. I've seen the same technique used in Jatra rehearsals. Performers work from the situations of the play, improvising, testing moves, gestures, arrangements, readings. I select blocking and line-readings from what's offered—my job is like that of a sculptor building up and whittling down material already there. Everything is kept fluid for many weeks. But it's not a question of vagueness: one concrete solution yields to another in an exploratory sequence of experiments.

For example, at first the wagon was a costume trunk on wheels to which we attached ropes. After a week this was rejected, and with it the whole idea of a rolling wagon. Any wagon of appropriate size would dominate our theatre as a centre-piece environment like the one we already had for *Tooth*. A rolling wagon automatically referred us to Brecht's (and every other) *MC* production making it impossible to investigate the play in a totally new American way. Soon we began to use the idea of a 'store' anchored against the west end of our theatre.

But then the problem was how to physicalize pulling, trekking the roads, back-bending labour; how to show one person exploiting another through oppressive labour and the transformation of human beings into animals dragging a load. Rojo, Clayburgh, and I discussed pulleys, ropes, blocks-and-tackle. One afternoon in May, Clayburgh arrived with this stuff—and immediately the performers tested it. Shelton ran his feet bloody trying to pull free from MacIntosh's hold—but the pulley system gave her a three-to-one advantage: here was the physical expression of exploitation and one person's control over another. Clayburgh hitched the tackle to the wall and put Borst on the hook. The visual-sonic effect was stunning: leaning out at a 45 degree angle, running with all his might but getting nowhere, the tackle jangling behind him, the ropes rising and falling in rhythm with his strides: scene 7 was born. The equipment was flexible: ropes could divide the space any way; they could be strung at any angle; they could hoist, drop, pull, and hold. From that afternoon Clayburgh began working out in detail how the rope-and-pulley system would be used in each scene. With only slight modification this system was used in India exactly as in New York. And from the beginning in 1974 it was clear that everyone would help in scene shifts—these were to be an integral part of the performance.

Paul Dessau's music was from the very start of rehearsals another backbone of the production. If the text and actions were experimented with freely, we applied ourselves with rigour to the Dessau score. Thus a dialectic operated at the centre of the rehearsal process. Richard Fire worked with us through June. Thereafter Ivanoff, a classical singer, became TPG's musical director. Her work went beyond teaching the Dessau score. She trained people in singing, combined traditional musical discipline with an appetite for new ways to make sound. Both these trends are heard in *MC*. They also reach back to TPG work in *Tooth, Concert* (1971), *Commune* (1970), and *Makbeth* (1969).

Brecht posits a dialectic between business, war, and dehumanization: the interaction of war and business results in dehumanization. No full-scale war has been fought in America since the Civil War and the wars against the American Indians of the nineteenth century. So I decided to emphasize business and through it to manifest the whole system. All details were organized accordingly. The south wall of the theatre was plastered with a mixture of super-market food ads and armed forces enlistment posters. As spectators enter the theatre they come to me where I sit behind a large cash-register collecting the admissions' charge—no tickets were sold in advance, everyone paid cash at the door. Each time money is taken, exchanged, or mentioned throughout the performance the register bell is rung: from the first spectator in to the moment when Courage gives the Peasant Woman some dollars to bury Kattrin the register bell itemizes each transaction. Vawter counts the night's receipts at his desk near his drum-set; real cash is used as props and about $50 is in circulation; a 'gold brick' monoprop is used to ikonize the valuable items Courage accumulates and sells, and as Swiss Cheese's cash box. In scene 6 Kattrin saves the 'gold brick' even at the cost of being raped. Courage curses the war and throws the brick down at the end of scene 6—but then she changes her mind and clutches the brick to her breast. Yvette takes cash from the soldiers who patronize her prostitute's business; and it is Poldi's money that Yvette loans to Courage to ransom Swiss Cheese. But Courage gets the money only when she mortgages the store-wagon, and her haggling costs Swiss Cheese his life. Courage is always doing business—yet the more business she does the poorer she gets.

In TPG performers develop roles on their own. As director I'm concerned with the continuity of training and, for each production, with the visual and sonic scores. Directing is mostly watching and selecting. I comment on rhythms, balance between silence and sound, gestures, groupings. I find in what the performers do things to be retained and things to be eliminated. I make suggestions—but my inventions are based on theirs. I move around to all the places where the audience will be: I'm not interested in a single-perspective picture but a whole environment. I don't talk much about the psychology of characters, feelings, motivations, or objectives. First of all, my colleagues are better trained and more competent in these matters than I; secondly, as Stanislavski showed in his 'method of physical actions', affects will arise on their own if the physical score is precise. What we do discuss is the physical score, the technical aspects—how everything is to be integrated, and the meaning of the play in social terms as it is worked out concretely in the production through the fundamental interaction between performers and spectators. I've given examples in the uses of ropes and money; but every aspect is worked through in meticulous detail. Improvisation is a valuable training and rehearsal tool, but in performance it is unreliable. Of course, performers working so close to spectators deal with contingencies—but these are best described as permutations on the score, not improvisations.

Triumphs of acting arise from patience, repetition, and the ability to re-do scenes that've been unchanged for months. In TPG we have no fear of developing idiosyncratic, divergent, or even contradictory interpretations if these are—or lead to—meeting places of an individual performer's impulses and the production's logic. So much fails, one or the other, and great performing happens only when the two meet. This method pulls us off-course for weeks as when we tried again and again to find a balance between Gray's one-syllable-at-a-time Swiss Cheese and Brecht's simpleton Christ. Once an action is accepted it is rehearsed ruthlessly. It took many hours to score Kattrin's death fall in scene 11 with the heel of her red boot caught on the edge of the ladder; or Yvette's sexual poses during the intercourse section of scene 3 so that the transfer of money from the soldiers to Yvette is visually prominent; or the cracked-voice lullaby Courage sings to Kattrin's corpse in scene 12 followed by her hyena-like stripping of the corpse of its resellable clothes. At the end of the play Courage is hitched to every rope in the theatre: she is enmeshed in her own web, she carries the audience with her, the whole space seems to be moving. To stage this Clayburgh worked backwards from scene 12 to scene 5 figuring how each rope had to be set so that all could be finally gathered at a single terminus. It was only after five months' work that scenes were run through without stopping—to run through too soon freezes work, reducing its experimental potential. Even after *MC* opened we met three hours before each performance for warm-ups, notes on the previous performance with suggestions for the show at hand, rehearsals of scenes and music. Months before *MC* opened— while it was very rough—spectators came to open rehearsals. In July these spectators were students from our NYU workshops; in November colleagues from other theatres and friends came; the general public was invited through newspaper ads in December. Thus *MC* developed under the public eye and retains the style of a tribunal. But also there is a sense of celebration—heightened by the full supper served after scene 3. In India this supper was more of a snack—but in America it is a full meal at a cheap price. Audiences at open rehearsals, and during the run too (performers talk to the spectators during the supper), share their reactions, make suggestions, and through their very behaviour help test the production as it develops. The spectator isn't a numb consumer welcome only after the creative work is done, but part of the process from its most formative stages. And the creative work is never ended—even during the fall of 1975—

while TPG was preparing four new works—changes were made in *MC*. And in India too changes were made.

The Schedule, The People

We arrived in Delhi on the morning of 3 February, twelve of us on the Air-India weekly charter from Amsterdam. Joan and I have been to India before, in 1971. At the airport were Suresh Awasthi who originated the idea of TPG coming to India, Rajinder Nath of Abhiyan our Delhi sponsors, and V. Ramamurthy (Murti), our Indian tech director. An immediate plunge into work: we accept the old gym at the Modern School as the place to build the environment; Clayburgh negotiates with Amrit Lal Nayar, a contractor, to supply us with 'slotted angles' and plywood and we decide to haul the environment around India rather than build from scratch at each site. The expense of acquiring the stuff and trucking it was not expected. Also we learned that our Delhi budget was to be met from box office—thus ticket prices would be at Rs 10, very high, and still there'd be a big loss. In fact, the same box office arrangement was made at Lucknow, while at Calcutta, Bhopal, and Bombay our sponsors took responsibility for meeting living and production costs. But everywhere the tickets ranged up to Rs 10. We had a grant of $21,000 from the JDR 3rd Fund—and with this we paid international and India travel, salaries, per diem allowances, and costs in Delhi and Lucknow. The grant didn't cover all these expenses, nor was it meant to; TPG's savings and other contributions added $13,000 to the kitty. The tour was very expensive, possibly too much so. In the future we ought to develop a simple, easily transportable or, even better, duplicatable environment. But nothing can save on the biggest expense, international air travel, which came to over $11,000.

With a hired crew of labourers, help from E. Alkazi and students of the National School of Drama (NSD) and volunteers from different Delhi theatres, work on the environment went well. Alkazi arranges for us to borrow lights not only for Delhi but for the whole tour. Then a big snag: Customs won't release our costumes, props, ropes and pulleys until we put up a Rs 81,000 bond. After two days of negotiations I personally guarantee the money underwriting a Letter of Credit TPG brought to India to cover expenses; my guarantee is in turn guaranteed by the United States Educational Foundation in India. (I'm a Fulbright scholar this year); and, finally, Grindlay's Bank puts up the Rs 81,000 bond and our stuff is liberated. Waiting for hours at the Palam customs shed I stare at a sign over the officer's desk: 'I am not interested in excuses for delay. I am interested only in a thing done'—Jawaharlal Nehru. We get our equipment on 7 February, two days before dress rehearsal.

On 10 February *MC* opens to a full house; but by the end about one-third had gone. Possibly they didn't expect a four-hour perform- ance during which they sat on hard wood planks, on the floor, or moved about. My immediate reactions as recorded in my notebook:

> Environment too long for its width. Acoustics bad. One-third of the audience left at intermission; one-third very appreciative. They rushed up to the performers and me after the show and showered us with congratulations. Mostly authentic, some just being polite. The show itself was slow and ragged. . . . Mistakes last night: Joan dropped her 'pulpit' speech in scene 3; I got the ropes wrong in scene 2; Griffiths went dry for lines in scene 9; the rope got stuck and Kattrin's ladder wouldn't go up for scene 11—we had to stop the show, fix it, and then go on. It was very hard to hear. People strained their voices. In the other places we should make the environment better proportioned. The theatre is filthy—the dirt road outside means dirt gets tracked in and the place gets suffocatingly dusty so it's hard to speak.
>
> *February 11*

And Joan said in her notebook:

> I was rolling in dirt. I breathed dirt, dry earth dirt. I strained my voice between a dirt-clogged throat and bad acoustics. I felt like I could have been anywhere on tour doing *MC* not in India. . . . I was exhausted, hungry, sick to my stomach. The wheelbarrow— used as a market basket—didn't work. I slipped and fell on the wagon steps. I spilled a bucket of water on an audience member in scene 3. And yet the Indians loved it. One man squeezed my hand so hard I thought he had broken my knuckles. Scene 12 took on a special meaning to me here of an Indian peasant woman beggar tromping through the dusty countryside, stumbling, enduring. . . . During the show I was not at all nervous, only angry or concentrated on what needed to be done: keeping the story clear. The audience's reaction was pleasing, but being a perfectionist I wasn't satisfied. It could've been better.
>
> *February 11*

It got better. The best performance in Delhi—and one of the best of the tour—occurred on 13 February, Friday night. It takes a great audience to make a great performance. They kept pushing in until there were too many of them, probably about 350. The performers bitched—but again and again I've seen that when something unexpected and hard happens—too big a house, a sudden error, a part of the environment that fails, etc.—the performance either collapses or overcomes the challenge luminously: through all the work the clarity of the play's themes and the skill of the performers, the sheer beauty of the event, comes through as it does in athletics.

At the same time that the performances were bringing TPG together, long-range problems troubled us all. On 11 February I wrote:

> New rhythms are needed: a theatre with (1) strong leadership working for (2) continuous training and opening up (3) doing performances in many places before different kinds of people (4) alternating between commercial and non-commercial work. . . . TPG is no longer the arena, if it ever was, where people (all, including me) can go beyond.

Instead of feeling encouraged-liberated by the group structure, I felt suffocated. I wasn't alone in thinking this way. Steve, Liz and Spalding wanted to direct and/or compose their own work; Joan wanted to find autonomy as a performer similar to what the others sought as directors and composers; Leeny wasn't sure what she wanted to do; etc. At the same time we didn't want to bust TPG up. We were looking for new arrangements. As often happens in our Group people began talking informally with each other about these feelings—and pressure built to have formal meetings.

In Delhi too the first inklings of the 'sex problem' appeared. In scene 3, Yvette and three soldiers perform a stylized mimicry of copulation while on the other side of the space Courage smears Kattrin's face with mud in order to make her unattractive to rapacious soldiers. The meaning is clear: in war a safe face is one smeared with filth, and love is mostly a business transaction. Two days after we opened Principal M. N. Kapur of the Modern School told me that this scene had repercussions among the governing board of the school. He also felt that it distorted our production—some people came to *MC* just to see it, others stayed away because of it. I discussed the issue with the Group. They argued that TPG hadn't come to India to show how Indians would stage *MC* but how Americans did. I felt torn because Kapur had been of great help to us, exceedingly generous. Just before a performance, as I was about to insist on some modifications in the scene, Kapur came up to me and said: 'No, don't change anything. Do what is right for your work.' My respect for him is deep.

The performances in Chandigarh were cancelled for lack of a suitable space. The Group went on to Lucknow while Steve and I went to Chandigarh to run a workshop. This and other workshops will be discussed later. When we got to Lucknow people were settled at the Government Tourist Bungalow only three blocks from the motor garage where the environment was being set up. Murti tells of delays up to six hours trucking the environment down from Delhi through octroi posts. Experience is teaching us about the local, regional, cultural, religious, political, and linguistic rivalries that both enrich and debilitate India. These rivalries shadowed us in Delhi and Calcutta, and affect us directly in Lucknow. Originally our Lucknow sponsors were Darpan, and the contact Awasthi gave me was Kunwar Narain. On 10 October 1975 I wrote a detailed letter to all our sponsors outlining exactly what TPG needed to stage *MC*. The three page single-spaced letter emphasized the following:

1. TPG does not perform in a proscenium theatre or in any way separate the audience from the performers. As the enclosed photographs show, the audience sits among the performers, or stands around them. . . . Thus instead of a regular theatre we need a large room for our performance. . . . When we do perform on a proscenium stage we put the entire audience on the stage—no one sits in the house, the curtain remains closed. Thus we can perform on a very large proscenium stage. Also we can perform in a gymnasium or a large banquet hall. In every case we need large quantities of scaffolding to build up the theatre.

2. The performance of *MC* takes nearly 4 hours. After scene 3 we serve a supper to the audience. . . . This meal is not 'entertainment' but still it is very much part of the performance; it is important to the themes of the play.

Incidentally, the supper did not work well at all in India. It was more an interval snack than a continuation of Courage's business. Indians don't eat at 7.30; they like to sit down; they eat in family groupings. Also all we could arrange to serve were snacks. In America the meal is actually a good bargain of bread, cheese, soup with meat and/or vegetables, fruit, and beverage. The performers assist in serving the meal. It was cooked by people from our workshops (who were paid for the job) upstairs at our theatre.

3. One of the scenes is played in the street outside the theatre. In New York a big door opens and the audience remains inside looking through the door at the performers who are standing in

the street. On tour we are sometimes able to play this scene as in New York—but we can also play it indoors if necessary.

In Delhi this scene worked well because the Modern School Gymnasium had a door that could be used like the one in New York. And in Bhopal where we performed on the large proscenium stage of the Kala Parishad's Ravindra Bhawan this scene was played in a field behind the theatre using an ox cart as MC's wagon. A special platform was constructed in Calcutta because the stage door was 12 feet above the street level. In Bombay the whole play was outdoors in the Cathedral and John Connon School courtyard and scene 9 was played within the regular performing space. In Lucknow the scene was played at the entrance to the motor garage, but not actually in the street. Nowhere did the scene work as well as in New York where Wooster Street carries light traffic and the scene gathers a small crowd of passersby. Also during winter the weather enters the theatre, spectators wrap themselves in their coats, the feeling of the final scenes (9 through 12) is very bleak. Courage's talk about winter is actualized.

On 29 October I had a long letter from Narain. 'I could not write to you immediately,' he said, 'as I waited for a confirmation from Darpan who wanted a little time to consider all your requirements and discuss them with their members so that they could make a definite commitment to you. They now assure me that adequate arrangements can be made.' I heard nothing from Darpan until 13 November when B. C. Gupta wrote agreeing to my proposed schedule and other details. That same day Gupta wrote Murti saying, 'the whole Darpan team will be at your disposal'. So I was surprised when I arrived in Lucknow to find out that Darpan wasn't sponsoring TPG at all. At the last minute Raj Bisaria and his Theatre Arts Workshop had taken over. I never found out what happened—only that no love was lost between the rival groups. Everywhere the Indian theatre is plagued by factionalism. But the modern theatre—particularly that wing that wants to do new work, experimental work—is not strong enough to afford factionalism. Throughout my week in Lucknow I split my time between Narain—who I found to be intelligent and perceptive—and Bisaria who worked day and and night with his crew to get *MC* up and going. Things were tense all around.

The environment was extraordinary, a motor garage, where amid piles of tyres, broken down cars, and steel girders we set up *MC*. We didn't use the whole 100 by 200 foot space but lashed slotted angles to girders. *MC* looked beautiful but the Lucknow audience was confused;

they lay back from the production. Bisaria explained that relatively few people in Lucknow know English, especially the American dialect TPG speaks. And environmental theatre was new for Lucknow— though I never tired of explaining the structural and conceptual links between it and traditional Indian theatre like Jatra, Kathakali, Ramlila. But a gap has opened between modern Indian theatre and traditional forms. The issue is complex because the traditional forms are exciting theatrically but ideologically and socially they are often reactionary; or, as in Jatra, commercial melodramas. Modern theatre's problem is how to use the staging and direct relation to the audience of the folk forms without at the same time falling into their reactionary *mythopoesis*. The answer is not in imitation or adaptation. Rather I suggest that writers, designers, and actors fully experience the folk forms, and get training in these forms—and then 'forget' what they've learned; fully digesting the techniques so that these become part of the muscle of their own work. It is at the level of body consciousness, integration of music and rhythmic movement, environmental staging, and direct contact with the audience that modern groups can use traditional theatre.

One of the best things at Lucknow was how about 75 poor people came to the show. At first they stood outside—they could see in because one side of the building had no wall. Not all the tickets were sold and during a scene change I gestured for the poor to come in. Most of the adults held back but the kids came. They found places on the floor and in the corners of the environment: they were skilled at fitting into crevices, spaces in the social structure rejected by richer people. And about 50 people scampered across the roof, peering down through the opening between the peaked roof and the horizontal walls. Paying spectators ignored this new group, or moved away slightly. I remembered my 9 years in the deep South of the USA where blacks were legislatively 'part of' and 'equal to' whites but actually kept 'apart from' in a conceptual if not physical sense.

By Lucknow TPG had come down from the high of first arrival in India. Almost everyone was sick. And problems that troubled us in America, but were put aside for the tour, reasserted themselves. These boiled down to the fact that TPG is 9 years old, its members are entering or in their 30s (and I'm 42). People want 'autonomy' and their own 'artistic identities'. They don't want to be known as 'members of Richard Schechner's Performance Group'. At the same time I want my leadership acknowledged within the Group. By the end of our stay in Lucknow everyone knew that we needed some full group discussions and these were set for Calcutta.

The Abhinav Bharati theatre off Shakespeare Sarani in Calcutta wasn't finished when we set up there. The audience entered through piles of junk, scraps from sets, hardware—and passed over a plank-boardwalk to the stage where we'd set up *MC*. The environment combined folk and modern elements—the grid was of bamboo, and bamboo railings lined the galleries. Everything went smoothly in Calcutta because of the superb organization led by Shyamanand Jalan and Bishu Sureka. They were of great help on the rest of the tour too. Also in Calcutta we picked up our relationship with Badal Sircar who'd come to North America and worked with TPG in 1972. Space limitations prevent me from discussing Sircar's newest work—done outdoors, in villages, in environmental spaces—*Spartacus, Michhil, Bhoma*. I say only that of the modern theatre I've seen in India Sircar's Satabdi and the Repertory Company of the NSD are doing the most important work. Performances in Calcutta went smoothly except for the 'sex issue' which came to a head after an unsigned review in the Hindi paper, *Vishvamitra*, proclaimed: 'The most daring use of this environment is made when the actors, both male and female, in full view of the audience and in full illumination strip down completely and change their costumes. In this manner they educate the audience —acting out everything, even the way a woman is disgraced as the soldiers fornicate with her.' The day this review appeared we were besieged by men who offered me up to Rs 100 for a ticket; women with tickets stayed away; men fought on the street in front of the theatre. At interval I said, 'The sex scene is over, so if that's what you came for, eat your supper and go.' Many left, maybe forty men.

The 'sex issue' exploded in Calcutta but it was there in Delhi and Bhopal too. Granted that standards vary greatly from USA to India, *MC* is not a sex show. Costume changes are done in the Green Room-dressing room which is intentionally visible for the same reason that we show every technical aspect of the production; but no one is naked —and there's absolutely no connection between the Yvette part of scene 3 and the costume changes. The scene itself balances Yvette's business of prostitution with Courage's smearing mud on Kattrin's face so that she'll appear unattractive to the sex-starved soldiers. Ironically, the males who stormed the Abhinav Bharati were like the soldiers of scene 3—and at root neither soldiers nor spectators are to be blamed. The fault lies with a repressive sexual censorship.

On 18 March, under arrangements made by Sircar and Barin Saha, we performed *MC* in Singjole, a village about 3 hours outside of Calcutta. In fact, however, one of our Calcutta sponsors (not Jalan or Sureka) opposed this performance. Shortly before leaving for India I got a letter from Calcutta dated 5 January 1976:

> I would strongly suggest, after consulting people in the theatre field, not to produce the play in any village as it will not only cost a huge amount of money and hard work, but also it will be very difficult to attract the required audience, as the atmosphere in our villages has not yet reached the standard to appreciate productions like yours. Please clarify the situation immediately.

I wrote back on 16 January:

> It is very important to us to be able to play in villages—we want our work to reach the people who live in the villages, no matter how difficult that may be. We are willing to adjust our staging to suit village conditions: outdoors spaces, courtyards, bad lighting or no stage lighting at all. . . . It is most important to us that we perform for a cross-section of the Indian public. This is the other reason why we insist on trying to perform, for no charge, in a village near Calcutta.

The production cost almost nothing because we set up under two large trees using them as the grid for our rope system; a trench was dug that came very close to the pit we have in New York; we lit the show with petromax lanterns; a harmonium substituted for the piano; the audience sat on the ground all around; there was no interval and no supper.

Instead of the 800 people we'd expected—two times the most we'd ever played *MC* for—about 2,000 people came. As elsewhere in folk theatre the women and young children sat on one side and the men and older boys on the other. The audience stayed for about 3 of the 4 hours (we began at 7.30); at the end there were maybe 750 people left. Sircar introduced the play and before each scene he outlined its action in Bengali. But we weren't skilled at projecting our voices to such a large crowd; and *MC* isn't the kind of play that can be suddenly shouted. I wrote in my notebook:

> Aesthetics went out the window. . . . We adjusted our staging and made it broad: telling the story through big actions. . . . We didn't contact this audience so much through our work as simply by our presence. It was a Fair and we were entertainment.

We cut large sections of scenes 6 and 8, and all of 9 and 10. The morning after the performance I went around Singjole with Saha talking to people. They liked the performance though they didn't understand its language or anything except the barest story outline. 'What did you like?' 'The songs, the falling, the fighting, the killing. The way Mother tried to save her children. The girl who couldn't talk.' But a Bengali director who saw the performance said, 'They were being polite. The only reason they didn't bust up the show was because you are white.'

Group members found the performance 'liberating'—they were free from the restraint that comes when an audience listens closely—they could go as far as possible in physicalizing their roles, and playing with words as sounds rather than as cognitive speech. As I've seen elsewhere spectators felt free to talk among themselves, wander to and from the performance, and pay attention only to what interested them. Peter Brook and Robert Wilson, among others, have experimented with this kind of rhythms—and I've seen it at performances of Chhau, Kathakali, and Ramlila. The performance at Singjole pinpointed the biggest shortcomings of the tour: (*i*) we didn't play to ordinary people in the cities; (*ii*) the one time we had a popular audience they couldn't follow the play.

My suggestions for future tours: (*i*) make tickets available free to theatre workers and students training for theatre. These people should see two or more performances so that they grasp the production at the professional level of techniques. After this close viewing, discussions are held between the visiting artists and the local people; these discussions are followed by workshops; (*ii*) either by extending the run or by direct subsidy at least one-third of the tickets are allocated for poor people at a cost no more than that of a front stall at the movies. Because TPG doesn't use fixed seating the poor, middle classes, and rich will either mix or segregate themselves; (*iii*) TPG must make productions that work visually if we are going to play for non-English speakers. And if we are going to play outdoors to large crowds then either microphones or clear loud speaking must be used. These suggestions are based on the fact that groups like TPG rarely visit India and the exchange must be managed so that both sides get the most out of it.

Before the meetings in Calcutta I made some notes about what kind of theatre I wanted, and my place in it:

Problems: (1) How to make a theatre for the poor, the workers, the office people and still survive and still do theatre that is important personally. (2) How to involve the audience at every level and still keep professional standards. . . . I want to get to these things: (1) Performances for 'people' on subjects or themes of importance to society—to do these shows free, where 'people' are. (2) Experiment with the whole range of what performance is—getting to, doing, going from—and to have performers and audience conscious of and participating in this whole range. It means opening not only rehearsals but pre-show notes and warm-ups and post-show discussions and parties to the audience. (3) Find or invent new kinds of psychophysical, psychosocial, and sociophysical exercises. To advance the knowledge of training —especially breathing and making sound.

These meetings are good because they open the possibility for change—even total liberation. For me the liberation can come in two ways: Control over TPG so it is an instrument of mine; or freedom from the Group so I can pursue these experiments on my own. In either case I can get free of the ego struggles. I no longer think the Group must reflect what I hope the coming society should be. I now think the instrument must be sharp and held in strong hands—and when it cuts it ought not cut into itself but into the world around it. Otherwise people will mostly sub-jectivize their lives, turn on or into each other, fail to do anything more than 'express' themselves—while not relating either to the society or to theoretical problems of performance theory, the art. It's the intersection of these two that interests me—not 'holding together' a group (whatever its reputation). Reputations come and go, even art passes. But certain theories and social systems abide, if not for all time, for a long time. I want to teach, change the order of society, and have-make fun.

The meetings took place on 16 and 17 March. The formality of a closed meeting extending over two days guarantees that everyone has a chance to say their say. When the Calcutta meetings were over we knew two things: people other than me would direct and in other ways seek their autonomy (this process began in 1973 with Borst directing *The Beard*), and more meetings were necessary after the tour to find out whether or not TPG should continue as a group and if so, how.

After Calcutta, Bhopal was like emptiness itself. It reminded me of the American southwest and the dry mountains of Mexico. But amid the feeling of newness was the sense that the trees had been cut down, erosion was clawing the land, gutting it. The organizing for TPG by

Ashok Bajpeyi and Satyen Kumar was a model of efficiency. Kumar visited Delhi on 14 February, saw a performance, met with me, Murti, Nath and Awasthi; he filed a report on 16 February that formed the basis of our Bhopal programme. Everything was covered, including TPG eating habits. Kumar estimated that our performances would cost Rs 10,000 of which Rs 6,000 could be earned at the box office if tickets were pegged at Rs 10. We set up at the Ravindra Bhawan. To encourage a breeze we left the auditorium open but permitted no one to sit there; we used the outdoor theatre and sloping lawn for scenes 9 through 12. The work at Bhopal went so efficiently that we invited Benu Ganguly, technical director, to come with us to Bombay.

If Calcutta is India's New York, then Bombay is her Los Angeles. All of TPG just slid into Bombay's luxury like falling into velvet. Except for one night at a Tamasha I saw nothing of Bombay's other side. In its segregation of the poor Bombay is very like American cities with their ghettoes and 'ethnic' neighbourhoods. The space for *MC* at the CJC School was a magnificent courtyard surrounded on three sides by galleried buildings. We adapted our environment to the large space making room for 500 spectators, and another 150 (at reduced prices) up in the galleries. I watched some of each show from up top: it was like looking at a terrain map on which figures made dance patterns, the sound rose splendidly so all the dialogue was heard. Everything arranged for us by Narayana Menon and K. K. Suvarna of the National Centre for the Performing Arts was first-rate. The shows were near perfect—we'd learned from Singjole to physicalize a bit more than in America, to speak a little slower, and to eliminate extraneous gestures. The audience understood English and knew Brecht.

On the last night's performance in Calcutta signs appeared in the theatre: 'Schechner Has No Right To Destroy Brecht's Epic Theatre.' 'We Want Brecht Not Environmental Theatre.' 'Environmental Theatre Is A Deliberate Distortion Of Brecht's Philosophy Of Theatre.' 'Long Live Bertolt Brecht, The Dramatist Of The People.' 'Brecht Dealt With War, Schechner Deals With Orgasm.' 'Schechner Preaches Community Involvement By Making You Pay For It.' 'Brecht Spoke of Reality And Struggle, Schechner Deals With Gags, Stunts And Sexual Perversion.' And on 5 April a review appeared in the (Bombay) *Times of India* that praised the production: 'Fantastic! Never before has a Bombay audience been exposed to such an enriching theatrical experience. . . . A summative statement on drama; an unforgettable event. Thrice tears welled up in my eyes. . . . Through it all, through the words and the action and the noise and the novelty and the enormous planning and intellection behind it Brecht's deep humanism emerges. . . . Mother Courage is Man [sic] confronting the absurd. As performed she is vigorous, harsh, pragmatic, tender, defiant, raw as a scoop of earth, ineluctably human.' These contradictory estimates of the production raise the same question: Is TPG true to Brecht, and if not, does it matter?

I don't think fidelity matters much, though I do think TPG's *MC* is true to Brecht. Most of the time the author's intentions aren't known. Who's to say what Sophocles, Kalidasa, or Shakespeare intended? Should Greek tragedies be performed only outdoors in semicircular theatres seating 17,000 spectators who attend as part of yearly civic celebrations? And should these plays be offered up as three tragedies followed by one satyr play? If so, the academies had better instruct us on how to recreate the Athenian city-state. And so on for every past epoch. And if fidelity means the 'interior meaning' of a text, then that is obviously a question of interpretation. Even garrulous Shaw didn't say everything about his plays; and most writers are mum. Fidelity is even less important with Brecht because he staged his plays as he saw fit, and left his 'model books' as evidence—while urging that these should not be slavishly followed. Of *MC* a film exists of the Brecht-Weigel production.

I have long taken the position, and hold it now, that a text is a skeleton, an outline, a plan, a map—but that the body, picture, structure, and territory of a play can be actualized only in performance, at the immediate and unique encounter of performers and spectators; and that rehearsal is a research process for unfolding and discovering what the performance will be. As for 'changing the text,' there are times when that's good and times when it's bad. A classic text that is in no danger of being forgotten is open to retelling, especially if it is to be translated anyway; also neglected plays that will rarely be done in their pristine form. Actually some of the great plays —Shakespeare's *Hamlet*, many of Molière's plays, Tulsidas' *Ramacharitmanas* (as chanted in Ramlila), not to mention Brecht's *Threepenny Opera*—are versions of older dramas or oral recitations. On the other hand, if a play is new I think the author's words should be respected—he has the right to see his play reach the public first as he wrote it. As a matter of fact, we made no text changes in *MC* except to cut all of scene 4 up to the 'Song of the Great Capitulation'.

But the objections, and praise, are based not on textual changes but on tone—on a sense that TPG didn't do Brecht as Brecht would have done it; and therefore we did it wrong. *MC* is not one of Brecht's hardline plays like *The Measures Taken*. It belongs to a later period along with *The Caucasian Chalk Circle* and *The Good Woman of Setzuan*. Written in 1938, premièred in 1939 in Zurich, *MC* is as much an anti-war play as a condemnation of capitalist greed. In the character of Courage, Brecht internalizes the dialectical conflict which breaks Shen Te and Shui Ta into two persons: Courage is both loving and cruel, generous and stingy, wise and stupid, the best humanity has to offer and an animal. At the end she is neither a hero nor a hyena, but both. Brecht's own *MC* production (I've studied the model book and seen the movie) is, if anything, more sentimental than TPG's: (*i*) the famous open-mouth silent scream of Weigel-Courage when she hears the rifle shots that kill Swiss Cheese but can't express (out loud) her grief; (*ii*) her mourning-lullaby sung over Kattrin's corpse: in Brecht's production Courage allows Kattrin to be buried fully clothed although her clothes are of market-value—in TPG's production we followed the logic of 'hyena of the battlefield' (Brecht's description of Courage) to its extreme by having Courage strip the outer garments off Kattrin; (*iii*) the final action of Brecht's production: on a gray, large, empty stage Courage alone lifts the heavy yoke of her wagon, hitches herself to it, and draws the vehicle two full times around the floor of the revolving stage. I don't criticize Brecht for these choices which point up Courage's humanity, grief, and (pardon) courage; the actions are balanced by others that show her bitterness, contempt, cynicism, and brutality. But I point out that Brecht the director knew different than Brecht the author. Whether different equals better I will not say.

At another level altogether, TPG has been 'true' to Brecht the author even when we've differed with Brecht the director. There is no rolling wagon, but instead a store which is more in the American tradition; we serve supper; the final scenes are played outdoors or with the theatre open to the street. We didn't set the play in seventeenth century Europe in a war between Protestants and Catholics; we use modern costumes and no make-up. We have no separate orchestra playing offstage or from the pit—the performers play the music and all technical people play dramatic roles too. In these ways we out-Brechted Brecht: not only is the work of the theatre shown but theatre

workers perform roles; and what is a better *verfrumsdungeffekt* than
seeing the performer playing Mother Courage play the flute, or the
man playing the Chaplain set the ropes between scenes? These choices
were made on the basis of how best to get the play across to our
audience, and in terms of an environmental theatre we advocate as
thoroughly as Brecht advocated his Epic Theatre. The underlying
idea of TPG's production—the actualization of the play's inscape—is
the same in TPG as with Brecht: a good woman who, in identifying
herself with the industrialists, the capitalists, makes choices against
her own class interest (which is lower middle, not rich as she gives
herself airs of being). Therefore she is systematically—not accidentally
—ground down, defeated, and transformed into an animal pulling her
own wagon. She is also a hyena of the battlefield, plundering corpses,
selling to both sides, cheating, haggling, saving her own skin at the
cost of her children's lives. But through all this, and Brecht knew it,
she shows grit, a sense of humour with her wise-cracks aimed unfail-
ingly at the generals, priests, kings, and popes. She has a sense of
values consistent with Brecht's: she is cynical about religion and
politics; she survives. As in *Circle* and *Good Woman* Brecht shows that
the only good person in bad times is a bad person (Azdak); good
people must act bad to survive in bad times. What the audience experiences is not a bad person getting worse—there's no educative value
in that, and Brecht is fundamentally optimistic—but a good person
forced to act bad in order to survive. What the audience learns to
condemn is the (capitalist and war-making) system that makes
Courage choose between her livelihood and a bribe to ransom her son
Swiss Cheese.

The Workshops, The Aftermath

Under USIS auspices TPG ran workshops in Calcutta and Bombay; we
also did workshops on our own in Delhi and in collaboration with our
sponsors in Bhopal and Chandigarh. Also I gave slide lectures about
our work and the films of *Dionysus in 69* and *The Tooth of Crime* were
shown. Workshop is the best introduction to TPG—but unfortunately
an introduction that can be given to only a few people. There are
other difficulties too. Our work is physical but Indian modern theatre
workers are not familiar with—and often are put off by—physical
work. I mean simple exertion, as well as self-expression through movement, singing, unstructured sound-making, and touching. Exercises
function as vessels—traditions actually—that contain and channel

energies, often sexual and aggressive energies (which are normally repressed or redirected). A jumping kick may metaphorize hurting, a deep release of sound and a pelvic thrust may metaphorize sexual intercourse. Unlike traditional forms that already have a grammar (either abstract or mimetic), I try to help performers find in workshop their own mode of expression; later some of these image-actions are used in performance. The workshop is a kind of group socio-psycho-analysis translated into theatrical terms: the space where the personal and the public intersect. I was afraid to go far with this kind of work in India: I didn't want to accept the responsibility of inviting the release of so much repressed energy when I was moving on in a matter of hours. Usually we taught breathing, panting, sound-making, a few of the psychophysical exercises (taken from Kathakali via Grotowski), and played theatre games and/or improvisations. Also a lot of discussion went on during the workshops—it was a healthy place to expound on TPG's work, demonstrate some of it, and invite participation. The deepest workshops took place after the tour when Joan and I could spend more time. In July we worked several times with Sircar's Satabdi. I watched and then participated in Debesh Chakravarty's work with his Epic Theatre. Joan and I exchanged work with The Puppets, directed by Raghunath Goswami in Calcutta. In September we did a five day (6 hours per day) workshop with the NSD Repertory in Delhi. This was very satisfying because the Rep people know each other well, are professionals, and wanted to go as far as they could. In October Joan worked more with them, as well as with students at the NSD.

One of the strangest workshops took place in Chandigarh on 23–4 February. Borst and I went there on the invitation of Balwant Gargi after *MC* performances were cancelled. Gargi had gathered theatre scholars and workers from India, Sri Lanka, Nepal, Afghanistan and other places to 'experiment with the translation of the folk ballad Mirza Sahiban into performing arts terms and the resultant production will be performed in a natural rural setting'. The time allotted was 23 February to 20 March. I don't know how it turned out, but it began like Alice's teaparty. Some of the visitors weren't performers; mixed in with them were Punjabi musicians who kept up a steady drumming and chanting behind many of the meetings. Gargi turned over the opening sessions to Steve and me, but I didn't have the foggiest idea what to do. We did standard voice work, warmups, and 'line exercises'—where people face each other and exchange gestures, sounds, ways of walking, etc. What bothered me was that on paper Gargi's programme read splendidly, but the participants didn't know how to break down the barriers between them—it wasn't their fault, there was no crucible prepared to melt down the divisions. And if Steve and I were supposed to provide the heat we found ourselves as disoriented as the others.

In my letter of 1 August 1974 to the JDR 3rd Fund's Porter McCray applying for the money to take TPG to India I outlined my aims:

> The entire Performance Group will participate in this tour. The tour will involve performing in Delhi, Calcutta, Madras and Bombay; studying at the Kathakali Kalamandalam in Kerala; observing traditional and ritual performances in various places in India; direct contact with Indian theatre and dance people; workshops and lecture-demonstrations at theatre centres. Along with Group projects several individual projects will also be worked out, including the possibility of a joint TPG-Indian production; various study projects in Indian arts.

Except for Joan and me the last TPG member left India on 21 June. Most of my programme beyond the performances, workshops, and lectures didn't happen. After the tour Clayburgh, Kas Self, Joan, and I saw Mayurbhanj, Purulia, and Seraikella Chhau, and studied Seraikella Chhau; later I studied Kathakali, Joan studied Hindustani singing, and we both studied yoga. Clayburgh was going to design a production in Delhi but the project collapsed. Discussions are going on that will bring me back to India to direct in Indian languages with Indian performers. Many Group members thought of staying in India till August, some even longer—so what happened? The meetings at Juhu actually stirred many people to go back to America and begin projects of their own. With me out of the USA until February 1977, time and facilities were available without danger of competition. Then during the tour there wasn't enough time at each centre to see Indian theatre or to follow-up initial contacts with Indian theatre workers. We nearly doubled our planned number of performances in order to earn more money and to respond to the great popularity of *MC*. Our sponsors concentrated on making *MC* a success and few arrangements were made for us to see modern, traditional, folk, or ritual performances. The tour got to be a grind, and at the end of it people were sick, exhausted, and worn out. Actually I didn't anticipate how hard being in India would be for some people—at the level of different food, living conditions, lack of family, friends, and familiar diversions.

Maybe I expected too much when I outlined my aims; or maybe those aims were mine and not TPG's. But the 'corollary items' are in the long run as important as the impact of our performing. I consider this tour a success—but for next time I want to guarantee those items —the joint productions, intensive workshops, experience of Indian theatre, studies—that make a tour more than hit-and-run.

Programme

Tour funded by JDR 3rd Fund, New York, who paid for overseas transportation, and contributed towards production and TPG living and travel expenses in India. Local sponsors in India paid for most of the local production costs and provided most of the living accommodation for TPG members. Local sponsors also donated in-kind work on publicity, the environments, and day-to-day running of the shows. United States Information Service paid for much of the advertising in India; also USIS paid TPG members for leading workshops in Calcutta and Bombay. TPG contributed money toward salaries while on tour and production expenses.

. . .

The Company, in order of speaking:

STEPHEN BORST as Recruiter, Chaplain, Lieutenant
JAMES GRIFFITHS as Sergeant, Cook, Poldi, Soldier
JOAN MACINTOSH as Mother Courage (Anna Fierling)
JAMES CLAYBURGH as Eilif, Man With A Patch Over His Eye, Clerk, Soldier
SPALDING GRAY as Swiss Cheese, Soldier, Peasant
ELIZABETH LECOMPTE as General, Yvette, Peasant
RON VAWTER as Ordnance Officer, Townspeople
BRUCE RAYVID as Soldier, Another Sergeant, Peasant
LEENY SACK as Kattrin

Environment designed by JAMES CLAYBURGH
Musical director and pianist, MIRIAM CHARNEY
Technical director, BRUCE RAYVID
Costumes, THEODORA SKIPITARES
Technical director in India, V. RAMAMURTHY
Associate technical director for Bhopal and Bombay, BENU GANGULY
Technical assistants, KAS SELF, MUNIERA CHRISTIANSEN
General Manager and drummer, RON VAWTER
Director, RICHARD SCHECHNER

Music by PAUL DESSAU
Translated from the German by RALPH MANHEIM

MOTHER COURAGE AND HER CHILDREN by BERTOLT BRECHT
(Written 1938; World Première, Zurich, 1939)

.   .   .

Tour Outline : 6 Localities, 23 Performances, 56 Days

Place	*Dates*	*Sponsors*

New Delhi
  Modern School
  Gymnasium
	February 10, 11, 12, 13,
	14, 18, 19, 20, 21:
	9 performances
		Abhiyan
		Rajinder Nath
		Som Nath Sapru
		M. N. Kapur, Principal
		of Modern School

Lucknow
  A private motor
  garage
	February 27, 28
	2 performances
		Theatre Arts Work-
		shop
		Raj Bisaria

Calcutta
  Abhinav Bharati
  Theatre
	March 9, 10, 12, 13, 14:
	5 performances
		Anamika Kala Sangam
		Shyamanand Jalan
		Bishwambhar Sureka
		Naveen Kishore

Singjole Under two trees	March 18: 1 performance	Tagore Society Barin Saha Badal Sircar
Bhopal Ravindra Bhawan	March 26, 27: 2 performances	Madhya Pradesh Kala Parishad Ashok Bajpeyi Satyen Kumar Benu Ganguly

Bombay
  Cathedral and John
  Connon School courtyard
	April 3, 4, 5, 6
	4 performances
		National Centre for
		the Performing Arts
		Narayana Menon
		K. K. Suvarna
		K. Kuruvila Jacob,
		Principal of Cathedral
		and John Connon
		School

3

Environmental Theatre: Space

This earth is my body. The sky is my body. The seasons are my body. The water is my body too. The world is just as big as my body. Do not think I am just in the east, west, south, or north. I am all over.

Killer-of-Enemies, Apache Hero

Not every place was good to sit or be on. Within the confines of the porch there was one spot that was unique, a post where I could be at my very best. It was my task to distinguish it from all the other places. The general pattern was that I had to 'feel' all the possible spots that were accessible until I could determine without doubt which was the right one.

Carlos Castaneda

In June 1970, I spent nearly three hours in the anechoic chamber at the Massachusetts Institute of Technology. After a period of very deep sleep, I awoke with no sense of how big the room was. I could see the walls, the floor, and the ceiling, but that wasn't enough to fix distance, and therefore size. How big was I? How big were the things in the room? When I spoke or shouted, there was no echo. I discovered how much I depended on echo to fix distance and how much I depended on distance to fix size. I crawled across the floor. It was like a big inner-spring mattress with no cloth covering. I measured the space with my body, but I had no assurance that, like Alice in Wonderland, I hadn't changed size. Then I lay still, and I heard gurglings in my stomach, my heartbeat, and an incredibly loud whirring and ringing in my ears. I felt my body try to expand to fill the space of the chamber, and I experienced my skin as a thin bag containing bones and a lot of sloshing fluid.

The fullness of space, the endless ways space can be transformed, articulated, animated—that is the basis of environmental theatre design. It is also the source of environmental theatre performer training. If the audience is one medium in which the performance takes place, the living space is another. The living space includes all the space in the theatre, not just what is called the stage. I believe there are actual relationships between the body and the spaces the body moves through. Much of workshop and rehearsal is devoted to discovering these relationships, which are subtle and ever-shifting.

The first scenic principle of environmental theatre is to create and use whole spaces. Literally spheres of spaces, spaces within spaces, spaces which contain, or envelop, or relate, or touch all the areas where the audience is and/or the performers perform. All the spaces are actively involved in all the aspects of the performance. If some spaces are used just for performing, this is not due to a predetermination of convention or architecture but because the particular production being worked on needs space organized that way. And the theatre itself is part of larger environments outside the theatre. These larger out-of-the-theatre spaces are the life of the city; and also temporal-historical spaces—modalities of time/space. At the start of the Open Theater's *Terminal*:

> 'We come upon the dying to call upon the dead.' We tried many routes to call up the dead: we invented some, and we studied procedures used by people who believe in invocation. What we chose finally was to knock on the door of the dead by tapping with the feet on the floor, the door of the dead. There is no ground where underfoot—below the wood, below the stone—are not the bones of someone who once lived. The guides invited the dead below the stage floor to come through and speak through the dying.[1]

There is no dead space, nor any end to space.

The Performing Garage is roughly fifty feet by thirty-five feet, with a height of twenty feet. Photograph 1 shows the environment for *Dionysus in 69* during the preperformance warmups. One of the two dominant towers is partially visible. The space is organized around a central area marked by black rubber mats. The audience sits on the platforms or on the carpeted floor. The only concentration of audience is a five-tier vertical structure on the north wall, which seats about one hundred persons. The lower levels of this tier can be seen in the upper left corner of the photo. Photograph 2 shows one of the dominant towers of the *Dionysus* environment. Pentheus, with his foot on the rail, is at the top of the tower addressing the audience and the performers. Spectators sit all around Pentheus. Diagonally across from this tower is its twin, separated by the black mats; about fifteen feet separate the towers.

The action of *Dionysus* occurs in several areas and in several ways.

1 TOP. Preperformance warmups for *Dionysus in 69*. Performers stretch out on their backs for breathing exercises. Warmups take about one hour. Photo by Fred Eberstadt.

2 BOTTOM LEFT. Pentheus addressing the citizens of Thebes from the top of one of the towers. The spectators are citizens of Thebes as well as theatregoers. They share this identification with the performers. Photo by Fred Eberstadt.

3 BOTTOM RIGHT. *Makbeth* environment, looking across the table to the stairway down which the audience comes entering the theatre from the second floor.

4 LEFT. Lady Makbeth as she appears while the audience is entering. Quietly she recites the text of Makbeth's letter to her.

5 BELOW. *Commune*, looking towards the west *pueblos*. In the foreground is the Wave, and at the right rear is the tub.

6 BOTTOM. *Commune*, from back in a *pueblo*.

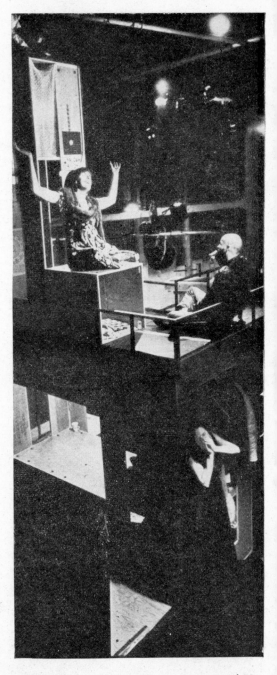

Left. Spectators and performers together in the final scene of *Commune*, as a reporter interviews Spalding/Polanski concerning the death of Sharon Tate.

Right. *The Tooth of Crime* environment, looking from the gallery to the centre structure. Performers are visible on four levels—all of which could contain spectators too. Spectators follow the action on foot around the theatre—moving either on floor level or along raised galleries. Stairs allow spectators to go from floor to galleries and back.

9 Top. Taking *Dionysus* out into Wooster Street—exploding the space of the theatre. Photo by Fred Eberstadt.

10 Bottom. Dionysus moving up Wooster Street as the performance continues. After about one block the performance dispersed. With the Living Theatre it continued for some time in their production of *Paradise Now*.

Dominant actions such as the birth of Dionysus, the seduction of Pentheus, and the death of Pentheus take place on the black mats. Choric actions such as the taunting of Pentheus by the chorus, the planning of Pentheus' murder by the chorus, and the soliciting of help from the audience take place in various areas around the periphery, mostly among the spectators. Some actions such as the sexual relations between Dionysus and Pentheus and the initial meeting between Cadmus and Tiresias take place entirely out of sight of the audience, privately. Underneath the visible environment is a pit 35' by 8' by 8'; two trapdoors allow access to the pit. There are good hiding places underneath some of the platforms back close to the walls. These 'secret' places were used as well as the public places.

Most of the action is single-focus, but significant actions take place simultaneously. While Pentheus is trying to make love with a person from the audience, the chorus is whispering to other spectators: 'Will you help us kill him in ten minutes?' After Pentheus is killed, all the women in the company rush into the audience and simultaneously tell about their part in the murder. At the end of the play, weather permitting, the large overhead garage door—just visible in the upper right hand corner of Photograph 1—is opened, and all the performers march out into Wooster Street, often followed by spectators.[2]

Photograph 3 shows the same space reconstructed for *Makbeth* (1969). Here a series of tightly connected rectangles rise from a central table. On this table much of the major action of the play takes place. But scenes are also acted high in the ramparts, back in corners out of sight of most spectators, and in the pit, which is wholly open, making a trench down the north side of the Garage. The rugs of *Dionysus* are gone, and the bare wood rises from a cement floor. Unlike the open feeling of the *Dionysus* environment, *Makbeth* suggested closed-in spaces, 'cabin'd, cribb'd, and confin'd'. Photograph 4 shows Lady Makbeth at the opening of the play sitting in her place reciting quietly to herself the text of Makbeth's fateful letter.

In *Dionysus* the audience is free to sit anywhere and invited to move around the environment. One scene is a dance with the audience. Spectators frequently join in the action at various times during a night's performance. In *Makbeth* the audience is restricted to a thirty-inch rim at the edges of the platforms. Action takes place in front and behind the audience, but not with them. On only one occasion during the run were spectators invited to participate. I told the audience of about fifty who were gathered upstairs before the performance that they should feel free to move around the space, following the action, exploring the complexities of the environment. I warned them that most of the actions were clustered in bunches performed simultaneously, so that following one action meant missing others. I asked them to remove their shoes so that their movements would not unduly disturb the performers. Nevertheless most of the performers felt that the movement of the audience was a distraction, and the experiment was not repeated. Audience movement is used extensively in *The Tooth of Crime*.

Photograph 5 is of *Commune*. Here 'pueblos' are built in two corners of the Garage; these are connected by a four-foot-wide 'road' elevated to eleven feet. The centre area is dominated by a gentle Wave that rises, falls, rises, and falls again. Next to the Wave is a tub three feet deep and six feet in diameter. The Wave and tub are used during the performance as many things: boat, sea, land, house, blood, village, beach, yard. The audience sat mostly high in the environment, though on crowded nights a number of persons sat on the floor. There was some audience movement through the space. For one scene all the audience was asked to sit on the Wave, and most did so. The action shown in Photo 5 is of Clementine leaping off a promontory into the arms of the other performers who then 'fly' her around the space.

Photograph 6 is a view of the *Commune* environment from a height of about five feet and looking out through the legs of a spectator sitting above. Most of the views are not obstructed. But more than in *Commune* or *Dionysus* spectators have the choice of sitting at the edge of a platform, deep in a pueblo, with other persons, or alone. The spectator can choose his own mode of involving himself within the performance, or remaining detached from it. The audience was offered real choices and the chance to exercise these choices several times throughout the performance. The spectator can change his perspective (high, low, near, far); his relationship to the performance (on top of it, in it, a middle distance from it, far away from it); his relationship to other spectators (alone, with a few others, with a bunch of others); whether to be in an open space or in an enclosed space. Surprisingly few spectators took advantage of the opportunities to change places. Even when the performers encouraged moves—such as saying to the audience when everyone was assembled on the Wave, 'When you return to your places, perhaps you want to go to a new place to get a different view of the events'—only a small proportion of the spectators went back to places different from where they'd come.

Photograph 7 shows a group of spectators assembled in the centre of the Wave during the play's final scene. The spectators had previously been invited into the centre of the Wave to represent the villagers of My Lai. (This scene has undergone many changes over the years *Commune* has been in TPG repertory; the play is still being performed and still being changed.) The scene photographed is of an interview between Spalding and several reporters. The character is being asked about his reactions to the murder of his pregnant wife.

Photograph 8 is of *The Tooth of Crime.* The view is from a gallery above the playing areas which are in and around a large houselike structure built entirely from plywood modules. For the first time TPG used a structure that blocks vision and has no single arenalike central playing space. Spectators move around the viewing gallery or on the floor in order to follow the action of the play. Also there are windows cut in the environment so that scenes can be seen framed in the environment—giving a filmlike shifting focus to the action. The patterns of movement in *Tooth* are irregular circles on the floor, with a lot of climbing into the modules. Each of the characters has a station in the environment; the characters move but often return to their stations. Some of the feel of *Tooth's* action is of a medieval play.

The *Tooth* environment is modular. Each of the plywood sides is perforated so that it can be joined to other sides in a variety of ways. Squares, rectangles, polygons, and near-circles can be built. Low, medium, and high platforms or towers rising to sixteen feet as in *Tooth* are possible. The modules can be reconstructed in numberless variations. The entire system is non-mechanical: It can be entirely reconstructed by hand. Jerry N. Rojo designed this modular system because TPG needed flexibility in order to stage a number of works in repertory.

Rojo, in collaboration with the Group, designed all the environments for TPG discussed in this essay. He is, in my opinion, the world's leading environmentalist. A large portion of his genius is in solving all the formidable artistic-technical problems we put to him in requiring a flexible, transformational space without the encumbrance of heavy or expensive machinery.

I met Rojo at Tulane University where he came in September 1966, on a leave of absence from the University of Connecticut. He had his master's from Tulane and came back to work for his doctorate. The New Orleans Group was working on *Victims of Duty.* I was teaching a seminar in performance theory. Paul Epstein, Arthur Wagner, and Rojo were among those who attended the seminar. We had before us some of the work of Jerzy Grotowski, Happenings, examples of ritual theatre, and game theory—of both the mathematical kind and Eric Berne's. Wagner was teaching acting, Epstein was a musician, Rojo a designer. I recall nothing specific about the seminar, but I know it acted on my ideas strongly. I remember that Rojo said little. Over the year we got to be friends. He was the one 'technical person' at Tulane who was interested in my ideas. Then when we were finishing rehearsals for *Victims*, we ran into some technical problems. We wanted a pile of chairs spiralling from the floor to the ceiling strong enough for Choubert to climb on. I asked Rojo to come down to the studio theatre of Le Petit Théâtre de Vieux Carré where *Victims* was being staged.

He liked the environment very much. He solved the problem of the chairs by building an armature of very strong plastic-coated wires from which the chairs blossomed like tree leaves. The next year in New York TPG was in the middle stages of *Dionysus* rehearsals. Mike Kirby had drawn some towers that I thought would be a good central image for the environment. But Mike wanted towers of a certain shape placed in a certain way; and I wanted something else. I phoned Rojo at Connecticut, and he said he'd help. He made new designs for the towers. I liked them immensely. He went ahead and built the towers.

So that is Rojo with hammer and saw. I think my deepest respect for him comes because he knows that environmental design = construction. The ideas are okay, the renderings beautiful, the models exciting—but it all comes down to hammers, nails, materials, and making the space into the shapes you need.

I think it's the same with performing. The daily physical commitment is what counts. The spirit is the body at work.

After *Dionysus* I invited Rojo to design *Makbeth*. I also asked Brooks McNamara who, like Rojo, had been a student at Tulane. During the winter of 1968–1969 they both worked on designs that ranged from Ziggurats to mazes to cattle runs. Finally, both Rojo's and McNamara's ideas were used. Then I asked Rojo to design *Commune*. Then he designed *The Tooth of Crime*.

These eight photographs give some indication of the flexibility possible in a small space such as the Garage. Each environment has a different feel, though all are made from simple wood structures. The audience is arranged in different ways and the action flows through the spaces differently for each production. In *Dionysus* there are many circular movements centred around the black mats; the flow is basically uninterrupted and with few turbulent eddies. In *Makbeth* the moves are angular, there are many private actions, much simultaneity, sharp, disjointed gestures, and harsh sounds coming from several directions at once. Heights were used much more than in *Dionysus*. *Commune* returns to some of the circularity of *Dionysus*, but the circles are incomplete, broken off. Most of the action takes place in the centre area, on or near the Wave. *Tooth* flows in tight eddies, circles, and figure eights, and the characters often spy on each other from heights or hidden vantage points.

Each environment grew from detailed work with the performers. Work with Rojo begins after the work with the performers is well under way. I try to make the environment a function of the actions discovered by the performers. Of course a reciprocity develops between space and idea, movement and characterization. In the case of *Makbeth* the fact that so much of the rehearsing was done in Yugoslavia far from the Garage led to a production style that hampered the performance.

Environmental design comes from daily work on the play. The environment develops from workshops, discussions, drawings, and models. Models are important because no two-dimensional rendering can give an accurate feel of space. Rehearsals are held in partially finished environments because the performers' work will revise the plans even during the construction phase. After opening, the environment changes as new aspects of the work are uncovered. The Performance Group's work with both the *Dionysus* and *Commune* environments was superior to work with the *Makbeth* environment because many rehearsals, open and closed, were held in the partially completed environments. The space and the performance developed together. On the other hand, the Group returned from Yugoslavia to a totally finished, extraordinarily strong *Makbeth* environment—a marriage between the environment and the performance was never consummated.

Work on an environment may begin long before a play has been selected or a script assembled. The basic work of TPG is with space: finding it, relating to it, negotiating with it, articulating it.[3] Whenever the Group arrives somewhere to perform, the first exercises put people in touch with the space.

Move through the space, explore it in different ways. Feel it, look at it, speak to it, rub it, listen to it, make sounds with it, play music with it, embrace it, smell it, lick it, etc.

Let the space do things to you: embrace you, hold you, move you, push you around, lift you up, crush you, etc.

Let sounds come out of you in relation to the space—to its volumes, rhythms, textures, materials.

Walk through the space, run, roll, somersault, swim, fly.[4]

Call to another person with words, with names, with unworded sounds, with unsounded breathing. Listen to the calls, try them from different places.

Then find a place where you feel most safe. Examine this place carefully, make it your home. Call from this place, this home, this nest. Then find a place where you feel most threatened. Call from there. Move from the bad place to the good place while singing softly.

I believe there is an actual, living relationship between the spaces of the body and the spaces the body moves through; that human living tissue does not abruptly stop at the skin. Exercises with space are built on the assumption that human beings and space are both alive. The exercises offer means by which people communicate with space and with each other through space; ways of locating centres of energy and boundaries, areas of interpenetration, exchange, and isolation, 'auras' and 'lines of energy'.[5]

An exercise based on these assumptions was developed by the Group at the start of a summer residency at the University of Rhode Island in 1971.

1. Performers move slowly towards each other until they are compressed into a living ball. They pack themselves together more and

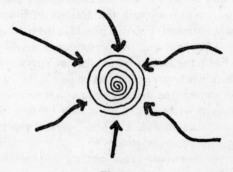

Fig. 1

more tightly until there is no room. They collapse towards no space, towards infinite inward pressure.   [Fig. 1]

2. Then, an explosion of the primal mass into the space; an explosion with sound. Ideally the primal mass is at the centre of the space, equidistant from walls, ceiling, and floor—so that the explosion goes in all directions.   [Fig. 2]

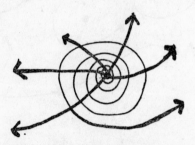

Fig. 2

3. Each person comes to rest in a place where he feels safe, centred, defined in relation to space and the others. From this centre each person marks out his boundaries, finds the points where he confronts others, where there are contested spaces, where he harmoniously shares space. The space is structured by fields of personal energies. [Fig. 3]

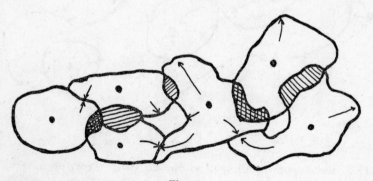

Fig. 3

4. Each performer determines for himself a route through the space. He keeps this map to himself, and once it is set, it cannot be changed. The reason for this rigidity is so that the experience of one performer

does not cause another performer to later alter his route, his own experience. Of course the exercise can be done with people choosing maps on the moment. The map of performer *A* is shown below. [Fig. 4]

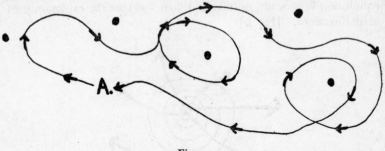

Fig. 4

5. Performer *A* passes through many different energy fields. Sometimes he is drawn in, sometimes pushed away, sometimes torn between two or more currents. As *A* makes his way, the others react with sounds, movements (without displacing the feet), and breathing rhythms. *A* moves either fast or slow, depending on the energies he feels; he makes sounds or remains silent.   [Fig. 5]

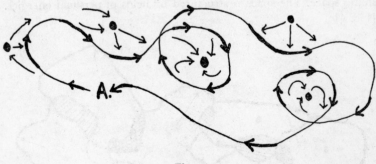

Fig. 5

This exercise with its allusions to the 'big bang' theory of universal creation and to the voyage home of Ulysses through seas of temptations, dangers, and pleasures gives performers a sense of *how full space is*. The problem is identifying the constantly changing patterns of energy that radiate through spaces—energy that comes from people, from things, from the shapes of the space.

Exercises like the two described help performers make space-maps—read space in many different ways. Western thought accustoms us to treat space visually. But acoustic, thermal, tactile, olfactory, and brain-wave maps can also be drawn. An olfactory map, for example, will not have the sharp edges of a visual map—it will be fluid, always changing, literally drifting on the wind, with eddies and intense centres shading off towards ill-defined edges.

In the spring of 1969 TPG explored the relationship between the snout—the nose and mouth, the cavities of the sinuses and throat—the gut, and the larger spaces in the theatre to the large gut spaces in the body. The work culminated with an exercise in June:

> Everyone in a circle. In the centre a basket covered with a white cloth. After two minutes of silence the cloth is taken away. The basket is full of peaches, strawberries, bananas, cherries, grapes, and blueberries.
>
> Everyone concentrates on the fruit. Imagine biting into it, tasting it, smelling it. Then, one at a time, performers go to the basket and using only the snout take one grape or berry. Roll it around your mouth, under your tongue; play with it as long as you can. Then bite into it, feel its juices and flavour, chew it as slowly as you can. Swallow.
>
> One performer goes back to the basket, takes a berry or grape with his snout. This piece of fruit is passed around the circle from mouth to mouth.
>
> Everyone goes to the basket and with your snouts, making as many trips as necessary, bring back a pile of fruit for yourself. Then put as many berries and grapes in your mouth as you can keep count of. When you lose count of how many you have, bite. Let the juices run down your chin. Sit quietly.
>
> Look at the basket. Everyone at once, animal-like, making sounds, using only snouts, rush to the basket and take the fruit. Carry it to a safe place and eat.
>
> Find each other. Clean each other with your tongues, cat-style. Relax, make sounds, take each other in. Take in the whole scene: empty basket, white cloth, stained clothing, scatterings of fruit-leavings.

This exercise took about three hours. The lighting in the Garage was a spotlight on the basket of fruit and scattered low-intensity lights elsewhere. The *Dionysus* environment was standing, and the soft rugs helped the exercise. I recall the fierceness with which people took the fruit and devoured it. Then they rushed from the centre of the theatre to dens, perches, nests, lairs. Only after a long while did they return to the open.

Through a process I don't understand but accept, the *insides of the body perceive space directly*. This visceral space-sense is activated by exercises like the fruit-eating. Exercises in smelling also activate the visceral space-sense. Visceral perception is related to the actual wash of the guts inside the body. To get at this you have to let go of sight, hearing, and touching with the skin. Things must be tasted and smelled, touched with the nostrils, mouth, lips, tongue, anus, and genitals: those places where the viscera is on or close to the surface. Visceral space-sense is not about edges, boundaries, outlines; it is about volumes, mass, and rhythm. The exercise in which a performer moves through spaces energized by others is about boundaries. 'Fruit-eating' is about rhythm.

I can't draw all this material into a neat bundle because I don't have a theory that can handle it. But let me throw a few more things at you. Richard Gould says that Australian aborigines perceive landmarks as 'nothing less than the bodies of the totemic beings, or items connected with them, transformed . . . into individual waterholes, trees, sandhills, ridges, and other physiographic features, as well as into rock alignments and sacred rock-piles.'[6] This is very much like what S. Giedion finds in the prehistoric art of the caves:

> One could give an almost endless list of instances showing how forms of animals, imbued with mystic significance, were born out of the rock: the bison in La Mouth (Dordogne), where the whole outline of the back, and to a certain extent even of the head, had been formed by the natural rock; the bison of the cavern of El Castillo (Santander), where major parts of the body had been seen in a stalactite and only a few lines were necessary to bring out the image; the group of polychrome bison on the ceiling of the cavern of Altamira, whose unusual recumbent positions stem from the form of the rock protuberances. . . . Rock, animal, and outline form an inseparable unit.[7]

Or the things Antonin Artaud saw in Mexico:

> Nature has wished to express itself over a race's entire geographic compass. . . . I was able to grasp that I was not dealing with sculpted forms but with a specific play of light, which *combined* itself with the outline of the rocks. . . . And I saw that all the rocks had the shape of women's busts on which two breasts were perfectly outlined.[8]

Artaud also saw heads, torsos in agony, crucifixions, men on horses, huge phalluses, and other images impressed on the rocks or rising from them. 'I saw all these forms became reality, little by little, in accordance with their rule.'

In all these cases not only is the separation between man and his environment transcended, but each is the image of the other. A recurrent claim of shamans is that they can take their guts out, wash them, and replace them; or that they have had their corruptible human guts replaced by eternally durable ones of stone.

The visceral space-sense is elusive, even for those who have experienced it. It is a communication from within the spaces of the body to within the spaces of the place one is in. You become aware of your body as a system of volumes, areas, and rhythms; as a coordinated collection of chambers, channels, solids, fluids, and gases; as a combination of resilient, hard, inner skeleton covered and held together by supple, tensile muscles and membranes—all this supporting and surrounding central, pulsating, life-source bays, gulfs, and bundles of mobile guts.

Donald M. Kaplan has carried these ideas to the point where he believes all theatre architecture is an expression of infant body-states. He thinks that the proscenium is a perfected form wherein the digestive guts seated in the darkened auditorium hungrily await the 'food' chewed and fed from the brilliantly illuminated stage (mouth). 'The interface of stage and auditorium is not a celebration of a maturational achievement, as certain other architectural forms are. A theatre reminds us of a dynamic condition.'[9] This condition is the digestive tract from mouth to stomach.

> Thus, as the theatre fills up and the performers prepare to go on, a voracity in the auditorium is about to be shaped and regulated from the stage by an active exercise of some kind of prescribed skill. At this point, we can begin to answer the question of what a theatre does kinesthetically, by observing that its geometrics and functions favour a juxtaposition of a *visceral* and *executive* experience.[10]

The visceral audience awaits satisfaction from the actors who feed the performance to them.

By putting everyone on stage, so to speak, the environmental theatre does away with the dichotomy Kaplan identified. The audience in environmental theatre must look to itself, as well as to the performers, for satisfaction of visceral needs. This less sharply delineated division of roles, actions, and spaces leads *not* to deeper involvement, not to a feeling of being swept away by the action—the bottomless empathy enhanced by darkness, distance, solitude-in-a-crowd, and regressive, cushioned comfort of a proscenium theatre—but to a kind of in-and-out experience; a sometimes dizzyingly rapid alternation of empathy and distance.

The orthodox theatre-goer is snuggled. He can keep his reactions to himself, and he is more likely to get utterly wrapped up in the experience on stage. This is even truer in the movies, where there is absolutely no responsibility to respond, because the actors in a film are not present at the theatre. In the environmental theatre the lighting and arrangement of space make it impossible to look at an action without seeing other spectators who visually, at least, are part of the performance. Nor is it possible to avoid a knowledge that for the others you are part of the performance. And in so far as performing means taking on the executive function, every spectator is forced into that to some degree by the architecture of environmental theatre.

Spectators experience great extremes—of deep, perhaps active involvement and participation; then critical distancing, looking at the performance, the theatre, the other spectators as if from very far away. Sometimes a spectator will freak out, go so far into the experience that he is lost inside it. More than a few times I have talked someone back from very far places. But the other extreme also occurs. I have spent many hours watching performances from a detached, disinterested point of view; and I have seen others do likewise. This is not a question of boredom, but of focusing on aspects of the performance other than the narrative, or the feelings of the performers. These aspects—technical, environmental, spectator behaviour—are masked in the orthodox theatre. You couldn't focus on them if you wanted to. In environmental theatre there are endless degrees of attention, subtle gradations of involvement. The experience of being a spectator, if you let yourself get into it, is not smooth but roller-coaster.

Many people, trained in the rigid reaction programme of orthodox theatre, are embarrassed by what they feel at environmental theatre. They think that the in-and-out reaction is 'wrong' or an indication that the play 'doesn't work'. People come up to me and say, 'I couldn't keep my attention focused on the play'. Or, 'I was moved by some of it, but I kept thinking my own thoughts. Sometimes I lost track of what was going on.' Or, 'Sometimes I felt good, but at other times I felt threatened.' Or, 'You know, I watched the audience so much I lost part of the play.' Or even, 'I fell asleep.' I think all of these responses are splendid.

If the body is one source of environmental theatre design, there are also historical and cultural sources. The body gives data for space-senses while historical or cultural studies give data for *space-fields*. Modern European-American culture is prejudiced in favour of rectangular, hard-edged spaces with clear boundaries and definite senses of right and left, up and down. There is only a blurry idea of what happens inside these boundaries. We fight wars to preserve boundaries, while letting the life inside our nations deteriorate.

Space may be organized without a single axis, as among the Eskimo where figures in the same field are 'upside down' relative to each other. Give an Eskimo child a paper to draw on, and he will fill up one side and continue to draw on the other side with no more thought of discontinuity than you have when you follow a sentence in this book from one page to the next. Space may be organized with a distorted or permutated axis as in surrealist art or topographic mathematics. Or it may be organized according to the X-ray technique of the North-west Coast Indians who see the inside and outside of an object with equal clarity—a cow with her unborn calf in her belly, a fish with a hook lodged in its throat, a man with his heart beating in his chest.

Space can be organized according to time, so that sequence in space = progression in time, as in Egyptian panels, medieval tryp-tichs, and the settings for morality plays in which the progress of history from the Creation to the Fall to the Crucifixion to Salvation or Hell was plain to all who had eyes to see. Space can be organized so that size, not distance, indicates importance. In Egyptian art the gods are biggest, the pharaohs next, and so on through many classes until we reach tiny slaves. Examples are without limit. Space can be shaped to suit any need.

The concept of *space-field* may be easier to grasp if I briefly present five kinds of performance space-fields: Egyptian, Greek, Balinese, Mexican, and New Guinean. The first two are historical, and the last three exist today.

The Egyptians staged periodic ceremonial spectacles. For these they built entire cities and floated great, ornate barges down the Nile. The river was not only the liquid, flowing stage for much of the Heb-Sed; it was itself the source of all Egyptian life, a living participant in the great drama of renewal. Time itself was stopped for the Heb-Sed festival. (We retain this idea of a holiday being time out.) The days of the Heb-Sed were not part of the calendar. The function of the mighty festival was to renew all of Egypt starting with the pharaoh. He himself played the major role in the drama. 'It was not a mere commemoration of the king's accession. It was a true renewal of kingly potency.'[11] The theatre event was performed in a special place that existed in a special time. But through this specialness flowed the eternal Nile which was both sacred and profane. And like the Nile, everyday Egyptian life was transformed by the Heb-Sed and renewed. [Fig. 6]

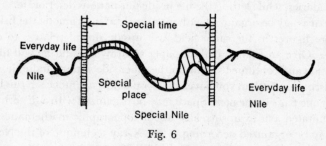

Fig. 6

Via Crete and other Mediterranean stepping-stones the Greeks took much from the Egyptians including the idea that the theatre is a festival: something that exists at a special time in a special place. But the Greeks were also influenced by prehistoric shamanistic ceremonies coming down from Central Asia and Europe. Animism, nature worship, and landscape were very important to the Greeks who, in this regard, were not so far from today's aborigines. The Greek theatre raised its audience in a semicircle around a full-circle dancing area. The audience area was made from a natural hill, and every Greek theatre gives a beautiful view over the skene to the landscape beyond. Thus the Greek arrangement included elements of holiday (= time out) and continuity with the landscape and the gods who dwelt therein. [Fig. 7]

Furthermore, the Greeks liked watching the dances not as discrete moves but as completed sequences, finished figures—a kind of stepped-out destiny in movement. In some surviving Greek theatres there are pavements of different-coloured stones tracing the dance routes: architectural scripts. These pavements help the memories of dancers and spectators alike. At any given moment the whole dance is known, and the dancers are seen as figures somewhere on the course. We tried for something like this in the *Commune* environment where different maps, figures, routes, and writing were marked on the floor and other parts of the environment. We used masking tape because that suggests the police reconstructing a crime and a stage manager marking the floor of a theatre.

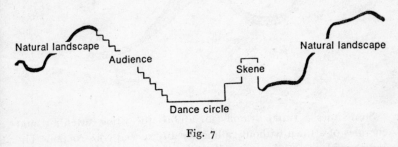

Fig. 7

Nothing could be farther from the Egyptian and Greek uses of space than the Balinese. The Balinese build nothing special for theatre. They do no seasonal plays. They perform in the village square, on temple steps, in courtyards, or on temporary stages thrown up for the occasion. And the occasion may be a marriage, a birth, a stroke of good fortune, a Hindu holiday, a need to placate the gods, or the means by which a rich man shows how rich he is. The performers are magnificently costumed and trained; they are professional in every sense except the commercial. But there is little formality surrounding a performance. Dogs eat some of the ceremonial food signalling the gods' acceptance of the offering, children play in the street in the midst of the trance-dancers, old men doze on their porches, women market, and those who want to watch the play do. Theatre in Bali accompanies everyday life. There is no time out for theatre. To the Balinese theatre happens anytime, anywhere, and its gestures are continuous with the rest of living.   [Fig. 8]

This integration of ceremonial and everyday is present in many Oriental cultures. M. C. Richards describes the Japanese Raku Ware where a person makes a teacup, fires it, and drinks out of it 'all in a single rhythm'.[12] The high formality of Japanese theatre is a refinement of daily, courtly, and military gestures. There is no break between theatre and the rest of life—only increasingly delicate stages of refinement. The Japanese theatre seems alien even to Japanese, because its gestures have been frozen in time. But at the beginning these gestures were not strange.

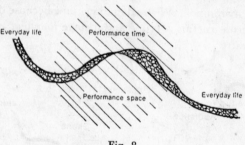

Fig. 8

Sometimes a ritual drama can absorb the whole attention and energies of a town without calling for any special construction. The existing village remains intact, but it is transformed by the drama into another time and place. Recently such a drama has been uncovered in coastal mountains of western Mexico. The Cora of Mesa del Nayar were converted to Catholicism by the Jesuits in the sixteenth century. Then in 1767 the Jesuits were expelled from Mexico. No priest appeared on the Mesa until 1969. During the two hundred years without contact these Cora maintained many Roman Catholic rites, among them a Holy Week passion play.

> But they had made them uniquely their own. For example, they had come to identify Our Lord Jesus Christ with their ancient deity Tayau, the sun god. . . . They took elements from the story of Christ's Passion, death, and Resurrection and made them into a ceremony apparently designed to ensure the renewal and continuity of their communal life.[13]

In the Cora play a boy of about seven plays Christ. There is no Pilate, no Judas. The villains are called *borrados*, which means 'erased ones' in Spanish. The borrados are the Judeans responsible for the crucifixion. For the three days of the festival 'all authority, civil and religious, passes to a man called the Captain of the Judeans. He and his borrados—young men of the region—darken themselves with soot and mud and thus "erase" their own personalities and their personal responsibility for whatever they do.' Fortified with peyote, the borrados hold forth for three days and nights. The crucifixion is preceded by a chase through the town with the boy-Christ doing his best to get away from the borrados. He is helped by a wooden cross that he brandishes. 'Three times—in the name of the Father, the Son, and the Holy Ghost—the borrados chased the boy, and three times they fell writing to the ground at the sight of the cross.' Then they catch him, tie him, and bring him to the church. There women groom him, and he sleeps overnight. The next morning he is brought out by the borrados and made to stand in front of a cross in the churchyard. This is the crucifixion. The next day at noon the village governor arrives on horseback. He plays the role of the centurion. He rides among the borrados and breaks their bamboo spears. They fall dead to the ground and then get up, go to the stream, and take a purifying bath. 'Near the church all was mirth and happiness.' Many things are interesting about the Cora play: how it is integrated into the life of the village, the changes made in the traditional Christ story, the double quality of drama and initiation ritual.

The Central Highlands of New Guinea provides the fifth model of using space. Catherine Berndt observed an all-night ceremony and noted the changes that occurred in a large open field.[14] 'At first there were distinct clusters of dancers, although the edges of the clusters blur as people greet kin, attend to ovens, or rest on the sidelines.' The blurring continues leading to wholesale intermingling 'until it becomes impossible to distinguish groups. Nevertheless, a certain nucleus is likely to resist this tendency to disperse.' Finally, as the time to set off for home approaches, 'the various units reform (though less compactly then before) and set off.' [Fig. 9]

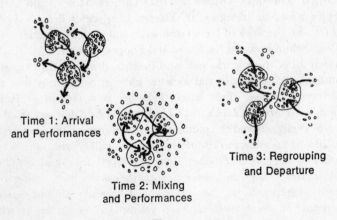

Time 1: Arrival and Performances

Time 2: Mixing and Performances

Time 3: Regrouping and Departure

Fig. 9

This is not unlike what happens at a party—except that in New Guinea the gathering is the occasion for performances of farces, dances, and songs. These are ornately costumed and often carefully staged.

Is the New Guinea use of space more 'primitive' than the Egyptian? The New Guinea use suits New Guinea ceremonial events which are also informal social gatherings like parties. The Egyptian use suits the great formality and impressive scale of the Heb-Sed. What the environmentalist learns in studying these examples—and many others—is that space-time-action is a single, flexible unit. The first obstacle to environmental design is preconception. The great enemy of preconception is a knowledge of cultures and periods other than one's own.

Thus far I've spoken of environmental design abstractly. I've said that it is related to body spaces, space-senses, and space-fields, but I have not been concrete in showing how. For one thing environmental design practice is ahead of theory. This is true partly because there are so many extraordinary examples of environmental design if we simply open our eyes to see. Whether the environmentalist looks at American Indian, Asian, Oceanic, African, Siberian, or Eskimo societies, he finds many models that may stimulate his creativity. Also he can look back in history as far as he can—to Altamira and the other caves; and then forward to Egypt, the Near and Middle East, Asia, and medieval Europe. In our own day he can study productions like Ludovico Ronconi's *Orlando Furioso*, Gilbert Moses' and Archie Shepp's *Slave Ship* (designed by Eugene Lee), Peter Brook's *Tempest* and *Orghast*, the work of Jerzy Grotowski, and the extraordinary work of Peter Schumann and the Bread and Puppet Theater.

What all of these works past and present, dramatic and ritual, in industrial and non-industrial societies have in common is that they each create or use whole space. Whether it is *Orghast* or Robert Wilson's *KA MOUNTAIN and GUARDenia TERRACE* set amid the ruins of Persepolis and the mountains near Shiraz, or the Heb-Sed on the Nile, or an initiation rite that starts in a village, moves to a road leading to the river, climaxes along the riverbanks, and concludes back in the village, or *Akropolis* with its environment being built out of stovepipes during the performance, or a pig-kill and dance at Kurumugl in New Guinea—each example is of an event whose expression in space is a complete statement of what the event is.

Sometimes the space is broken into many spaces. Sometimes the audience is given a special place to watch from. Sometimes the space is treated fluidly, changing during the performance. Sometimes nothing is done to the space. The thing about environmental theatre space is not just a matter of how you end up using space. It is an attitude. *Start with all the space there is and then decide what to use, what not to use, and how to use what you use.*

Work on *Makbeth* began in October 1968, with workshops exploring Shakespeare's *Macbeth*. We did a lot of exercises about prophecy, laying on hands, witchcraft. We took the text apart and reassembled it in funny ways. We tried to find the main threads of action from both an individual and a group point of view. In December we had Rojo and McNamara down to the Garage. Both of them sat in on workshops and talk. Many models of the environment were proposed. We selected, finally, Rojo's—but did not discard McNamara's. After modification it became the Makbeth Maze: the way into the theatre from the second floor of the Garage. The Maze was a bit of Madame Toussaud, a bit of fun house, scraps of theatre history, mirrors, and information about the performance. It ended at an open hole in the floor, a narrow descent into Makbeth's hell.[15]

The mise-en-scène for *Makbeth* was worked out in six phases, the environment in five.

Mise-en-scène

1. October 1968–February 1969. Improvisations without keeping to Shakespeare's text. Search for basic actions, basic movement patterns. First determination of space-field as 'cabin'd, cribb'd, and confin'd.'

2. March–June 1969. Making of scenes not in Shakespeare. These expressed some actual situations in the Group. Using Shakespeare's text as raw material. Demystifying Shakespeare. First character groupings: Dark Powers, Founders, Doers, Avengers.

3. July–August 1969. Cast assignments. Decisions about the shape of the space, the nature of the music. Much work with Rojo and Epstein. End of group workshops. I worked alone assembling what we had into a coherent script.

4. September 1969. Rehearsals in Baocic, Yugoslavia, while Rojo built the environment in the Garage. Composition of music by Epstein in Philadelphia.

5. October–November 1969. Rehearsals in the Garage. Revision of script. Integration of music into the production. Opening.

6. December 1969–January 1970. Run. Few changes except tightening. Closing.

The second phase of work didn't yield an acceptable performance text, but it gave performers a handle on the language. The work overcame the scared feelings people have when first approaching sacred Shakespeare. Also the second phase made it clear how to organize the story and divide the roles.

Environment

1. October 1968–February 1969. Rojo, McNamara, and I discussed the themes of the play and possibilities for the environment. They came to a few workshops.

2. March–May 1969. Rojo and McNamara attended Wednesday night workshops devoted to text construction and environment. Drawings and models, many rejected ideas including ziggurats, corrals, and wire fences. Finally, Rojo's design is accepted, and McNamara's is transformed into the Maze.

3. June–August, 1969. Construction of working models. Decision to move Maze upstairs and use it as the way into the environment downstairs. Approval of final building plans before my departure for Yugoslavia in August. Also approval of costumes.

4. September 1969. Construction of about 90 per cent of the environment while the Group rehearsed in Yugoslavia.

5. October 1969. Completion of environment, lighting, costumes.

The big mistake with *Makbeth* was that we rehearsed it in Baocic, and the space-field of that outdoor meadow stayed with us. It was impossible to work effectively in the Garage environment. The Yugoslavian rehearsals broke in two our work on the play; and yet the rehearsals in Yugoslavia gave us the fundamental scenic actions. The production could not survive the contradiction. Ultimately the magnificent Garage environment was alien to a mise-en-scène worked out in Yugoslavia.

The Baocic meadow was large; performers looked across at adversaries who could be seen but not heard. There was a limitless ceiling of sky, the play of natural light, the sweet smell of clean air. In the meadow the Dark Powers transformed into birds hiding in the trees or woodchucks in the underbrush. The Makbeths lived atop a knoll near a large tree. Malcolm and Macduff, after the murder of their father, Duncan, took a long semicircular route through forests and shrubs to get at the Makbeths. I directed by running from one side of the meadow to another, ducking behind trees or rocks, flattened on my belly in the grass, watching, yelling directions, just keeping up with the action. I saw Banquo, trapped by the Dark Powers in a blind alley of shrubbery, vainly struggle before they bashed her head in with a rock. I hid nearby as the Dark Powers lured Makbeth into a dusky gully cut by a brook and whispered to him that he would never be slain by a man of woman born. I watched as Malcolm and Macduff, assisted by the Dark Powers, camouflaged themselves with grass and branches and advanced on Dunsinane. Only a few of these scenes were translatable into the Garage environment. The long, deep pit against the north wall served well as the gully-home of the Dark Powers; Banquo was trapped amid the wood columns supporting the environment; the advancing Malcolm and Macduff darted from column to column as in a forest as they approached Dunsinane. But the amplitude of the Baocic meadow could not be stuffed into Rojo's magnificent Garage environment. Furthermore, this amplitude did not suit the play we started the previous winter in New York.

What happened during the month's rehearsals in Baocic was that the performers developed the action according to the space-field there while Rojo built from what he perceived from workshops. The space-field of Baocic contradicted the space-field of Rojo's environment. Disunity within the Group made it impossible to overcome or live with this contradiction. We could not use it creatively. I remember William Finley saying, when he first saw the Garage, 'It's great, really marvellous, but how do we work in it?' I panicked and resorted to blocking. Instead of taking the time to let the performers feel their way around, through, and into the space, I imposed actions and rhythms. Throughout its run *Makbeth* never felt at home in the Garage. I hope I've learned the lesson: *Text, action and environment must develop together*.

Rojo's environment had one supreme quality: it incorporated the tensions he sensed in the Group, conflicts that led to the dissolution of TPG early in 1970. The rehearsals of *Makbeth* coincided with the undoing of the Group. Daily, heavy personal things came down, and although no one said so out loud, I think we each knew that *Makbeth* was our last play together. Because of the way TPG works, our conflicts fed into the structure of *Makbeth*. It became an angry play of blood, power struggles, betrayals, fleeting contacts, brief flashes of quiet punctuated by screams. All of this is in Shakespeare's script. It also characterized the environment. Gone were the soft carpets and suffused lighting of *Dionysus* replaced by a concrete floor, bare wood platforms framed by iron piping, lighting that came in fitful bursts. The bare feet of *Dionysus* gave way to boxing shoes, nakedness to unisex costumes of crushed corduroy.

It was better with *Commune*. Rojo and I met during the spring of 1970 to talk over the play while it was in its very early stages. He visited New Paltz several times during the summer to watch workshops and present and revise his drawings and models. Sculptor Robert Adzema made several models that were helpful in getting the environment together. Everyone in the Group went over the models and made suggestions. At the end of July the Wave was built in New Paltz, and we rehearsed with it for the rest of the summer. We appropriated scaffolding and built an approximation of the environment Rojo was designing. He saw enough rehearsals to change his plans according to what was happening to the play. There were weekly open rehearsals to see how the audience reacted to the environment. By the end of August a plan was agreed on, and during September while TPG and Wave were in residence at Goddard, Rojo built about one-third of the environment in the Garage. In October we did a few open rehearsals in the Garage working in the partially finished environment. Rojo learned from watching us work. He completed the environment in October while the Group was on tour—still with the Wave, our cumbersome environmental security blanket. When the Group returned to New York in November, everyone pitched in to paint the Garage. We painted the ceiling sky blue and the walls desert red-brown. The environment was finished. Later, during performances, spectators—given chalk—added much interesting graffiti.

Some of the graffiti is still on the ceiling, even for *The Tooth of Crime*. And lumber, fittings, scraps of every environment ever built in the Garage comprise part of whatever is most current. This is not only a matter of economy. Like new cities built on the rubble and from the rubble of older ones, the present recapitulates and transforms the past: there is a tangible tradition in the Garage.

There is no such thing as a standard environmental design. A standard design mocks the basic principle: *The event, the performers, the environmentalist, the director, and the audience interacting with each other in a space (or spaces) determine the environment.* Having said that, I offer a 'standard environmental design'. A theatre ought to offer to each spectator the chance to find his own place. There ought to be *jumping-off places* where spectators can physically enter the performance; there ought to be *regular places* where spectators can arrange themselves more or less as they would in an orthodox theatre—this helps relieve the anxieties some people feel when entering an environmental theatre; there ought to be *vantage points* where people can get out of the way of the main action and look at it with detachment; there ought to be *pinnacles, dens, and hutches*: extreme places far up, far back, and deep down where spectators can dangle or burrow or vanish. At most levels there ought to be places where people can be alone, be together with one or two others, or be with a fairly large group. Spaces ought to be open enough so that in most of them people can stand, sit, lean, or lie down as the mood directs. Spaces ought to open to each other so that spectators can see each other and move from one place to another. The overall feel of the theatre ought to be of a place where choices can be made. The feel I get from a successful environment is that of a *global space*, a microcosm, with flow, contact, and inter-action.

This long list of 'ought to be's' is obliterated by the specific needs of a production. None of the TPG environments meets all of these 'requirements'.

As the environmentalist works, particularly if he is new at the game, he should ask himself questions. These questions are implicit in the work, different from questions an orthodox designer might ask.

1. Does the mass, volume, and rhythm of the whole environment express the play? Not the play as I abstractly conceive it, but as I have watched it develop in rehearsals?

2. Does the material out of which the environment is built—texture, weight, colour, density, feel—express the play?

3. Can spectators see each other? Can they hide from each other? Can they stand, sit, lean, lie down? Can they be alone, in small groups, in larger groups?

4. Are there places to look down on most of the action, to look across at it, to look up to it?

5. Where are the places for performing? How are they connected to each other? How many places are used both by the audience and by the performers?

6. Are there efficient ways of moving up and down as well as in all horizontal directions?

7. What does the environment sound like? How does it smell?

8. Can every surface and supporting member safely hold as many people as can crowd onto it? Are there at least two ways in and out of every space?

The thing about safety is that nothing should be disguised. If a ladder is hard to climb, make it look like it's hard to climb. In five years' working in the Garage there have been no major accidents and only a few scrapes and sprains. The worst that's happened has been a broken foot that occurred to William Shephard when he made a spectacular leap changing his course in midair to avoid demolishing a spectator.

The environmentalist is not trying to create the illusion of a place; he wants to create a functioning space. This space will be used by many different kinds of people, not only the performers. The stage designer is often concerned with effect: how does it *look* from the house? The environmentalist is concerned with structure and use: how does it *work*? Often the stage designer's set is used from a distance —don't touch this, don't stand on that—but everything the environmentalist builds must work. Stage designing is two-dimensional, a kind of propped-up painting. Environmental design is strictly three-dimensional. If it's there, it's got to work. This leads to sparseness.

Have you ever thought how *stupid* the proscenium theatre is architecturally? Start with the auditorium, the 'house'. A silly name for row after row of regularly arranged seats—little properties that spectators rent for a few hours. Nothing here of the freedom of arrangement in a house where people live—and can push the furniture around. And most of the places in the 'house' are disadvantageous for seeing or hearing. The first few rows are so close that the actors—in their effort to project to the back and up to the balconies—spit all over you; the seats to the side give a fun-house mirror view of the stage, all pulled out of proportion; the seats at the back of the orchestra under the balcony are claustrophobic and acoustically murder; the view from the second balcony makes the stage look like a flea circus. Only a few seats in the orchestra, mezzanine, and first balcony offer anything like a pleasing view of the stage. But this is no surprise. The proscenium theatre was originally designed to emphasize differences in class and wealth. It was meant to have very good seats, medium seats, poor seats, and very bad seats.

When people come late or leave early, they all but step on you, push their asses in your face, and disrupt whole rows of spectators. There is no chance to readjust your body, take a seventh-inning stretch, or extend your arms. During intermission everyone runs to the lobby to gobble food, drink, smoke, talk. Intermission is just about the only human thing going on. Also, of course, to see who's here—which undeniably is one of theatre's chiefest and oldest joys. Not just to look at or for famous people—but to look over the crowd, see who's out with you this evening. This looking is impossible in the darkened house that cruelly makes you focus straight ahead, as in church or at school, at a performance that, finally, may not interest you at all.

The worst thing about the 'house' is that it imprisons you away from the stage where there are many interesting things to see if you were only allowed. What's visible of the stage from the house is only a fraction of its total area and volume. For me the wonderful direction is up. To gaze up into the flies through rods and curtains and lights and ropes and catwalks and galleries into the immense space! Whenever TPG is asked to perform in a proscenium, I accept with enthusiasm. 'Bring everyone on stage,' I say, 'and turn a few lights upward so that people can see how high the flies are.' Also in newer theatres there are vast chambers to the left and right of the playing stage, and often behind the playing area, too. These are for 'wagons', a term as old as medieval theatre, meaning rolling platforms on which whole sets are built and then brought into place. And sometimes there is a turntable—a device Brecht loved. Usually there are trapdoors leading to a cellar under the stage, and doors going to the backstage, the shop, the dressing rooms, the greenroom. So the proscenium stage is a focused space surrounded on every side by other spaces attending on the stage like an old queen. How mean that audiences should be exiled from this royal realm of magic. Such exclusion is pitiable, cheap, unfair, and unnecessary.

My own preference is to do away with most of the machinery. It makes the theatre worker like a soldier trapped inside his burning tank. But I would keep the spaces—the overs, unders, and arounds.

Some new theatres designed by people who want to keep up to date try to keep 'the best' from previous ages. These theatres are like old trees weighted down by so many branches that they break. Such a theatre is the brand-new job at the University of Rhode Island, where TPG was in residence in the summer of 1971. The theatre wasn't even open to the public when I saw it. In the semicircular arrangement of seats in the house is the Greek amphitheatre, in the vomitoria leading from the house to the foot of the orchestra pit is the Roman stadium, in the space for wagons are the medieval moralities and pageants, in the fly system are the Italian scenic conventions of the Renaissance, in the slightly thrust stage is the Elizabethan theatre, in the proscenium

6

posts is the eighteenth-century theatre, in the orchestra pit is the nineteenth-century opera, in the turntable is the early twentieth-century, in the bank after bank of computerized lighting controls are contemporary electronics. Pity the poor student actor!

When the Group took one look at this monster, we decided to work in the scene shop—an honest, large, irregular space that could be made into anything. Not by building scenery or pushing buttons, but by putting down a plywood floor we could dance and run and jump on, some scaffolds to climb over, a few velours to soak up extra noise, and fewer than twenty lights to make it bright enough to see. The rest is performing.

The simple fact that in most theatres actors enter through their own door at one time and audience enters through another door at a later time architecturally expresses a strong aesthetic and class consciousness. The separate doors are entrances literally to different worlds. The stage door leads to all the equipment and facilities backstage. This stuff is not at all dressed up. Layers of paint, raw pipes, old scenery, costume racks, lights, wires, tools, are all laid out in ways that facilitate use and accessibility. Except on the stage things are arranged according to systems that make for easy indexing and use. On the stage, of course, things are arranged for the audience's eyes. The audience enters the theatre door into a plush, often ornate, and stylish lobby. This is so even off off-Broadway where, in their own way, the lobbies are modish. The house itself is as plush as the producers can afford to make it. From the house the audience views the stage where an illusion has been created. From the front the stage presents its false but pretty face. From backstage the scenery is ugly (if you like illusions) but working—supports, nails, ropes, and wires are visible— and the view of the stage from behind or the sides reminds me of nothing so much as a ship: a lot of equipment focused in a small space.

What if the audience and the actors were to enter through the same door at the same time? What if all the equipment of the theatre, however arranged, were available to public view at all times? What if we eliminated the distinctions between backstage and onstage, house and stage, stage door and theatre door? No theatre that I know of has done this, not absolutely. Once in Vancouver in August 1972, TPG experimented with a 'real-time' performance of *Commune*. I announced to our workshop and to some university classes that anyone would be welcome to come to the theatre at 6 P.M.—at the time of the performers' call. About ten students showed up, and they entered the theatre together with the performers. The visitors were free to go wherever they pleased. They watched warmups, listened to notes, helped the tech director check the lights, set the props, fill the tub, clean up the theatre. They watched the performers put on their costumes and saw the regular audience arrive at 7:45. Then the performance. After, the routine of closing up the theatre for the night: removing costumes and putting them in the laundry bag for washing, re-collecting props, emptying the tub, and all the other routines of ending. Out of the ten students only two or three stuck for the whole process that was over about 10:30. (*Commune* itself takes only about ninety minutes.) The performers were a little uneasy at their presence for warmups and notes. After the performance no one minded who was there. I felt funny, too, and performed a little for the 'real-time' audience. I wanted them to have a good time. Removing the 'magic' from theatre won't be easy.

A further experiment in this line is part of *The Tooth of Crime* production. Performers man the box office, greet spectators as they enter the theatre, explain aspects of the production: particularly the fact that spectators can get as close to a scene as they wish by moving throughout the theatre during the entire performance. At intermission performers prepare and sell coffee, talk to spectators, socialize, and let everyone know when the second act is beginning. The difference between show time and intermission is clear, but there is no attempt made at hiding the non-performing life performers lead even in the midst of a night at theatre. Strikingly enough, I find that the performers' concentration on their work and the audience's interest in the story is not at all diminished by the socializing. If anything, the playing of the play is enhanced. Roles are seen as emerging from a full constellation of activities that include economics, logistics, hostings, and one-to-one relationships. The performers are seen not as the magic people *of* the story but as the people who *play* the story.

When I design an environment, I try to take into account the space-senses of the performers, of the text-action, and of the space we're working in. These make an irregular circle, an interconnected system that is always changing.   [Fig. 10]

In time the space gets set as the environment is built. Or doesn't get set. The finest thing about *Orlando Furioso* was the way the environment itself kept changing because the environment was the audience. As the big set pieces crawled or hurtled across the floor, the audience scattered or followed. I climbed a lighting tower and looked down from about twenty feet. Not knowing Italian helped me concentrate on the changing figures of movement. I thought I detected a pattern.

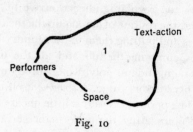

Fig. 10

For gentle, quiet scenes the audience pressed in, heads and shoulders forward. Running away from a careening platform, they seemed to run in front of it instead of to the sides as one might expect. In other words, they challenged the platform to run them down—they played a game with the platform. They stood back from declamations, with hips thrust forward, head and shoulders back.

Once the audience is let into the environment, the basic relationship is changed. There are four points on the circle.   [Fig. 11]

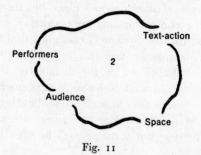

Fig. 11

This is as simple as ABC except that in orthodox theatre the audience is outside the circle. Fixed seating, lighting design, architecture: everything is clearly meant to exclude the audience from any kind of participation in the action. Even their watching is meant to be ignored. The spectators are put into the semi-fetal prison of a chair, and no matter what they feel, it will be hard to physicalize and express those feelings.   [Fig. 12]

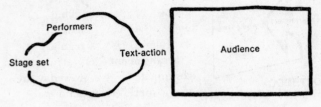

Fig. 12

I don't see any middle ground. Either the audience is in it or they are out of it. Either there is potential for *contact* or there is not. I don't deny that the spectator in the orthodox theatre feels something. Sure he does. *But he cannot easily, naturally, unconsciously, and without embarrassment express those feelings except within idiotically limited limits.*

When we say of a great performer that he or she has *presence*, that we are *moved* by the performance, that we have been *touched*, we are not speaking nonsense or entirely metaphorically. Many times I've seen an audience collectively catch its breath, shift position, become very still, change their points of contact and orientation to each other, or to the performers, quite unconsciously, without thought or intention. These changes in body positions, in expressive poses—the way a person fronts himself (or sidles, or turns his shoulder, or his back) on another—on an action is a delightful part of every performance in an environmental theatre. The theatre ought architecturally to offer a rich field for this kind of communication—not only to occur but to be observed by whoever has eyes for it. The orthodox theatre lets the audience see the actors making this kind of movement. But what about letting spectators see spectators and performers see spectators? Such open architecture encourages a contact that is continuous, subtle, fluid, pervasive, and unconscious. Lovely.

Three major tendencies of contemporary Western theatre are exemplified by the ways audiences are arranged and treated. In the orthodox theatre, including so-called open stages, such as arenas, thrust stages, and calipter stages, the stage is brightly lit and active; from it information flows into the darkened auditorium where the audience is arranged in regular seats. Feedback from the house to the stage is limited.   [Fig. 13]

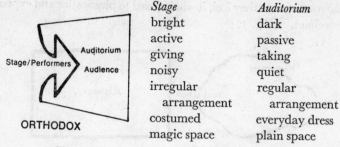

Stage	Auditorium
bright	dark
active	passive
giving	taking
noisy	quiet
irregular	regular
arrangement	arrangement
costumed	everyday dress
magic space	plain space

Fig. 13

Confrontation theatre, as in the Living Theatre's *Paradise Now*, uses orthodox theatre space for unorthodox ends. Many local scenes or confrontations take place both on the stage and in the auditorium. The traditional uses of stage and house are frequently inverted. The aim of confrontation theatre is to provoke the audience into participating or at least to make people feel very uncomfortable about not participating. Confrontational theatre is a transitional form depending heavily on an *épater le bourgeois* attitude and the need among the bourgeois to experience suffering as a relief of guilt.   [Fig. 14]

Stage	Auditorium
bright	alternately bright and dark
active	forced into activity
giving-taking	taking-giving
noisy	noisy
irregular arrangement	regular arrangement changed by attempts to use the whole space
usually in street clothes, sometimes naked	usually in street clothes, but sometimes provoked to nakedness or exchange of clothes
magic space made plain	plain space made magic

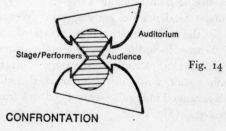

Fig. 14

CONFRONTATION

Environmental theatre encourages give-and-take throughout a globally organized space in which the areas occupied by the audience are a kind of sea through which the performers swim; and the performance areas are kinds of islands or continents in the midst of the audience. The audience does not sit in regularly arranged rows; there is one whole space rather than two opposing spaces. The environmental use of space is fundamentally *collaborative*; the action flows in many directions sustained only by the cooperation of performers and spectators. Environmental theatre design is a reflection of the communal nature of this kind of theatre. The design encourages participation; it is also a reflection of the wish for participation. There are no settled sides automatically dividing the audience off against the performers. [Fig. 15]

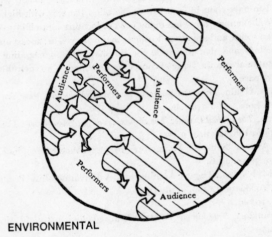

ENVIRONMENTAL

Fig. 15

I end this essay by proposing a few principles of environmental design. These have all been discussed. I gather them as a way of easy reference and summary.

1. For each production the whole space is designed.
2. The design takes into account space-senses and space-fields.
3. Every part of the environment is functional.
4. The environment evolves along with the play it embodies.
5. The performer is included in all phases of planning and building.

1. Joseph Chaikin, *The Presence of the Actor* (New York: Atheneum, 1973), p. 30.

2. For a complete account of the production see *The Performance Group, Dionysus 69*, ed. Richard Schechner (New York: Farrar Straus and Giroux, 1970). A film of the play taken in the Garage is also available.

3. Articulating a space means letting the space have *its* say. Looking at a space and exploring it not as a means of doing what you want to do in it, but of uncovering what the space is, how it is constructed, what its various rhythms are. Maybe staying still in it, as in the spaces of some cathedrals.

4. When an action is literally impossible—such as swimming or flying—the performer does it sonically, or in action with the help of others. If a person cannot fly by himself, he can be carried in such a way that he gets a sense of flying. If he cannot swim through air, he can make his breath find the rhythms of swimming.

5. Much work needs to be done in pinpointing the exact relationships between the human body and space. Many apparently mystical concepts will, I think, be found to have roots in fact. Just as the blind bat sees with high-frequency sound, so the human being has many ways of locating himself in space; means other than seeing and sounding. I believe that energy is broadcast and received very precisely and that we are at the threshold of understanding what and how. Also we are on the verge of conceding that there is no such thing as dead or empty space.

6. Richard A. Gould, *Yiwara: Foragers of the Australian Desert* (New York: Charles Scribner's Sons, 1969), p. 128.

7. S. Giedion, *The Eternal Present: The Beginnings of Art* (New York: The Bollingen Foundation, 1962), vol. 1, p. 22.

8. Antonin Artaud, 'Symbolic Mountains' (1945), tr. Victor Corti, in *TDR*, 1965, vol. 9, no. 3, pp. 94–6.

9. Donald M. Kaplan, 'Theatre Architecture: A derivation of the Primal Cavity', in *TDR*, 1968, vol. 12, no. 3, p. 113.

10. Ibid. pp. 107–8.

11. Henri Frankfort, *Kingship and the Gods* (Chicago: University of Chicago Press, 1948), p. 79.

12. M. C. Richards, *Centering* (Middleton, Connecticut: Wesleyan University Press, 1970), p. 29.

13. Guillermo E. Aldana's extraordinary *National Geographic* article (June 1971), 'Mesa del Nayar's Strange Holy Week', has many unforgettable photographs. All quotations are from Aldana's article.

14. Quotations and drawings from Catherine H. Berndt, 'Ascription of Meaning in a ceremonial context in the Eastern Central Highlands of New Guinea', in *Anthropology in the South Seas* (1959), pp. 161–83.

15. The New Orleans Group had something similar in the lobby for *Victims of Duty* in 1967. The exhibit was mounted on billboards and contained hundreds of photos, newpaper articles, letters, birth certificates and other personal crap dealing with the private lives of the performers and directors—a takeoff on the trivia in theatre programmes. Also there was a short film, slides, and taped

music counterpointing the Tulane NROTC band with Hitler marches. During the performance the exhibit was changed so that when the audience left, people were forced to duck under a sheet on which was written the famous Eichmann quotation: 'I am a victim of the actions of others and obedience to duty'. From the ceiling hung pictures of Eichmann all neat in his uniform.

4
Performers and Spectators
Transported and Transformed

By using masks, costumes, and physical actions arranged in a set way, or improvised according to known rules; by performing following a script, scenario, or set of rules; by performing in special places or places made special by performing in them; by performing on holidays or at times set aside 'after work' or at crises in the life cycle such as initiations, weddings, and funerals: by all these means, and more, theatrical reality is marked 'non-ordinary—for special use only'. Furthermore, what is performed is encoded—I want to say nested, trapped, contained, distilled, held, restrained, metaphorized—in one, or more, special kinds of communication: either as a mixture of narrative and Hindu temple service as in Ramlila; or as fixed narrative and individual creativity as in any of the productions of, say, Chekhov's *The Cherry Orchard*; or as a well-known sequence of events better known to connoisseurs than to common spectators as in the *kuse mai* of the Noh drama *Yorimasa* as performed by the Kanze school; or as closely guarded secrets revealed to initiates during the performance itself as in the vomiting and bleeding that is part of the initiation of Gahuku boys in Papua–New Guinea; or as a script imposed by a single writer-director-scenographer such as with Richard Foreman's *Pain(t)*; or as words and actions devised collectively as with *Mysteries and Smaller Pieces* of The Living Theatre; or as a scenario sent to hundreds of people, some of them friends, some strangers, to be acted (or discarded) separately, and in many different styles, by recipients of one of Allan Kaprow's happenings. This Homeric list may exhaust you, reader, but not the field. They are mere smatterings of evidence of the incredible diversity of performance events. And I have pointedly omitted events like the Mass, professional football, psychodrama, whirling dervishes in devotion, Sumo wrestling: a wide variety of performative rituals, games, sports, and hard-to-define activities that lie between or outside established genres. After all, 'established genre' indicates a record of what has found its place, while performance activities are fundamentally processual: there will always be a certain proportion of them in the process of transformation, categorically undefinable. But all performances—defined and undefined—share at least one underlying quality. Performance behaviour isn't free and easy. Performance behaviour is known and/or practised behaviour—or 'twice-behaved behaviour', 'restored behaviour'[1]—either rehearsed, previously known, learned by osmosis since early childhood, revealed during the performance by masters, guides, gurus, or elders, or generated by rules that govern the outcomes as in improvisatory theatre or sports.

Because performance behaviour isn't free and easy it never wholly 'belongs to' the performer. In Euro-American theatre (Stanislavski and after) much of the work of training and rehearsal makes performance behaviour seem 'as if' it belongs to the performer.

> Because the very best that can happen is to have the actor completely carried away by the play. Then regardless of his own will he lives the part, not noticing *how* he feels, not thinking about *what* he does, and it all moves of its own accord, subconsciously and intuitively.[2]

But Stanislavski well knew that this kind of intuitive flow is unreliable. Thus the 'Stanislavski system' is largely devoted to training the actor so that flow can be generated through a conscious process. But such a seamless knitting of the 'life of' the character and that of the actor is not the goal of all theatre everywhere. In the West, Brecht distrusted it, but Brecht himself modelled his ideal actor—one who alternated between flow and reflexivity, between 'being the character' and speaking about the character—after what he had learned of Asian theatre, especially Chinese theatre. And in the Ramlila of Ramnagar, India's best-known Ramlila, the directors of the spectacle, the *vyases*, stand behind the performers, open regiebuchs in hand, correcting words and actions: making certain that everything happens according to the book. Interestingly, the crowds at Ramlila are not troubled into supposing that the actions of Rama or Hanuman are any less 'real' due to the presence of the *vyases*, or even their intervention. But clearly the 'life of' Rama and Hanuman intersect but are not identical to the 'life of' the actors. Like the presence of director-author T. Kantor during the performances of his *The Dead Class*—where Kantor makes slight adjustments in the performance by lowering a performer's hand, or whispering to another to speed up the delivery of some lines—the corrections of the performance become part of the performance. The stage—and I don't mean only the physical place, but the time/space/spectator/performer aggregate—generates a centripetal field that gobbles up whatever happens on it or near it. This absorption into the centre is the chief parallel between performance process and ritual process; it's what Kafka meant when he wrote the mini-parable:

> Leopards break into the temple and drink to the dregs what is in the sacrificial pitchers; this is repeated over and over again; finally it can be calculated in advance, and it becomes part of the ceremony.[3]

After some performances Kantor's corrections became predictable; people who saw *The Dead Class* many times say that Kantor's gestures are no longer free but part of the performance score. But even the intervening-when-needed, and therefore unpredictable, actions of the *vyases* at Ramlila are part of the performance score—just as the officials moving in and out of a football game intervene only when there is an infraction but still play decisive and well-defined roles in the game.

As Kafka says, accidents become part of the ceremony, even adding a special thrill. During the 1980 Ringling Brothers Circus at Madison Square Garden, a trapeze artist attempts to rise from a position where she is hanging by her ankles. She starts, hesitates, reaches, almost falls. The music stops, the crowd gasps—if she cannot reach the bar she will drop forty feet. Finally, inching her way up, grabbing her left forearm with her right hand, she reaches the bar. The music crescendos, the crowd sighs relief and then cheers. The whole bit is repeated each show. It doesn't matter whether this bit actually happened once and then was kept as business, or whether it was invented wholesale. It is now 'calculated in advance': part of the show. And each show—of theatre, sports, ritual—is a palimpsest collecting, or stacking, and displaying whatever is, as Brecht says, 'the least rejected of all the things tried'. But the performance process is a continuous rejecting and replacing. Long-running shows—and certainly rituals are these—are not dead repetitions but continuous erasings and superimposings. The overall shape of the show stays the same, but pieces of business are always coming and going. This process of collecting and discarding, of selecting, organizing, and showing, is what rehearsals are all about. And it's not such a rational, logical-linear process as writing about it makes it seem. It's not so much a thought-out system of trial and error as it is a playing around with themes, actions, gestures, fantasies, words: whatever's being worked on. From all the doing, some things are done again and again; they are perceived in retrospect as 'working', and they are 'kept'. They are, as it were, thrown forward in time to be used in the 'finished performance'. The performance 'takes shape' little bit by little bit, building from the fragments of 'kept business' so that often the final scene of a show will be clear before its first scene—or specific bits will be perfected before a sense of the overall production is known. That is why the text of a play will tell you so little about how a production might look. The production doesn't 'come out' of the text, but is generated in rehearsal in an effort to 'meet' the text. And when you see a play and recognize it as familiar you are referring back to earlier productions, not to the playscript. An unproduced play is not a homunculus but a shard of an as yet unassembled whole.

During the run of a play—or over the calendrically fixed course of the performances of a ritual—even in the most traditional genres (I've seen Noh, Ramlila, Kathakali, and Balinese dance-drama do this) new business is accumulated and stale business eliminated. A person going to a particular performance only once, as is the habit in our culture, can't notice the process of continuous change. Sometimes, where a performance is frozen tight, it takes great effort, and ceremony, to update the show: as when a Pope summons a Council to revise the Mass. But on the local level, the Mass is always being adjusted to suit the living relationship between priest and parishioners. This relationship is as much one between performer and participating spectators as between religious leader and faithful. Individual performative variation will be appreciated even more when you recognize that a performance of the Mass far transcends the recitation of a set text: it involves the particular and peculiar styles of the performers. And as with the Mass, so with all ceremonies/rituals everywhere.

I wrote before that performing isn't free and easy: it is behaviour that is 'put on'. This is what gives theatre its bad name. Theatre is that art where the master teacher says, 'Truth is what acting is all about; once you can fake truth you've got it made.' This is not a wholly cynical statement, as can be seen in the story Lévi-Strauss tells of Quesalid, a Kwakiutl who wanted to expose the quackery of the shamans.[4] 'Driven by curiosity about their tricks and by the desire to expose them, he began to associate with the shamans until one of them offered to make him a member of their group. Quesalid did not wait to be asked twice.' He was thoroughly trained in acting, magic, singing; he learned how to fake fainting and fits, how to induce vomiting and to employ spies who would tell him about the lives of his patients. He learned how to hide a wad of down in the corner of his mouth and then, biting his tongue or making his gums bleed, to produce this bloody evidence before patient and spectators as 'the pathological foreign body extracted as a result of his sucking and manipulations'. Quesalid mastered the art so well that he not only exposed the other shamans as quacks but built a powerful reputation for himself as a true shaman. Over the years he began to believe in his cures, even though he always knew that they were based on tricks. But he reasoned that the ill got better because they believed in him, and they believed in him because he knew his art so well and performed it so stunningly. Finally he thought of the bloody down and all his other tricks as manifestations of his own authentic powers. As Lévi-Strauss says: 'Quesalid did not become a great shaman because he cured his patients; he cured his patients because he had become a great shaman.' Quesalid, like the leopards in Kafka's parable, was absorbed into the field of his own performing. He was transformed into what he had set out to expose.[5]

At the Ramlila of Ramnagar, India, one of the best actors is the man who plays the semi-divine sage, Narad-muni. When Narad-muni speaks or sings the audience—sometimes of more than twenty-five thousand—listens with special care; many believe the performer playing Narad-muni has powers linking him to the sage/character he plays. This man is no longer called by his born name, not even by himself. Over the thirty-five years he has performed Narad-muni he has increasingly been identified with the legendary sage. Because he is a Brahmin, and any Brahmin can perform priestly ceremonies, Narad began some years ago to practise priestcraft. Now he is the *mahant*—owner and chief priest—of two temples in Mirzapur, a city about forty miles from Ramnagar. He is rich. People come from far away to his temples because they know Narad-muni speaks through Narad-priest. Narad never claims to be an incarnation of Narad-muni. But each year at Ramlila his connection to Narad-muni is renewed, displayed, deepened, and ritualized before an audience of thousands. This man is not Narad-muni, but also he is not not Narad-muni: he performs in the field between a negative and a double negative, a field of limitless potential, free as it is from both the person (not) and the person impersonated (not not). All effective performances share this 'not—not not' quality: Olivier is not Hamlet, but also he is not not Hamlet: his performance is between a denial of being another (= I am me) and a denial of not being another (= I am Hamlet). Performer training focuses its techniques not on making one person into another, but in permitting the performer to act in-between identities; in this sense performing is a paradigm of liminality.

Indian culture with its tradition of reincarnation encourages this kind of multiplication of impersonations. When the beautiful black god Krishna was desired by all of the *gopis*, he multiplied himself so that each woman had Krishna with her: this theme is a favourite of Indian artists, both visual and performative, and forms the praxis-core of many kinds of Krishna worship.[6] And who is the 'genuine' Hamlet? Olivier? Burton? Bernhardt? Or Burbage, who played it first in 1603? Or a nameless English actor who toured France even earlier in a lost play now known only as the *ur-Hamlet*? This question of multiple realities, each the negativity of all the others, does not merely point to a peculiarity of the stage, but rather locates the essence of performance: at once the most concrete and evanescent of the arts. And in so far as performance is a main model for human behaviour in general, this liminal, processual, multi-real quality reveals both the glory and the abyss of human freedom.

Few are the performers who have experienced Narad's transformation. Even at Ramlila most performers don't get absorbed into their roles. This is not to say the roles don't deeply affect the performer's lives. In approaching the village where the family who have played the demon-king Ravana lives, I was told that 'Ravan-raj [King Ravana] lives over there'. Everyone knows Ravana: he is royalty among peasants. The family has grown rich since the time in the 1860s that a forefather was picked through audition by the Maharaja of Benares to play Ravana. And over the years the situation of that family has become more and more a structural antithesis to that of the boys who play Rama and his brothers, the protagonists of the Ramlila and arch-enemies of Ravana, whose role is roughly analogous to that of Satan in *Paradise Lost*. The boys are picked by audition yearly; they mostly come from city families and are educated; after their stint in Ramlila most enter professions ranging from the priesthood to journalism and acting. During the thirty-one days of the cycle play the boys playing Rama and his brothers live in seclusion in three different dharamsalas in Ramnagar—moving along with the play itself to different locations; Ravana returns each night the several miles to his native place: like his mythic Lanka he lives away from Rama, Hanuman, Sugriva, or any of their party. But at the climax of the cycle, when Ravana is killed in battle by Rama, the performer signifies this moment by taking off his ten-headed mask and prostrating himself before Rama, kissing his feet. But again, I ask, who is doing the kissing? The actor without his mask is doing devotion to the boy who, with his sacred crown, is Rama-incarnate. Both man and boy are 'between personae', in that liminal, double-negative field where they are neither themselves nor their roles. And if few performers have experienced Narad's transformation, most have felt Ravan-raj's and Rama's doubling: the sense of being taken over by a role, of being possessed by it—in its 'flow', or in the flow of the audience's appetite for illusion: *ludus*, *lila*: play.

This surrender to the flow of action is the ritual process. Here it is that the two root meanings of *ri* converge: the action is orderly, even numerical—'play it by the numbers'—but the sense of being in it is, as Csikszentmihalyi says, 'the merging of action and awareness. A person in flow has no dualistic perspective: he is aware of his actions but not of the awareness itself.'[7] 'The steps for experiencing flow . . . involve the . . . process of delimiting reality, controlling some aspect of it, and responding to the feedback with a concentration that excludes anything else as irrelevant.'[8] Or as Ryczard Cieslak, the great actor who performed in many of Grotowski's works, told me:

The score is like a glass inside which a candle is burning. The glass is solid; it is there, you can depend on it. It contains and guides the flame. But it is not the flame. The flame is my inner process each night. The flame is what illuminates the score, what the spectators see through the score. The flame is alive. Just as the flame in the glass moves, flutters, rises, falls, almost goes out, suddenly glows brightly, responds to each breath of wind—so my inner life varies from night to night, from moment to moment. . . . I begin each night without anticipations. This is the hardest thing to learn. I do not prepare myself to feel anything. I do not say, 'Last night, this scene was extraordinary, I will try to do that again.' I want only to be receptive to what will happen. And I am ready to take what happens if I am secure in my score, knowing that, even if I feel a minimum, the glass will not break, the objective structure worked out over the months will help me through. But when a night comes that I can glow, shine, live, reveal—I am ready for it by not anticipating it. The score remains the same, but everything is different because I am different.[9]

Cieslak is the Zen master for whom the moment of action is when all the preparation falls away: what remains is readiness. As Shakespeare says, 'ripeness is all'.

When the performance is over Cieslak 'cools down'. Often he drinks vodka, talks, smokes a lot of cigarettes. Getting out of the role is sometimes harder than getting into it. Little work has been done on the 'cool-down', at least in the Euro-American tradition. Here the emphasis is on training, rehearsal, and warm-up. In Bali, by contrast, there are rituals for cooling down including sprinkling with holy water, inhalation of incense, massage, and even sacrifice of animals and blood sprinkling. What the cool-down does is return the performer to an ordinary sphere of existence: to transport him back to where he began. Acting, in most cases, is the art of temporary transformation: not only the journey out but also the return. Quesalid and Narad both, over the long run, gave in to their roles; Cieslak knows how to prepare and be ready to flow with his role. But he has hardly an inkling of what to do afterwards. And some roles effect a swift and permanent transformation, as in initiation rites and other 'rites of passage'. I am interested in these different kinds of changes that occur within performers—and the concomitant changes that happen in an audience —not from a psychological point of view, but as a baseline from which to project several stops along a continuum of performance types. This continuum will tell something about performance in a number of cultures, and also interculturally. The continuum runs from those performances where the performer is changed through the 'work' of the performance to those in which he is transported and returned to his starting place. A vertical axis of this continuum would show whether transformation occurs gradually, as with Quesalid and Narad, or suddenly, as when a Gahuku boy is changed into a man through the work of a single set of initiatory performances. And also I will show how often these two kinds of performances—transportative and transformative—occur together, working together.

I call performances where performers are changed 'transformations' and those where performers are returned to their starting places 'transportations'. 'Transportation' because during the performance the performers are 'taken somewhere' but at the end, often assisted by others, they are 'cooled down' and re-enter ordinary life just about where they went in.   [Fig. 1]

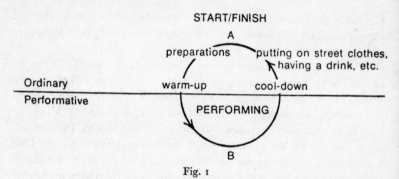

Fig. 1

The performer goes from the 'ordinary world' to the 'performative world', from one time/space reference to another, from one personality reference to one or more others. He plays a character, battles demons, goes into trance, travels to the sky or under the sea or earth: he is transformed, enabled to do things 'in performance' he cannot do ordinarily. But when the performance is over, or even as a final phase of the performance, he returns to where he started. Otherwise he is left hanging—as some movie actors, not all happily, have found out. If John Wayne was satisfied in becoming (like Narad) what he portrayed, Bela Lugosi was not. I do want to point out that if a change occurs within the performer, or in his status, it happens only over a long series of performances, each of which moves the performer slightly.   [Fig. 2]

A series of transportations results in a transformation

Fig. 2

This is what happened to Narad and John Wayne. Thus each separate performance is a transportation, ending about where it began, while a series of transportation performances can achieve a transformation. It's not my task here to describe the ways the ordinary world is different from the performative world. In some kinds of performances —trance dancing, for example—extreme care is exercised in bringing the performer out of trance. This is so because trance exhibits both a quality of personality change and involuntariness: the trancer clearly needs help 'coming back', while the character actor appears to be in control of himself. We might even say that there are two kinds of transportations—the voluntary and the involuntary—and that character acting belongs to the first category and trance to the second. However, in watching trance—and seeing many films depicting it—I suspect that the difference between these kinds of transportations has been overemphasized. The character actor is self-starting (at least if he has orthodox Euro-American training), but once warmed-up and in the flow of things he is quite deeply involved in what Keats called the 'negative capability' and what I've schemed out as the 'not me— not not me'. The character actor in flow is not himself but he is not not himself at the same time. Also, trance performers are frequently very conscious of their actions even while performing them; and they too undergo training and warm-up. The difference between these kinds of performance may be more in labelling and cultural expectations than in their performance processes.

Transformation performances are clearly evidenced in initiation rites, whose very purpose it is to transform people from one status or social identity to another. An initiation not only marks a change but is itself the means by which persons achieve their new selves: no performance, no change. Kenneth E. Read tells how a Papua–New Guinea boy, Asemo, was taken from his mother's home, secluded in the bush for several weeks, put through with his age-mates initiatory ordeals and training, and finally brought back to his village (along with his age-mates) transformed into a man. Read lets us know that the underlying action of the initiation is performative. To give but two examples, after two weeks of seclusion the boys are brought back to Susuroka, their village:

The noise and movement were overwhelming. Behind us, the shrill voices of women rose in keening, ritual, stylized cries informed by genuine emotion that were like a sharp instrument stabbing into the din around me. The ululating notes of male voices locked with thumping shouts, deep drumbeats expelled from distended chests counterpointed the crash of bare feet on the ground, and, rising above it all, came the cries of the flutes.[10]

Asemo and his age-mates were somewhere in the middle of the throng, almost certainly blinded by the dust, carried along by the press of stronger bodies. . . . Other youths had told me, laughing, of their panic during these opening minutes of their day-long ordeal.[11]

This ordeal included forced vomiting and nosebleeding. Read describes how Asemo and the other boys were 'sadly bedraggled' and 'dejected' and 'limp'. Literally exhausted, the boys were carried, dragged, and pushed into running a gauntlet where Gahuku women attacked the men and boys with 'stones and lethal pieces of wood, an occasional axe, and even a few bows and arrows'. The men picked the boys up and put them on their shoulders and together they ran through no-man's-land.

> The men had bunched together as they ran, so closely packed that they struck each other with their legs and arms. In the centre of the throng the initiates, riding the shoulders of their escorts, swayed precariously from side to side, their fingers clutching the feathered hair of the head between their legs.[12]

Read says 'there was no mistaking the venom in the assault' of the women; and the men didn't think of the attack as a 'ceremonial charade' but recognized that it 'teetered on the edge of virtual disaster'. On the edge, but not over: the attack was contained within its performative boundaries much the way a bloody hockey game barely but reliably remains a game. The ordeal, the gauntlet, the attack: these are all 'twice-behaved behaviours'—scored, expected, performed.

Six weeks later the 'final act was played out in the . . . village'. Asemo spent those weeks absorbing training. The day of his coming out—a day of feasting and dancing—culminated in the presentation of the initiates to the whole village. This time the women didn't assault the men but greeted them with a 'rising chorus of welcoming calls'. Then the initiates danced as a group, without the assistance or protection of the older men.

> They moved unsteadily under the ungainly decorations, and I failed to see the splendid stirring change that had been apparent to their elders' eyes. But dignity touched them when they began to dance, a slow measure based on the assertive stepping of the men but held to a restrained, promenading pace by the weight [of their headdresses] they carried on their heads. For a moment I was one with the crowd of admirers.[13]

Asemo and his age-mates had become men in the Gahuku scheme of things. During and after his day of dancing Asemo was a male

Gahuku with the responsibilities and privileges of that status. Abolition of the initiation rites—and Read thought when he wrote *The High Valley* in 1965 that they would not be performed again—signals a shift in the whole basis of Gahuku society. That is because the initiation doesn't merely mark a change that has occurred elsewhere in the social scheme—as bar-mitzvah, graduation, or entrance into a professional association usually do in the Euro-American context—but is in its whole duration the machine that works the changes transforming boys into men. Without this machine Gahuku boys will be different kinds of men. To be taken from Susuroka, to undergo the ordeals, to be trained in lore and dancing, to return and dance: that process equals becoming a Gahuku man. This status—whatever its personal meanings and effects, whatever private styles it accommodates—is fundamentally social, public, and objective. It does not determine what kind of Gahuku man Asemo will be, or even how he feels about it, any more than a wedding ceremony determines what kind of husband the groom will be. But definite acts have been performed. These acts accomplish a transformation.

People are accustomed to calling transportation performances 'theatre' and transformation performances 'ritual'. But this neat separation doesn't hold up. Mostly the two kinds of performances coexist in the same event. Just as Asemo and his age-mates were being transformed, the Gahuku men who vomited and bled with them, who carried them on their shoulders through the attack by the women, who trained them to dance—these men were transported, not transformed. They were trainers, guides, and co-performers. Those who no longer change—or who do not change 'this time', through the work of this performance—effect the changes wrought in the transformed. This relationship can be figured this way.   [Fig. 3]

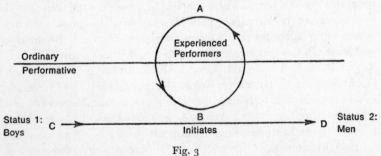

Fig. 3

The experienced performers enter the performance and share in its actions of bleeding, vomiting, gauntlet-running. But when the performance is over, the already-initiated Gahuku men re-enter ordinary life approximately where they left it. If any change among them occurs, it is subtle: the way persons achieve more respect, or lose it, through doing what is necessary in their social lives. When the performance is over the transported have been returned to their place of entry and the transformed have been changed. The system is analogous to a printing press, where information is imprinted upon a piece of paper as it is fed through. The performance—and the training leading up to it—are points of contact between the 'press' (transported) and the 'paper' (transformed). Point B—the performance witnessed by spectators who are far from casual seekers of entertainment—is the decisive contact between transported and transformed. What the transported imprint upon the transformed at that point of contact is there to stay: circumcision, scarring, tattooing, and so on; or the giving of special clothes, ornaments, and artifacts, such as wedding bands, the sacred four-strand thread of Hindu initiation, the *teffilin* to be bound and unbound daily by Jewish males, and so on. Or something is taken from the transformed: the bloody down Quesalid displays, the foreskin taken from the circumcised, a ceremonial haircut, or, as in the Gahuku case, blood and vomit. These markings, additions, and subtractions are not mere arrows pointing to deeper significance; they are themselves loaded with power: they bind a person to his community, anchor him to a social identity; they are at once intimate and public. Theatre people especially ought to be sensitive to the force of the surface. The surface of the social being is like the surface of the sun: always seething, throwing up from the depths material heretofore hidden, and sucking down into the depths what just now was surface.

For the system to work the transported must be as unchanged as the transformed is permanently changed. The work of the transported is to enter the performance, play his role, wear his mask—usually acting as the agent for larger forces, or possessed directly by them—and leave. In this process the transported is identical to the actor. Or to put it another way, the actor in Euro-American theatre is an example of a transported performer. For reasons that will be made clear later, the Euro-American theatre is one of transportation without transformation. Much activity from 1960 onwards has sought to introduce into Euro-American theatre the process of transformation.

And the audience? Spectators at transformation performances

usually have a stake in seeing that the performance succeeds. They are relatives of the performers, part of the same community. Thus in transformation performances the attention of the transported and the spectators converges on the transformed.   [Fig. 4]

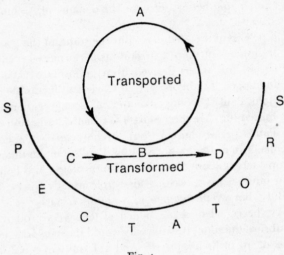

Fig. 4

This convergence of attention, and direct stake in the performance, is why so many transformation performances use audience participation. All of Susuroka gathered for the final day of dancing as Asemo and his age-mates made their debut as men. At first only the boys-now-men dance, but then everyone joins in a general celebration. So it is also with bar mitzvahs, weddings, and even funerals.

In a transformation performance the stars of the show may not be the best performers, technically speaking. Asemo and his age-mates can't dance as well as the older men, any more than a bar mitzvah boy sings his part from the Torah as well as the *chazan*. Throughout the initiation process the older men have concentrated on getting the boys through—doing what must be done for the initiation to be completed, for it to work. And on that last day, the concentration of the village is on what has been made: new men, the work done. Interestingly, the word 'drama' derives from the Greek root *dra*: to do, to make. Similarly, at a wedding the attention is on the marrying couple, at a bar mitzvah it's on the bar mitzvah boy, and so on. This isn't to say that the transported need not be skilled performers. Everywhere the pleasure an audience gets from a transformation performance depends greatly on the skills of the elders and/or professionals who train, guide, officiate, and often co-perform with the transformed. The bar mitzvah boy is praised for his singing, but the *chazan* better sing better; ditto for the dancing of Asemo's father and uncles.

It would be easy if it ended here. But the status of the transported can be more important than their skills as performers—even if, as in Quesalid's case, this status derived from performative skill. Think what would happen if the Pope played Christ at Oberammergau. As it is, Pope John Paul II cooing to an audience/congregation of 17,000 teenagers bussed into Madison Square Garden is flashed on national TV. John Paul's performance is 'out of character' for a Pope, but mushy evidence of his 'humanness'. John Paul's 'human image' often makes people forget about his conservative theology. And Polish John Paul is an unusual bit of casting for a role usually reserved for an Italian. But what would happen to a common parish priest if, on national TV, he cooed to a big bunch of teenagers brought before him? An absurd question, because why would the networks broadcast the doings of an ordinary priest? And yet this same parish priest celebrating Mass is more powerful, in the Church's view, than an actor playing the Pope in *The Deputy*. And how about the unlikely possibility that a priest (or the Pope himself) play the role of Pope in a play? However unlikely these combinations are, they point to the four variables operating in every performance: (1) whether the performance is efficacious, directly making changes in ordinary life (initiations, weddings, and so on), or whether it is fictive, even about 'real events' (*The Deputy*, ordinary plays, documentaries); (2) the status of the roles *within* a performance; (3) the status of the persons playing the roles—whether they are playing themselves (as in initiations), are possessed by others, or have, in the Stanislavskian sense, 'built a role'. (Remember that Quesalid started by playing the role of unmasker/investigator and ended behind the mask he wanted to rip off others, and that Carnival and other celebrations pivot upon the inversion of roles where fools play the king and the king is required to act foolishly.) And, finally, (4) the quality of the performance measured by the mastery performers have over whatever skills are demanded (and these vary from society to society, occasion to occasion)—even, sometimes, the skill to feign a lack of skill as in many

con games. None of these four variables is absent from any performance, transformative or transportational.

My model of transportation/transformation performance is open. It
can be applied across cultures and genres. I have already applied it to
the initiation rites of Gahuku boys in Papua–New Guinea. And
presently I will apply it to a few more kinds of performances selected
not only to be representative but also because I have had some
personal experience with most of them. In the Greek case, obviously
I wasn't around in the fifth century B.C., but I have directed versions
of Euripides' *The Bacchae* and Sophocles/Seneca's *Oedipus*. I will also
look at theatre according to the Indian treatise *Natyasastra* (fourth
century B.C.–second century A.D.), the Noh drama according to the
writings of Zeami (thirteenth century), and as practised today in
Japan; the *Elephant Man* currently on Broadway; and my own production of *Dionysus in 69* as an example of environmental theatre and
audience participation.

   First let me show how the model looks when applied to that period
of Athenian theatre when writers alone received prizes.   [Fig. 5]

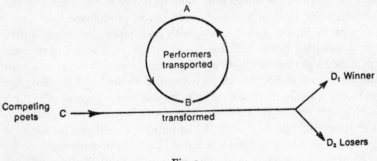

Fig. 5

This is the opposite of what happened in the village of Susuroka.
There people of different statuses were transformed by the initiation
performance into people of the same status: boys + men became all
men. Here people of the same status, poets competing, are transformed by the performance into unequals: a winner + losers. This
competitive differentiation is of course that of the *agon*: the core action
of each Greek tragedy is identical to that of the City Dionysia as a
whole. The revelation through direct competition among agonists
(pro- and ant-) of who wins and who loses is deep not only in Greek

tragedy but, by derivation, in Euro-American theatre, whose narratives until very recently always involved conflict and resolution into winners and losers.

The Greeks so loved competition that they preferred it over aesthetics. At first, prizes were given only to the writers, and each formed an ensemble of who he thought could best present his play. Aeschylus was noted for training his own chorus. But commencing in 449 B.C., prizes were also given for the best actor. From then on writers were not allowed to select their own protagonists—these were assigned by lot and paid by the archon out of public funds. This lessened the possibility that writers and actors would form teams—certainly a strange regulation from the modern viewpoint because it foreclosed one of the ambitions of twentieth-century theatre: to form an aesthetically balanced company. But the Greeks wanted to reduce the possibility that the two competitions—one in writing, the other in acting—although they occurred at the same time and used the same medium, and clearly affected one another, would in practice be reduced to one. What happened was that writers were transporters for actors and actors for writers: each was the means the other used to achieve victory. The model thus could be drawn twice: once with the writers as the 'straight line' and once with the protagonists.

In Susuroka the men compete with each other. But even as they do they collaborate to help the boys through. The object of the performance is to eliminate winners and losers—the boys helped the most are those least able to do what's needed. Ultimately, all the boys are initiated, all win, all dance together on the village ground. This isn't saying that among the Gahuku there aren't better or worse dancers; but these differences, during the initiation, are effaced as much as possible, or at least not made a formal part of the ceremonies. With the Greeks the differences are displayed as much as possible—though even they made mistakes: Sophocles lost the year he entered with *Oedipus*.

I said that among the Greeks competition was preferred over aesthetics. That may be hard to swallow because Euro-American aesthetics, thanks to the Greeks, is a function of competition. If aesthetics is a concern for how well (= how beautifully) a thing is done, it developed among the Greeks when they ceased looking at a group in the process of being transported—as in the dithyrambic dances—and began selecting from the group individuals who 'do better' than others. [Fig. 6]

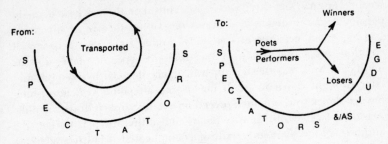

Fig. 6

Only by observing the details of performance—the what and how—could the Greeks, and any who follow the Greek model, discern winning poets and actors from losers. This process of differentiation is even more demanding when it's possible for a winning actor to perform in a losing play and a losing actor in a winning one. Spectators and judges—who actively claim to represent the 'whole city', just as the judges who award Obies and Tonys claim to represent the 'theatrical community'—confront the artists directly; they are neither absorbed into the performance as participators nor simply 'enjoying' it. Critics must, and spectators often do, rank performances in relation to other performances, even separating out within a given performance the 'good' from the 'bad'. And writers and players—knowing they are being judged, that something important is at stake—react by playing up to the audience or intentionally scorning it. Rare is the performance, especially on opening night when the critics are there, in which performers feel the audience working with them, mutually absorbed in the task of making the show go. Instead, the mutuality is of confrontation—the radical separation of audience and judges/critics on one side and performers, playwrights, and other theatre people on the other. This basic confrontation leads to the accumulation of 'values' by which artists are transformed into winners and losers. Again, much of the experimental work during the last twenty years has been directed—through devices of audience participation, environmental staging, and collective creativity—at abolishing this agony.

Aesthetics need not be built from competition—as is clear when you look at theatre according to the *Natyasastra*. This book, called the 'Fifth Veda', was compiled between the fourth century B.C. and the second century A.D. It is almost certainly not the work of a single person. And the details it contains describing theatre architecture, staging, exact gestures of the body, limbs, face; its discussion of emotions, of acting styles, of the different types of plays; and its mythical frame of a theatrical performance decreed by the gods and later brought down to earth for people all point to a flourishing theatre-dance tradition long preceding extant Sanskrit drama. Unlike Aristotle, who wrote from a philosophical-literary perspective, the author(s) of the *Natyasastra* write of a complicated, sophisticated living performance genre. The book is so full of details, of exact descriptions and specifications, that it can be nothing else than a manual, a how-to-do-it text. Out of all this I want to look very closely at the relationship between the means of theatrical production—gestures, dance steps, mode of dialogue delivery, costumes, make-up, masks, theatre architecture and stage design, and so on—and the particular kind of 'entertainment' enjoyed by the spectators.

This relationship is epitomized in the Sanskrit notion of *rasa*. *Rasa* literally means 'flavour' or 'taste', and Indian theatre—like the Indian painting and sculpting of roughly the same period, especially the caves at Ajanta and the sculptural group at Mahabalipuram—is, in Richard Lannoy's McLuhanesque term, 'synaesthesic'. As Lannoy says:

> The Ajanta style approaches as near as it is likely for an artist to get to a felicitous rendering of tactile sensations normally experienced subconsciously. These are felt rather than seen when the eye is subordinate to a total receptivity of all the senses. . . . The seated queen with the floating hand is drawn so that we obtain information which cannot be had by looking at her from a single, fixed viewpoint. . . . The logic of this style demands that movements and gestures can only be described in terms of the area or space in which they occur; we cannot identify a figure except by comparing its position with others around it. . . . It could be said that the Ajanta artist is concerned with the order of sensuousness, as distinct from the order of reason.[14]

Lannoy shows how the Sanskrit drama, based on the *Natyasastra* (or probably vice versa), is analogous—especially in its synaesthesic technique—to the cave art and even to the caves themselves. 'The structure and ornamentation of the caves were deliberately designed to induce total participation during ritual circumambulation. The acoustics of one Ajanta *vihara*, or assembly hall (Cave VI), are such that any

sound long continues to echo round the walls. The whole structure
seems to have been tuned like a drum.'[15] This tuning was not fortuitous
—these caves are human-made, excavated and carved out of a solid
mountain wall.

> In both cases [the caves, the theatre] total participation of the
> viewer was ensured by a skilful combination of sensory experience.
> The 'wrap-around' effect [of] the caves was conveyed on the
> stage by adapting the technically brilliant virtuosity of Vedic
> incantation and phonetic science to the needs of the world's most
> richly textured style of poetic drama.[16]

What the *Natyasastra* supplies are the concrete details of that style
which is not at its core literary but theatrical. Even today in such
popular forms as Ramlila, Raslila, and the Krishna *bhajans*, there is
circumambulation, trance dancing, sharing of food, open or cyclical
rather than confrontational narrative, wrap-around environmental
theatre type staging, processions; phases of the performance where the
spectators watch and phases where they participate: a total blending
of theatre, dance, music, food-sharing, religious ceremony, and a
resulting sensuous overload that convinces me that the *Natyasastra*
informs not only the classical Sanskrit drama, extinct for twelve
hundred years, but also dozens of living forms beloved by the Indian
people.

I said that *rasa* is the essence of the performance theory of the
Natyasastra. And that *rasa* means taste or flavour: a sensuous essence
that enters through the snout—nose, mouth, tongue—and engages the
eyes and ears the way a sumptuous meal does, ultimately satisfying
the belly which, to minds conditioned by yoga, is the seat of breath.
Thus *rasa* is neither gross nor leaden, but highly sophisticated and
subtle. Food-sharing symbolism is a paradigm of more than Indian
theatre. Food, with accompanying oblations of ghee (clarified butter),
water, flowers, bells, fire: these are the integers linking Indian
theatre and *puja*, the basic Hindu ceremony whose roots reach down
to pre-Aryan Harappa. At the core of *puja* is the offering of *prasad*,
food, to the gods. This food is sanctified by the gods and returned to
the people. The food makes a circular journey but is transformed in
the process from human offering to divine gift. Different foods—
different flavours and textures, different references and associations—
have different functions and meanings; fruits, sweets, rice, and so on,
prepared in various ways, constitute a language of food. Indian
theatre, derived from the entertainments among the gods (according

to the *Natyasastra*), also is an offering to the gods: a food for the gods, which the gods return to people for their enjoyment. And the gods are frequent characters in the plays, as well as spectators of the human show. In Ramlila at Ramnagar long poles topped by effigies represent the gods on high looking down at the performance. This appearance of the gods as performers and spectators is natural and easy among a people who believe in reincarnation and whose basic religious texts, the Vedas, depict gods modelled on 'primal man' and not the other way round. Also, the occasion for theatre in India is not, nor was it ever, a competition among poets and actors. Performances occur for any number of reasons ranging from the celebrations of fixed annual events like Ramlila, Raslila, and Chhau to pure enjoyment at commercial theatres like Jatra and Tamasha to the marking of auspicious events like marriages, the visit of a dignitary, or recovery from an illness. The performance is sometimes thought of as an offering. Need I add that these occasions and functions overlap? At the Ramlila of Ramnagar the outskirts of the performing area are occupied by sellers of food, trinkets, clothes and the operators of games of skill and chance. Everyone attends the Ramlila, from the nursing infant to the highest god. On one night, from a tower later to be occupied by the Maharaja of Benares's family, performers representing Visnu and Laksmi watch as Rama and Sita are displayed; these are all manifestations of the same deity, scattered abundantly in time and space like flower petals or tossed rice and saying the same thing: This is an auspicious event.

Rasa is the flavour of the performance—how it tastes, how it appeals to the tastes of people from different *jati*, 'castes', and experience; and Indians use the word 'taste' with a great deal more subtlety and range of socio-aesthetic signification than we do. If some theatres need an audience to hear it, and some need spectators to see it, Indian theatre needs partakers to savour it. I don't have the time here to discuss exactly how *rasa* is used. What I do want to point out is that according to the *Natyasastra*—and in many Indian performances of today—the enjoyment of the performance is shared between the performers and the spectators, or as I shall say from this point, between the preparers and the partakers. *Rasa* happens where the experience of the preparers and partakers meet. Each, using skills that have to be learned and that are not easy, moves towards the other. The experience of the performance is like that of a banquet where the cooks and servers must know how to prepare and serve, but the diners must know how to eat. And, as in Asian banquets in general, there is more food than can possibly be consumed: a great part of the skill is in knowing how and what to select for any given occasion. This relationship can be depicted as in Fig. 7.

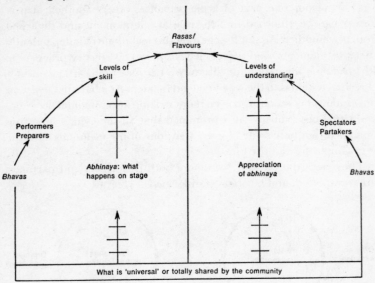

Fig. 7

A successful performance is one where both the levels of skill (preparers) and understanding (partakers) are high and equal. If the partaker expects more than the preparer can deliver, the performance is inadequate; if the preparer does more than the partaker can savour, the performance is wasted. Low skill matched by low understanding is preferable to an imbalance. Perfect *rasa* is a meeting at a very high level of preparer and partaker. Noh drama in Japan works in a similar way, except that the root metaphor is gardening and what is shared is *hana*, 'flower'. More on that later.

This Indian system of participant enjoyment—a system exported to Southeast Asia, China, and Japan—is one of the main things that attracted Brecht to Asian theatre. This system involves the audience in a very active way while at the same time enhancing its enjoyment. The system works with relations among four variables:

$$
\begin{array}{cccc}
\text{I} & 2 & 3 & 4 \\
\text{performer/performed} & \longrightarrow \text{RASA} \longleftarrow & \text{savoured/spectator} \\
\text{preparer} & & \text{partaker}
\end{array}
$$

Rasa is the interface of 1/2 :: 4/3. *Rasa* doesn't exist independently: it is a function of the interface. And each term of the system can be varied independently of the others. That is, for example, some spectators can savour one part of a performance, others another; a performer can be absorbed into his role at one moment and detached from it at another. Again, Brecht took this technique of independently variable elements and developed from it his theory/practice of *Verfremdung*—'alienation' or 'distance'. Let me emphasize again how close this system is to the way fine food is eaten. At a banquet, feast, or fine restaurant—and this is even more striking at ceremonial occasions and ritual observances—it is presumed that all the food is superb or sanctified, but only some of it is eaten: one of the meanings of 'taste' is to sample only a little bit.

Thus, according to the *Natyasastra* both performers and partakers are transported, and no one is transformed. [Fig. 8]

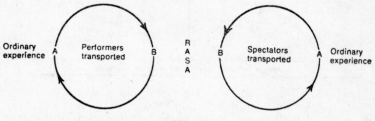

Fig. 8

Rasa is the mutuality, the sharing, the co-creation of preparers and partakers. Every detail of the presentation is worked out, but variable: theatre architecture, mise-en-scène, gestures, music, types of plays, spectator comportment, the proper occasions for theatre, et cetera, et cetera, et cetera. If Aristotle's *Poetics* is so laconic as to be considered only notes towards a text, the *Natyasastra* is so detailed as to be thought collectively authored, compiled over four or five centuries, a collective lore-book of performance. But while the details are worked out to a degree unknown in the West, there is much liberty within the scheme because the parts are variable.

For example, how much should be presented at one time? There is a 'start' and 'finish' to each night's performance—and many plays in the Sanskrit and folk traditions extend over a number of days and/or nights—but there isn't any definite 'beginning' or 'end' as there is in Greek drama. Where to stop in a given series again depends on circumstances. At Ramlila the size of the crowds, the weather, the energy of the performers, and the wishes of the Maharaja all can determine how much is done on a given day. Like post-modern performance in Europe and America, the Indian system is a braid of several strands of activities and demands that performer and partaker attend together to the here and now of the ever-changing relations among the strands. The two systems, Greek and Indian, can be diagrammed as in Fig. 9.

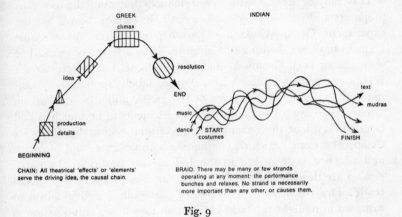

Fig. 9

This difference affects not only the performance but training, rehearsals, and the means of transmitting performance knowledge. Paradoxically, the Greek system—as it has worked itself out in Western theatre historically—is freer than the Indian in training and rehearsal but more fixed in performance. Through training and rehearsal the 'idea' or 'action' of the performance is 'discovered', and this takes searching; in performance this idea is 'shown', and this takes a fixed score. In the Indian system training and rehearsal are fixed because what is being transmitted is not a means of discovery but the performance elements themselves broken into learnable segments. The performance, however, is truly contingent. The more experienced and respected the performer, the more he is permitted to vary elements of the show during performance. The performance is truly contingent, an ever-changing *lila* ('play', 'sport', 'illusion') created between preparer and partaker. But these days, as even classical and folk arts are restored according to Westernized training methods, Indian theatre is losing its quality of contingency.

This view of the difference between causal chains and braided

8

relations also helps explain why Western theatre develops from crises that it is then the business of the performance to resolve, while Sanskrit drama, and much contemporary Indian theatre, 'doesn't go anywhere'. It's not supposed to go somewhere, it's not a 'development-resolution' kind of drama, but an expository, synaesthetic, and playful set of variations much more akin to the *raga* system of music than to anything Aristotelian.

This 'playing around with'—performances that mutually transport preparers and partakers—describes not only Indian theatre but the experiments Grotowski made in 'paratheatre' and the 'rituals' Anne Halprin has been devising in California for nearly thirty years. The weakness of both Grotowski and Halprin is that they rely on the I-Thou immediacy, what Victor Turner labels 'spontaneous communitas', to generate the rules of the game, and they depend on 'group creativity' to come up with the elements to be bunched and braided. Without the benefit of a worked-out, culturally elaborate theatrical system (which the *Natyasastra* both describes and provides, and which is ever-present in the Indian oral tradition) the participants are thrown back on their own 'sincerity', their own 'personal truth'. This truth is but a version of that radical individualism so rampant in twilight capitalist culture: all too often a combination of clichés of intimacy, unexamined cultural fact, and romantic distortions of pre-industrial religious experience. The results—as I've witnessed them and heard them described—are actions like staring deeply into your partner's eyes, swaying or moving in circles in 'ritualistic' dances, passing fire, telling personal stories during long hours spent quietly in candlelight, running through the woods at night, and so on.[17] Yet the underlying tendency of this kind of experiment is, I think, valid: to restore to performance, or invent anew, that quality of mutuality so powerfully present in *rasa*.

Nothing could be further from the narcissistic experiments of today's theatre than Japanese Noh—a form that is describable by the figures I devised for the *Natyasastra*. In Noh there is a close relationship between highly skilled performers—many of them apprenticed in the art from early childhood by their fathers, uncles, and grandfathers—and an audience of connoisseurs. Zeami and his father, Kannami, gave Noh its definitive shape in the fourteenth and fifteenth centuries. Zeami, in a series of monographs, is very specific about how Noh performers are to be trained, how Noh is to be performed, and what the underlying theory of the art is. I can, in this essay, only touch on this rich literature—one of the most detailed accounts ever written by an individual on theatre. And Zeami was not only a director and actor of great force, but the author of the largest number of Noh plays still in the repertory. His output and range is roughly that of Brecht and Stanislavski combined.

Zeami is specific about how a performance of Noh is to be adjusted according to a number of circumstances outside the mise-en-scène: the season, weather, quality and comportment of the audience. For example:

> When Noh is performed in a shrine or in the presence of a noble, there are many people assembled, and it is very noisy with the buzz and murmur of their voices. In that case, the performer better wait until they become calm and quiet and all their eyes are concentrated on the entrance. . . . If he begins to sing *issei* [entrance music] immediately, the atmosphere of the theatre will take on the tone of the performance, the attention of the audience will be concentrated on the movements of the shite [main actor] and the noisy voices will become quiet. . . . But as one of the principles of Noh is that it should be performed in front of nobles, if the noble arrives at his box earlier than usual, the shite must begin the play as soon as possible. In this case, the audience has not yet become quiet, or latecomers are entering the boxes, and everyone's mind is not yet prepared to see the Noh, some standing, others sitting in their boxes. In this case, one will not have a sufficiently calm atmosphere in which to perform. At such a time . . . the player had better be clad in more ornamental dress than usual, sing more strongly, step more loudly on the floor, and his carriage should be much more vivid and attractive. This will calm down the atmosphere of the theatre. . . . So to judge whether the audience is ready for the play to begin, or whether their minds are not yet concentrated on it, is very difficult. Only the experienced shite can do it.[18]

The audience whose eyes are not sharply appreciative will not praise the talented shite, and, on the other hand, the audience who can really appreciate Noh cannot endure to see an immature shite performing. It is natural that the unskilled shite is never admired by a cultivated audience; but that the real master sometimes cannot hold the attention of an unappreciative audience is partly because these people do not have enough taste to recognize the master's talent.[19]

The purpose of this art is to pacify and give pleasure to the minds of the audience and to move them, both nobles and the common people, and this will also assure prosperity and long life [for the actor].[20]

So close and immediate is the relationship between performers and spectators that if the audience is noisy the costumes are changed at the last minute, a kind of homeopathy is tried where brighter costuming is used to calm a too-flashy audience. Noh's apparent solemnity and fixity are deceptive. At its core is a set of contingencies unmatched elsewhere in world theatre. The shite rehearses only with the chorus. The *waki* (second character), *kyogen* (comic actor), flutist, and drummers are each from different families, and rehearse separately from each other. The whole group of actors, chorus, musicians meets only once or twice before a public performance. The shite outlines his plans. Rehearsals as such are rarely held. The performance itself is the meeting place of the strands—singing, chanting, dancing, reciting, music-making—that are braided into the public Noh. And the performance is variable not only in the ways Zeami describes but also because the shite can signal the musicians to indicate that a dance will be repeated or shortened. Again, like Indian raga music, Noh takes advantage of the immediacy of the encounter among artists and between the ensemble and the audience. An audience of connoisseurs is aware of, and delights in, these contingencies. Noh—the very word means 'skill'—is like a sport, and the spectator's enjoyment is increased if, like the baseball fan who can read the third-base coach's signs to batter and runners, he knows the details of the interplay on stage. Today many spectators of Noh also study its chanting or dancing, and are attached to one school or other. For their part, Noh performers complain of boredom when, for tours, a company is assembled to repeat a fixed repertory. The onceness of Zen—a meditation and a martial art—is the heart of Noh.

Not *rasa*, flavour, but *hana*, flower, is the root metaphor of Noh. To understand *hana* you must see many sumi-i paintings, where each stroke of the brush is allowed just once, there are no corrections, so that a great work, when it occurs, is what happens when all training drops away in an unrevised meeting of artist and medium. Zeami speaks of *hana* often, but at no time more cogently than here.

My father Kannami died on the nineteenth of May [1384] at the age of fifty-two. On the fourth day of the same month he gave a dedicatory performance in front of Segen Shrine in the province of Suruga. His own performance on this programme was especially brilliant, and the audence, both high and low, all applauded. He had ceded many showy plays to uninitiated shite, and he himself performed easy ones, in a subdued way; but, with this additional colour to it, his flower looked better than ever. As his was *shin-no-hana* [*hana* acquired through training, literally 'true flower'] it survived until he became old without leaving him, like an old leafless tree which still blossoms.[21]

Pure Beckett: an art of distilled discipline. Not only sumi-i, but Zen rock gardens and bonsai trees are analogues to Noh. *Hana* exists between performers and spectators; when it is there both performers and spectators are transported.   [Fig. 10]

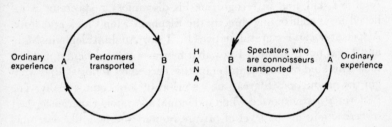

Fig. 10

But unless the spectators know what's going on through specific instruction in Noh the *hana* is missing. As in the Tea Ceremony the ability to appreciate the service and the objects shown is directly proportional to what the guests know. This is different from the Indian situation where mutuality but not special knowledge is required. Living in a north Indian village will give a person by the age of five all that he needs to participate in Ramlila; from then on the experience will deepen year by year. But the Noh spectator must become a connoisseur or he will fail the performance. And that is why so many newcomers to Noh find it impenetrable.

It doesn't take special training to like Broadway theatre, or to dislike it. But in this trait Broadway is like experimental theatre. Almost all Euro-American theatre prides itself on its popularity: what it asks of its audience is not special knowledge but responsivity. The historic sources of this theatre are not so much religious ritual or initiatory ordeals but popular entertainments. I saw *The Elephant Man* on Broadway in 1979. Philip Anglim's portrayal of the title role was a model of professionalism as understood in the American theatre:

physical, restrained, precise, and according to the conventions of a stylized naturalism. By holding his right arm extended and twisted from the shoulder and again at the wrist, by dropping his right shoulder and turning his neck to the left, by rotating his left wrist and clenching his fist—and then keeping this excruciating position for more than two hours (except when off-stage)—Anglim gave the impression of deformity without help from the costumer or makeup artist. This is in contrast, say, to Lon Chaney's *Hunchback of Notre Dame* in the movies—or dozens of other films—where the actor is an armature for a construction. But Anglim's work on himself serves another purpose too. It allows individual spectators to sympathize with the character Anglim is playing and not be repulsed. In admiring Anglim's skill, and in recognizing his discomfort, a spectator is relieved from confronting directly the Elephant Man's look and stink. A spectator can congratulate herself: 'I saw Anglim/Elephant Man, and I was not disgusted. I saw that he was a human being, just like me.' This kind of sentimental empathy, earned by acting skill, is what got the production its great success critically and commercially. The performer is transported while individual spectators experience their own reactions at the level of private responses. Some, like me, may simply respond to Anglim's skill. There is no collective work set out for the audience to do or participate in.   [Fig. 11]

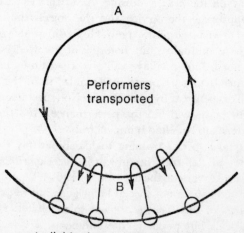

Fig. 11

The difference (can I say emptiness?) between this experience, these sets of individual experiences—parallel but not collective—and Asemo's initiation, Greek theatre, *Natyasastra*, and Noh is clear. In each of the others the audience has a definite collective role to play. The tie-ins do not stop with responsivity but go on to include consciously articulated and practised interactions. Asemo and his agemates exist as initiates between the men and the rest of Susuroka, somewhat the way *rasa* and *hana* are co-created by audience and performers in Indian and Japanese theatre. And in the Greek theatre, a particular performance determined who won the prize. The only thing close to this kind of celebratory play/work in our culture is what fans do at football, baseball, boxing, or other sports events.

Brecht knew this and wanted people to attend theatre with the same critical/supportive mind they take to sports. It was this lack of mutuality, a symptom of the audience's lack of power, and the performances' lack of transformative potential, that led to the experiments of the 60s and 70s. These involved audience participation, creation of new kinds of spaces for theatre, a widespread interest in shamanism: performances that heal, transport, transform. And conscious links were forged between theatre and religion. I do not have space to investigate these experiments here. I have written extensively about them elsewhere.[22] But I do want to say that in regard to some of my own work—*Dionysus in 69, Commune,* and *Mother Courage* especially—I positioned my company, The Performance Group, somewhere between the individualist practice of Broadway and the collective social process of Susuroka. Also I had the ambition to develop a performing style as precise as that described in the *Natyasastra*. I even sought to train the audience by holding many discussions after performances, giving public workshops, holding open rehearsals, and lecturing/writing a lot about the work. I didn't know it at the time, but I used workshops with The Performance Group as a way of transforming individuals into a group and then used The Group as transporters in an attempt to make out of the individuals who constitute an audience a collective, if only a temporary collective—a community for the time being.   [Fig. 12]

I treated the members of the audience as if they were joining a workshop, and I tried to condense the workshop into a single performance. Grotowski, recognizing as early as 1967 that this couldn't be done, did away with the audience altogether. In his paratheatrical work he has broken his acting company into subgroups who lead

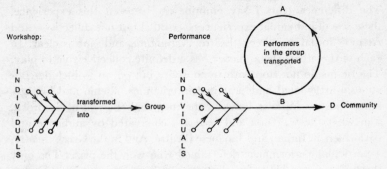

An attempt, in American society, to duplicate the initiatory/transformative process.

Fig. 12

people in attempts to generate 'spontaneous communitas'. Eugenio Barba started in 1980 the International School of Theatre Anthropology to bring together master teachers from Asia and students from Europe and America. He doesn't want to teach oriental techniques but get at 'certain laws that determine organic tensions in the actor's organism. . . . The study and understanding of these laws, going beyond the styles and conventions of their theatrical forms, can, for the European actor, facilitate an awareness of his own energy processes.'[23] Barba says that 'theatre anthropology is the study of the biological and cultural behaviour of man in a theatrical situation, that is to say, of man presenting and using his physical and mental presence in accordance with laws differing from those of daily life.' My own attention has turned, temporarily I think, from actually making performances to the writing of 'performance theory'.

Today there is a quiet in the American theatre. But the surface calm lies. Tectonically there is movement bringing a collision of cultures. And where traditions collide—or separate radically—up bursts creative magma. If this is not happening right now on the 'art front', it is happening in the social sciences—disciplines undergoing transformation. In the spring 1980 issue of *The American Scholar*, Clifford Geertz writes about 'blurred genres'—his attempt to catch up to, and criticize, movements in social thought dealing with cultures in terms of games, dramas, and texts. Geertz, a pioneer of these processes (they are not yet frozen into 'methods'), recognizes them as ways of handling the new world that has borne itself since World War II: a world of colliding cultures no longer dominated by Europeans and Americans, and no longer dominable by anyone. Dominance, of course, can be political, economic, cultural, scientific, philosophical, artistic. In none of these spheres is there going to be hegemony. Soon enough, as the changed relations among peoples are manifested, the term 'international' will be replaced by 'intercultural'. This phase of human history will not bring the 'retribalization' of industrial societies. But it will see the coexistence of metaphoric and linear knowledge. Metaphoric knowledge—the kind of knowledge released by the arts— is gaining an equal footing: it is not inferior to 'realer' facticities but a primary reality, one of several that braid into the human helix. And theatrical metaphor—restored and reactualized behaviour—is the root metaphor. It is the root because theatre = action = transportation/ transformation. Chased from Plato's republic as nonrational and subversive, but existing always, sometimes marginally, theatre is now showing itself everywhere: in social dramas, personal experience, public displays, political and economic interaction, art. So now: on with the show.

1. I discuss this idea of 'twice-behaved behaviour' extensively in 'Restored Behaviour'; see below, pp. 164–237. I see in the rehearsal process itself the paradigm of ritual, and in 'restored behaviour' the operation linking such diverse activities as ritual, theatre, psychotherapy, shamanism, and reflexivity.

2. From K. Stanislavski, *An Actor Prepares* (N.Y.: Theatre Arts, 1946), p. 13. This sense of being 'carried away' is what M. Csikszentmihalyi calls 'flow', and it characterizes a number of activities, such as sports, mountain climbing, chess, surgery (for the surgeon), theatre, dance. It is the opposite of reflexivity. Probably many human activities are dialectical, depending on a wavelike alternation of flow and reflexivity. It may also be that some activities— theatre being among them—have a reflexive rehearsal phase followed by a flowing performance. For more on flow, see Csikszentmihalyi's *Beyond Boredom and Anxiety* (San Francisco: Jossey-Bass, 1975).

3. F. Kafka, *Wedding Preparations in the Country and Other Posthumous Prose Writings* (London: Secker and Warburg, 1954), p. 40.

4. C. Lévi-Strauss, 'The Sorcerer and His Magic', in *Structural Anthropology* (N.Y.: Basic Books, 1963), pp. 167–85.

5. It is another example of the peculiar power of performance to invert causal progressions so that effects precede causes. That is, the 'power' of a performer is *both* cause and effect of his performance. Performance—and its effect on the audience—and feedback comprise a synchronic bundle that, paradoxically, unfolds during the performance according to a diachronic progression.

6. The best discussions I know of are of M. Singer's 'The Radha–Krishna *Bhajanas* of Madras City', in *When A Great Tradition Modernizes* (London: Pall

Mall Press, 1972), pp. 199–244, and N. Hein, *The Miracle Plays of Mathura* (New Haven: Yale University Press, 1972).

7. Csikszentmihalyi, *Beyond Boredom*, p. 38.
8. Ibid. pp. 53–4.
9. Quoted in R. Schechner, *Environmental Theater* (N.Y.: Hawthorn, 1973), p. 295.
10. K. E. Read, *The High Valley* (N.Y.: Charles Scribner's Sons, 1965), p. 159.
11. Read, *High Valley*, p. 160.
12. Ibid. p. 172.
13. Ibid. p. 177.
14. R. Lannoy, *The Speaking Tree* (London: Oxford University Press, 1971), pp. 48–9.
15. Ibid. p. 43.
16. Ibid. p. 54.
17. Grotowski's work is complicated—combining as it does elements of old-fashioned Polish Catholicism with the new religions of California. Also Grotowski's own position inside communist Poland is not easily defined. He is, or was, a member of the Party; and he is, or was, an avant-garde theatre director. His work is not anti-government in any sense, concentrating as it does on the inner life of his followers. Grotowski's work can be divided into two parts: up until 1967, when he concentrated on presenting public performances according to a technique described in his book, *Towards a Poor Theatre*; and from 1967 to the present, when he has experimented in para-theatrical activity, some of which is described in a pamphlet, 'On the Road to Active Culture', ed. Leszek Kolankiewicz, trans. Boleslaw Taborski (unpublished manuscript; Wroclaw, Poland, 1978).
18. Zeami, *Kadensho*, trans. Chuichi Sakurai, Shuseki Hayashi, Rokuro Satoi, and Bin Miyai (Kyoto: Sumiya-Shinobe Publishing Institute, 1969), pp. 36–9.
19. Ibid. p. 63.
20. Ibid. pp. 64–5.
21. Ibid. pp. 23–4.
22. See especially R. Schechner, *Environmental Theater* (1973) and *Essays on Performance Theory* (N.Y.: Drama Books Specialists, 1977).
23. From a three-page announcement of the first session of the International School of Theatre Anthropology, held in Bonn, West Germany; Holstebro, Denmark; and Stockholm, Sweden from 1 October through 30 November 1980. Barba's school is only the most recent of a very extensive set of exchanges among the world's theatres, both ritual and aesthetic. Peter Brook has run his International Centre for Theatre Research in Paris for more than ten years, using performers from Africa, Asia, Europe, and America and experimenting with forms as diverse as Shinto worship and African storytelling, and texts ranging from the *Mahabharata* to the *Ik*, adapted from Colin Turnbull's *The Mountain People*. Ellen Stewart at La Mama ETC in New York sponsors the Third World Institute of Theatre Arts Studies which, for example, in October 1980 ran performances and workshops of traditional theatre and rituals from Nigeria, Japan, the Dominican Republic, the Philippines, Korea, Indonesia, India, and Haiti. This work, and much more like it, is laying the foundation for an extensive reconstruction of theatricality—what it means, how it works—

on a world-wide basis. The exchange is not one-way: a Nigerian explained how TV is used to reawaken among children interest in traditional games and ceremonies. The Performance Group's tour of India in 1976 had an effect on directors, actors, and writers in India.

5

From Ritual to Theatre and Back: The Structure/Process of the Efficacy-Entertainment Dyad

The *kaiko* celebration of the Tsembaga of Highlands New Guinea is a year-long festival culminating in the *konj kaiko*—pig *kaiko*. *Kaiko* means dancing, and the chief entertainments of the celebrations are dances. During 1962 the Tsembaga entertained thirteen other local groups on fifteen occasions.[1] To make sure that the *kaiko* was successful young Tsembaga men were sent to neighbouring areas to announce the shows—and to send back messages of delay should a visiting group be late: in that case the entertainments were postponed. The day of dancing begins with the dancers—all men—bathing and adorning themselves. Putting on costumes takes hours. It is an exacting, precise and delicate process. When dressed the dancers assemble on the flattened, stamped-down grounds where they dance both for their own pleasure and as rehearsal in advance of the arrival of their guests. The visitors announce their arrival by singing—they can be heard before they are seen. By this time many spectators have gathered, including both men and women from neighbouring villages. These spectators come to watch, and to trade goods. Finally,

the local dancers retire to a vantage point just above the dance ground, where their view of the visitors is unimpeded and where they continue singing. The visitors approach the gate silently, led by men carrying fight packages,[2] swinging their axes as they run back and forth in front of their procession in the peculiar crouched fighting prance. Just before they reach the gate they are met by one or two of those locals who have invited them and who now escort them over the gate. Visiting women and children follow behind the dancers and join the other spectators on the sidelines. There is much embracing as the local women and children greet visiting kinfolk. The dancing procession charges to the centre of the dance ground shouting the long, low battle cry and stamping their feet, magically treated before their arrival ... to enable them to dance strongly. After they charge back and forth across the dance ground several times, repeating the stamping in several locations while the crowd cheers in admiration of their numbers, their style and the richness of their finery, they begin to sing.[3]

The performance is a transformation of combat techniques into entertainment. All the basic moves and sounds—even the charge into the central space—are adaptations and direct lifts from battle. But the Tsembaga dance is a dance, and clearly so to everyone present at it. The dancing is not an isolated phenomenon—as theatre-going in America still is usually—but a behaviour nested in supportive actions. The entry described takes place late in the afternoon, and just before dusk the dancing stops and the food which has been piled in the centre of the dancing ground is distributed and eaten. It might be said, literally, that the dancing is *about the food,* for the whole *kaiko* cycle is about acquiring enough pigs-for-meat to afford the festival.

> The visitors are asked to stop dancing and gather around while a presentation speech is made by one of the men responsible for the invitation. As he slowly walks around and around the food that has been laid out in a number of piles, the speechmaker recounts the relations of the two groups: their mutual assistance in fighting, their exchange of women and wealth, their hospitality to each other in times of defeat. . . . When the speech of presentation is finished they gather their portions and distribute them to those men who came to help them dance, and to their women.[4]

After supper the dancing resumes and goes on all night. By dawn almost everyone has danced with everyone else: and this communality is a sign of a strong alliance.

With dawn the dancing ground is converted into a market place. Ornaments, pigs, furs, axes, knives, shells, pigments, tobacco are all traded or sold (money has come into the Tsembaga's economy).

> The transactions that take place on the dance ground are completed on the spot; a man both gives and receives at the same time. . . . At the men's houses, however, a different kind of exchange takes place. Here men from other places give to their kinsmen or trading partners in the local group valuables for which they do not receive immediate return.[5]

This orchestrated indebtedness is at the heart of the *kaiko.* At the start of the celebration the hosts owe meat to the guests and the guests owe items of trade to the hosts. In the first part of the *kaiko* the hosts pay meat to the guests; in the second part of the *kaiko* the guests pay the hosts trade items. But neither payment ends in a balance. When the *kaiko* is over the guests owe the hosts meat, and the hosts owe the guests trade items. This symmetrical imbalance guarantees further *kaikos*—continued exchanges between groups. Often trade items are not given back directly, but traded back through third or fourth parties. After the public trading and the gift-giving, some dancing resumes which ends by midmorning. Then everyone goes home.

The *kaiko* entertainments are a ritual display, not simply a doing but a *showing of a doing*. Furthermore, this showing is both actual (= the trading and giving of goods resulting in a new imbalance) and symbolic (= the reaffirmation of alliances made concrete in the debtor-creditor relationship). The entertainment itself is a vehicle for debtors and creditors to exchange places; it is also the occasion for a market; and it is fun. The *kaiko* depends on the accumulation of pigs and goods, and on a willingness to dress up and dance; neither by itself is enough. The dancing is a performance—and appreciated as such, with the audience serving as frequently acerbic critics—but it's also a way of facilitating trade, finding mates, cementing military alliances and reaffirming tribal hierarchies.

> The Tsembaga say that 'those who come to our *kaiko* will also come to our fights'. This native interpretation of *kaiko* attendance is also given expression by an invited group. Preparations for departure to a *kaiko* at another place include ritual performances similar to those that precede a fight. Fight packages are applied to the heads and hearts of the dancers and *gir* to their feet so that they will dance strongly, just as, during warfare, they are applied so that they will fight strongly. . . . Dancing is like fighting. The visitors' procession is led by men carrying fight packages, and their entrance upon the dance ground of their hosts is martial. To join a group in dancing is the symbolic expression of willingness to join them in fighting.[6]

The *kaiko* dance display is a cultural version of territorial and status displays in animals; the rituals of the Tsembaga are ethological as well as sociological. They are also ecological: the *kaiko* is a means of organizing the Tsembaga's relationships to their neighbours, to their lands and goods, to their gardens and hunting ranges.

A *kaiko* culminates in the *konj kaiko*. The *kaiko* lasts a year, the *konj kaiko* a few days, usually two. Kaiko years are rare. During the fifty to sixty years ending in 1963 the Tsembaga staged four *kaikos*, with an average of twelve to fifteen years between festivals.[7] The whole cycle is tied to the war/peace rhythm which, in turn, is tied to the fortunes of the pig population. After the *konj kaiko*—whose major event is a mass slaughter of pigs and distribution of meat—a short peace is followed by war, which continues until another *kaiko* cycle begins. The cycle itself lasts for enough years to allow the raising of sufficient pigs to stage a *konj kaiko*. The *konj kaiko* of 7 and 8 November 1963 saw the slaughter of 96 pigs with a total live weight of 15,000 pounds, yielding around 7,500 pounds of meat; eventually about 3,000 people got shares of the kill.[8] What starts in dancing ends in eating; or, to put it in artistic-religious terms, what starts as theatre ends as communion. *Perhaps not since classical Athenian festivals and medieval pageants have we in the West used performances as the pivots in systems involving economic, social, political and religious transactions.* With the re-advent of holism in contemporary society at least a discussion of such performances becomes practical. It is clear that the *kaiko* dances are not ornaments or pastimes or even 'part of the means' of effecting the transactions among the Tsembaga. The dances both symbolize and participate in the process of exchange.

The dances are pivots in a *system of transformations which change destructive behaviour into constructive alliances*. It is no accident that every move, chant and costume of the *kaiko* dances are adapted from combat: a new use is found for this behaviour. Quite unconsciously a positive feedback begins: the more splendid the displays of dancing, the stronger the alliances; the stronger the alliances, the more splendid the dancing. Between *kaikos*—but only between them—war is waged; during the cycles there is peace. The exact transformation of combat behaviour into performance is at the heart of the *kaiko*. This transformation is identical in structure to that at the heart of Greek theatre (and from the Greeks down throughout all of Western theatre history). Namely, characterization and the presentation of real or possible events—the story, plot or dramatic action worked out among human figures (whether they be called men or gods)—is a transformation of real behaviour into symbolic behaviour. In fact, *transformation is the heart of theatre, and there appear to be only two fundamental kinds of theatrical transformation*: (1) the displacement of anti-social, injurious, disruptive behaviour by ritualized gesture and display, and (2) the invention of characters who act out fictional events or real events fictionalized by virtue of their being acted out (as in documentary theatre or Roman gladiatorial games.) These two kinds of transformation occur together, but in the mix usually one is dominant. Western theatre emphasizes characterization and the enactment of fictions; Melanesian, African and Australian (aborigine) theatre emphasize the displacement of hostile behaviour. Forms which balance the two tendencies—Nō, Kathakali, the Balinese Ketchak, medieval moralities, some contemporary avant-garde performances—offer, I think, the best models for the future of the theatre.

Much performing among communal peoples is, like the *kaiko*, part of the overall ecology of a society. The *Engwura* cycle of the Arunta of Australia, as described by Spencer and Gillen in the late nineteenth century,[9] is an elegant example of how a complicated series of performances expressed and participated in a people's ecology. The fact that the *Engwura* is no longer performed—that the Arunta, culturally speaking, have been exterminated—indicates the incompatibility of wholeness as I am describing it and Western society as it is presently constituted. In so far as performing groups adapt techniques from the *kaiko* or *Engwura* they are bound to remain outside the 'mainstream'. But the chief function of the avant garde is to propose models for change: to remain 'in advance'. The *Engwura* was an initiation cycle that spanned several years; the last phase consisted of performances staged sporadically over a three-to-four-month period. Each phase of the *Engwura* took place only when several conditions meshed: enough young men of a certain age gathered in one place to be initiated; enough older men willing to lead the ceremonies (particularly important in a non-literate culture); enough food to support celebration. Then the sacred implements and sacred grounds were prepared painstakingly and according to tradition. Finally, there had to be peace among neighbouring tribes—but the announcement of a forthcoming *Engwura* was sometimes enough to guarantee a peace.

The daily rhythm recapitulated the monthly rhythm: performance spaces were cleared, implements repaired and laid out, body decorations applied, food cooked. Each performance day saw not one but several performances, with rest and preparations between each. Each performance lasted on an average ten minutes, and was characteristically a dance accompanied by drumming and chanting. Then the performers rested for about two hours; then preparations for the next performance began, and these preparations took about two hours.[10] The whole cycle recapitulates the life cycle of the Arunta male; and during his life he could expect to play roles co-existent with his status in society: initiate, participant, leader or onlooker. Thus on each day performers enacted condensed and concentrated versions of their lives; and the three-to-four-month culminating series of performances also replicated the life cycle. The whole cycle was, in fact, an important—perhaps the most important—set of events in an Arunta life.[11] Each phase of the cycle was a replication (either an extension or a concentration) of every other phase.

The subject matter of each brief dance-drama was life events of mythical Dreamtime beings who populated the world 'in the beginning'.[12] These mythic events were very important to the Arunta and constituted for them a history and, since each Dreamtime event was connected to specific places and landmarks, a geography.[13] The rituals are a concrete symbolization and re-enactment of Dreamtime events, and to this extent the *Engwura* is familiar to us: it is not unlike our own drama except that we accept the reactualization of past events only as a convention. The Arunta, like the orthodox Catholic taking the Eucharist, accepted the manifestation of Dreamtime events as actual. [Fig. 1]

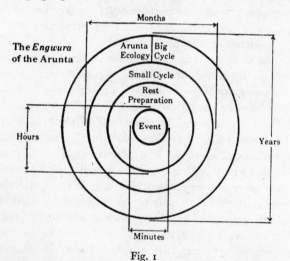

Fig. 1

The overall structure of the *Engwura* is analogic, while its interior structure is dramatic. The two structures are integrated because the Arunta believed concretely in the Dreamtime and experienced their own lives as divided between 'ordinary' and 'super-ordinary' realities. They experienced an interaction between these realities, and *Engwura*

9

performers were the navel, or link, or point-of-time-and-place where the two realities meshed.

I saw an ecological ritual similar to the *konj kaiko* (but much less inclusive than the *Engwura*) in March 1972, at Kurumugl in the Eastern Highlands of New Guinea.[14] Surrounding the performance of the *kaiko* is no special self-conciousness—that is, the ritual functions without the Tsembaga being explicitly aware of its functions; and aside from commendatory or critical comments on the dancing no aesthetic judgments are passed. In other words there are neither performance theorists nor critics among the Tsembaga. At Kurumugl the people know what the ritual does and why it was established—to inhibit warfare among feuding groups. The ritual at Kurumugl is already travelling along the continuum towards theatre in the modern sense. Knowing what the ritual does is a very important step in the development of theatre from ritual.

It's my purpose to outline a process through which theatre develops from ritual; and also to suggest that in some circumstances ritual develops from theatre. I think this process ought to be documented from contemporary or near-contemporary sources because so often the jump from ritual to theatre is assumed, or attributed to ancient events the evidence for which is suspect.[15]

Unlike the *kaiko* dancing grounds, the 'council grounds' (as they are called) at Kurumugl are near no regular village. The colonial Australian government set them up as a place where former enemies assemble to *sing-sing* (pidgin for drama-music-dance). The difference between the Tsembaga and the people at Kurumugl is that the *kaiko* brought together traditional allies while the Kurumugl *sing-sing* assembles traditional enemies. The performances at Kurumugl are always in danger of tipping over into actual combat, even though the performances are very much like those of the *konj kaiko*: dance movements adapted from combat, war chants, the arrival of a guest group at a dance ground piled high with freshly slaughtered, cooked pork. The celebration at Kurumugl that I saw took two days. The first consisted of arriving, setting up temporary house inside long rectangular huts, digging cooking ovens. All the people gathered— about 350—were of one tribal group. They awaited the arrival of their guests, a group comparable in size, but recently their enemies. The second day began with the slaughter of about two hundred pigs. These are clubbed on the snouts and heads. As each owner kills his animal he recites—sings—a speech telling how difficult it was to raise the pig, who it is promised to, what a fine animal it is, etc. The *pro forma recitatives* are applauded with laughs and roars, as they often contain jokes and obscene invective. The orations are accompanied by the death squeals of the pigs. Then the animals are gutted, butchered and lowered in halves and quarters into earth ovens to cook. Their guts are hung in nets over the ovens and steamed. Their bladders are blown into balloons and given to the children. The sight and smell of so much meat and blood excites the people, including me. No special clothes are worn for the killing. The only ritual element I detected was the careful display of pig jawbones on a circular altar-like structure in the middle of the dance grounds. From each jaw flowers were hung.

As the cooking starts, the men retire to the huts to begin adorning themselves. From time to time a man emerges to try on a towering headdress of cassowary and peacock feathers. The women cook and tend to the children. After about four hours the meat, still nearly raw, is taken from the ovens and displayed in long rows. Each family lays out its own meat—the women doing most of the work—like so much money in the bank: pork is wealth in the Highlands. As more and more men finish dressing they emerge from the huts to show off and admire each other in a grudging way—the adorning is very competitive. Some women also adorned themselves, dressing much like the men. I couldn't determine if this was traditional or an innovation. A man invited Joan MacIntosh[16] and me into his hut to watch him put on his makeup. He set out a mirror and tins of pigment (bought from a Japanese trading store) and then applied blue, red and black to his torso, shoulders, arms and face. He painted half his nose red and the other half blue. I asked him what the patterns meant. He said he chose them because he liked the way they looked. The Australian aborigines, by contrast, adorn their bodies with patterns each detail of which is linked to ancestral beings, sexual magic or recent events. Aborigine body painting is map-making and myth-telling.

Our performer showed us his headdress of four-foot-long feathers, and stepped outside to try it on. As he emerged from the hut his casual air dropped and he literally thrust his chest forward, gave a long whooping call, put on his headdress and displayed himself. He was costumed for a social not a dramatic role—that is, not to present a fictional character whose life was separable from his own, but to show himself in a special way: to display his strength, his power, his wealth, his authority. It is not easy to distinguish between these kinds of roles, except that in drama the script is already fixed in its details, the precise gestures of the role are rehearsed for a particular occasion (and other occasions, other 'productions', might eventuate in different gestures), while 'in life' the script is 'replaced by an ongoing process, this process is set in motion by the objective demands of the role, and the subjective motives and goals of the actor'.[17] An awareness that social and dramatic roles are indeed closely related to each other, and locating their points of convergence in the mise-en-scène rather than in the mind of the playwright, has been one of the major developments in contemporary theatre. This development has been helped by film and television—by film because it presents dramatic actions on location, as if in 'real life', and by TV because all so-called news is staged. It is staged not only by the obvious editing of raw footage to suit TV format and the need to sell time (that is, to hold the viewer's attention), but also as it is actually made. Many guerrilla activities, terrorist raids, kidnappings, assassinations and street demonstrations are theatricalized events performed by groups of people in order to catch the attention of larger masses of people by means of TV. This is the main way today in which powerless groups get a hearing. In response, the authorities stage their repressive raids, their assaults and their reprisals: to show the world how the insurgents will be dealt with, to display the power of authority and to terrorize the viewer. Thus an apparent two-person exchange between activist and authority is actually a three-person arrangement with the spectator supplying the vital link. Thus are we continually being educated to the histrionic structure of communication.[18]

The seeds of this histrionic sense are at Kurumugl. As these people are 'technified' (already they have planes before cars, TV before newspapers) they will leap not into the twentieth century but beyond, going directly from pre-industrial tribalism to automation-age tribalism. The big difference between the two is that pre-industrial tribalism scatters power among a large number of local leaders, there being no way for people to maintain themselves in large masses; automation-age tribalism is a way of controlling megalopolitic masses. I mean by tribalism the shaping of social roles not through individual choice but by collective formation; the substitution of histrionic-ritualized events for ordinary events; the sacralization or increasingly closely codified definition of all experience; and the disappearance of solitude and one-to-one intimacy as we have developed it since the Renaissance. Automation-age tribalism is medievalism under the auspices of technology. Such tribalism is good for the theatre—if by good one means that most social situations will be governed by conventional, external gestures loaded with metaphoric/symbolic significances. Anomie and identity crisis are eliminated and in their places are fixed roles and rites of passage transporting persons not only from one status to another but from one identity to another. These transportations are achieved by means of performances. I call these kinds of performances 'transformances' because the performances are the means of transformation from one status, identity or situation to another.

When the performer at Kurumugl stepped outside his hut he joined a group of envious males whose costumes were, like his, peculiar amalgams of traditional and imported stuff: sunglasses and bones stuck through the septum; cigarette holders and homemade tobacco pipes; khaki shorts and grass skirts. But despite the breakdown in traditional costume an old pattern was being worked out. An ecological ritual where the pig meat was a 'payback' (pidgin for fulfilling a ritual obligation) from the hosts to the guests. As among the Tsembaga every adult male at Kurumugl was in a debtor relationship to persons arriving in the afternoon of the second day. The nature of the payback is such that what is given back must exceed what is owed. (This is true even of war, where a perpetual imbalance in casualties must be maintained.) The payback ceremony involves an exchange of roles in which creditors become debtors and debtors become creditors. This insures that more ceremonies will follow when the new debtors accumulate enough pigs. Never is a balance struck, because a balance would threaten an end to the obligations, and this would lead to war. As long as the obligations are intact the social web transmits continuous waves of paybacks back and forth. The visitors approaching Kurumugl came not as friends but as invaders. The afternoon's performance was not a party but a ritual combat with the guests assaulting Kurumugl in a modified war dance, armed with fighting spears, and the campers at Kurumugl defending their ground and the immense pile of meat piled in the centre of it. Instead of a secret raiding party there were dancers; instead of taking human victims, they took meat. And instead of doubt about the outcome everyone knew what was going to happen. Thus a ritualized social drama (as war in the Highlands often is) moves toward becoming an aesthetic drama in which a script of actions is adhered to—the script being known in advance and carefully prepared for.

Again, differences between social and aesthetic drama are not easy to specify. Social drama has more variables, the outcome is in doubt —it is more like a game or sporting context. Aesthetic drama is almost totally arranged in advance, and the participants can concentrate not on strategies of achieving their goals—at Kurumugl, to penetrate to where the meat was, or to defend the meat pile—but on displays; aesthetic drama is less instrumental and more ornamental than social drama. Also, it can use symbolic time and place, and so become entirely fictionalized.

Early in the afternoon of the second day I heard from outside the camp the chanting and shouting of the invaders. The people in camp returned these shouts so that an antiphonal chorus arose. Then the men in camp—and a contingent of about twenty women who were fully armed—rushed to the edges of Kurumugl and the ritual combat began. Both sides were armed with bows and arrows, spears, sticks and axes. They chanted in a rhythm common to the Highlands—a leader sings a phrase and is overlapped by the unison response of many followers. This call-and-response is in loud nasal tones, a progression of quarter and half notes. Such chants alternate with Ketchaklike staccato grunts-pants-shouts. From about one to five in the afternoon the two groups engaged in fierce ritual combat. Each cycle of singing and dancing climaxed when parties of warriors rushed forward from both sides, spears ready for throwing, and, at apparently the last second, did a rapid kick-from-the-knee step instead of throwing their weapons. The weapons became props in a performance of aggression displaced, if not into friendship, at least into a non-deadly confrontation.

The assaults of the invaders were repeated dozens of times; a lush and valuable peanut field was trampled to muck; each assault was met by determined counterattack. But foot by foot the invaders penetrated to the heart of the camp ground—to the pile of meat and the altar of jaw bones and flowers. All the meat previously laid out in rows was now piled three feet deep—a huge heap of legs, snouts, ribs and flanks all tangled together. Three live white goats were tethered to a pole at the edge of the meat pile. Once the invaders reached the meat they merged with their hosts in one large, whooping, chanting, dancing doughnut of warriors. Around and around the meat they danced, for nearly an hour. I was pinned up against a tree, between the armed dancers and the meat. Then, suddenly, the dancing stopped and orators plunged into the meat, pulling a leg, or a flank, or a side of ribs, and shouted-sung-declaimed things like:

> This pig I give you in payment for the pig you gave my father three years ago! Your pig was scrawny, no fat on it at all, but my pig is huge, with lots of fat, much good meat—much better than the one my father got! And my whole family, especially my brothers, will remember that we are giving you today better than what we got, so that you owe us, and will help us if we need you beside us in a fight!

Sometimes the speechifying rises to song; sometimes insults are hurled back and forth. The fun in the orating, and the joking, stands on a very serious foundation: the participants do not forget that not so long ago they were blood enemies. After more than an hour of orating, the meat is distributed. Sleds are made to carry it shoulder high and whole families, with much singing, leave with their share of meat.

The performance at Kurumugl consists of displaying the meat, ritual combat, the merging of the two groups into one, orating and carrying the meat away. Preparations for this performance are both immediate, the day before at the camp (and at the visitors' residence), and long-range: raising the pigs, acquiring costumes and ornaments. After the performance comes the cleanup, the travel home, the distribution of the meat, feasting and stories about the *sing-sing*. By means of the performance the basic relationship—one might say the fundamental relationship—between the invading and the host groups is inverted.

ACTUALITY 1 → TRANSFORMANCE → ACTUALITY 2
Group A is debtor Group B is debtor
to Group B to Group A

As in all rites of passage something has happened during the performance; *the performance both symbolizes and actualizes the change in status*. The dancing at Kurumugl is the process by which change happens and it is the only process (other than war) recognized by all the parties assembled at Kurumugl. Giving and taking the meat not only symbolizes the changed relationship between Group A and B, it is the change itself. This convergence of symbolic and actual event is missing from aesthetic theatre. We have sought for it by trying to make the performer 'responsible' or 'visible' in and for his performance—

either through psychodramatic techniques or other psychological means. This use of psychology is a reflection of our preoccupation with the individual. Where performances have been sociologically or politically motivated—such as happenings and guerrilla theatre— the authenticating techniques have included emphasis on the event in and for itself, the development of group consciousness and appeals to the public at large. But a fundamental contradiction undermines these efforts. At Kurumugl enough actual wealth and people could be assembled in one place so that what was done in the performance focused actual economic, political and social power. In our society only a charade of power is displayed at theatrical performances. When this is recognized, authenticating theatres preoccupy themselves with symbolic activities, feeling helpless in the face of the hollowness of the authenticating tasks they set up for themselves. So-called real events are revealed as metaphors. In a society as large and wealthy as ours only aesthetic theatre is possible. Or authenticating theatres must seek a basis other than economics; or fully ally themselves with established authority. None of these options is as easy as it sounds.

At Kurumugl the change between Group A and B is not simply the occasion for a celebratory performance (as a birthday party celebrates but does not effect a change in age). The performance effects what it celebrates. It opens up enough time in the right place for the exchange to be made: it is liminal: a fluid mid-point between two fixed structures. Only for a brief time do the two groups merge into one dancing circle; during this liminal time/place *communitas* is possible—that levelling of all differences in an ecstasy that so often characterizes performing.[19] Then, and only then, the exchange takes place.

war parties	——————transformed into———	→dancing groups
human victims	——————————————————	→pig meat
battle dress	——————————————————	→costumes
combat	——————————————————	→dancing

debtors	→creditors
creditors	→debtors
two groups	→one group

The transformations above the line convert actualities into aesthetic realities. Those below the line effect a change from one actuality into another. It is only because the transformations above the line happen that those below the line can take place in peace. All the transformations—aesthetic as well as actual—are temporary: the meat will be eaten, the costumes doffed, the dance ended; the single group will divide again according to known divisions; today's debtors will be next year's creditors, etc. The celebration at Kurumugl managed a complicated and potentially dangerous exchange with a minimum of danger and a maximum of pleasure. The mode of achieving 'real results'—paying debts, incurring new obligations—was performing; the dancing does not celebrate achieving results, it does not precede or follow the exchange, it is the means of making the transformations; the performance is effective.

The Tsembaga, Arunta and Kurumugl performances are ecological rituals. Whatever enjoyment the participants take in the dancing, and however carefully they prepare themselves for dancing, the dances are danced to achieve results. In religious rituals results are achieved by appealing to a transcendent Other (who puts in an appearance either in person or by surrogate). In ecological rituals the other group, or the status to be achieved, or some other clearly human arrangement is the object of the performance. An ecological ritual with no results to show 'below the line' would soon cease. The 'above the line' transformations change aggressive actions into harmless and pleasure-giving performances (in the cases cited). One is struck by the analogy to certain biological adaptations among animals.[20]

In the New Guinea Highlands, at first under the pressure of the colonial police, later under its own momentum, warfare is transformed into dancing. As above-the-line activities grow in importance, entertainment as such takes over from efficacy as the reason for the performance. It is not only that creditors and debtors need to exchange roles, but also that people want to show off; it is not only to get results that the dances are staged, but also because people like dancing for its own sake. Efficacy and entertainment are opposed to each other, but they form a binary system, a continuum.

EFFICACY ←——————→	ENTERTAINMENT
(Ritual)	(Theatre)
results	fun
link to an absent Other	only for those here
abolishes time, symbolic time	emphasizes now
brings Other here	audience is the Other
performer possessed, in trance	performer knows what he's doing
audience participates	audience watches
audience believes	audience appreciates

| criticism is forbidden | criticism is encouraged |
| collective creativity | individual creativity |

The basic opposition is between efficacy and entertainment, not between ritual and theatre. Whether one calls a specific performance ritual or theatre depends on the degree to which the performance tends towards efficacy or entertainment. No performance is pure efficacy or pure entertainment. The matter is complicated because one can look at specific performances from several vantages; changing perspective changes classification. For example, a Broadway musical is entertainment if one concentrates on what happens onstage and in the house. But if the point of view expands—to include rehearsals, backstage life before, during and after the show, the function of the roles in the careers of each performer, the money invested by backers, the arrival of the audience, their social status, how they paid for their tickets (as individuals, expense accounts, theatre parties, etc.) and how this indicates the use they're making of the performance (as entertainment, to advance their careers, to support a charity, etc.)—then the Broadway musical is more than entertainment; it reveals many ritual elements.

Recently, more performances have been emphasizing the rehearsal and backstage procedures. At first this was as simple as showing the lighting instruments and using a half-curtain, as Brecht did. But within the last fifteen years the process of mounting the performance, the workshops that lead up to the performance, the means by which an audience is brought into the space and led from the space and many other previously automatic procedures, have become the subjects of theatrical manipulations. These procedures have to do with the theatre-in-itself and they are, as regards the theatre, efficacious: that is, these procedures are what makes a theatre into a theatre regardless of themes, plot or the usual 'elements of drama'. *The attention paid to the procedures of making theatre are, I think, attempts at ritualizing performance, of finding in the theatre itself authenticating acts.* In a period when authenticity is increasingly rare in public life the performer has been asked to surrender his traditional masks and be himself; or at least to show how the masks are put on and taken off. Instead of mirroring his times the performer is asked to remedy them. The professions taken as models for theatre are medicine and the church. No wonder shamanism is popular among theatre people: shamanism is that branch of doctoring that is religious, and that kind of religion that is full of ironies and tricks.[21]

At present efficacy is ascending to a dominant position over entertainment. It is my belief that theatre history can be given an overall shape as a development along a core which is a *braided structure* constantly interrelating efficacy and entertainment. At each period in each culture one or the other is dominant—one is ascending while the other is descending. Naturally, these changes are part of changes in the overall social structure; yet performance is not a passive mirror of these social changes but a part of the complicated feedback process that brings about change. At all times a dialectical tension exists between efficacious and entertainment tendencies. For Western theatre, at least, I think it can be shown that when the braid is tight—that is, when efficacy and entertainment are both present in nearly equal degrees—theatre flourishes. During these brief historical moments the theatre answers needs that are both ritualistic and pleasure-giving. Fifth-century Athenian theatre, Elizabethan theatre, and possibly the theatre of the late nineteenth century and/or of our own times show the kind of convergence I'm talking about. When efficacy dominates, performances are universalistic, allegorical, ritualized, tied to a stable established order; this kind of theatre persists for a relatively long time. When entertainment dominates, performances are class-oriented, individualized, show business, constantly adjusted to suit the tastes of a fickle audience. The two most recent convergences—the rise of entertainment before the Elizabethan period and the rise of efficacy during the modern period—are necessarily opposites of each other. The model that I offer is of course a simplification. I present it as a help in conceptualizing my view of the progression of theatre history, which I think has its own logic and internal force. The late medieval period was dominated by efficacious performances: church services, court ceremonies, moralities, pageants. In the early Renaissance these began to decline and popular entertainments, always present, gained, finally becoming dominant in the form of the public theatres of the Elizabethan period. The private and court theatres developed alongside the public theatres. The private theatres were for the upper classes. Although some professionals worked in both public and private theatres, and some spectators attended both, these entertainments were fundamentally opposed to each other. The conflicts between the public and private theatres never worked themselves out because all the theatres were closed in 1642. When theatres reopened at the Restoration the Elizabethan public theatre was gone and all the theatres resembled the private theatres and masques, the property of the upper classes. During the eighteenth and nineteenth centuries this aristocratic theatre developed into the bourgeois theatre, as that class rose to displace the aristocracy. The dominant efficacious mode of the medieval centuries went underground to re-emerge in the guise of social and political drama during the last third of the nineteenth century. This new naturalistic theatre opposed the commercialism and pomposity of the boulevards and allied itself to scientific theatrical styles and techniques. The avant garde identified itself both with Bohemianism—the outcasts of bourgeois society—and science, the source of power. Avant garde artists used terms like 'experimental' and 'research' to characterize their work, which took place in 'laboratories'. Efficacy lies at the ideological heart of all aspects of this new theatre.   [Fig. 2]

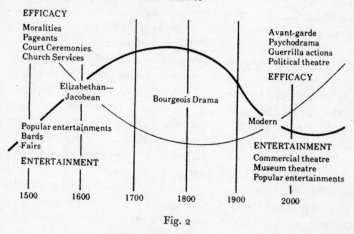

Efficacy/Entertainment Braid:
Fifteenth to Twenty-First Centuries
in the English and American Theatres

EFFICACY

Moralities
Pageants
Court Ceremonies.
Church Services

Avant-garde
Psychodrama
Guerrilla actions
Political theatre

EFFICACY

Elizabethan—
Jacobean

Bourgeois Drama

Modern

Popular entertainments
Bards
Fairs

ENTERTAINMENT
Commercial theatre
Museum theatre
Popular entertainments

ENTERTAINMENT

1500   1600   1700   1800   1900   2000

Fig. 2

In the twentieth century the entertainment theatre, threatened with extinction, broke into two parts: an increasingly outmoded commercial theatre typified by Broadway and a subsidized community museum typified by the regional theatres. The FACT meeting at Princeton[23] was an attempt by commercial interests to ally themselves with the regional theatres. Although such an alliance is inevitable, it's most likely that the regional theatres will absorb the commercial theatres. Whatever the outcome, the entertainment theatres remain fundamentally opposed by the avant garde—which has itself, by mid-twentieth century, expanded to include direct political action, psycho-therapy and other manifestly efficacious kinds of performances. It is my opinion that efficacious theatres are on the upswing and will dominate the theatrical world within the next 20 years.

Up to here I've said this: (1) in some social settings ritual performances are part of ecosystems and mediate political relations, group hierarchy and economics; (2) in other settings ritual performances begin to take on qualities of show business; (3) there is a dialectical-dyadic continuum linking efficacy to entertainment—both are present in all performances, but in each performance one or the other is dominant; (4) in different societies, at different times, either efficacy or entertainment dominates, the two being in a braided relationship to each other.

O. B. Hardison quotes Honorius of Autun's twelfth-century view of the Mass as evidence that people at the time saw this ceremony as drama:

> It is known that those who recited tragedies in theatres presented the actions of opponents by gestures before the people. In the same way our tragic author [i.e. the celebrant] represents by his gestures in the theatre of the Church before the Christian people the struggle of Christ and teaches to them the victory of his redemption. [Honorius then compares each movement of the Mass to an equivalent movement of tragic drama.] . . . When the sacrifice has been completed, peace and Communion are given by the celebrant to the people. . . . Then, by the *Ite, missa est*, they are ordered to return to their homes with rejoicing. They shout *Deo gratias* and return home rejoicing.[24]

What is extraordinary about Honorius' description is that it is a medieval view, not a backwards glance by a modernist. Honorius' Mass is more familiar to those who have attended avant garde performances than to those whose experience is limited to orthodox theatre. The twelfth-century Mass employed many avant garde techniques: it was allegorical, it used audience participation, it treated time teleologically, it extended the scope of the performance from the church to the roadways to the homes. But for all this I still think it is fair to call this Mass a ritual rather than theatre. My opinion is founded on the almost totally efficacious nature of the Mass. As

Hardison says, 'The service . . . has a very important aesthetic dimension, but it is essentially not a matter of appreciation but of passionate affirmation.'[25] The Mass was a closed circle which included only the congregation and the officiants; there was literally and figuratively no room for appreciators. The Mass was an obligatory action entered into either joyfully or sullenly, through which members of the congregation signalled to each other and to the hierarchy their continued participation in the congregation. What I say of the twelfth-century Mass, Rappaport has said of the Tsembaga:

> While the scope of the social unity is frequently not made explicit, it would seem that in some studies it is what Durkheim called a 'church', that is, 'a society whose members are united by the fact that they think in the same way in regard to the sacred world and its relations with the profane world, and by the fact that they translate these common ideas into common practices.' . . . Such units, composed of aggregates of individuals who regard their collective well-being to be dependent upon a common body of ritual performances, might be called 'congregations'.[26]

Because of its all-inclusive hold on its congregation the Mass was not theatre in the classical or modern sense. Theatre comes into existence when a separation occurs between audience and performers. The paradigmatic theatrical situation is a group of performers soliciting an audience who may or may not respond by attending. The audience is free to attend or stay away—and if they stay away it is the theatre that suffers, not its would-be audience. In ritual, staying away means rejecting the congregation—or being rejected by it, as in excommunication, ostracism or exile. If only a few stay away, it is those who are absent who suffer; if many stay away, the congregation is in danger of schism or extinction. To put it another way: *ritual is an event upon which its participants depend; theatre is an event which depends on its participants.* The process is not cut-and-dry. But evidence of the transformational steps by which theatre emerges from ritual—by which an efficacious event in which the participants depend on the performance is transformed into an entertainment in which the entertainers depend on an audience—is not locked in ancient or medieval documents. The transformation of ritual into theatre is occurring today.

Asaro is a village about seventy miles east of Kurumugl. There the famous dance of the Mudmen is performed as a tourist entertainment three times a week. It was not always so. The villagers originally performed only when they felt threatened by attack. Before dawn village men went to a local creek, rubbed their bodies with white mud (the colour of death) and constructed grotesque masks of wood frames covered by mud and vegetation. Emerging from the creek at dawn, possessed by the spirits of the dead, the dancers moved in an eerie, slow, crouching step. Sometimes they went to the village of their enemies and frightened them, thus preventing attack; sometimes they danced in their own village. The dances took less than ten minutes; preparations took most of the previous night. (This ratio of preparation to performance is not unusual; it is present even in modern Western theatre in the rehearsal-performance ratio.) The dance of the Mudmen was performed occasionally, when needed. After pacification by Australian authorities there was less need for the Mudmen. However, in the mid-sixties a photographer from the *National Geographic Magazine* paid the villagers to stage the dance for him. These photos became world famous—and it was not long before tourists demanded to see the Mudmen. (Even the name 'Mudmen' is an invention for tourists; I don't know the original name of the ceremony.) Because Asaro is near the Mount Hagan-Goroka road it was easy to arrange for minibuses to bring spectators to the village. Tourists pay up to $20 each to see the short dances; of this sum the Asaroans get 10 per cent. Because the 10-minute dance is not a long enough show by Western standards, the dancing has been augmented by a display of bow-and-arrow marksmanship, a photo session and a 'market'. But Asaro is not (yet) a craft village, and the few necklaces and string bags I saw for sale were pathetic—the day I was there no one bought anything.

The people of Asaro don't know what their dance is any more. Surely it's not to frighten enemies—it attracts tourists. It has no relationship to the spirits of the dead who appear only before dawn, and the tourists come a little after midday. The social fabric of Asaro has been torn to shreds, but the changes required of the Mudmen dance are a result of the deeper disruptions of Highlands life and only in a minor way a cause of these disruptions. In fact, despite the exploitation of the village by the tourist agencies, the meagre sums paid the Asaroans are needed desperately during a period when the barter economy has fallen apart. I expect future changes in the dance will make it longer, more visually complicated, possibly adding musical accompaniment; the craft skills of the villagers will improve, or they will import stuff to sell; their percentage of the take will rise. In short, the dance will approach those Western standards of entertainment represented by the tastes of the audience, and the benefits will rise accordingly. Presently, the Asaroans perform a traditional ritual emptied of its efficacy but not yet regarded as a theatrical entertainment.

Joan MacIntosh and I arrived before the tourists and stayed after they left. The villagers looked at us curiously—we were taking pictures of the tourists as well as of the dancers. After the other whites left, a man came up to us and in pidgin asked us to come with him. We walked four miles along a ridge until we got to Kenetisarobe. There we met Asuwe Yamuruhu, the headman. He wanted us to go to Goroka and tell the tourists about his dancers; he wanted tourists to come and watch a show which, he assured us, was much better than the Mudmen. It began to rain very hard as we squatted in the entrance to a round hut—around us, in the rain, a few villagers watched. We agreed on a price—$4 a person—and a time, the next afternoon; not only would we see dances but we could tape-record songs too.

The next afternoon we arrived with two friends, paid our $16, and saw a dance consisting of very slow steps, as if the dancers were moving through deep mud, their fingers splayed and their faces masked or tied into grotesque shapes. (Peter Thoady, headmaster of the Goroka Teachers' College, told us that the distortion of the faces probably was in imitation of yaws, a disfiguring disease common in the area.) The dancers moved in a half-crouch and occasionally shouted phrases and expletives. The Grassmen of Kenetisarobe were very like the Mudmen of Asaro. After the dancing we spent about an hour recording music, talking and smoking.

The Kenetisarobe dance was adapted from ceremonial farces of the region. Asuwe staged them for us—he knew that Asaro was making money from its dance, and the Kenetisarobe show was modelled on the Asaro formula: slow dance, grotesque masks, plenty of opportunity for photographs and a follow-up after the dance. What the people of Asaro did with a minimum of self-awareness, Asuwe did with a keen sense of theatre business. Examples of the same pattern abound. In Bali tourist versions of Barong and Ketchak are everywhere—along the Denpasar to Ubud road signs advertising these performances are as frequent as movie marquees in America. Signs, in English, often read: 'Traditional Ketchak—Holy Monkey Dance Theatre—Tonight at 8', or 'Barong—Each Wednesday at 8 on the Temple Steps'. The Balinese, with characteristic sophistication, make separate tourist shows and keep authentic performances secret—and, more important, far from the main road. Tourists want to drive to their entertainments; they want a dependable schedule; and they want a way to leave conveniently if they choose to go early. Most authentic performances—of Ketchak and of other actual ritual performances—are accessible only on foot, through rather thick jungle and only with the permission of the village giving the performance. During my two weeks in Bali I saw two such performances. We stumbled on a Ketchak while walking through the monkey forest near Ubud—we followed some women carrying offerings of food. Once we entered Tigal we stayed there for ten hours before the Ketchak began a little after 9 P.M. At Tenganan we saw the final two days of the annual Abuang. Some of the ceremony was public and about fifty tourists joined the villagers to enjoy the afternoon dancing. These people were asked to leave by 5 P.M. We were quietly told to remain in the town office. Then, after dark, we were taken to different compounds in the village for different aspects of the ceremony. We were also allowed to listen to special gamelon music played before dawn. We weren't allowed to photograph, and only a limited amount of tape recording was allowed. The daytime ceremonies definitely had the feel of an entertainment: outsiders came in, shops were open and doing a brisk business, the dances were carefully choreographed to the gamelon music. At night the operation was different: each aspect of the ceremony was privatized and done not with an eye to its prettiness but to its correctness; time gaps between elements were longer and more irregular; many discussions concerning how to do certain things were held, and this delayed the ceremonies. The subject matter of the Abuang—if I can use that phrase—is the presentation of all the unmarried males to all the unmarried females. The daytime dances showed everyone off; the nighttime ceremonies concerned actual betrothal.

Surely the tourist trade has influenced so-called 'genuine' performances in Bali and elsewhere. I have no contempt for these changes. Changes in conventions, themes, methods and styles occur because of opportunism, audience pressures, professionalism (itself often a new concept) and new technology. Tourism has been really important and worldwide only since the advent of cheap air travel. Theatre historians will regard tourism as of as much importance to twentieth-century theatre as the exchange between England and the Continent

10

was in the sixteenth and seventeenth centuries. Theatre people imitate popular imported modes, and the locals respond to the demands of rich visitors—or local audiences demand changes because they've absorbed the tastes of alien cultures. From one point of view these changes are corruptions—a clamour is raised to establish cultural zoos in which the original versions of age-old rituals can be preserved. But even traditional performances vary greatly from generation to generation—an oral tradition is flexible, able to absorb many personal variations within set parameters. And the cultural-zoo approach is itself the most pernicious aspect of tourism. I hate the genocide that has eradicated such cultures as that of the Australian Aborigines. But I see nothing wrong with what's happening in Bali and New Guinea, where two systems of theatre exist. The relationship between these is not a simple division between tourist and authentic. More studies are needed on the exchange between what's left of traditional performances and emerging tourist shows. And at what moment does a tourist show become itself an authentic theatrical art?

Tourism is a two-way street: travellers bring back experiences, expectations, and, if the tourists are practitioners, techniques, scenes and even entire forms. The birth ritual of *Dionysus in 69* was adapted from the Asmat of West Irian; several sequences in the Living Theatre's *Mysteries* and *Paradise Now* were taken from yoga and Indian theatre; Phillip Glass's music draws on gamelon and Indian raga; Imamu Baraka's writing is deeply influenced by African modes of storytelling and drama. The list could be extended, and to all the arts. Many innovators since World War II (a great war for travel) have been decisively influenced by work from cultures other than their own; this means, for Western artists, Asia, Africa and Oceania. The impact of communal-collective forms on contemporary Western theatre is like that of classical forms on the Renaissance. The differences, however, are also important: in the Renaissance all that remained of classical culture were architectural ruins, old texts and relics of the plastic arts. This material was frequently fragmented and corrupt. Also, Renaissance scholars looked with universal respect, even awe, at what they found of classical Greece and Rome. Today's cross-cultural feed is mainly in the area of performances; the shows have been seen intact; the originators of the performances are former colonial peoples, or peoples who were considered inferior by populations around the north Atlantic basin. In other words, it is logical that today's influences should be felt first in the avant garde.

A very clear and provable Asian influence on contemporary Western theatre is seen in Grotowski's work, particularly its 'poor theatre' phase, from around 1964 to around 1971. This period includes several versions of *Akropolis, The Constant Prince* and the first versions of *Apocalypsis Cum Figuris*. The foundation of this work is the psycho-physical/plastique exercises which Grotowski and Ryszard Cieslak taught in many of their workshops in Poland and abroad. Ever since I learned some of these exercises in 1967, I felt they were influenced not only by yoga, which Grotowski acknowledges, but by the south Indian dance-theatre form, Kathakali. In 1972, while visiting the Kathakali Kalamandalam in Kerala, I asked about Grotowski's visits to the school. No one remembered him, but Eugenio Barba was remembered, and in the school's visitors' book I found the following entry:

29 September 1963

The Secretary
Kalamandalam
Cheruthuruthy

Dear Sir:
I had not the occasion, last night at the performance, to thank you for all the kind help you have given me during my stay here. To you, and to the Superintendent, and to all the boys who were so willing to be of service, I would like to express my gratitude and sincerest thanks.

My visit to Kalamandalam has greatly helped me in my studies and the research material I have collected will surely be of the greatest assistance to those people working at the Theatre Laboratory in Poland.

Many thanks once again,

Yours sincerely,
Eugenio Barba [signed]

Barba brought Kathakali exercises to Grotowski in Poland—they form the core of the plastique and psychophysical exercises. When Barba founded his Odin Teatret he used these exercises—as modified by the Polish Lab—as the basis of his own work. Grotowski has visited India on several occasions, the first in 1956–57, when he also travelled to China and Japan.

Peter Brook's three-month trip in 1972–73 with a troupe of 30 persons through Algeria, Mali, Niger, Dahomey and Nigeria is another version of the 'trading partner' idea. Brook, even more consciously and fully than Grotowski-through-Barba, went to Africa to trade techniques, perform, observe performances. In Brook's words:

> Once we sat in Agades in a small hut all afternoon, singing. We and the African group sang, and suddenly we found that we were hitting exactly the same language of sound. Well, we understood theirs and they understood ours, and something quite electrifying happened because, out of all sorts of different songs, one suddenly came upon this common area.
>
> Another experience of that same sort occurred one night when we were camping in a forest. We thought there was no one around for miles, but as always, suddenly, children appeared from nowhere and beckoned. We were just sitting and doing some improvised song, and the children asked us to come down to their village, only a couple of miles away, because there was going to be some singing and dancing later in the night and everyone would be very pleased if we could come.
>
> So we said 'sure'. We walked down through the forest, found this village and found that, indeed, there was a ceremony going on. Somebody had just died and it was a funeral ceremony. We were made very welcome and we sat there, in total darkness under the trees, just seeing these moving shadows dancing and singing. And after a couple of hours they suddenly said to us: the boys say that this is what you do, too. Now you must sing for us.
>
> So we had to improvise a song for them. And this was perhaps one of the best works of the entire journey. Because the song that was produced for the occasion was extraordinarily moving, right and satisfying, and made a real coming together of the people and ourselves. It is impossible to say what produced it, because it was produced as much by the group that was working together in a certain way, with all the work that has gone into that, and as much by all the conditions of the moment that bore their influence: the place, the night, the feeling for the other people, so that we were actually making something for them in exchange for what they had offered us.[27]

Throughout Asia, MacIntosh and I found this same 'exchange policy'. We were invited to stay at Tenganan because the people knew we performed, and at the main public performance the chief insisted that I do a dance.[28] At Karamui in New Guinea—far from any road (we flew in)—we were shown funeral ceremonies (a villager, with much laughter, played the role of the corpse), but we were expected to sing songs in exchange. In the Sepik River village of Kamanabit

the headman insisted that MacIntosh be awakened and brought to
his house to sing even though she was exhausted from a day's travel;
his demand came after I'd been listening to village women singing.

The kind of influence through observation and trading reflected
in Barba's letter, Brook's trip and my own experiences is different
from Artaud's reaction to Balinese theatre. Artaud was influenced,
but the Balinese didn't care; there was no exchange. In the more
recent examples work was consciously traded, professionals sought
to expand their knowledge.

Whatever the ritual functions of Kathakali within the context
of Kerala village life, the Kalamandalam is a professional training school and its troupe performs for pay in India and overseas.
Foreigners come to study at the Kalamandalam (while I was there
about five Westerners were studying). This training does not eventuate
in the establishment of Kathakali troupes outside India—rather the
work is integrated into existing styles. It remains to be seen how the
presence of outsiders at the Kalamandalam, and the frequent tours
of the troupe, affect the work in Kerala. The situation with Brook
is different. The African villagers were in the midst of a religious
ritual (a funeral ceremony) but they were also eager to share their
entertainment (trading songs) to use their ritual as an item of trade.
That the exchange was mutually moving is no surprise—entertainment and ritual co-exist comfortably.

Touring ritual performances around the world—and thereby converting them into entertainments—is nothing new: the Romans were
fond of importing exotic entertainments, the more authentic the
better. Every colonial or conquering power has done the same. In
1972, at the Brooklyn Academy of Music the following show took
place (I quote from the programme):

THE BROOKLYN ACADEMY OF MUSIC
in association with
Mel Howard Productions, Inc.
and
Ninon Tallon-Karlweis
in cooperation with
The Turkish Ministry of Tourism and Information

Present
THE WHIRLING DERVISHES OF TURKEY
(THE PROGRAMME IS A RELIGIOUS CEREMONY. YOU ARE
KINDLY REQUESTED TO REFRAIN FROM APPLAUSE.)

The audience had to be told that what they paid money to see as an entertainment retained enough of its ritual basis to require a change in conventional theatrical behaviour. The performance was simple and moving—I suppose a fairly accurate presentation of the dervish ritual. I know that several theatre groups in New York were influenced by it. Both Robert Wilson's Byrd Hoffman group and The Performance Group have used whirling.

In October 1973, the Shingon Buddhist monks came to the Brooklyn Academy of Music with 'ceremonies, music and epics of ancient Japan'. The dervishes whirled on a stage facing the 2,000-seat opera house. The monks performed in a room designed for Brook's appearance after his African trip—a space 75' × 40', with a height of about 30'. The audience numbered around two hundred, seated on cushions scattered on the floor, and on bleachers. As at Asaro and Kenetisarobe the Buddhist rituals were not long enough to constitute an entertainment by Western standards. So the programme was augmented by performers of Japanese contemporary music and a recitation of Japanese war tales from the twelfth to fourteenth centuries. Only after the intermission did the monks perform their temple service. The programme described in detail what the monks were doing, what it meant and how the ceremony is used in Japan. Thus the audience was treated as if it were attending Grand Opera, where the libretto is summarized, or a new kind of sport in which the rules, equipment and structure are explained. It seemed to me that the monks, like the dervishes, were deeply into what they were doing. They were 'in character'—and it was impossible to distinguish what they were doing from what Stanislavski required of actors. I was convinced: these dervishes were Dervishes, these monks were Monks. A defined interface between spectators and performers existed; on one side was authenticity, efficacy and ritual, on the other side was entertainment and theatre.

Any ritual can be lifted from its original setting and performed as theatre—just as any everyday event can be.[29] This is possible because context, not fundamental structure, distinguishes ritual, entertainment and ordinary life from each other. The differences among them arise from the agreement (conscious or unexpressed) between performers and spectators. Entertainment/theatre emerges from ritual out of a complex consisting of an audience separate from the performers, the development of professional performers and economic needs imposing a situation in which performances are made to please the audience rather than according to a fixed code or dogma. It is also possible for ritual to arise out of theatre by reversing the process just described. This move from theatre to ritual marks Grotowski's work and that of the Living Theatre. But the rituals created were unstable because they were not attached to actual social structures outside theatre. Also, the difference between ritual, theatre and ordinary life depends on the degree spectators and performers attend to efficacy, pleasure or routine; and how symbolic meaning and effect are infused and attached to performed events. In all entertainment there is some efficacy and in all ritual there is some theatre.[30]

The entire binary 'efficacy/ritual—entertainment/theatre' is performance: performance includes the impulse to be serious and to entertain; to collect meanings and to pass the time; to display symbolic behaviour that actualizes 'there and then' and to exist only 'here and now'; to be oneself and to play at being others; to be in a trance and to be conscious; to get results and to fool around; to focus the action on and for a select group sharing a hermetic language and to broadcast to the largest possible audiences of strangers who buy tickets.

At this moment The Performance Group is working on Brecht's *Mother Courage and Her Children*. Most of our rehearsals have been open—when weather permits, the big overhead front garage door of our theatre has been raised and people off the street, students and friends have come in to watch us work. Every rehearsal has had from five to forty people watching. The rehearsals have a feeling of stop and go, with nothing special planned to accommodate the spectators. Yet their presence makes a deep difference: work on the play now includes a public social core; and the work is about showing-a-way-of-working. This theme will be worked into the formal performances. The space for *Courage*—designed by Jerry N. Rojo and James Clayburgh, collaborating with all the other members of the Group—expresses the interplay between Brecht's drama and the larger performance in which it takes place. A part of the room has been made into a Green Room wholly visible to the audience. When a performer is not in a scene he or she goes into the Green Room, gets some coffee, reads, relaxes. The rest of the theatre is divided into three main spaces: an empty cube 30′ × 30′ × 20′ (including an open pit 20′ × 8′ × 7′); a 20′ × 20′ × 20′ cube filled with irregular scaffolding, platforms, and ropes; galleries, walkways and a bridge about 11 feet off the ground. The audience can move freely through the entire space, continually changing perspective and mood. It is possible to see everything from a single vantage, but only if one looks through other structures. Scene Nine takes place outside the theatre in Wooster Street, with the large Garage door open. The door stays open for the final three scenes—in winter this means that the temperature in the theatre plunges.

Our production has one intermission, after Scene Five. During intermission supper is sold, and the performers mix with the audience. During supper the 'Song of the Great Capitulation' (Scene Four) is sung, as in a cabaret, without insistence that people pay attention. When the drama resumes after supper I think it is experienced differently because of the hour of mingling, talking and sharing of food and drink.[31] Another shift in the mode of experiencing the play comes when the performance moves outside, and the theatre takes on the feeling of the outside. *Mother Courage* is treated as a drama nested in a larger performance event. The ideas behind The Performance Group's production of *Courage* are common to *ritual performances: to control or manipulate the whole world of the performance, not just present the drama at its centre.* In this way a theatrical event in Soho, New York City, is nudged a little way from the entertainment end of the continuum towards efficacy. Without diminishing its theatricality, I hope to enhance its ritual aspects.

Orthodox theories say that ritual precedes theatre, just as efficacy and monism ('primitive oneness') precede entertainment. It is a cliché of interpretations of Paleolithic cave art that some kind of 'ritual' generated the art—and by ritual is meant a serious, efficacious, result-oriented performance either to insure fertility, to placate the powers who control the hunt, to maintain a balance between male and female or something. These things, or some of them, may be true; but they are not the whole truth: entertainment, passing time in play and fun (not the passive and cut-off feeling of 'art for art's sake', but an active involvement with the process of making art) are interwoven with and inseparable from any efficacious aspects of the earliest art. The idea of a primitive oneness is a combination of Edenic fantasy and the Protestant work ethic supported by the projections of early ethnographers too many of whom were missionaries. Accumulating evidence from Paleolithic, early historical, classical, Asian, African and contemporary communal peoples suggest that a

1 Top. Eilif, the lazy animal, resting; in the background Swiss Cheese, the good boy, looks round. At the Modern School, New Delhi. Photo by Pablo Bartholomew.

2 Bottom. Mother Courage, dressed as a lower middle class American housewife, scolds Swiss Cheese (scene 3) and warns him always to be lowest and careful. Photo by Pablo Bartholomew.

13 TOP LEFT. Courage looks at Swiss Cheese's body (scene 3)—and then denies she knows him. Modern School, New Delhi. Photo by Pablo Bartholomew.

14 TOP RIGHT. Kattrin and the Cook prepare to march off hauling Courage's Wagon. Modern School, New Delhi. Photo by Pablo Bartholomew.

15 BOTTOM. Courage, beaten down, looks at dead Kattrin (scene 11). It is cold in the theatre in the Performing Garage, New York. The big garage door is open, and it is winter—that's why spectators have their coats on. Photo by Clem Fiori.

16 Top. Kattrin beats her drum (scene 11). Modern School, New Delhi.
Photo by Pablo Bartholomew.

17 Bottom. Courage mourns Kattrin (scene 11). Modern School, New Delhi.
Photo by Pablo Bartholomew.

18 TOP LEFT. Between scenes : The director hauls scenery. Modern School, New Delhi. Phot by Pablo Bartholomew.

19 TOP RIGHT. Eilif bragging (scene 2). A motor garage, Lucknow.

20 BOTTOM. Courage marches on, as the performers sing the final song facing her (scene 12 Modern School, New Delhi. Photo by Pablo Bartholomew.

complicated social life and rich, symbolic art are co-existent with the human condition. The idea of the 'simple primitive'—either noble or savage—has been killed by Lévi-Strauss, La Barre and others. Shamans were artists and performers and doctors and trance-possessed (temporary) psychotics and priests and entertainers. To argue that because several roles are played simultaneously by one person (or class of people), or that because a single performance expresses many contradictory impulses that the art of such people (and their societies) is simple is to look at things upside down.

Industrial societies separate/standardize functions/expressions; communal societies combine many functions/expressions in single often extended complicated events. The experience of urban life is to move from one 'pure' event to another—only over time and by means of a synthesis managed by each individual (and many people can't manage it) is there a sense of unity emerging from the multiplicity and pluralism. I personally enjoy this pluralism, but it can go too far and fragment people, not cut them off so much as cut them up. Communal life, on the other hand, includes in each event—even a ceremony as short as the ten-minute Arunta dance—a bundle of meanings/functions/expressions. These are not implicit: each participant knows the connections, and the initiate is taught them. The leader of the dance is also the leader of his band, is also a skilled hunter, is also related to the boys being initiated, etc. And, as I've shown, the dance is nested in a complex of ceremonies where each part is a synecdoche. Much of the post-war avant garde is an attempt to overcome fragmentation by approaching performance as a part of rather than apart from the community. Sometimes this community is the community of the artists making the work; this has been the pattern in New York, London, Paris and other Western cities. Sometimes—as in the general uprisings of 1968—the art is joined to large political movements. Sometimes, as in black and Chicano theatre, and more recently in other 'special interest' theatres, the artists identify with—even help to form—a sense of ethnic, racial or political identity. This community-related avant garde is not only a phenomenon of the industrialized West, but also of countries that are industrializing or undergoing great changes in social organization. In Eastern Europe, Japan and in the work of people like Rendra in Indonesia, Soyinka in Nigeria, Boal in Brazil and Argentina we see the same process.

This work is not simple atavism, it is not a wild attempt to dismantle industrialism, or to halt its spread. It is an active seeking to find places within industrial societies—even within the industrial process itself—for communities to exist; and to demand a restructuring of the social order in terms of community, collectively and person-to-person interaction, or 'meetings', as Grotowski says. The problems of industrialization and fragmentation are clearly not problems of capitalism alone. Experiments of the kind I've been talking about are taking place in socialist states too. These experiments—still relatively scattered and tentative, and always facing a hostile establishment, are showing signs of taking root; they address themselves to the audience not as a collection of money-paying individual strangers, or forced participants in a show of solidarity (as in mass rallies or coercive church-going), but as a community, even as a congregation, as Turner calls them. And the object of such performances is both to entertain—to have fun—and to create *communities*: a sense of collective celebration. This contemporary movement originated in the avant garde theatre and is moving towards ritual.

Performance doesn't originate in ritual any more than it originates in entertainment. It originates in the binary system: efficacy-entertainment which includes the subset ritual-theatre. From the beginning—logically as well as historically—both terms of the binary are present, are required. At any historical moment there is movement from one pole towards the other. This oscillation is continuous—performance is in an active steady-state.

The whole binary system efficacy/ritual—entertainment/theatre is what I call 'performance'. Performance originates in impulses to make things happen and to entertain; to collect meanings and to pass the time; to be transformed into another and to be onself; to disappear and to show off; to bring into a celebratory space a transcendent Other who exists then-and-now and later-and-now and to celebrate here-and-now only us who are present; to get things done and to play around; to focus inward on a select initiated group sharing a hermetic language and to broadcast out to the largest possible collection of strangers. These oppositions—and all the others generated by them—comprise performance: it is an active situation, a steady process of transformation. The move from ritual to theatre happens when a participating audience fragments into a collection of people who pay, who come because the show is advertised, who evaluate what they are going to see before they see it; the move from theatre to ritual happens when the audience as a collection of separate people is dissolved into the performance as participants. These opposing tendencies are present in all performances. Brecht, and Meyerhold before him, worked to keep the tension between these extremes working throughout each performance by moving an audience back and forth moment to moment. The deep effect of Brecht's *verfremdung* is to unexpectedly shift modes, styles, rhythms, perspectives; and at the moment of change, when the affective part of a scene abruptly stops, or when a distanced beat suddenly becomes moving—the dramaturgic structure allows the writer/director/performer to make a 'statement', to insert an ironic comment, to encourage the spectator to think about what he's seen and/or felt. The structure of the performance is obliterated by its anti-structure and in the liminal moment a direct communication, a deep contact, with the audience is made. Of all the experiments with theatrical structure over the past century this one is most likely to stick. It resonates back to medieval theatre, and to many folk theatres existing now.

I can best summarize by drawing four models, explaining each as I go.

Actuality 1 ←———ENCOUNTER/EXCHANGE———→ Actuality 2

A meeting takes place at a market or on a battlefield. Goods are traded, money is earned, territory taken, a group routed. The encounter is intended to be entirely efficacious—even though sometimes nothing is traded or battles end in stand-offs. The rituals in this kind of activity are ethological and/or sociological. That is they are based on 'fixed-action patterns', and they are intended to regulate human interaction so that what is supposed to happen, or be determined, by the meeting of individuals and/or groups actually happens. The entertainment/theatrical elements in these kinds of meetings are reduced to a minimum, though they are present. The job is to get through the encounter/exchange as efficiently as possible and arrive at Actuality 2. But even this model doesn't show all that really happens. Markets are places of display, joking, gossiping, singing; they often attract mountebanks and other popular entertainments. Battlefields are places to show the colours, parade strength and in general scare your opponent off the field. Guerrilla war and mass combat work against these theatrical qualities. Thus even at this level the ethological and sociological rituals are embroidered with entertainment. There is a tendency towards:

Actuality 1 <——— PERFORMANCE ———> Actuality 2

This is the case with ecological rituals such as those among the Arunta and Tsembaga. Their performances effect changes both in the status of some people participating (through initiation, marriage and other rites of passage) and in economic matters (pigs, sago, trade items). In fact, how good a performance is can be an important element in determining social status. The Greeks offered prizes to their tragedians; our society offers wealth and fame. Among Aborigines and New Guinea people high status is conferred on the better performers. A shaman among the American Indians or in Siberia is honoured for his or her tricks and style.

This process can itself become highly advanced resulting in:

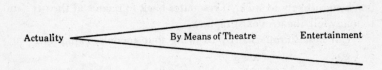

Actuality ⟨⟨ By Means of Theatre   Entertainment

This is what happened when the Dervishes or the Monks performed at the Brooklyn Academy. Rituals which have efficacy in a defined setting become entertainments in another setting. *The Yoshi Show*, presented at the Public Theatre in New York in 1975, included a Buddhist monk, a Shinto priest, a martial arts expert and a Tibetan monk performing along with Yoshi, a Japanese actor who had studied extensively with Peter Brook. The show combined elements of different religious ceremonies with theatrical performing. The event was very confusing because it was neither the presentation of a ritual as theatre nor an entertainment. On the other hand this ambiguity gave it a special power, almost as sacrilege because of the clash of different kinds of worship. In shows of this kind money is exchanged for a peek at ritual. And 'new rituals' are synthesized for the sake of entertainment.

Another example of this model is its reverse:

Entertainment ⟨⟨ By Means of Ritual   Actuality

This is what Grotowski is doing. This tendency has been present in his work for the last 10 years. He sets many of his performances in churches, selecting audiences either on an individual basis, or by some means (including very high prices) that limit the number of people making audiences into elites. In *Fire on the Mountain* each *ul* was peopled by invited participants only. And the nature of the work in the *uls* was to bring about a kind of intimacy and quasi-religious solidarity by means of performance exercises, group encounter/therapy techniques and submission to the will of a strong leader.[32] Grotowski's experiments are like EST in America where groups of people are 'broken down' over a weekend's experience of extreme intensity, often an ordeal of shouting, physical work and direct confrontation. Although this subject won't be explored here the means of encounter therapy are very close to traditional initiation rites where the young boy is broken down and re-made in a short period of time through a series of instructions and ordeals.

During the appearance in Philadelphia in 1973 of the Polish Laboratory Theatre the performances of *Apocalypsis cum Figuris* were only the first step in a more elaborate ceremony. During the performances Grotowski literally 'tapped' 5 to 10 students and asked them to remain after the performance. These were then invited to go with Grotowski and his company to a retreat in the hills not far from Philadelphia where the students and the performers would meet 'on a one-to-one basis'. Clearly the performance of *Apocalypsis* was an entry into some other kind of experience, one which can't be called theatre in the usual sense.

In *Paradise Now* the Living Theatre attempted a similar transformation of entertainment into actuality—in their case a political rather than religious actuality. By challenging the audience where they sit, by inviting them onto the stage, by not presenting a drama or even a set of incidents but rather a plan and a series of provocations, the Living undercut orthodox theatre, even avant-gardism. Then, after many spectators left, often the majority—a winnowing similar to Grotowski's but carried out in a different way: where Grotowski selected who was to go with him, the Living allowed the spectators to individually select themselves—the performers led some of the remaining spectators into the streets. An actual political event arose out of the entertainment event by means of a theatrical confrontation. In the streets the performers and spectators were often met by the police. While Grotowski's work eventuates in religious meetings the Living's eventuates in public acts.

The origins of theatre—considered since Aristotle's day to be found in ritual—look different when seen from the perspective of popular entertainment. E. T. Kirby sees theatre beginning in shamanism, certainly a ritual system. But shamanism itself—as Kirby notes—is closely connected to magic acts, acrobatics, puppetry and other popular entertainments. La Barre points out that the Asiatic-American Trickster—a figure that can be traced back to Paleolithic times—is a 'mixture of clown, culture hero and demigod'. La Barre reminds us of the connections between the Trickster and the Greek origins of theatre:

> The great antiquity of the trickster should be suggested first of all by his being much the same in both Paleosiberian and American hunting tribes; and again by the fact that the more a tribe has been influenced by agriculture in America, the less important he becomes in the total tribal mythology as compared with his pre-eminence among both Siberian and American hunters. [. . .] We must not forget the element of *entertainment* in Old World shamanism: were tales of the erotic escapades of eagle-Zeus once told in the same tone of voice as those of Sibero-American Raven? And did not shamanistic rivalry develop into both the Dionysian bard-contests of Greek drama in the Old World and into *midewewin* medicine-shows in the New? As for that, have modern medicine-men entirely lost the old shamanic self-dramatization?[33]

So wherever we look, and no matter how far back, theatre is a mixture, a braid, of entertainment and ritual. At one moment ritual seems to be the source, at another it is entertainment that claims primacy. They are a twin-system, tumbling over each other, and vitally interconnected.

Even at this more or less quiet moment, 1976, it's clear that the orthodox dramaturgy—the theatre of plays done in fixed settings for a settled audience relating stories as if they were happening to others—is finished. At least this kind of theatre doesn't meet the needs of many people—needs as old as theatre itself, combining ritual and entertainment. These needs also include actual group interaction as a remedy for a runaway technology. I am not reacting against technology—I have not bought a cabin in Vermont yet. But I know an authentic need exists for encounters that are neither just informal person-to-person gatherings like parties nor formal, mediated, programmed routines like office or factory work—or watching television and films, for that matter. Theatre is a middle world where actual group interaction can happen—not only through

audience participation but by subtler means of audience inclusion
and environmental staging; theatre combines artistic-composed behaviour with everyday-spontaneous behaviour. Theatre people are
moving into areas once solely occupied by religion and politics.
Priests and politicians will doubtlessly pick up new techniques from
theatre. But whether they will be able to restore public confidence
in their professions is questionable. Will theatre then become a big
avenue rather than the sideroad it's been for the past 300 years?

1. In describing the *kaiko* I followed the account in Roy A. Rappaport's *Pigs
   for the Ancestors* (New Haven: Yale University Press, 1968). His study is a
   paradigm of how to examine ritual performances within an ecological context.
2. A fight package is a small bundle containing 'the thorny leaves of the males
   of a rare, unidentified tree growing in the *kamunga*, called the "fight tree" and
   personal material belonging to the enemy, such as hair, fragments of leaves
   worn over the buttocks, and dirt scraped from the skin' (Rappaport, op. cit.
   p. 120). It is said that pressing the packages to the heart and head will give
   a man courage and improve his chances of killing an enemy. Materials used
   in fight packages are acquired from neutrals who have relatives among the
   enemy; fight packages are items of trade. Their use in peaceful dancing shows
   the relationship between the dancing and combat; in many parts of Asia
   performance forms have arisen from martial arts.
3. Rappaport, op. cit. p. 187.
4. Ibid. p. 188.
5. Ibid. p. 189.
6. Ibid. p. 195–6.
7. Ibid. p. 156.
8. Ibid. p. 214.
9. B. Spencer and F. J. Gillen, *The Native Tribes of Central Australia* (N.Y.: Dover
   Publications, 1968, reprinted from 1899). This study has the advantage over
   later ones that the tribes described were relatively intact, having just been
   contacted by the invading Europeans. In Australia contact meant extermination both demographically and culturally.
10. This rhythm of relatively long preparations followed by a brief performance,
    with a series of performances given on a single day, is common in Australia.
    See also A. P. Elkin and Catherine and Ronald Berndt, *Art in Arnhem Land*
    (Chicago: University of Chicago Press, 1950); and Ronald and Catherine
    Berndt, *The World of the First Australians* (Chicago: University of Chicago
    Press, 1964). Although we accept this rhythm in dance and music, it has not
    yet found acceptance in theatre. Still dominated by Aristotelian injunctions
    we act as if a work has to be of a certain length to acquire seriousness.
11. In Oceania it is not unusual—or was not until the eradication of traditional
    ways—for ritual performances to form the core of a person's life. Van Gennep's
    classic analysis of rituals into crisis moments preceded and followed by long
    periods of relative calm is not wholly descriptive of the situation in New

Guinea and Australia. Although the performances are peak experiences, preparations for them continuing over months and years dominate the lives of the people. See F. E. Williams, *The Drama of the Orokolo* (London: OUP, 1940), and Richard Schechner, 'Actuals: A Look into Performance Theory', in *Essays on Performance Theory 1970–76* (N.Y.: Drama Books Specialists, 1977). See also V. W. Turner, *The Ritual Process* (Chicago: Aldine Publishing Company, 1969); and V. W. Turner, *Dramas, Fields and Metaphors* (Ithaca: Cornell University Press, 1974).

12. See the discussion of 'reactualization' and its relation to the Dreamtime in Mircea Eliade, *Rites and Symbols of Initiation* (N.Y.: Harper Torchbooks, 1965).

13. An excellent account of the intimate association among events, landmarks, and body decorations is given in Richard A. Gould, *Yiwara: Foragers of the Australian Desert* (N.Y.: Charles Scribner's Sons, 1969). See also Geza Roheim, *The Eternal Ones of the Dream* (N.Y.: International Universities Press, 1969; reprinted from 1945).

14. The Highlands consist of a central valley, and many spur valleys, surrounded by mountains rising to 15,000 feet. The whole area is about three hundred miles long and one hundred and fifty miles wide. It is sparsely populated, by less than three million; villages average four hundred inhabitants. Because of the terrain many local groups have little contact with each other—and there is much local warfare and feuding. There are about five hundred languages, most of them mutually unintelligible, and the largest of them spoken by only 130,000 people. English and pidgin are the basic *linguae francae*.

15. By now criticism of the Cambridge Anthropologists' thesis concerning the ritual origins and structure of Greek theatre is well known. See, for example, E. R. Dodds, *The Greeks and the Irrational* (Berkeley: University of California Press, 1951).

16. Joan MacIntosh, a performer with The Performance Group and my wife, was my partner on the trip to Asia in 1971–72 which forms the experiential background to this piece.

17. Elizabeth Burns, *Theatricality* (N.Y.: Harper and Row, 1972), p. 132. This way of looking at ordinary experiences as theatre has roots, of course, in literature. But its systematic application has only recently begun. The key observations have been made by Erving Goffman, *The Presentation of Self in Everyday Life* (Garden City: Doubleday Anchor Books, 1959), and *Relations in Public* (N.Y.: Basic Books, 1971).

18. According to Robert Brustein, 'News Theatre', in *The New York Times Magazine*, 16 June, 1974, pp. 7ff., news theatre is 'any histrionic proceeding that results from a collaboration between newsworthy personalities, vast public, and the visual or print media (television, films, book publishing, magazines and newspapers). News theatre, in other words, is any event that confuses news with theatre and theatre with news.' I think Brustein's description is accurate, but that he is wrong when he says that 'news' and 'theatre' should be kept distinct. Certainly there are areas of independence, but the two are inherently interdependent. Both are public, action-centred, and crisis-dominated. Furthermore, as the means of news transmission abandons print and uses visual media they approximate the means of theatre. The problems stirred up are not solved by bemoaning the inevitable. Only in finding ways

of controlling what's happening will a satisfactory process occur. Take one limited, but decisive, area—the ethics of news reporting. I refer to the ways in which reporting shapes people's responses to events. We all know that so called 'objective' reporting is anything but objective. But is it distorted simply through the evil designs of the news managers, or is there at work a deep structure which makes even attempts at objectivity impossible? Drama has long had an ethical purpose which is expressed not only overtly but in dramatic structure. News broadcasting used the same structures but without consciousness of the ethics inherent in them. And it is axiomatic that an unconscious ethic will automatically reinforce the *status quo*; or, as Brecht put it, to remain neutral is to support the stronger side. The need then is to make the structures of news reporting—especially its dramatic structures—more conscious; this will lead to greater control over what is being said. Whether these new powers will be used to advance the causes of the people or to repress them remains in doubt.

19. For extended discussions of the concepts of liminality and *communitas* see Turner, *The Ritual Process* and *Dramas, Fields and Metaphors*.

20. Konrad Lorenz, *On Aggression* (N.Y.: Bantam Books, 1967), discusses at some length the development of 'appeasement ceremonies' in animals. More technical descriptions are offered by Irenaus Eibl-Eibesfeldt, *Ethology: The Biology of Behaviour* (N.Y.: Holt, Rinehart and Winston, 1970). Lorenz's description of a special kind of ceremony is almost exactly what I saw in New Guinea, and what so many others have described. 'Of all the various appeasement ceremonies, with their many different roots, the most important for our theme are those appearing or greeting rites which have arisen from redirected aggression movements. They differ from all the already described appeasement ceremonies in that they do not put aggression under inhibition but divert it from certain members of the species and canalize it in the direction of others. This new orientation of aggressive behaviour is one of the most ingenious inventions of evolution, but it is even more than that: wherever redirected rituals of appeasement are observed, the ceremony is bound to the individuality of the participating partners. The aggression of a particular individual is diverted from a second, equally particular individual, while its discharge against all other, anonymous members of the species is not inhibited. Thus discrimination between friend and stranger arises, and for the first time in the world personal bonds between individuals come into being' (pp. 131–2). Or, as the Tsembaga say, 'those who come to our *Kaiko* will also come to our fights'. It is also important to note that the ceremonies Lorenz focused on were greeting ceremonies; the dances in the Highlands may correctly be called greeting dances.

21. E. T. Kirby, 'The Shamanistic Origins of Popular Entertainments', in *TDR*, 18: March (1974). Kirby sees shamanism as 'The "great unitarian artwork" that fragmented into a number of performance arts' (p. 6). See also E. T. Kirby, 'The origin of Nō Drama', in *Educational Theatre Journal*, 25: October (1973) and Schechner, *Environmental Theatre* (N.Y.: Hawthorn Books, 1973), the chapter 'Shaman'.

22. George J. Becker, ed., *Documents of Modern Literary Realism* (Princeton: Princeton University Press, 1963). See especially Emile Zola's 'Naturalism in Theatre' and Strindberg's 'Naturalism in Theatre'.

23. The First American Congress of Theatre met in Princeton, 2–6 June 1974. It brought together more than 200 leaders of the American theatre—very heavily weighted towards producers, managers of regional theatres, and professional administrators. Also the conference was weighted towards New York, organized as it was by Alexander H. Cohen, the New York producer. Eleven panels discussed various problems confronting the theatre, but the real action was in the interaction among individuals and interest groups. It seems likely that a second Congress will be held, one which is less New York dominated. However, it does not appear as if theatre artists will be given any more prominence—that is, writers, directors, actors, and designers will still be under-represented in relationship to the overall number of delegates. The fundamental theme of the Congress—and future Congresses as well—is a growing recognition of a contradictory reality: theatre is marginal, economically speaking, but it seems also to have enduring roots in society. Means are therefore necessary to bring the disparate wings of the theatre together for a common rumination of basically economic issues. Whether politics can, or should, be kept out of these meetings is another question. As for aesthetics, forget it.

24. O. B. Hardison, *Christian Rite and Christian Drama in the Middle Ages* (Baltimore: University of Maryland Press, 1965), p. 40.

25. Ibid. p. 77.

26. Rappaport, op. cit. p. 1.

27. Peter Brook, 'On Africa', in *TDR*, 17: September (1973), pp. 45–6. Brook's anecdote is a fine example of what I mean by 'preparations' rather than rehearsals. Rehearsal is a way of setting an exact sequence of events. Preparations are a constant state of training so that when a situation arises one will be ready to 'do something appropriate' to the moment. Preparations are what a good athletic team does. Too often those interested in improvisation feel that it can arise spontaneously, out of the moment. Nothing is further from the truth. What arises spontaneously is the moment itself, the response is selected from a known repertory and joins with the moment to give the impression of total spontaneity. Most performances among communal peoples are not rehearsed, they are prepared.

28. His invitation was based on my reputation on the island. Although I was there for only two weeks I used to play games with children in which I would imitate animals. I did one act that especially amused the children: making my hands into horns I would charge at them as if I were an enraged bull. On several occasions while riding a bus to a remote village some children would spot me and make the horn gesture. At Tenganan the dance I did at the public performance was a variation on the animal game. MacIntosh's singing was appreciated everywhere, and people would actually get very angry if she refused to sing. In New Guinea especially, almost anything—an object, a relationship, an event, a performance—is made into an item of trade; there are no neutral or valueless events.

29. The late sixties and early seventies saw a number of performances based on this premise. A family in Greenwich Village sold admission to their apartment where spectators watched them in their daily lives. Of course the Loud Family epic on television carried this style of documentary drama to its

logical end: The feedback from the weekly series actually affected the lives the Louds lived, and so we watched the family change under the impact of their knowledge that they were being watched. The theoretical foundations of this kind of art lie in Cage's assertion that theatre is actually an attitude on the part of the spectator—to set up a chair in the street and to watch what happens is to transform the streets into a theatre. These ideas are still very much with us in Process Art.

30. The kind of classification I'm indicating for performance is one which is being increasingly used in the sciences, and is replacing older forms of classification where one class of events excludes another. 'Classifications need not be hierarchies and the clusters may overlap (intersect). The whole idea of hierarchic, nonoverlapping (mutually exclusive) classifications which is so attractive to the human mind is currently undergoing re-examination. From studies in a variety of fields the representation of taxonomic structure as overlapping clusters or as ordinations appears far preferable.' (Robert R. Sokal, 'Classification: Purposes, Principles, Progress, Prospects', *Science*, 27 September 1974, p. 1121). One 'locates' a performance by using the co-ordinates of efficacy and entertainment.

31. In *Commune*, there was one night an interruption of more than three hours. During that time the spectators and performers came to know each other in a way much more intimate and actual than is usually possible in a theatre. When the play resumed there was a feeling surrounding the performance that added power to it. The supper sequence in *Mother Courage* is an attempt at building-in the kind of relationship between performers and spectators that accidentally occurred that night at *Commune*. See Richard Schechner, *Environmental Theatre*, pp. 49–56.

32. This experiment, now called 'Mountain Project', has been revised and is still going on. It is part of Grotowski's 'paratheatrical phase' which began in 1969. In the paratheatrical work there are no spectators, the form is not fixed, the process is what emerges from each participant. Members of the Polish Lab working alone or in teams lead this work. Each project has its own title, such as: *Acting Therapy, Vigil, Meditations, Aloud, Soundings*, etc. The events take from a few hours to several weeks, and use all kinds of space from rooms to large sections of the countryside (pilgrimages).

33. Weston La Barre, *The Ghost Dance* (N.Y.: Dell Publishing Company, 1972), pp. 195–6.

6

Restoration of Behaviour

I

Restored behaviour is living behaviour treated as a film director treats a strip of film. These strips can be rearranged, reconstructed; they are independent of the causal systems (social, psychological, technological) that brought them into existence: they have a life of their own. The original 'truth' or 'motivation' of the behaviour may be lost, ignored, or contradicted. How the strip of behaviour was made, found, developed may be unknown or covered over, elaborated, distorted by myth. Originating as a process, used in the process of rehearsal to make a new process—a performance—the strips of behaviour are not themselves process but things, items, 'material'. The strips can be of long duration as in some rituals, or of short duration as in some gestures, dance movements, or *mantras*.

Restored behaviour is used in all kinds of performances from shamanism, exorcism, and trance to ritual theatre and aesthetic theatre, from initiation rites to social dramas, from psychoanalysis to newer therapies such as psychodrama, transactional analysis, and primal. In fact, the use of restored behaviour is the main characteristic of performance. The practitioners of all these arts, rites, and healings assumed that some kinds of behaviour—organized sequences of events, scripted actions, known texts, scored movements—exist separately from the performers who 'do' these behaviours. Because the behaviour is separate from those who are behaving, the behaviour can be stored, transmitted, manipulated, transformed. The performers get in touch with, recover, remember, or even invent these strips of behaviour and then rebehave according to these strips, either by being absorbed into them (playing the role, going into trance) or by existing side-by-side with them (Brecht's *Verfremdung Effekt*). The work of restoration is carried on in rehearsals and/or in the transmission of behaviour from master performer to novice. Understanding the work of rehearsals, and the subjunctive mood used there, is the surest way to link ritual process to aesthetic process.

Restored behaviour is 'out there', distant from me in time as in the psychoanalytic abreaction, or in sphere of reality as in the encounter between Rangda and Barong in Balinese dance-drama, or by aesthetic convention as when Hamlet rejects his mother, Gertrude, or by tradition as in the brave way a Gahuku boy during his initiation accepts the ordeal of having sharp, jagged leaves slice the inside of his nostrils bringing much blood, or the shy way a New Jersey 'blushing bride' behaves at her wedding even though she and her groom have lived together for three years.

Restored behaviour is symbolic and reflexive. These difficult terms are reducible to the same principle of self-in/as-other: the social or transindividual self. Symbolic and reflexive behaviour is the hardening into theatre of social, religious, medical, educational, and aesthetic process. Performance means: never for the first time; it means: for the second to the nth time. Reflexive means to see the self in the self-and-other.

Neither painting nor sculpting, nor even writing, uses behaviour in actual flow. But thousands of years before movies, rituals were made from strips of restored behaviour so that action and stasis could coexist in the same act. Great comfort flowed from ritual: the deeds of people, gods, ancestors participated simultaneously in being and becoming, in having been, are, and will be. These strips of behaviour were replayed many times. Mnemonic devices ensured that the performance was 'right'—as rehearsed or as received—and some performances have been transmitted across many generations with few accidental variations. Even now the terror of the first night is not the presence of the public but that mistakes are no longer forgiven.

This constancy of transmission is all the more astonishing when you realize that restored behaviour involves choice. Animals repeat themselves, and so do the cycles of the moon, but only when the actor can say 'no' to an action is there the possibility of restored behaviour. Even the shaman who is called—the trancer falling into trance—gives over or resists; and there is general suspicion of he who too easily says yes. There is a continuum from the not-much-choice of ritual to the lots-of-choice of aesthetic theatre. But in aesthetic theatre this freedom is narrowed during rehearsals. Rehearsals function to build a score, and this score is a 'ritual by contract' limited to the duration of the run.

Restored behaviour can be put on as a mask or costume is put on. Its shape can be seen from the outside, and changed. That's what theatre directors, councils of bishops, master performers, and great shamans do: change the performance score. The performance can change because it is not a 'natural event' but one, as Turner says, in the subjunctive mood, in what Stanislavski called the 'as if'. Existing as second nature, restored behaviour is always subject to revision. Its 'secondness' is also its negativity, subjectivity, 'anti-ness'.

II

Put in personal terms, restored behaviour is 'me behaving as if I am someone else'. But this someone else may also be 'me in another state of feeling/being'. Performing my dream, re-experiencing my childhood trauma, showing you what I did yesterday. Also social actions: the enactment of events whose origins can't be located in individuals, if they can be located at all. Sometimes these events are attributed to collective individuals like the Books of Moses, the Iliad of Homer, the Mahabharata of Vyas; sometimes they belong anonymously to folklore, legend, myth. Restored behaviour offers to both individuals and groups the chance to become someone else 'for the time being', or the chance to become what they once were. Or even, and most often, to rebecome what they never were.

Three performative systems are shown in Figure 1. In 1→2, I become someone else, or myself in another state of being. There is only moderate displacement—a few rehearsals, sometimes none— and my performance is a solo. Two or more individuals can perform 1→2 simultaneously, as when several people fall into trance together. The astonishing thing about Balinese *sanghyang* is that each dancer has by herself/himself so incarnated the collective score that solo dances cohere into a group performance. Upon recovering from the trance, dancers are often not aware that others were dancing; sometimes they don't remember their own dancing. I've seen similar meshing of solo performing into a group event in a black church in Bedford-Stuyvesant during Easter week, 1978. As the gospel singing reached a climax, more than a dozen women and men 'fell out' into the aisles at the same time. Each was dancing in trance alone—but the whole group was dancing together. The heat of the event was controlled by the singers who definitely were not in trance. Peter Adair's film of a snake-handling sect in West Virginia, *The Holy Ghost People*, shows the same thing.

In 1→3→4 a restored event is created from a distant place or an actual past. This is common enough when the action is frozen, as in

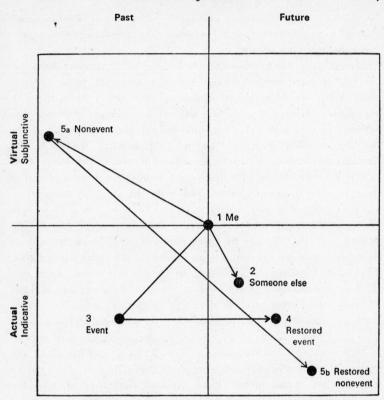

Fig. 1 Restored events are placed in the future because rehearsals are a means of collecting behaviour and 'keeping' it for the performance-to-be. Once performances begin these are, of course, in the present. Presence is an essential quality of live performance. The model is drawn from the perspective of rehearsal or training and practice: whatever goes on 'before' performance that makes performance possible.

the dioramas of animal and human habitats at the American Museum of Natural History. Strictly speaking, these are restored environments, not behaviours. But recently, and increasingly, action is being added to the environments. I will have a lot more to say later about 'restored villages' and 'theme parks', where fact and fantasy are freely mixed. Some zoos, reacting to the disappearance of species in the wild, now run 'breeding parks' that replicate the vanishing wilderness. It soon may be that the African veldt is better preserved near San Diego than in Africa. In the breeding park near Front

Royal, Virginia, the concern to keep the environment pristine is such that all visitors are excluded. Of course, the breeders, veterinarians, and ethologists are allowed in.

Many traditional performances are $1 \to 3 \to 4$—or performances that are kept in repertory according to a strict adherence to the original score. When the Moscow Art Theatre visited New York in the mid-1960s they claimed to present Chekhov according to Stanislavski's original *mise en scène*. When I saw several plays of Brecht at the Berliner Ensemble in 1969, I was told that Brecht's *Modelbuchs*—his detailed *mise en scène* instructions—were followed to the letter. Certainly classical ballets have been passed on through generations of dancers with minimal change. But even the strictest attempts at $1 \to 3 \to 4$ frequently are in fact examples of $1 \to 5a \to 5b$; $1 \to 3 \to 4$ is very unstable simply because even if human memory can be improved upon by the use of exact notation, a performance always happens within several contexts, and these are not easily controllable. The social circumstances change, as indeed is obvious when you think of Stanislavski's productions at the turn of the century and the Moscow Art Theatre today. Even the bodies of performers—what they are supposed to look like, how they are supposed to move, what they think and believe—change radically over relatively brief periods of time. Not to mention the reactions, feelings, and moods of the audience. Performances that were once current, even avant garde, soon become period pieces. These kinds of contextual changes are not measurable by labanotation[1] or visible in the written musical score. Even identical performances, in time, are not identical.

Nō drama is a very intriguing example of a performance that is both $1 \to 3 \to 4$ and $1 \to 5a \to 5b$ simultaneously and consciously. The whole score of a Nō play—its *mise en scène*, music, text, costuming, masking—is transmitted within a school or family from one generation to the next with only minor variations. In this sense, Nō, at least since the Meiji Restoration in the nineteenth century, is a clear example of $1 \to 3 \to 4$. During his lifetime a Nō *shite*—the main actor, literally the 'doer', the one who wears the mask—moves from one role to another in a progression. He accepts the score of the role he approaches and leaves behind the score of his earlier role which is taken over by another. Only the greatest masters of Nō are permitted to change the score, and then these changes become part of the tradition: they are passed on to the next generation. The roles, and their place within the *mise en scène*, and the *mise en scènes* themselves

within the progression of Nō plays that makes up a lifetime of performing, is a complicated but decipherable system. But each individual Nō performance also includes surprises. The groups who come
together to do a Nō play are made up of representatives of many
different families, each with their own traditions, their own 'secrets'.
The *shite* and chorus work together; the waki, the kyogen, the flutist,
the drummers each work separately. True to its Zen roots, a Nō
drama staged traditionally occurs only once, finding in the absolute
immediacy of the meeting among all its constituent players a unique
power. A few days before a scheduled performance the *shite* calls all
the participants together and outlines his intentions. The first time
the whole thing is done is before the audience during the actual performance. Like the Zen archer, the *shite* hits his mark or he doesn't.

During the performance—through signals coming from the *shite*
to the musicians and others—variations occur: routines are repeated
or cut, emphases changed, tempos accelerated or slowed. Even the
selection of what costume and mask to wear depends on the *shite's*
opinion regarding the mood of the audience—an opinion he forms
by watching the audience assemble or by gauging their reactions to
the first plays of a full Nō programme, which may include five Nō
and four comic kyogens and last seven hours or more. Those Nō
performers, made into a 'company' for foreign tours, where they
repeat the same plays over and over, performing with the same people,
complain of boredom and the lack of creative opportunity. Traditionally, then, each performance of Nō, and every variation during a
performance, is the leading edge of a long tradition formed in the
thirteenth and fourteenth centuries, almost extinguished by the mid-
nineteenth, and flourishing again now. This leading edge is both
$1 \rightarrow 3 \rightarrow 4$ and $1 \rightarrow 5a \rightarrow 5b$.

As interesting as Nō, though much more local, is Shaker dancing.
Shakers, a religious sect brought from England to America in 1774,
are nearly dead now, but about the time of the Civil War numbered
about 6000 members. Its ritual included song and dance. Originally
these were done for the Shakers themselves. But:

> As Shakerism grew, the religion and the social organization it
> engendered became less ecstatic and more rigid and institu-
> tionalized. The dances and songs, which were the main form of
> worship, also changed from involuntary ecstatic and convulsive
> movements with glossolalia occurring during spells of altered
> states of consciousness to disciplined choreographed marches with

symbolic steps, gestures, and floor plans. These rituals became elaborate and fixed dance 'exercises'. A steady stream of tourists came to the Shaker communities to watch these spectacles.[2]

The Shakers had stopped dancing by 1931 when Doris Humphrey, one of the pioneers of modern dance in America, choreographed *The Shakers*. I don't have the time to go into the details that Youngerman assembles demonstrating the deep affinities between the Shakers and *The Shakers*. Clearly Humphrey did her research. Youngerman says: 'Humphrey's choreography embodies a wide range of Shaker culture incorporating many direct references to actual Shaker dances.'

Humphrey's dance is still in the repertory of the José Limon Dance Company, where I saw it in 1979 and again in 1981. The dance is also labanotated, which means that other companies can dance Humphrey's dance much the way any orchestra can play a Beethoven symphony. In fact, in 1979, the Humphrey dance was performed by the Louisville Ballet at Shakertown, a reconstructed Shaker village at Pleasant Hill, Kentucky. This may not be the only example of an aesthetic dance being a main way of physically re/membering (= putting what has been dis/membered back together) an extinct behaviour. Shakers dancing is $1 \rightarrow 3 \rightarrow 4$; Humphrey's dance is $1 \rightarrow 5a \rightarrow 5b$. The Humphrey dance as a way of finding out what the Shakers did is restored behaviour. The Shaker story goes on. Not only is the Humphrey dance in existence, both through the Limon Company where she danced and through labanotation, but some people have reconstructed the actual Shaker dances from original sources.

Robin Evanchuk visited a few surviving Shakers in 1962 and 1975. They had long since stopped dancing, but by eliciting their memories and those of people who knew Shakers, and by drawing on the research of Edward Deming Andrews,[3] Evanchuk reconstructed the 'authentic' dances. As of 1977 three groups 'have learned and presented this reconstruction', including her own group, the Liberty Assembly. Evanchuk is always bringing new dancers in; she does this by thorough orientation:

> During the teaching sessions, the dancers must overcome their fear of appearing ridiculous due to the strangeness of the movements and the intense emotion. In addition to a strong orientation, I find that constant repetition of the movements, which allows the dancers to gradually become comfortable with them, tends to lessen their embarrassment and moves the emphasis from

how the dancers feel to concern for how the Shakers themselves felt when they were involved in the exercises.[4]

So we have three different but related performance traditions: the Shakers themselves, an art dance by Humphrey that continues to be performed both by her company and others, and an 'authentic' reconstruction of Shaker dancing by Evanchuk. Of Shaker dancing in the nineteenth century I can say nothing, except to guess that it started as a performance of the $1 \rightarrow 3 \rightarrow 4$ type but soon became a $1 \rightarrow 5a \rightarrow 5b$ as tourists visited the Shakers to watch them dance. Clearly both Humphrey's *The Shakers* and Evanchuk's reconstructions are performances of the $1 \rightarrow 5a \rightarrow 5b$ type. For these are performances based on performances. One is 'art'; but dance anthropologist Youngerman feels that Humphrey's dance comes close to the heart of the sect, and she reports that

> One of the last two Shaker brothers, Ricardo Belden, then 87 years old, saw the 1955 reconstruction of *The Shakers* at Connecticut College and reportedly was 'enthralled' by the performance. He later wrote to Humphrey offering to come to New London the following summer to teach Shaker dances. What greater tribute could there be?[5]

The notes of this same Ricardo Belden were used by Evanchuk in her work. And it is clear from Evanchuk's writings that her wish is not just to re-create the dances but the feelings: the fervour, ecstasy, and joy that go with the dancing. In a real way she wants to reconstruct not Shaker dancing but the Shakers themselves. Humphrey doesn't call her dance an ethnographic reconstruction, and Evanchuk doesn't call hers artworks; they both fall between these too neat categories. They are both restorations of behaviour of the $1 \rightarrow 5a \rightarrow 5b$ type.

$1 \rightarrow 5a \rightarrow 5b$ is a performance based on previous performances—so much so that the totality of all previous performances is called 'the original'. Just as Evanchuk says she is reconstructing 'authentic' Shaker dances, I can ask: which dances, on which occasions, before what audiences, with whom as dancers? 'The original' is almost always a bundle of performances conventionally represented as 'an' original. Where there is an original, and it has been scored and notated, contextual and historical changes make even the exact replication of the original event different than the original event. Thus technically the Moscow Art Theatre productions, the Brecht productions, the Humphrey *Shakers* danced by the Limon Company are $1 \rightarrow 3 \rightarrow 4$. But in practice they are all $1 \rightarrow 5a \rightarrow 5b$. Other examples of $1 \rightarrow 5a \rightarrow 5b$ include theatre when the *mise en scène* is developed during rehearsals; rituals that actualize,[6] commemorate, or summarize myth (though probably it's the other way around: myths are word-versions of rituals); ethnographic films shot in the field and edited at home; versions of ancient forms, neoclassical or other, that purport to recover old works for modern audiences. In $1 \rightarrow 5a \rightarrow 5b$ the event restored has been forgotten, never was, or is overlaid with so much secondary stuff that its historicity is lost. History is not what happened (that's its press) but what is encoded and performed.

$1 \rightarrow 3 \rightarrow 4$ is unstable. Many performances that start out as, or seem to be, $1 \rightarrow 3 \rightarrow 4$ are really $1 \rightarrow 5a \rightarrow 5b$. Sometimes masters of an art reconstruct the scores they receive; these changes enter the score and become part of the tradition. This ability to accept change is a characteristic of a living tradition. Nō drama is fixed, but performers who achieve *hana* ('flower' or mastery of their roles) introduce changes some of which are passed on to their successors: Nō actors are also Nō directors and teachers. But $1 \rightarrow 5a \rightarrow 5b$ is not restricted to these kinds of changes.

It's the work of rehearsals to prepare the behaviour of performers so that it seems spontaneous, authentic, unrehearsed. I don't mean only in the psychological way familiar to Western naturalism. Authenticity is a question of harmony/mastery of whatever style is being played, Chekhov or Chikamatsu. For the Brechtian actor to show he is acting is no less difficult than for the Stanislavskian actor not to show he is acting. A story-teller like Bob Carroll plays with his audience—joking, offering them beer, stopping in mid-sentence to welcome a latecomer. Watching Carroll many times, I learned that these gestures, these genuine interactions, are part of a set scheme, strips of behaviour. What Carroll does/says is fixed, the moments where he inserts these strips, the persons he directs them to, change according to circumstances. When planning an open rehearsal, a time when spectators can see the work process in raw form, I discuss with the performers what should and should not be shown. The presence of the public not only changes the way I work but what I work on. If a performer says she's not ready to show something, I don't force the issue, as I might in closed rehearsal.

During rehearsals a past is invented or assembled out of bits of actual experience, fantasies, historical research; or a known score is

recalled. Earlier rehearsals and/or performances quickly become the
reference points, the building blocks of performances. Useful recollections are not of 'how it was' but of 'how we used to do it'.
The 'it' is not of the event but of an earlier rehearsal. Soon reference
back to the original, if there is an original, is irrelevant. How Christ
offered his disciples wine and matzo at the Last Supper (a seder) is
irrelevant to the performance of the Eucharist. The church ceremony
has its own history. The language of church ceremony has never
been the language Christ spoke, Aramaic-Hebrew. Nor are the
gestures or costume of the priest modelled on Christ's. And if the
church had chosen another of Christ's gestures as the keystone of
the mass—say, the laying-on of hands to heal the sick—this would
have developed its own traditional script. Indeed, in some pentacostal
churches the laying-on of hands is the key representation of Christ,
the demonstration of His presence. Or the taking-up of serpents.
And each of these gestures has developed its own way of being performed. What happens over centuries to the various church services,
happens much more quickly during rehearsals.

This is not just a thing of the West. John Emigh[7] reports an example
of $1 \rightarrow 5a \rightarrow 5b$ from the Sepik River area of Papua–New Guinea. In
the village of Magendo, some time before the performance Emigh
saw, an uninitiated boy named Wok wandered into the House
Tamboran (men's house, forbidden to the uninitiated) and was killed.
The story goes that a bird came to the boy's mother in a dream and
told her what had happened and where to find Wok's body. The
mother accused her brother of causing Wok's death. She said her
brother had painted a dangerous spirit image in the House Tamboran.
The brother accepted the blame, the House was torn down, a new
one built, and the spirit of Wok resided in the new house. Wok is
also credited by the villagers with teaching them how to build better
canoes, how to catch fish, and how to plant crops. Emigh goes on:

> Now there are several things about this story and its preparation
> for the event at hand that I find fascinating. First is the im-
> mediate and physical sense of relationship between past and
> present. The old House Tamboran stood *there* across the swamp.
> The reeds the child was found in was over *here*—people are very
> specific about the geography involved, and also about improve-
> ments in village life made possible by the intervention of Wok's
> spirit. Performing the dance at this time would be an act of
> renewal, of reconnection of past and present.

But what's rehearsal at Magendo like? How does it use the material of Wok's story?

> As the rehearsal proceeded an old man would stop the singing from time to time to make suggestions on style or phrasing, or, just as often, just as much a part of the event being rehearsed, he would comment on the meaning of the song words, on the details of the story. The rehearsal was at once remarkably informal and absolutely effective.

Questions of performing style are combined with interpretations of the story. The historical-legendary Wok is being transformed into his dance. A virtual or nonevent in the past—which, I grant, may have been itself based on something that happened, the death of a child—is made into a concrete, actual present. But this is rehearsal: the present is something being made 'for tomorrow', for the future when the dance will be danced.

> As the rehearsal proceeded men and women would occasionally drift by. The assembled singers, drummers, and witnesses practised the movements of the dance that accompanies the mother's lament. Lawrence, a school-teacher who spoke English, explained that this was an 'imitative' dance, a dance in which both men and women imitated the movements of birds performing activities that loosely correlated to the events described in the mother's lament.

Wok is represented by his mother's lament, and the lament is represented by dancers, both men and women—and they are dancing as birds.

> The dancers imitate birds because the clan the story is significant to is a bird clan, has a bird as its totem. The story is at once distanced—put at an artistic remove—by the translation of the women's lament into gestures performed by both men and women acting as birds and made more immediate in its impact to all the people of the village by this artistic displacement.

More immediate because the bird clan exists now. A woman's lament for a murdered son is transformed into a dance of men and women imitating birds. A nonevent of the past—the killing of Wok (by a spirit?)—is used as the jumping-off place for a theatrical event of the future: a bird dance commemorating a mother's lament. I say 'nonevent' because the killing of Wok, however it happened, even if it happened, is not what makes him significant to Magendo. It's as if the role of hero culture-bearer was there waiting for someone to play it, and Wok was selected. Wok's spirit taught the people how to fish, plant, build ceremonial houses. We don't know whether Wok's murder was the precipitating event or whether his role as culture-bearer meant that he had to be killed. It doesn't much matter. It can't be found out. And the Wok who is the hero bears no necessary relationship to that other Wok who was murdered, except that by now they are both part of the same script, the same strip of behaviour. The important event—the event that Magendo needs—is neither Wok's death, nor his skills, nor his mother's lament: yet the performance of the dance that is none of these brings them all together. The performance is itself the text.

The rehearsal Emigh saw is, like so many performances elsewhere, doubly reflexive. The scheme of time is worked with as a single fabric, to be rewoven according to needs uncovered during rehearsals. And the attention during rehearsal is as much towards the technique of the dance as it is towards what the dance signifies. The rehearsal looks backward to Wok and forward to its finished performance. Rituals disguise themselves as restorations of actual events, when in fact they are restorations of earlier rituals. The ritual process as rehearsal is a shuttling back and forth between the nonevent and the restored event to be performed, between the significance of the event (as story, obligatory act, prayer, etc.) and the details of technique that make up the performance as performance. The rehearsals create the nonevent even as the nonevent is apparently creating the rehearsals. It is not because of Wok that the people of Magendo dance, but because of their dance that Wok (still) exists.

Look again at Figure 1. The fetch, or distance travelled, increases so that the trip $1 \rightarrow 5_a \rightarrow 5_b$ is greater than either $1 \rightarrow 2$ or $1 \rightarrow 3 \rightarrow 4$. This increase is in scope of time as well as scope of mood. $1 \rightarrow 5_a \rightarrow 5_b$ links past, rehearsal time, and performance time both in the subjunctive and indicative moods. (I use '$5_a \rightarrow 5_b$' because the nonevent and the restored nonevent are versions of one another, not independent events.) Doing a known score is $1 \rightarrow 3 \rightarrow 4$. But even this known score has behind it a $1 \rightarrow 5_a \rightarrow 5_b$: a time when the score was being invented, being put together, in flux.

The model has implications for a unified theory of ritual. The repetition of individual or social facts in the future indicative ($1 \rightarrow 2$) is ritual in the ethological sense. The repetition of a given or traditional performance score ($1 \rightarrow 3 \rightarrow 4$) is ritual in the social and religious sense. It is also those aesthetic performances—Nō drama, a performance of medieval music on original or facsimile instruments by the Pro Musica Antiqua—that share a necessity for unchangeability. The collective invention of new performances, or the substantial revision of traditional performances, that draws together all times and moods ($1 \rightarrow 5a \rightarrow 5b$) is ritual in the symbolic sense. A particular performance can combine or be between modes—especially between $1 \rightarrow 3 \rightarrow 4$ and $1 \rightarrow 5a \rightarrow 5b$; that's what Nō drama does. The model is meant to provide guideposts in a dynamic system. Performances of the type $1 \rightarrow 5a \rightarrow 5b$ may seem to be recollections of the past, but actually they are conjunctions whose centre cannot be located in any time or mood but only in the whole bundle, the full and complex interrelation among them all. As performances they are played in the indicative mood, but as performances of something they are in the subjunctive mood. The difference between animal ritual and human ritual is that animals are always performing what they are, while humans almost always perform what they are not.

III

A very clear example of a restoration of behaviour of the $1 \rightarrow 5a \rightarrow 5b$ type is the *agnicayana* that Frits Staal and Robert Gardner filmed in 1975 in Panjal, Kerala, India. Staal writes:

> This event, which lasted 12 days, was filmed, photographed, recorded, and extensively documented. From 20 hours of rough footage, Robert Gardner and I produced a 45-minute film, *Altar of Fire*. Two records are planned with selections from the 80 hours of recorded recitation and chant. Photographs of the ceremonies were taken by Adelaide de Menil. In collaboration with the chief Nambudiri ritualists and other scholars, I am preparing a definitive account of the ceremonies, which will appear in two illustrated volumes entitled: *Agni—The Vedic Ritual of the Fire Altar*. . . . Vedic ritual is not only the oldest surviving ritual of mankind; it also provides the best source material for a theory of ritual. . . . Hubert and Mauss . . . used the Vedic animal sacrifice as source material for a construction of a ritual paradigm. However, they did not know that these rituals are still performed, so that many data were inaccessible to them.[8]

This was written in 1978; by now most of Staal's programme has been executed. Note also that he regards the agnicayana as a chief source of ritual paradigm: the performance exists to feed scholarship. Indeed, in his work Staal develops a theory of ritual based on the 1975 performance. I am not concerned here with that theory because of an irony: were it not being filmed, photographed, and recorded the agnicayana would not have been performed. The impetus for the 1975 agnicayana came from America, not India; and most of the funding originated outside India. I doubt that various agencies would have responded with cash to pleas by Nambudiri Brahmans for support of a ritual that was too expensive for them to mount unaided. In fact, it was the threat of extinction, the sense that 'this is the last chance to record this event', that created the event.

Yet, accurately, the film's narrator proclaims that the viewer is seeing 'probably the last' of its kind. Actually the 1975 agnicayana was either the one after the last of a series or the first of a new series. Before 1975, agnicayana was last performed in the 1950s. Behind them is an undocumentable but safely presumed set of performances reaching back maybe the 3000 years Staal and Gardner claim. But maybe not: it's not clear when agnicayana was performed before the 1950s. The transmission of the ritual—both its *mise en scène* and its text—was largely oral, from man to boy, older Brahman priest to younger, employing a number of mnemonic devices used by Vedic reciters.

The ritual is very expensive by Kerala Indian standards. Many priests are employed, a ritual enclosure has to be built, an altar of fired brick assembled, implements gathered, and so on. The rite itself is archaic: long ago Vedic ritual gave way to later forms of Hinduism; Brahman priests had to reconstruct the agnicayana from a variety of sources: memory, Sanskrit texts, local opinion. Also, and decisively, the agnicayana involves animal sacrifice, now repugnant to many, if not most, Indians in Kerala. A great row erupted over whether or not to include the required sacrifice of fourteen goats. The debate was sharp, often political, with local Marxists being most strongly opposed to blood sacrifice. Finally, the goats were spared, and rice wrapped in leaves was substituted. It's therefore ironic when Staal speaks of 'Vedic animal sacrifice . . . still performed'.

Thus the whole contextual situation of the performance of the agnicayana in 1975 is more multiplex than Staal says. For the 1975 performance re-presents the earlier performances while being the single seed of a whole forest of future possibilities. And many of these possibilities are far from Kerala in time, place, and ideational style. This multiplexity is depicted in Figure 2.

Time	Original events	in between	Media events	in between	Scholarship
"Then" 1	Agnicayana, 1950s and earlier: the oral tradition				
"Now" 2		Deciding how to do the ritual: consulting priests, scholars, locals, filmmakers, etc.			
2		The shooting script			
2		Agnicayana, 1975			
2			Rough footage being shot; Still photos being shot; Recording sound		
2		People who came to see the ritual			
			People who came to see the filming		
2		People who came both for ritual and filming			
2		Row over sacrificing the goats			
"Later" 3			Finished film Finished book Finished recording		
"Indefinite Future" 4					Theory of ritual

Fig. 2

In this figure time is relative to events. The film of the 1975 agnicayana becomes the 'now' for all future persons who experience the ritual performance through this medium. And, as Staal says, it is likely that most people will experience agnicayana this way. Even if a living tradition continues, it is probable that the stagers in Kerala will refer to the film. The filming, as distinct from the film—that is, the process of 'getting the 1975 performance on film'—is in fact a generating event. It generates events behind it: planning, consultations with ritual specialists, assembling people, material, and animals; and it generates events ahead of it: items of Euro-American culture like films, books, cassettes, and items of scholarship, such as theories of ritual shared by Euro-Americans and Indians. The media event— the actual shooting of the film in 1975—attracted locals and inter- nationals, many of whom came as much to see the film being made as the agnicayana being performed. The whole bundle in Figure 2 between original events and scholarship is, in Turner's vocabulary, both liminal (an authentic ritual event) and liminoid (a voluntary performative event). In so far as the 1975 agnicayana is liminoid it serves purposes far beyond what the agnicayana was when it was solely part of the Kerala oral tradition. Furthermore, in restoring the agnicayana considerations of how best to document the per- formance were always in the minds of Staal–Gardner; after all, they are as much movie producers as anthropological observers. Their shooting script shows how deeply their instruments intervened in the event. Not that passive recording of events is possible, even with the notebook and pencil; read your Heisenberg. Like many rituals the agnicayana involves some very dense hours of theatricality—much simultaneous action occurring over a fairly wide range of spaces. But the camera and microphone are instruments of focus; and certainly finished film and sound cassettes are outcomes of a rigorous selective/ editing process. As performed in 1975 the agnicayana took 120 hours, plus many more hours of preparations. Staal–Gardner could shoot only 20 hours, and their script says that for 'numerous episodes filming depends on remaining quantity of raw stock'.[9] Exigency *über alles*. The 20 hours of raw footage were edited into a 45-minute film.

As best I can gather—and by analogy with other ritual events I've attended in India—agnicayana flows unevenly over its 120 hours. It has the feel often of synchronous not diachronous time; spatially it gathers itself in climaxes and is dispersed among several points: the main altar, the subsidiary altars, the home of the chief sacrificer, the purifying waters, and so on. But filmmaking works by taking bits and then later assembling them, and recombining them, into a dia- chronous whole. Filmmaking is a Frankenstein process of breakdown and stitched-together assemblage. Staal–Gardner's shooting script is no exception to this process. The 12-day ceremony is broken into episodes convenient to the camera. And the script is very specific about who the main performers are, and what's of interest:

Advaryu 1 [chief priest]: as stage manager he performs most of the rites and commands the others. He is where the action is. . . .

The final killing of the goat within the Camitra will not be filmed on this occasion [day 1] since this would upset many people; but hopefully on a later occasion. . . .

[For day 2] No more than 30 minutes of filming for the·entire day.

These procedures—the media event itself—are only faintly perceived in *Altar of Fire*. Edmund Carpenter, one of the visiting scholars lassoed for the filming, says on camera that three kinds of events are going on simultaneously: the agnicayana, the social event surrounding the ritual (common in India), and the media event. *Altar of Fire* spends virtually all its time on the agnicayana. There is a saying in India: 'Every *lila* [performance] is surrounded by a *mela* [fair and market]'. Media events are even more rare than *lilas*: so the 1975 agnicayana attracted a large number of onlookers, merchants, soothsayers, beggars, entertainers. But *Altar of Fire* is carefully nonreflexive. Except for a few feet here and there, concentrating on the visiting Western scholars, Staal–Gardner used the old fly-on-the-wall technique: 'Gosh, it sure is lucky we got here in time to shoot this.'

No one in the film goes into the controversy surrounding the sacrifice of the fourteen goats. Can there be agnicayana without blood sacrifice? How did the priests feel about the issue? What were the political questions surrounding the argument—that is, were 'progressive' Marxists pitted against 'reactionary' ritualists; and did the 'ugly American' come in for a beating? Kerala has long had a Marxist government; Kerala's literacy rate, 80 per cent, is the highest of any Indian state. The issue of the goat sacrifice was debated hotly in the area, and its press, during the filming.

Altar of Fire doesn't hint at any out-of-sequence filming, but as the script indicates the sacrifice was put off from day 1 to a later time; and then effigies were used instead of goats. Was the ceremony using these effigies filmed out of sequence and later edited into sequence? The film is mute on this; everything seems to be 'in place in time'. And, most importantly, except for the shots of the visitors there is no sense that a film is being made. *Altar of Fire* is designed to make the viewer feel 'I am here at the enactment of a rare, ancient ritual'. But after I saw the movie several times, more questions arose. There is an old priest—a Walter Huston of a man, with a scraggly beard and a canny sparkle—a casting director's dream of a 'wise old folksy priest' who explains in English much of what's going on. But he isn't the chief priest, who is much younger and doesn't look the part (to American eyes). Why was the old man chosen? There are other evidences of 'film logic' as understood by American filmmakers taking over.

Such procedures raise important questions. We need no renewed educating to the idea that the instruments and means of observing and recording things so deeply affect what's being observed that a new situation arises, one in which the observer is included in the same bundle as the observed. And we are used to questioning the authenticity of performances like the 1975 agnicayana, as Robert A. Paul did and as Stall answered.[10] But if the discussion stops here, we miss a chance to recognize in the Staal-Gardner film another harbinger of an important shift towards the theatricalization of anthropology. I mean this in a double sense.

First, by replacing the notebook with the tape recorder, the still camera with the movie camera, the monograph with the film, a shift occurs whereby we understand social life as narrative, crisis and crisis resolution, drama, person-to-person interaction, display behaviour, and so on. As Staal–Gardner say succinctly in their shooting script: 'the advaryu 1 as stage managers . . . is where the action is.' More than that, media create action.

Second, this shift of paradigm has direct consequences in the world it maps. The shift in anthropology is part of a larger intellectual movement in which understanding of human behaviour is changing from clear differentiation between cause and effect, past and present, form and content—and the literary, linear modes of discovery, analysis, and presentation—to the theatrical paradigm. The theatrical paradigm uses editing, rehearsal, deconstruction/reconstruction of actuality: the creation and organization of strips of behaviour. These techniques blur temporal and causal systems, creating in their stead bundles of relations that attain only relative clarity, and that only within contexts that themselves need definition. An effect may precede its cause. Something that happened later—in the shooting of a film, in the rehearsal of an event—may be used earlier in the finished performance, as when effigies of goats are edited into the sequence of the agnicayana with the result that they appear before it was actually decided to use them at all.

Look at the chart (Figure 2) mapping the time scheme of the agnicayana. The original events—the ritual as performed in the 1950s and earlier—and the scholarship purporting to interpret this ritual are separated by a cluster of performance events. The ritual was not a function of Kerala culture 1975, but of Euro-American culture. Scholars now writing on Vedic ritual, however, will turn to *Altar of Fire*, and the book and recordings. Probably scholars will talk of the agnicayana, not of the 'restored agnicayana'. Scholars will assume that original events of the class $1 \rightarrow 3 \rightarrow 4$ are being discussed. But actually the 1975 agnicayana is $1 \rightarrow 5a \rightarrow 5b$ event. It was restored in order to be filmed. It exists liminally between the original series that ended in the 1950s and the media events of the Staal–Gardner project. *Altar of Fire* ends with the narrator announcing that the viewer has seen what is probably the last performance of agnicayana. Not true. The viewer has seen the first of a new series of performances, one in which the event has been restored, compressed, edited; and in which the event will never change because it is 'on film'. When people want to 'see' the agnicayana, they will not go to Kerala: they will rent *Altar of Fire*. Scholarship using the agnicayana will not be based on the series that ended in the 1950s, about which very little is known, but on the material gathered by Staal–Gardner. And few, if any, scholars will examine the raw footage, the full set of tapes; they will instead look at the movie and listen to the recordings released by Staal–Gardner. Theories will be built on items extrapolated from strips of restored behaviour.

But is this any different than building theories on writings? Writings are more easily recognized as interpretations than restorations of behaviour are. Theories are presented in the same bundle as the data on which these theories rest. References are freely made to earlier interpretations and theories. Often, writing is clearly reflexive. I don't prefer writings to restorations of behaviour as a way of scholarship. But restorations are not yet understood as thoroughly as writing. Therefore, at present restorations leave more mess than writing. People use restorations and consider them $1 \rightarrow 2$ or $1 \rightarrow 3 \rightarrow 4$ when actually they are $1 \rightarrow 5a \rightarrow 5b$. $1 \rightarrow 5a \rightarrow 5b$ is hard to deal with, ambivalent, with no clear temporal sequence, no fixed causal system.

Why not think of Staal–Gardner as film producers-directors? Their work in India is more easily understood when seen in performative terms. An earlier event is 'researched' and/or 'remembered'—actions equivalent to rehearsals. A performance is arranged that presumably duplicates this earlier event. An event created in the future (the film *Altar of Fire*, 5b) is projected backward in time (the 'original' agnicayana, 5a) and restored 'now' in order to be filmed (what happened in Kerala in 1975, 1). The items in this bundle cannot be separated; they must be considered as a unit. The so-called prior event—the 'original' agnicayana is not strictly prior—certainly did not 'cause' the 1975 performance. The 1975 performance was caused by the project of making a film. So in a sense the future is causing the present which, in turn, makes it necessary to research, remember—rehearse— the past. But this past—what is turned up by the rehearsal process— determines what is done in 1975, and those events are used to make the movie. The movie then replaces the 'original' event; the movie is what we have of the past.

Sometimes the restored event can spark a new series of original performances. Alan Lomax reports the experience of Adrian Gerbrands:

> Gerbrands by chance screened a documentary on Eastern New Guinea mask-making for a native group in New Britain. The audience reacted powerfully during and after the screening. They, too, had once known how to make such masks and should, they felt, try their skill again, especially if their art too would be filmed. After Gerbrands had filmed the group's mask-making, a lone native approached him with the offer to perform a very important and defunct ceremony if he would film it. Naturally again Gerbrands used his camera. On his next trip to New Britain, the other men in the village insisted on seeing the film and were so distressed at the poor quality of the filmed ceremony that they vowed forthwith to re-enact the whole ceremony, masks, costumes, ballet, feasting, and all, but at a length suitable for filming. This event and its resultant film were such a success locally that the ceremony is now being celebrated every year just as in former times.[11]

Ceremonies like this, and like the agnicayana, exist between fact and fiction: they are a new class of facts. Simulations, models, and theatricalizations are part of this new class. Their in-betweenness links them to Turner's Talmud on Van Gennep's idea of 'liminality' and to what D. W. Winnicott calls 'transitional objects and phenomena'. More on these later.

Sometimes restorations clash with the very agencies that promote them:

> In an effort to boost tourism, tribesmen in New Guinea have offered to turn cannibal again. They told committee members of

the Mt. Hagan Show, the big territorial festival, that they were prepared to eat human flesh at the show in August [1975]. The tribesmen added, however, that they did not want to kill any of their enemies and would make do instead with a body from the local hospital morgue. A government officer at the meeting politely but firmly declined the tribesmen's suggestions.

The rhetoric of the Los Angeles *Times* story is the key to the cultural contexts in conflict here. To American readers 'tribesmen' = savages, 'committee members' = Europeanized savages, 'government officer' = the New Civilized Power. The story is full of sly humour, delectably alluding to a taboo appetite. That's why it was picked up by a major American paper. But the locals have logic on their side. If old dances are being restored, why not the cannibal feast? The locals know how far they can go: the body will come from an approved repository of corpses, a hospital, a representation of the New Civilized Power. The Power has its role to play too: it must demonstrate far and wide that, well, New Guinea is and isn't New Guinea anymore. So the story 'gets out', and the sponsors of the Mt. Hagan Show have their cake without having to eat it too.

IV

Restorations needn't be exploitations. Sometimes they are arranged with such care that after a while the restored behaviour heals into its presumptive past and its present cultural context like a well-set bone. In these cases a 'tradition' is rapidly established and judgments about authenticity hard to make. Let me give two examples from India.

Bharatanatyam, the classical Indian dance, is traced back not only to the ancient text on theatre, *Natyasastra* (*ca.* second century B.C.–second century A.D.), that describes dance poses but also to temple sculptings that show these poses. The best known of these sculptings is the group at the fourteenth-century temple of Nataraja (Siva, king of dancers) at Chidambaram, south of Madras. Most writings assume a continuous tradition connecting *Natyasastra*, temple sculptings, and today's dancing. According to Kapila Vatsyayana, India's leading dance theorist and historian:

Bharatanatyam is perhaps the oldest among the contemporary classical dance forms of India. . . . Whether the dancer was the devadasi of the temple or the court-dancer of the Maratha kings of Tanjore, her technique followed strictly the patterns which had been used for ages.[12]

Whenever the contemporary forms of Bharatanatyam and Manipuri and Odissi evolved, two things are clear: first, that they were broadly following the tradition of the *Natyasastra* and were practising similar principles of technique from their inception, and, second, that the stylization of movement began as far back as the 8th and 9th century. . . . Some contemporary styles preserve the characteristic features of this tradition more rigorously than others: Bharatanatyam uses the basic adhamadali [postures] most rigorously.[13]

But in fact it's not known when the 'classical' Bharatanatyam died out, or even if it ever existed in the form in which it is described by scholars and danced by contemporary dancers. The old texts and the sculptings surely show that there was some kind of dance, but nothing was remembered of this dance, not even its name, when moves were made to 'revive' it at the start of the twentieth century.

There was a temple dance called *sadir nac* danced by women of families hereditarily attached to certain temples. According to Milton Singer:

> The dancing girls, their teachers, and musicians performed not only on the occasion of temple festivals and ceremonies, but also for private parties, particularly weddings, and at palace parties. Special troupes of dancing girls and musicians were sometimes permanently attached to the courts.[14]

Some dancing girls were prostitutes: temple prostitution was widespread. The British and some Indians campaigned from the start of the twentieth century to stop temple dancing. In 1947 Madras State outlawed it. Long before that the number of *devadasis* (dancing girls) dwindled. Connected with the campaign to outlaw *sadir nac* Dr V. Raghavan, scholar and critic, coined the term Bharatanatyam to describe the dance he and dancer Rukmini Devi were developing. They wanted to use *sadir nac* but not be identified with its bad reputation. They cleaned up *sadir nac*, brought in gestures based on the *Natyasastra* and temple sculptings, developed standard teaching methods. They claimed that Bharatanatyam was very old. And, of course, a conformity to ancient texts and art could be demonstrated: every move in Bharatanatyam was measured against the sources of which it presumed to be a living vestige. The differences between *sadir nac* and the old sources were attributed to degeneracy. The new dance, now legitimized by its heritage, not only absorbed *sadir nac*, but attracted the daughters of the most respectable families to practise it. Many study Bharatanatyam as a kind of finishing school. It is danced all over India by both amateurs and professionals. It is a major export item.

The 'history' and 'tradition' of Bharatanatyam—its roots in the ancient texts and art—is actually a restoration of behaviour of the $1 \rightarrow 5a \rightarrow 5b$ type. $5a =$ the 'ancient classical dance'. But this dance is a construction based on the restoration work of Raghavan, Devi, and others. They used *sadir nac* not as a dance in its own right but as a faint image of some ancient glory. But that 'ancient classical dance' is a projection backward in time: we know what it looks like because we have the Bharatanatyam. Soon people believed that the ancient dance led to Bharatanatyam when, in fact, the Bharatanatyam led to the ancient dance. An original ancient dance is created in the past in order to be restored for the present and future. There is no single source for Bharatanatyam, only the whole bundle $1 \rightarrow 5a \rightarrow 5b$.

Purulia Chhau, a masked dance of the semiarid region of rural Bengal adjoining Bihar and Orissa, is an athletic dance-drama of many leaps, somersaults, and stampings. The drummers of the Dom caste beat huge kettle drums and long oblong drums, taunting the dancers into frenzied twisting jumps, screams, and mock battles. Rivalry among villages competing at the annual festival at Matha is fierce. According to Asutosh Bhattacharyya, Professor of Bengali Literature at Calcutta University, who has devoted himself entirely to Chhau since 1961, the Purulia region is inhabited by many aboriginal tribes whose

> religious customs and social festivals show very little resemblance with those of Hinduism. . . . But, it is also a fact that the Mura of Purulia are very ardent participants in Chhau dance. With practically no education and social advancement the members of this community have been performing this art which is based on the episodes of the Ramayana and the Mahabharata and the Indian classical literature most faithfully, in some cases, for generations. . . . Sometimes an entire village, however poor, inhabited exclusively by the Mura, sacrifices its hard-earned resources for the cause of organizing Chhau dance parties.[15]

This presents a problem for Bhattacharyya: 'the system which is followed in Chhau dance today could not have been developed by the aboriginal people who practise the dance. It is indeed a contribution of a higher culture keenly conscious of an aesthetic sense.'[16] He guesses that the drummers, the Dom, an outcaste group, originated Chhau, for the Dom were at one time a 'highly sophisticated community . . . brave soldiers in the infantry of the local feudal Chiefs'.[17] Thrown out of work when the British pacified the region in the eighteenth century, failing to farm because of what Bhattacharyya calls the 'vanity of their past tradition of warriors', they were reduced to their present untouchable status: workers of hides, drummers. But their war dance lives on as Chhau.

Some interesting prejudices sparkle from Bhattacharyya's story. Aboriginal peoples have no developed aesthetic sense; high-caste dancers are transformed into low-caste drummers because warriors are too proud to farm (how about using their swords to steal land and then becoming landlords, a time-honoured practice?); great amounts are spent on dance parties, but these compete at Matha, the annual festival initiated by Bhattacharyya in 1967, not an ancient tradition at all. As he says:

> In April 1961 I visited an interior village in the Purulia District with a batch of students of the Calcutta University and for the first time observed a regular performance of the Chhau dance. . . . I found that there was a system of this dance and a definitely established method which was well-preserved. But it was on the decline due to lack of patronage from any source whatsoever. I wanted to draw attention of the world outside to this novel form of dance.[18]

And that he did. All-star parties of Chhau dancers have toured in Europe in 1972, in Australia and North America in 1975, and in Iran. They have danced in New Delhi, and as Bhattacharyya exults:

> I attracted the notice of Sangeet Natak Akademi, New Delhi [the Government agency established to encourage and preserve traditional performing arts] to this form of dance. It took immediate interest and invited me to give performances of the dance in New Delhi. In June 1969, I visited New Delhi with a batch of 40 village artists for the first time outside their native district. Performances were held there before very distinguished Indian and foreign invitees. . . . Performances were also shown on TV in Delhi. Only three years later it was also shown on BBC television in London and five years later on NBC in New York, USA.[19]

Note how Bhattacharyya refers to the dances as his: 'invited me to give performances of the dance'. This is not bragging but acknowledgment of the circumstances: without a patron the villagers would have gotten nowhere. And these days a patron needs more than money— or maybe he doesn't need money so much as knowledge, and a wish to devote himself to the form he's restoring. Government comes up with the cash.

Chhau 1961 and after is a creation of the mixture of what Bhattacharyya found and what he invented. But his invention was of the $1 \rightarrow 5a \rightarrow 5b$ type. As a folklorist-anthropologist he dug into the past and constructed a history of Chhau, and a technique, that he then proceeded faithfully to restore. His annual festival at Matha coincides with the Chaitra Parvan celebrations common to the area, and the occasion of the annual Chhau festivals of Seraikella and Mayurbhanj (related forms of the dance). These festivals, once paid for by maharajas, are now sponsored, less lavishly, by the government. In 1976 I went to Matha, a hill station, not a town, but only a few buildings and an open field. The dances go on there all night for two nights. Villagers, arriving from towns as far as a two-day journey, set up camps. Roping together *charpois* (sleeping cots made of wood and twine) a theatre is jerrybuilt. Women and children watch, and sleep, sitting and reclining on the *charpois* elevated to a height of 8 feet or more. Men and boys stand on the ground. A narrow passageway leads from the area where performers put on costumes and masks to the roughly circular dancing ground. Parties enter down the passageway, stop, present themselves, then leap into their dancing. All dancing is done with bare feet on bare earth, swept clean of large rocks but still raw, pebbled, with turned-up clods and scrub grass. To me it felt like a rodeo in a backwater town. Torches and petromax lanterns throw shadowy light, the drums bark and roar, the *shenais* (clarinet-like instruments) shriek, as party after party compete. Most parties consist of five to nine dancers. Some masks adorned with peacock feathers rise 3 feet over the dancers' heads. The mask of 10-headed Ravana is more than 4 feet long. Wearing these masks dancers make full somersaults and twisting leaps. The dances are vigorous, and it's very hot inside the papier-mâché masks. Each dance lasts less than 10 minutes. Every village dances twice. There are no prizes but there is competition, and everyone knows who dances well, who poorly.

Just in case there are doubts, on each afternoon following the night's dancing Bhattacharyya critiques the performances. During the dancing he sits behind a desk, two petromax lanterns making him the best-lit figure of the event; and next to him are his university assistants. All night he watches and writes. The next day, one by one the villages appear before him. I listened to what he said. He warned one party not to use story elements not found in the Hindu classics. He chided another for not wearing the standard basic costume of short skirt over leggings decorated in rings of white, red, and black. Bhattacharyya selected this basic costume from one village and made it general. When I asked him about it he said that the costumes he chose were the most authentic, the least Westernized. In a word, Bhattacharyya oversees every aspect of Purulia Chhau; training, dance themes, music, costuming, dance steps. He selects individuals from different villages to make up the all-star teams that tour. He rehearses the touring parties and they, of course, return to their home villages with enhanced reputations. Touring, in fact, has had deep effects on Chhau. Three 'foreign parties' came into existence since the first tour in 1972: 19 people went to Europe, 16 to Iran, and 11 to Australia and North America. Because foreigners won't sit through 9 hours of dancing, Bhattacharyya made a programme of 2-hour duration. And because he didn't think that bare chests looked good on the male dancers he designed a jacket based on an old pattern. Both these changes have become standard back in Purulia. Many of the people who went abroad formed their own groups at home. Each of these groups are called 'foreign parties', and bill themselves as such; this gives them status, drawing power, and the ability to charge more. There is demand now for performances as performances, not as part of the ritual calendar. A performance can be hired for about 1000 rupees—a lot cheaper than Jatra, the most popular form of entertainment in rural Bengal. But 1000 rupees is still a lot of money for performers of Chhau. In Bhattacharyya's opinion, as the financial opportunities have increased the subtlety of the art has declined. John Emigh spoke to Bhattacharyya in the summer of 1980. In reflecting on the tours, Bhattacharyya told him that he thinks they saved a form otherwise doomed, but at the expense of stirring jealousies and rivalries and generating irreversible changes in the form. Chhau is a masked dance, and one side effect of its popularity abroad has been the demand by tourists for masks. Many masks are shipped that have never been worn by a dancer.

These changes can be traced back to Bhattacharyya. He is the big Chhau man, and his authority is rarely questioned, never overturned. He's a professor, a scholar from Calcutta. When he writes about Chhau he emphasizes its village base and ancient origins; he even suggests a possible connection between Chhau and the dances of Bali. (The Kalinga Empire of Orissa, *ca*. third century B.C., possibly traded across the seas as far as Bali.) But he hardly mentions his own role in restoring the dance. Rather he speaks of himself as 'discovering' it. His 1980 conversation with Emigh is the first acknowledgment of the changes consequent to his discovery.

In 1977, along with Suresh Awasthi, former Secretary of the Sangeet Natak Akademi, the man who introduced me to Chhau, and Shyamanand Jalan, a theatre director of modern plays and a Calcutta lawyer, I helped organize a Chhau Festival in Calcutta. This was the first time ever that all three kinds of Chhau were seen on the same programme. And the first time many of the dancers from Purulia, Seraikella, and Mayurbhanj saw each others' dances. Traditionally, Chhau is danced only on Chaitra Parvan (in March–April), so all the dancing parties are occupied simultaneously and tied to their home territories. But in 1937–1938, when maharajas had plenty of cash, dancers of Seraikella Chhau toured to Europe. They also danced for Gandhi in Calcutta. The patron, teacher, and choreographer of the Seraikella troupe was Bijoy Pratap Singh Deo, brother to the maharaja. And the star dancer was Suvendra, the crown prince (he died at age 23). After Independence and the abolition of the Privy Purses the dances declined for lack of patronage. The three forms of Chhau are related, though more scholarly work needs to be done to establish exactly what the connections are. Dancing masters from Seraikella were imported into Mayurbhanj by its maharaja early in the century. Both Seraikella and Purulia Chhau use masks, though these look very different from each other. Seraikella style is also influenced by Western ballet. Remember that maharajas were often culturally as much European as Indian. At the 1977 Calcutta festival there were 3 days of dancing, demonstrations of techniques, and talk. A second Chhau Festival, under government sponsorship, was held in Bhubaneswar, Orissa, in 1978. Festivals such as these are themselves hybrids, crosses between the Indian love of jatra-lila-mela (pilgrimage, performance, and fair-ground) and the Western taste for collecting behaviours as 'items' of culture, then dissecting the collection in a scholarly way at conferences-cum-junkets. Who ever pays his own way to a scholarly meeting? In 1980 Kedar Nath Sahoo—

the Seraikella Chhau master dancer-teacher, and the last man alive who danced under Bijoy—went to Europe and the United States demonstrating the art and teaching. It's neither possible nor desirable to keep forms 'pure'. The question is to what degree should cross-breeding be managed, and to what degree promiscuous?

Sometimes, actually, changes are insisted upon by insiders and not imposed from without. One of the best-known films concerning non-Western performance is the Mead–Bateson *Trance and Dance in Bali* (1938). At one of the showings of this film at the American Museum of Natural History in New York, Mead said that in preparing the confrontation between Rangda and Barong for filming, the trance club of Pagutan decided that foreign viewers would rather see young women go into trance and stab at their breasts with krises. Customarily only men and old women perform this. The women often go with their breasts bare—naked breasts do not suggest the same erotic significance in Bali as in New York. But, also I suppose to please, or at least not offend, foreigners, the Balinese women's breasts were covered. Without telling Mead or Bateson, the men of the trance club instructed the young women in the proper techniques for entering trance; the women were also taught how to handle the krises. Then the men of the club proudly announced to the filmmakers the changes made for the special filming. In *Trance and Dance*, as the narrator says, one old woman who 'said she wouldn't go into trance' is unexpectedly deeply possessed. The camera follows her: she is bare-breasted, she is deep in trance, her kris is powerfully turned against her own chest; later, slowly, she is brought out of trance by an old priest. Members of the trance club were angry at this old woman because they felt that her trance disturbed the aesthetic refinements they had rehearsed for foreign eyes.[20] Which is 'authentic'—the young women prepared by the Balinese themselves, or the solitary old woman doing the traditional thing? Cases abound where, as in Pagutan Baji District, local performances are adapted to suit foreign tastes. Hula dancers, for example, are traditionally heavy—that is, powerful and mature—middle-aged women. But tourist hula, now almost traditional in its own right, features slim-hipped young women. It's precisely when changes feed back into the traditional forms, actually becoming these forms, that a restoration of behaviour of the $1 \rightarrow 5a \rightarrow 5b$ type occurs.

Sometimes even, knowing the money that tourists have to spend, performances are invented and foisted upon tourists as traditional when they are not. I was in the Papua–New Guinea Highlands in

1972 where I saw the tourist performance of the famous Mudmen of Asaro, whose story is sad indeed. These white-clay-covered dancers, with their grotesque masks of hardened clay, originally depicted ghosts arising from a stream. Their performance was very effective in scaring away enemies. But when photos of their masks appeared, in the *National Geographic*, I believe, a demand was created for their dancing. The whole performance was dislocated. The dancers danced at midday instead of dawn; they were visible in the centre of the small village instead of lurking in the bush near the stream; they performed twice weekly instead of only when necessary, that is, when threatened by enemies. And, naturally, they were exploited: when I saw them they kept 10 per cent of the tourists' dollars. Because I was photographing the tourists disembarking from their Volkswagen minibus, and because I arrived before the ordinary tourists and remained after, I was approached by a villager. He asked me to come with him to his village, Kenetasarobe, not far from Asaro. Once there he showed me his group of dancers, with their spectacular masks; and he put on a display of fire-making. He made it clear that he had devised this performance and believed that I was a tourist agency booker. I took a few photos, paid some money, accepted a bamboo smoking pipe as a souvenir. Regretfully I told my local choreographer that I could not help him sell his dance.

With both Bharatanatyam and Purulia Chhau a modern version of an old art is born through the intervention/invention of one or a few dedicated persons from outside the class of those they are leading. This is, maybe, a version of the Moses myth or the Marxist fact; revolution comes to a group from the outside, typically brought in by a lost member of the tribe who rediscovers his origins. As Indians, Raghavan, Devi, and Bhattacharyya are not outsiders the way Staal, Gardner, and Gerbrands are. But Raghavan and Devi were not from *devadasi* families, and Bhattacharyya is no aboriginal tribesman.

I see nothing amiss in the restorations of behaviour called Bharatanatyam or Purulia Chhau. Artforms and rituals too are always in the process of development. And sometimes the impetus comes by way of restored behaviour. Bharatanatyam and Chhau are analogous to the works of the French dramatists of the seventeenth century, who were conforming to what they thought were the rules of Attic tragedy. Or to those of Renaissance architects restoring what they thought were classical styles. These people had at hand Aristotle, the Greek plays, architectural ruins, and Vetruvius. Today we have at hand relics of behaviour, ancient texts, sculptings, and the memories of Hindu priests. We also have ways of getting, transmitting, storing, and broadcasting information that makes a one-world information network a reality. 'Nativistic movements' seek to restore the old ways. I'm talking about something else. There is something postmodern in restoring behaviour. Scholars and specialists fear a disruption of historical variety brought about by world monoculture. Just as physical well-being depends on a varied gene pool, so social well-being depends on a varied culture pool. Restored behaviour is a way of guaranteeing a varied culture pool. It is a strategy that fits within, and yet opposes, world monoculture, It's not the 'natives' who practise restored behaviour. The *devadasis* were content to dance their *sadir nac*, even if it was doomed; the Mura and Dom danced and drummed their Chhau before Bhattacharyya arrived in 1961, even if it was 'in decay'. But the moderns want to bring into the postmodern world 'authentic cultural items'. Within the frame of postmodern information theory—all knowledge is reducible/transformable into bits of information, and therefore potentially reconstructible in new orders, new beings in fact—an illusion of diversity is projected: backward in time to 5_a, forward to 5_b. This illusion is artful because it is art itself, pure theatre. And the underlying idea that information, not things, is the basic material of nature, not just culture, is at the root of such recent explorations as recombinant DNA, gene-splicing, and cloning. What is created through these experiments is a liminal existence between nature and culture. It suggests that nature and culture might be a false dichotomy, representing not opposing realms but different perceptions of identical processes.

When Bhattacharyya goes to the field and finds Chhau 'in decay', or when Raghavan finds 'vestiges' of a classical dance in *sadir nac*, is what they find incomplete? Only with reference to a presumed past and a rehearsed-restored future is it incomplete; only when measured against the whole bundle $1 \rightarrow 5_a \rightarrow 5_b$. The restorers view the behaviours they restore through a wider time-lens, a wider conceptual-lens, than the dancers of 'native' *sadir nac* and Chhau. Restored behaviour is not a process of scraping away dead layers of paint to reveal the original artwork; it is not discovering an unbroken—dare I say, unconscious?—tradition, but of research and fieldwork, of rehearsals in the deepest sense. There is more of this kind of thing coming. Already the past 70 years are available on film. Waves of styles return regularly because of this availability. We are not going to 'lose' behaviour from the 1920s, for instance, in the same way or to the same extent as we've lost previous epochs. We're in a time when traditions can die in life, be preserved archivally as behaviours, and later be restored.

V

Although restored behaviour seems to be founded in the past and follow a linear chronology—'Bharatanatyam is perhaps the oldest among the contemporary dance forms of India', 'Vedic ritual is . . . the oldest surviving ritual of mankind'—it is in fact a synchronic bundle, $1 \rightarrow 5_a \rightarrow 5_b$. The past, 5_a, is recreated in terms not simply of a present, 1, but of a future, 5_b. This future is the performance being rehearsed, the next showing, the 'finished thing' made efficient, graceful, and perfect through rehearsals. Restored behaviour is both teleological and eschatological. It joins original causes and what happens at the end of time. It is a model of destiny.

VI

Restorations of behaviour are not limited to New Guinea or India, that world of the non-Western other. All over America restorations of behaviour are common, popular, and making money for their owners. Maurice J. Moran, Jr., has written an account of theme parks and restored villages. Their diversity is undeniable: Renaissance Pleasure Fairs in California and New York, restored villages in almost every state, Disneyland and Disneyworld, safari and wildlife parks, amusement parks organized around single themes, Land of Oz in North Carolina, Storyland in New Hampshire, Frontierland, Ghost Town in the Sky, even L'il Abner's Dogpatch. The Marriott Corporation, operators of parks and owners of hotels, describes the parks as 'a family entertainment complex oriented to a particular subject or historical area, combining a continuity of costuming and architecture with entertainment and merchandise to create a fantasy-provoking atmosphere'.[21] These places are large environmental theatres. They are related to get-togethers like the Papua–New Guinea kaiko, the Amerindian powwow, and the Indian Kumbh Mela: pilgrimage centres where performances, goods, services, and ideologies are displayed and exchanged.

In this essay I concentrate on only one kind of theme park, the restored village. As of 1978 there were more than sixty such villages in the United States and Canada, and, it seems, more are coming. Millions of people visit them each year. Typically they restore the Colonial period or the nineteenth century; they reinforce the ideology of rugged individualism as represented by early settlers of the Eastern states (Colonial Williamsburg, Plimoth Plantation), the shoot-'em-up West (Buckskin Joe and Cripple Creek, Colorado, Cowtown, Kansas, Old Tucson, Arizona), or romanticized heroic industries like mining and whaling. Some, like Amish Farms and Homes in Pennsylvania, present a spectacle of people actually living their lives; a few, like Harpers Ferry in West Virginia, commemorate historical confrontations. The scope of the architectural reconstructions and the behaviours of the persons who work in the villages make these restorations more than museums.

At Columbia Historic Park, California,

> the tour of a still functioning gold mine is a major attraction— where would-be spelunkers are warned of the dangers of cave-ins and claim jumping. The miners are two retired men who can actually make a living from the little bit of gold left in the vein.[22]

Historic Smithville in New Jersey covers 25 acres on which stand a cluster of 36 buildings including a gristmill, schoolhouse, Quaker meetinghouse, cobbler's shop, and firehouse,

> most of which are original structures from the Jersey shore area. 'Residents' of the town are dressed in period costume and work at the tasks of the 18th and 19th century citizens.[23]

Old Sturbridge Village in Massachusetts was started in 1946. By 1978 there were more than 35 buildings on the 200-acre tract. The crafts people are dressed in period costumes. On Sundays

> a Quaker meeting is held. There is village dancing on Wednesday evenings. School is actually taught in the little faded schoolhouse two days a week, and there are presentations of plays from the period (*The Drunkard*, 1840, *Ever So Humble*, 1836). On July 4th the entire village celebrates as it may have been then.[24]

At Louisbourg, Quebec, the employees of the village

> assume the names of people who actually inhabited the village. The visitor is stopped at the gate and instructed to proceed only after an informal search, conducted in French. If you reply in English, a wary eye is kept on you as you proceed.[25]

Given the present temper of relations between English and French speakers in Quebec, this entrance initiation reverberates across several centuries.

> One woman asked this writer if he had met her 'husband'. She was referring in the present tense to the man who had served as the chief engineer in the original Louisbourg. Her 'maid' and 'children' ('I had five, you know, but one died this past winter') cavort in the kitchen, smiling at the strangely clothed visitors with their magic boxes [cameras].[26]

The performance is carried further at Plimoth Plantation in Massachusetts. According to materials sent to me by Judith Ingram, director of marketing at the Plantation, an attempt is made at a total re-creation, including performing actual residents of Plimoth in the seventeenth century:

> Our efforts on this behalf began in the late 1960s. Since that time, visitors to our Pilgrim Village have been afforded the opportunity for total immersion in 17th century life. Staff members are trained in what might be termed 'non-programmatic' interpretation which stresses the ability to converse with visitors naturally while putting in a hard day's work running the community in a holistic way. This approach assures that all the senses are brought to bear in the learning process. . . . No one who has entered the small, cluttered houses in our village in July and had to contend with the flies and dust, who has seen a fire on the hearth on a hot scorching day, or who has observed the difficulties just keeping the food edible, will come away with the traditional stereotype of the starched Pilgrim intact.
>
> In 1978 interpretation in the Pilgrim Village took another important step forward with the introduction of first person interpretation. Within the palisaded walls of the village no trace of the modern world can be found [except for special paths and access to several structures for the handicapped]. Now, we have recreated not only the houses and furnishings, but also the residents of 1627 Plymouth. Great care has been taken in replicating the attire, the personalities, and even regional English dialects of the Pilgrims.[27]

The Plimoth staff are careful to point out that the Plantation is not a 'restoration', but a 're-creation'. 'We have no surviving original houses', says Ingram, 'we do not know the exact design of the houses and must recreate structures typical of the period.'[28] These 're-creations' are built after much research. The same care goes into building roles—and these are modelled not on 'typical' people of the period but on actual residents of the colony.

According to Bob Marten, cohead of the Plantation's Interpretation Department, ads are placed each January to fill about 30 roles to represent the actual 200 persons who lived in the colony in 1627. That is, 30 out of 200 villagers are actually represented by what Marten calls 'cultural informants':

> Marten said the Plantation tries to find people who are similar to the characters they will play. 'We're looking for the 20th-century counterparts of 17th-century people. If casting for the part of Elder (William) Brewster, we'll look for someone of approximately the same age with a gracious manner of expression and ready vocabulary. . . . John Billington was a rogue, a con man. So we'll find someone who's capable of being in this role. He's usually played by a character actor who could sell a man his own shoes.'[29]

As in movie acting, a lot of type-casting is done. 'A truck driver makes a better yeoman than a teacher', says Marten.

Interestingly there is little group rehearsal—this is not a play the performers are preparing for, but a more improvisatory world of interaction not only among themselves but with the tourists who visit the Plantation daily. (The Plantation is open seven days a week, 9 to 5, from 1 April through 30 November.) Each performer is given a 'Documentary Biograph' and a 'Personation Biograph'. The documentary biograph tells what is known about the character to be portrayed: age in 1627, place of origin, parents, social status, and so on. Some of these data are noted as 'current opinion' (rather than established fact), and some as 'learned fabrication'—a category that means invented, but according to probability. The personation biograph includes dialect specimen, signature, names of the character's friends, some suggested readings, and, very importantly, a paragraph or two of 'notes'. For example, Phineas Pratt, we are told, is 34, comes from Buckinghamshire, arrived at Plimoth aboard the Sparrow in 1622, and is a yeoman. The notes on Phineas's personation biograph tell the performer, in part:

> P. Pratt is a man of Character; he cannot Lie, nor swear, nor suffer one heard—Quicker Master P. would unscabbard his temper a' his sword than tolerate a false-hood or an dissembilating

man. Nor ought he, by his own Code of Good Word and Valient Deed. One doesn't find him continually Defending his or others verity, however, for the same disposition which causeth him to believe in his own Truth Telling, causeth him to trust the truth of Others—unless he find ample cause to Doubt. . . . He has lived as close to the red men—friends & foes—as anie English Man & accepted—nay, even *adopted* to his open ways, their customs & believs—but his animated telling of the sagacities & civilities of *The Beaver* causes some of the more canny & doubtful of the community to wince at 'Finyuz's' acceptance of what they deem heathan apocrypha.

These notes are written in what I suppose is a seventeenth-century hand, in seventeenth-century grammar. The biograph also has a drawing of Phineas in his clothes—or costume, depending on whether you take his point of view or that of the performer playing him. Along with the biographs a performer is given a cassette tape of someone talking in the proper dialect.

Moran visited Plimoth:

In each building a member of the household that would have resided there greets you and asks 'How be ye?' Within a few minutes you find yourself responding in a language that was foreign only moments ago. 'I be well, thank ye.' One little girl is asked, 'Where be ye from?' 'New Jersey', she answers. 'I'm afraid I don't know that place.' A parent intervenes. 'You see, Susie, New Jersey isn't invented yet.' . . . As the day proceeds, the villagers go about their work. Food is prepared in black kettles over hot coals, while they explain to their visitors the difference between pottage and ragout. . . . One young lad is helping build Mr. Allerton's house. With Irish brogue he explains, 'I was in a shipwreck on my way to Virginia colony. When I washed ashore the Indians took me here. I was surprised to find anyone speaking English in these wilds.' . . . One goat insisted on coming into the Standish household, only to be shooed away by the maid. The houses are all hand-constructed, some with wooden floors, some with clay (damp in the spring thaw). The streets are uneven, rocky. . . . Many special events continue the theme of historic reenactment. There is the opening of the Wampanoag Summer Settlement, staffed by native Americans in the style of the 17th century. There is a village barnraising and a reenactment of a typical wedding in the colony and also in the Indian camp. But the classical attraction, and one of the chief fundraisers for the village, is the Harvest Festival in October. . . . Here the villagers renew 17th century harvest customs with cooking and feasting, songs, dances, and a general show of high spirits. Native Americans from the summer settlement join in friendly challenges of skill and chance.[30]

In the information sheet I got from Ingram the 'first person interpretation' technique is celebrated:

First person interpretation not only encourages the personal involvement of visitors, it also facilitates the discussion of difficult concepts and ideas. Indeed, it has been our experience that since the implementation of this technique in the Pilgrim Village the frequency of questions dealing with matters that can collectively be termed the 17th century world view has risen. There has also been a corresponding decrease in the questions that fall into the 'What is that?' category. By speaking in the first person, our staff can respond to questions in personal rather than abstract terms.[31]

Much effort is made to separate the seventeenth from the twentieth century. 'Unlike places like Sturbridge and Williamsburg', says Ingram, 'no items whatsoever are sold aboard the Mayflower or in the Pilgrim Village. . . . Our program carefully separates modern element from period element, using the former to prepare the visitor for a suspension of doubt as he steps into the past.'[32] This is somewhat like Disneyworld, and other theme parks, where a radical separation is attempted between the ordinary world and the world of the park. At Disneyworld the backstage is actually underground, and central control areas are several miles from the part of the park that visitors stroll in. All employees at Disneyworld enter and leave the area underground and out of sight: they are seen in the Magic Kingdom only in costume and in character.

But despite—even because of—these attempts at separating realities, or spheres of experience in time/space, spectators enjoy what can best be described as a postmodern thrill at the mix or close coincidence of contradictory categories. At Plimoth hosts are twentieth-century persons trained in seventeenth-century English (more or less); the visitors are tourists who have paid to be treated as guests dropping in from another century. A brochure emphasizes the reality of the seventeenth-century world, while encouraging the visitors to break that frame:

The people you will meet in the village portray—through dress, speech, manner and attitudes—known residents of the colony in

1627. Their lives follow the seasonal cycle of all farming communities—planting and harvesting crops, tending animals, preparing meals, preserving food—what you see will depend upon the time of your visit. Busy as they are, the villagers are always eager for conversation. Feel free to ask questions; and remember, the answers you receive will reflect each individual's 17th century identity.

The give-away phrase is 'busy as they are'. It's not true: they are paid to respond to the visitors. I doubt that a villager who refused to talk to the tourists would last long in the seventeeth century, for he will have violated a rule laid down by his twentieth-century employers. The little one-page map and flyer is also full of the contradictions. The Village is entered only after the tourist has gone through a reception centre and an orientation centre. The reception centre is where business is done: restaurant, gift shop, bookstore, tickets for the Village itself; also telephones, toilets, a picnic area. The orientation centre includes a multi-image slide show which is, the flyer tells us, 'an essential part of your visit'. It gives historical background and lays out what's offered. The orientation to the seventeenth century 'lasts about 15 minutes'.

There is some cuteness amidst the insistence on stepping back into the seventeenth century. Spanish and French persons, 'if unarmed', are welcome at the Plantation even though England was at war with Spain and/or France for much of the seventeenth century. The architecture of the Village is totally re-created indoors and out—nothing survives from the original colony. Thus an unusual situation obtains at Plimoth. It is known who was there, and background information has been researched; consequently, the characters have a kind of authenticity that the architecture lacks. The buildings and furnishings are 'typical' of the period, but the people are 'actually from' 1627. At Plimoth restored behaviour is ahead of re-created architecture. And performers who have been at it awhile identify closely with their roles. Marten has played Myles Standish from 1969:

> After living with Myles Standish for all these years, Marten said he's 'more supportive and defensive' in his attitude toward the historical figure than a historian might be. Aside from appreciating Standish's virtues, Marten has gained an understanding of why the soldier committed some of his more controversial acts. 'He killed a number of Indians—not in fair combat, but

in ambush', Marten said. 'If he had to knock off a few Indians for the good of the colony, he would do it without question. I don't think I'd have the stomach to do what he did, but in the context of that time, what Myles did made sense.'[33]

What happened to Marten happens to all actors: they build roles, filling in from their own feeling what can't be located in any background study. I don't know Marten's ethnic roots, but Native Americans are hired to portray Indians at Plimoth. And the brochure tells visitors to 'meet the Native American people who lived for centuries along the New England coast'. And an avowed aim of the Plantation is to provide 'the opportunity for members of the Native American community to learn about aspects of their own culture that are in danger of being lost'.[34] I suppose that such authenticity as is needed at Wampanoag is not necessary for the Pilgrim Village. Or is it illegal? Are there any blacks playing pilgrims? And if not do they have the basis for a class-action suit? State health codes prohibit visitors from tasting the ragout boiling in the stew-pots, though one visitor reports that this law is not always observed. The point is that there is no way of avoiding anachronisms at the deepest level: authenticity is a question of stage convention, of respecting the sponsors' implicit request not to question too far, and to enjoy contradictions: real Indians not real British colonists.

Inside the fence a seventeenth-century village atmosphere is kept up. As it is aboard the Mayflower II and in the Indian settlement. But a visit to the whole complex—reception centre, orientation centre, re-created environments alive with restored behaviour—is a thoroughly anachronistic experience, a theatrical experience, made even more sharply so by the use of restored behaviour as the key element. Spectators-participants generally go along with the seventeenth-century reality. John S. Boyd plays Stephen Hopkins, assistant to Governor William Bradford. Hopkins is also the Village's first tavern keeper.

Right now, that is in 1627, Hopkins is a 'husbandman' or farmer who spends much of his time working in the fields around the plantation, when he is not answering the questions of modern tourists. 'You are meeting people from all over the world', Boyd says. 'I have met people from five different countries in one day.... Most visitors enter into the spirit of the Plantation', Boyd says, but a few are nonplussed when a plantation resident will claim never to have heard of Pennsylvania or ask visitors if they have a 'good king'. Most of them, though, 'really do accept us as from another century'.[35]

Accept in the same way that Robert De Niro is accepted as Jake La Motta in *Raging Bull*. In fact, in the Pilgrim Village it's the logic of the movies that dominates, not theatre as Artaud, Brecht, or Richard Foreman conceive it.

Looking at the Plantation's programmes over a full year: the meetings held on location by local groups, the films, the winter education programmes, the information distributed explaining how the Plantation works, the flyers, brochures, even the handsome Annual Report detailing attendance (590,000 in 1979), sales, contributions, and costs (about $1.5 million a year), we have a uniquely late-twentieth-century American phenomenon. Everything is as authentic as possible, but the day ends for visitors at 5, and the Plantation is closed for the winter. By closed I mean the performers are no longer about their daily chores, no longer living in the seventeenth century. The Plantation is open for special programmes and as a show business gearing up for an early spring opening. Maybe the Village is closed for the winter because those early Pilgrim winters were hard. The ordeals of hunger and cold, of death, can't yet be shown—or, rather, re-created. The limits of theatre end with Thanksgiving. Or maybe it's that outdoor entertainment in Massachusetts would be a loser in the winter. Probably it's both. The contradictions and anachronisms —framed and carefully kept separate (all gifts and books, restaurant and toilets, slide projectors and brochures, are outside the Village proper)—are what gives Plimoth and its sister restored villages their special kick. The contradictions are hidden, almost, and revealed at special times and places: like the magician who shows a little bit of his magic. It keeps the appetite whetted. So inside the Village it is all naturalism; but taken as a whole the Plantation is, after all, somewhat like Brecht and Foreman. The people who make Plimoth are aware that what they're doing isn't 'just' mounting static exhibits à la the dioramas at the American Museum of Natural History. They may not say it in these terms, but Plimoth is restored behaviour mixing 1→3→4 and 1→5a→5b.

But what of villages that specialize in restoring fantasies? More than one Old West town features regular *High Noon* shootouts or an attack by 'savage' Indians. These events are not taken from history, at least not directly. They are not researched the way data about the early settlement of New England are by people at Plimoth. They are played back from the movies. They are reflexions not reflections of the American experience. Sometimes, curiously, they double-back into movies. Buckskin Joe, Colorado, was created by Malcolm F. Brown, former art director at MGM. The town has been the setting for more than one movie, including *Cat Ballou*, a parody of Westerns. At Buckskin Joe a shootout takes place in front of the saloon, and the spectators, who are actual customers at the bar or other stores, duck for cover. At King's Island in Cincinnati a passenger train is held up, the conductor taken hostage, and passengers asked to intervene to save the day. Audience participation, on the decline in theatre, is increasing at theme parks and restored villages.

Considered theoretically, restored villages, even those built on fantasies and/or movies, raise hard questions. How are they different from the Staal–Gardner agnicayana? Staal–Gardner based their Vedic ritual on a reconstruction of an 'old India' as distorted, and as true, as the Old West of America where Amerindians attacked settlers and shootouts occurred in front of saloons. The Brahman priests went to texts, their own memories, and what old people could recall of the agnicayana, just as architects, performers, and craftspeople of restored villages research their stuff. And as for things taken from pop mythology, as at Buckskin Joe, there are parallels in Chhau where the stories re-enacted are from the Ramayana and Mahabharata, sacred in Sanskrit and very popular in numberless other versions including movies and comic books. No, the difference between the American restored villages and the agnicayana and Chhau is that the performers and spectators in the restored villages know it's all make-believe (Figure 3).

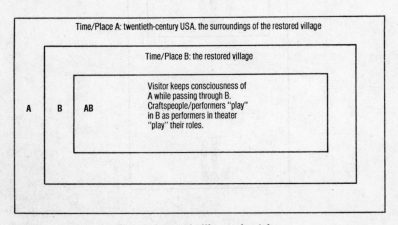

Fig. 3   Restored villages: time/place.

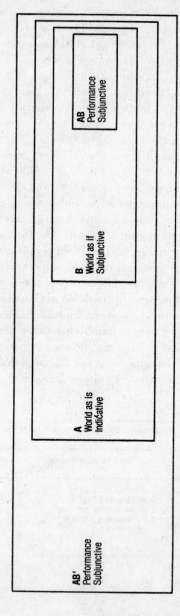

Fig. 4 Subjunctive/indicative.

There is a move from frame A into frame B resulting in a special consciousness, AB. AB is another way of stating the subjunctive mood of restored behaviour: the overlaying of two frames that cannot coexist in the indicative: 'being in' the nineteenth and twentieth centuries simultaneously, 'being' Rama and Ravana and two village persons, 'doing' a Vedic ritual before cameras and tape recorders. What happens is that the smaller subjunctive frame temporarily and paradoxically expands and contains the indicative frame. Everything is 'for the time being' (Figure 4).

The indicative world is temporarily isolated, surrounded and penetrated by the subjunctive: on the outside is the environment of the performance; on the inside is the special consciousness of performing and witnessing/participating in a performance. The famous 'suspension of disbelief' is the agreement to let the smaller frame AB become the larger frame AB'.

At Plimoth, after a few hours in the village, the visitors leave the seventeenth century; at the end of the day the craftspeople pack up and go home. Even those who make their home in the village keep an awareness of the world outside. But sometimes the anachronistic choice is radical, affecting a person's whole being. I met a number of families living in the mountains surrounding Santa Cruz, California, without electricity and other 'modern conveniences'. But the most studied, most extreme examples of anachronistic living are those done for the media, like the agnicayana, or like the Celtic encampment near London:

> Five young couples and their children lived together in a house made of sticks, grass and mud, lighted only by fire and the daylight that came through two low doors. They grew vegetables, raised boars, cows, chickens and goats, and kept a polecat for catching rabbits. They shaped pottery, forged tools, built cartwheels, wove cloth, cured the skins of animals. They sound like the Celtic tribesmen who lived not far from what is now London 2,200 years ago; they are actually 20th century Britons who have been living like Iron Age Celts for almost a year. Their experiment was conceived by John Percival, a BBC producer, to dramatize archeology for a series of 12 television documentaries. ... Cameramen arrived at the Wiltshire village southwest of London every week to make films. Otherwise the 'Celts' were well insulated from the modern world. ... Kate Rossetti, a Bristol teacher, had a long list of what she missed: 'My family and friends, chocolate, comfy shoes, Bach and Bob Dylan, being

able to zoom up to Scotland'. But she said she does not think she
will ever live in a city again.[36]

This kind of thing is no Arcadian return to nature. Contemporary
Arcadians live in the Santa Cruz mountains. The BBC Celts are more
like breeding zoos—places where images of bygone life can be bred
and recaptured (in this case on film); a convergence of archaeology,
anthropology, and media. It stands between the obvious fakery of a
restored village and the not so obvious fakery of the 1975 agnicayana.
By fake I mean something unable to live on its own, something that
needs a media push or seems out of joint with contemporary life. Of
course theatre is fake, but it celebrates its fakery, while restored
villages slyly try to hide theirs. This sly faking is on the increase.

The BBC Celts are close to the Brahman priests who restored the
agnicayana for Staal–Gardner. For the 1975 agnicayana there were
two audiences: an immediate one of locals, many of whom treated
the ritual as a media event (this happens whenever a film is shot on
location, even outside my window on Sullivan Street in Manhattan);
and an audience of Americans who see *Altar of Fire* mainly as a
documentary of an actual ritual. But ritual with a difference—ritual
for study, for entertainment: a 'specimen'. The inversion is ironic.
The audience in Kerala sees the agnicayana as media; the audience
in America sees the media (version of agnicayana) as ritual. Both
audiences are alienated from the 'pure' agnicayana. But was there
ever a pure agnicayana? Isn't every instance of it $1 \rightarrow 5a \rightarrow 5b$? The
narrator of *Altar of Fire* tells the audience that the performance they
are seeing is probably the last ever of this ritual. This adds a P. T.
Barnum flavour. And at Plimoth nothing (new) is going to happen;
life there is finished. These examples of restored behaviour are very
much like theatre in a theatre: the script is set, the environment is
known, the actors play set roles. But Bharatanatyam and Chhau are
different. These restorations have healed seamlessly into their cultural
surround: they are living arts. As such these dances will change; their
future isn't predictable. Plimoth Plantation either continues as it is
or ceases to be what it is: its very existence is knotted into its specific
historicity. Each production of aesthetic theatre is like Plimoth, but
the theatre as a genre is like Bharatanatyam and Chhau. The simi-
larities and differences among various performance systems are summarized in Figure 5.

One of the big differences among performance systems is the
physical environment—what contains what. In ordinary theatre the

	A	B	C	D
1	**Arts** Theatre, dance, etc.	**Restored arts** Bharatanatyam, Purulia Chhau, etc.		

Between these there is little or no phenomonological distinction making it very hard to tell A1 from B1 without doing historical research — B1 heals seamlessly into A1. Both A1 and B1 have a "life of its own." In both, performers know they're "in a show" and audiences know they're "watching a show."

	A	B	C	D
2	**Media fiction** Regular movies	**Media simulation** Recreated especially for media, as were the BBC Celts	**Media "push"** Without media there would be no event, as the 1975 agnicayana	**Media "there"** Documentaries, news

A move to the right = decreasing dependence on media to make the event, though news items are edited creating a feedback between what "is" news and what media "makes into" news. Also a move to the right = an increase in narration, in suggesting an independent event that needs an observer outside "objectively" explaining it. B2, C2, and D2 merge into one another. Only in A2 is the performer sure he is "in a show" and the spectator sure he is "watching a show." A recent form, "docudrama," combines A2 and D2

	A	B	C	D
3	**Theme parks** Disneyland, Land of Oz, Dogpatch, etc.	**Restored villages made from fantasy and history** Buckskin Joe, Frontierland, Columbia Historic Park, etc.	**Restored villages made from history** Plimoth, Smithville, Louisbourg, etc.	

In A3 everyone knows they are "in a show" as spectator-participants or performers. In B3 and C3 even the performers begin to feel they are "in life." But, paradoxically, B3 and C3 are very close to A1 and B1 where the event begins to have a "life of its own." In A3 most of the machinery — mechanical and human — is hidden from the spectator creating a fictive environment. In B3 and C3 there is an attempt — as at museums — to show as much as possible. But these days even museums are fictionalizing. For example, the Ice Age Art exhibit at the American Museum of Natural History (1978–1979) was made mostly from simulated items.

Fig. 5 Performance systems: a comparative chart.

domain of the spectator, the house, is larger than the domain of the performer, the stage, and distinctly separate from it. In environmental theatre there is a shift in that the spectator and performer often share the same space and sometimes exchange spaces, and sometimes the domain of the performer is larger than that of the spectator, enclosing the spectator within the performance. This tendency is taken even further in restored villages and theme parks, where the visitor enters an environment that swallows him. Every effort is made to transform the spectator into a participant. And while the visitor keeps a consciousness of his own time and place, he simultaneously enjoys a temporary surrender of them. The 1975 agnicayana combines the qualities of film with those of a restored village. There are two frames working: that of the ritual and that of the film being made of the ritual. The Brahman priests are performers of the agnicayana and 'visitors' absorbed into it (Vedic ritual being older and different from Brahman Hindu ritual); the local people watch both the ritual and the filming of it—neither event is familiar. If the priests had been totally absorbed into the agnicayana, they would have insisted on sacrificing the goats, or they would have stopped the performance because in Vedic terms the goat sacrifice is essential. But the priests, too, wanted the film to be made. The priests acted in regard to animal sacrifice not as Vedic priests but as modern Indians. More: they acted as performers in a film with a big stake in seeing that the shooting came off well. Using their authority as priests they devised the substitute effigies as a way of making the film, performing the agnicayana, and not offending the values of modern Kerala Indians. Thus the priests played three roles: Vedic ritualists, Brahman priests arbitrating a living tradition, and film performers. In a way the film performers convinced the Brahman priests that it was OK to tamper with the Vedic tradition. Or, as film performers Brahman priests were asked to play the role of Vedic ritualists. This double, or triple, life is typically that of theatre actors; it is the theatrical brand of truth. And between the frame of the agnicayana and the frame of the filmmaking stood the local audience, enjoying both spectacles.

But is it fair to say that the priests were play-acting? From the perspective of Euro-American conventions, 'acting' means make-believe, illusion, lying. Even Goffman, who has studied acting in ordinary life, identifies it most directly with con men and others who must maintain a 'front' separate from their 'true' selves. This understanding of acting derives from our Platonic view of a hierarchy of realities in which the most real is the most distant from experience and from our Aristotelian view of art, which is an imitation of a reflection. But from the perspective of Indian conventions—and the system of maya/lila underlying them—acting is playful illusion, but so is the world itself, so that in India acting is both false and true. In fact, in Asia the mask is often credited with being closer to the way things are in the world than the face behind the mask can be: acting becomes not a species of lying but a means to the truth. Since Stanislavski at least this has been the ambition of theatre in the West; and it is this ambition—this wish to have art search out and represent truth—that has fired much theatrical experimentation. And driven artists to seek non-Western cultures, Asian especially, ways of making theatre that are not Aristotelian. Brecht, Meyerhold, Grotowski, Artaud, Cage—seminal figures all—used Asian practices as models for their own work.

But back to the priests officiating at the Staal–Gardner agnicayana. I might think they were acting, and Kerala villagers might think they were doing what priests always do—mediating between ordinary and nonordinary experience, both of which need acting. The priests are trained/prepared by birth and education to restore the behaviour of the agnicayana. It is not accurate to call them actors and it is not accurate to not call them actors. They were between 'not actors' and 'not not actors'—a realm of double negativity that precisely describes the process of theatrical characterization, a liminal realm. As for American restored villages, anyone with proper training can demonstrate colonial crafts and speak English in a seventeenth-century Yankee dialect. At the end of the workday, craftspeople and performers take off their costumes, put down their tools, and go home. The visitors assume this divestiture of roles is taking place even if they don't see it with their own eyes. At Plimoth some of the conventions ordinarily followed in an American theatre are dropped. The performers are not on a stage, not rewarded by applause, and don't strictly follow a word-by-word script called a drama. In some of the villages the actors interact with spectators, making the visitor enter into the world of the village, thereby further blurring the seam between the performance and its nonacting surround. The performers at Plimoth are acting, but they may not seem to be acting. In America we say someone is 'only acting' when we detect the seams between the performance and the nonacting surround. We also say someone is acting when he or she is performing on a stage. We say someone is not acting when he or she is doing what one ordinarily would do were there no audience. Documentary film imposes an acting frame around a nonacting situation. But documentaries like Curtis's *In the Land of the Head Hunters* or Flaherty's *Nanook of the North* combine people sometimes going about their ordinary tasks, sometimes restoring behaviours of a recent past, and sometimes acting for pay in fictive situations in an 'on location' set wearing costumes and saying lines written for the occasion.

In some cases, in the restored villages, and from the effect of people like Curtis, matters have grown more complicated. Some performers at restored villages have become permanent residents of the village, live off the income from their crafts, eat the food they have cooked that day in the presence of the visitors. Their 'lived lives' mesh with their 'performed lives' in so strong a way that it feeds back into their performances. Their roles become their 'ordinary life', supplying their restored behaviour with a new source of authenticity. When this happens, the residents of the restored villages can no more comfortably be subsumed under the category of 'play actors' than can the Kerala Brahman priests.

In T. McLuhan's 1974 film, *The Shadow Catcher*, a few of the original participants in Curtis's 1914 *Head Hunters* explain how Curtis's interest in the 'old ways' rekindled their own interest—and led to their restoring some ceremonies previously abandoned. Thus the value frame of the new dominant culture encouraged the enactment as fiction of what was previously performed in fact; while other actions —masked dancing, shamanic healing—were done in fact but before the rolling camera. Later a new cultural whole emerged combining fiction and fact and including performances invented for tourists. Younger Kwakiutls said Curtis's movie helped them learn about the old life, because seeing something 'really being done' is so much more powerful than just hearing about it. But what was 'really being done' even the old-timers didn't do anymore by the time Curtis arrived. Who knows if they ever did it the way he filmed it. Curtis paid performers 50c an hour—$5 when there was danger, like rowing the huge war canoes or hunting sea lions.

Increasingly, American theatre of all kinds is like *Head Hunters* (whose title was changed to *Land of the Long Canoes* because Curtis thought American audiences would find head-hunting repulsive; the movie failed commercially anyway)—combining documentary, fiction, and history: in other words, restored behaviour, $1 \rightarrow 5a \rightarrow 5b$.

From the 1970s into the 1980s experimental theatre has put acting and nonacting side by side, as in the work of Spalding Gray, Leeny Sack, Robert Wilson–Christopher Knowles, and Squat Theatre. In contrast, such strongholds of 'fact' as network news programmes are anchored by people selected for their ability to perform, not to gather or edit news. A suitable aesthetic theory doesn't exist to handle these crossovers and juxtapositions. They are all $1 \rightarrow 5a \rightarrow 5b$.

Taken as a whole, the performances I'm discussing belong to the subjunctive, not the indicative, mood. And the spectators, too, by virtue of their being physically inside the action instead of standing outside looking in, give over to the subjunctive—to behaving 'as if' they were really there in that negotiated space-time-event I call restored behaviour. Negotiated because it takes an agreement among all parties to keep the thing up in the air, moving, alive. The restored village and Curtis's half restoring, half inventing for the sake of his feature film are performances intermediate in type between the Brahman priest restoring an archaic and nowadays unperformed ritual for the benefit of the cameras and Olivier playing Hamlet on the orthodox Euro-American stage. Intermediate also are performances like those of Wilson–Knowles, Gray, and Squat. The most interesting work of the past ten years is intermediate, liminal: work that illuminates its own ambivalence, that is explicitly reflexive, and that is very difficult to categorize. In orthodox theatre the domain of the spectator ('the house') is larger than and separate from the domain of the drama ('the stage'). This framing helps maintain the objectivity and critical/aesthetic distance of the orthodox theatre-goer. But in restored villages, as in environmental theatre, the domain of the performance surrounds and includes the 'spectator'. Looking at becomes harder; being in, easier. There is no house, and spectators are thrown back on their own resources for whatever assurance they need to maintain who/where they are. How to behave, what to do or not to do, are troubling questions in this situation. Although work like Wilson–Knowles's and Gray's does not include the spectator physically, it undermines his psychic distance by presenting nonacting as performance. The same uneasiness results.

VII

The theory explaining all this will come from theatre specialists or from social scientists learned in theatre. Theatre is the art that specializes in the concrete techniques of restoring behaviour. Turner's theory, like Goffman's, is actually a theatrical one generalized to suit social process. Working the same field are Geertz, Rappaport, and Myerhoff. The field is fertile because individual cultures and world monoculture are increasingly theatrical.

Preparing to do theatre includes memorizing a score of gestures, sounds, and movements and/or achieving a mood where apparently 'external' gestures, sounds, and movements 'take over' the performer as in a trance. This basic theatrical process is universal. Whether the performer is in a Broadway musical, an experimental theatre workshop in Soho, a shingeki performance in Tokyo, a Nō drama in Kyoto, the Bolshoi ballet, or the Moscow Art Theatre, a Balinese trance drama, Ramlila in India, the dances of the pig kaiko of Papua–New Guinea, or Yoruba theatre—anywhere—behaviour that is other is transformed into the performer's alienated or objectified parts of his own self—either his private self or his social self—then reintegrated and shown publicly in a total display. The process has two parts and a conclusion; these are strictly analogous to what Van Gennep and Turner describe as the ritual process. First there is the breaking down, where the performer's resistance is overcome, where he is made open and vulnerable, 'ready': then there is the building up, or the filling up, where at first short and then increasingly long and integrated strips of behaviour are added to what the performer can do. At a certain point in the process—a point that differs widely from culture to culture, artistic form to form—a public is required before whom, or in collaboration with, the new behaviour is displayed.

This process has been described from the social perspective by Turner and from the individual-psychological perspective by Winnicott. Turner's key idea is his elaboration of Van Gennep's term, liminality:

> Liminal entities are neither here nor there, they are betwixt and between positions assigned and arrayed by law, custom, convention, and ceremonial. As such, their ambiguous and indeterminate attributes are expressed by a rich variety of symbols in the many societies that ritualize social and cultural transitions.[37]

> The neophyte in liminality must be a *tabula rasa*, a blank slate, on which is inscribed the knowledge and wisdom of the group, in those respects that pertain to the new status.[38]

Theatre is an 'artificial species' of ritual, a hothouse version often created by individuals or temporary groups. Turner calls the arts and some other leisures of modern society 'liminoid', suggesting that they share some of the functions and processes of liminal acts, but that they are also characterized by a voluntariness—a conscious subjunctivity—that is not present in liminal actions. In theatre the performer induces in himself, or has induced for him, replications/restorations of those life-crises most people avoid or undergo only when pressed by necessity. Comedy as well as tragedy deals with difficult, anxiety-ridden crises. The pleasure comes because of the subjunctive mood of the activity, the learned ability to experience an action without suffering its consequences. Hamlet dies, not Olivier. Of course, as I've noted, contemporary theatre skirts or even crosses the boundaries, and some of our recent Hamlets have suffered a real wound or two.

The workshop-rehearsal phase of performing, the 'preperformance', is designed to make the performer a *tabula rasa* with regard to what is going to be performed. The performer is stripped of his everyday identity or learns how to put it aside. Then, once cleansed, the performer brings out of himself, or is inscribed upon, or filled up with, Another, a 'character', or some special aspect of himself, his 'persona'. Workshop-rehearsal passes through three distinct steps that coincide with the ritual process: (1) separation or stripping away, reducing, eliminating, or setting aside 'me'; (2) initiation, or revelation, or finding out what's new—in 'me' or in/from Another, or what's essential and necessary, and (3) reintegration, or building up longer and longer meaningful strips of behaviour; making something for the public—preparing to re-enter the social world but as a new and/or different 'self'. The time spent in these three steps, and the place where this work is done, is liminal. Not the finished performances but this multiphasic process of 'making up' performances are what need to be compared to ritual. Little comparative work of that kind has been done because few anthropologists have participated in, or closely observed, the workshop-rehearsal process.

How do workshop-rehearsals work? There are two basic methods. In the first, actual items of performance are passed on directly from master to neophyte. There is no 'technique' separate from parts of the performance to be learned. I've watched Kakul, the dance guru of Batuan, Bali, as he stood behind a young girl, maybe 8 years old, manipulating her wrists, hands, and shoulders with his hands; her torso with his body; her legs with his knees and feet. He used her as a puppet transferring directly his own body-sense of the dance. She gave her body over to him. Eventually, Kakul says, the dance 'goes into' her body; she learns it in much the same way that spoken language is learned, by being surrounded and immersed in it. She may never know the 'grammar' of her dancing, just as many fine speakers of English never know its grammar. Also this way of training prepares her for trance possession where culturally known beings will go into her body using it in much the way that Kakul used it to train her. In this method of 'direct acquisition' by manipulation, imitation, and repetition there is the paradox that the 'creativity' of the performer comes only after he has mastered a form by rote learning. Kakul, at the end of his career, after he gained a reputation as a great performer, began to improvise and introduce new material; just as a Nō performer who has achieved *hana* (flower) can modify what he has learned from his father. Experimentation which literally means 'going outside the boundaries' is reserved for the most experienced, most respected and often the oldest performers. In Euro-American theatre, experimentation is mostly the work of the young. And this is because the initial phases of workshop-rehearsal are the freest; and it is the youthful performer who is encouraged to 'do something new'.

In the method of direct acquisition there is no reference during training to any generative grammar of performance. Nor do training or exercises stimulate 'creativity' or encourage experimentation or the discovery of new material or patterns. I've watched the *vyas* (director) of the Ramnagar Ramlila employ direct acquisition in teaching the texts and gestures to the teen-age boys who perform the *swarupas* (the gods Rama, Bharata, Lakshmana, and Satrughna). Learning the score 'prepares' the boys to be entered by the gods during moments of the actual performance. The last thing a *vyas* wants of such performers is 'creativity'. The *swarupas* must be receptive, even passive. When the boys are not wearing the crowns that signify the activation of the godhead within them, they are just boys, lectured by the *vyas*, scolded by their mothers. At the same time, however, they are fed a special diet of godly foods: pure milk, sweet rice, fruit, nuts, yoghurt. This diet not only gives them strength but makes them feel like gods. Through the method of direct acquisition two tasks are accomplished simultaneously. Performance texts—I mean not only the words but the whole *mise en scène*—are passed on from generation to generation, and particular performances are made ready for the public. There is no way to separate these tasks, for the texts are both written and oral: the libraries where these texts are kept are the bodies of the performers.

The second method of workshop-rehearsal is to teach a grammar, a set of 'basic exercises' out of which, through transformation, the particular, and often very different, *mise en scènes* will come. Some great texts do not exist as performances but only as words. There is no one way to play *Hamlet*, nor even any 250 ways. There is no continuity of performing *Hamlet* from 1604 to now. Not only were the theatres closed during the Cromwell era, but the Euro-American modern tradition locates continuity in the written text and innovation in the performance. Recent 'violations' of this tradition—for example, my collaging and rearranging classic texts, or the attempt to build in theatre 'performance texts' as is seen in the work of Brecht and Mabou Mines—have had tough going. In the 'learn a basic alphabet/grammar' method students learn how to 'use' their mind-bodies in order to invent the particular gestures that will make up this or that production. A radical separation of written text and performance text has occurred. The written text is preserved separately from any of its performances. A large body of criticism dealing with the written text arises, and this criticism tends to dominate the field. There is also a separation between training and rehearsal. Training is generalized, in the sense that techniques are learned that can be applied to any number of performances. Schools brag that their graduates can act in any number of styles. It would be absurd for a Nō actor to perform modern naturalism. However, Kanze Hideo, a leading Nō actor, has worked with experimental theatre director Tadushi Suzuki, who bases much of his training on Nō (as well as martial arts and kabuki). In the 'alphabet method' an actor pants, not so that he may be able to pant in performance, but in order to strengthen his diaphragm, get in touch with the different ways the voice can resonate, control his breathing so that difficult physical exertions can be accomplished without losing breath, and so on. Or scenes from plays are practised in training not because they will be performed soon or in that way, but so that the student can learn to 'build a character', evoke genuine emotions or effectively feign them on stage, or deal with his fellow actors.

But just as there are intermediate or liminal performance styles, so are there some training methods that occupy a position in between these extremes, combining elements of both. Guru Kedar Nath

Sahoo, master dancer of masked Seraikella Chhau, teaches first a set of sword and shield exercises that will later be transformed into moves used within the dance-drama. These exercises also strengthen the body and familiarize the performers with Chhau's martial roots. And in Kathakali, the dance-drama of Kerala, training begins with a series of massages administered by the guru's feet to the student's whole body. These massages literally erase old body stances and help bring the student's body to a new alignment. The massage period coincides with a series of rigorous exercises that are later used with some variation in the Kathakali itself. Neither in Chhau nor in Kathakali are the exercises used as the basis for invention; they are there to help the student use his body in the necessary way. Thus the exercises can be looked at as part of the 'breaking down' phase of training. They do not help a student grasp the underlying logic of the performance. That can come only after years of experience as the student deciphers for himself what he is doing. Many excellent performers never come to this kind of theoretical knowledge. But some do, and those are the ones most likely to introduce changes.

In the Euro-American method rehearsal is not a matter of transmitting a known performance text but the invention of a new text. This new text is arrived at during rehearsals. It is necessary to teach performers a generative code. In the method of direct acquisition rehearsals consist not in inventing a new performance text but in mastering a known one. But performance itself can be more flexible. Nō drama appears very formal and set. But during performance subtle cues pass between the *shite* (principal actor) and musicians, chorus, and *waki* (second actor). These cues tell the others that the *shite* has decided to repeat a section, or will increase the tempo, or slow it down, and so on. If, however, a performer goes beyond what is given him to vary—if he performs publicly without mask or traditional costume—a storm breaks: is this 'new thing' actually Nō? In the Euro-American method rehearsals are 'explorations' that lead to a 'fixed score' during performance. Only shows advertised as improvisatory change markedly night to night. And most improvised shows are mere rearrangements of fixed routines. But the physical details of shows can vary greatly as long as the written text is recognizable. Shakespeare has been done in period costume, modern dress, eclectic mixed dress. Yet when I staged plays environmentally, and introduced audience participation, journalists publicly demanded, 'Is this theatre?'

During rehearsals of the Euro-American type the grammar of techniques is used to discover and 'keep' items that will later appear in the performance. That which is already known in the direct acquisition method is discovered or invented. Something happens that is 'right', and the director says 'keep that'. What he means is, not to do it again, but to put it ahead in time—to literally throw it forward in the hope that the item of action will be used later, that it will provide a clue as to what the finished *mise en scène* will look like. During rehearsals the shape and feel of the performance being discovered/invented/restored lies in a liminal area between present and future, and between past, present, and future as personal associations from performers and director are added to the scheme. Thus a 1 →5a →5b situation occurs. To the outside observer, the bits of performance being 'thrown forward', being 'kept', may appear haphazard. But sooner or later a pattern emerges as when, through a fog, a coastline is first sensed ('I smell land'), then vaguely discerned as a darkness, then seen as a blurred image, and finally resolved with increasing detail. So too, in this method, depicted in Figure 6, the performance evolves out of rehearsals. As Brecht said, the performance is the least rejected of all the things tried.

Early rehearsals are not only jerky and disjointed; they are laden with anxiety. The actions of the rehearsal have a high information potential but a very low goal orientation. 'What are we doing?' 'What are we looking for?' 'Why are we doing this?' are the common questions. The director doesn't know; he too is hunting. A director may maintain confidence by imposing order in the guise of known

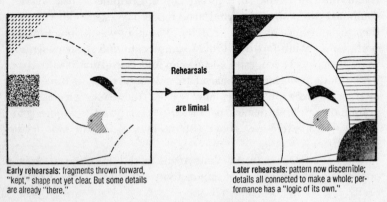

Early rehearsals: fragments thrown forward, "kept," shape not yet clear. But some details are already "there."

Rehearsals are liminal

Later rehearsals: pattern now discernible; details all connected to make a whole; performance has a "logic of its own."

Fig. 6 Rehearsals.

exercises, or he will introduce new basic techniques, expanding the range of the group's generative grammar. But if, by a certain time, a target is not visible (not only a production date but a vision of what's to be produced), if not enough has been thrown forward to provide an outline, a goal, the project falters, then fails. The possibilities for failure are great enough when, as in the case of *Hamlet*, it's a matter of generating a performance text that suits a written one. Where there is no pre-existing text whatsoever—as with much contemporary theatre—the likelihood of failure is still greater.

During the past 50 years, since Artaud at least, the two kinds of workshop-rehearsal process—transmission of whole items by direct acquisition and transmission by means of learning a generative grammar—have been linked. This linkage is, in fact, the great work of experimental theatre in this century. Richard Foreman, for example, transmits to relatively passive performers a complete performance text in a method parallel to that used by the Ramlila *vyases*. Foreman writes his plays, makes a schematic of how they are to be staged, designs the setting, and often is present as chief technician at each performance. And the 'grammatical' methods of Guru Sahoo and the teachers at the Kathakali may be due to extensive contact with European methods. Also techniques such as yoga, martial arts, and mantra chanting, transmitted as whole texts in their cultures of origin, are now used in the West as training of the generative grammar kind. In 1978, at a meeting outside of Warsaw convened by Grotowski, I saw Kanze Hideo put on a Nō mask, crawl on the floor, and improvise actions having nothing to do with classical Nō. And his friend, director Suzuki, in a production of Euripides' *Trojan Women*, combined Nō, kabuki, martial arts, modern Western experimental theatre, and ancient Greek tragedy. The play was as much about post-atomic-bomb Japan as Troy. Examples multiply, bearing witness to exchanges between, especially, Asian and Euro-American theatre. Three kinds of workshop-rehearsal are now occurring: (1) those based on transmitting a total performance text; (2) those based on generative grammars resulting in new performance texts; and (3) those combining 1 and 2. This last is not a sterile hybrid, but the most fertile of the three.

There is another way of looking at the workshop-rehearsal process connecting Turner's ideas of subjunctivity/liminality to Stanislavski's 'as if'.

Figure 7 shows that the deep structure of workshop-rehearsal inverts

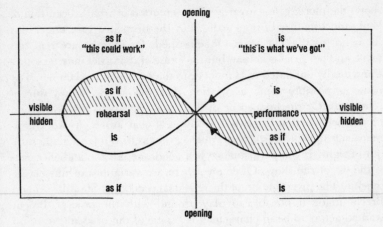

Fig. 7[39] 'As if'.

the deep structure of performance. In workshop-rehearsal real work is being done, work that is serious and problematical. Workshop-rehearsal ironically belongs to the indicative, to the realm of the 'is', but on a deep, hidden level of structure. The visible aspect of workshop-rehearsal, its processual frame, is 'as if', subjunctive, tentative—'let's try that', 'this could work', 'what would happen if?'—play. Techniques of 'as if'—exercises, games, improvisation, therapy—bring up material from within those making the show or from the outside. The work of workshop-rehearsal is to find, reveal, express these deep things, and then to integrate them into a new whole. Even while deep things are 'brought up' the workshop-rehearsal must be kept open—that is, liminal. The 'as if' is a scalpel cutting deep into the actual lives of those making the work. And the most serious crises of performance—the things that can destroy a work most surely—happen during workshop-rehearsals. This is the period during which performers throw tantrums, directors fire persons who disagree, and writers phone their agents in terror. For during this time every small change can have immense consequences on the 'work as a whole'.

The performance is the inverse of the workshop-rehearsal. The show becomes 'real', part of history, when it opens; certain public rituals such as reviewing, attendance by an audience of strangers, an opening night party mark the transition from rehearsal to performance. The frame and visible structure of the performance is an 'is', the finished show, the more or less invariable presentation of what's been found, kept, and organized into a score. But the deep structure under this 'is' is an 'as if'. The tears Ophelia sheds for Hamlet are real salt tears, and her grief is actual, but the cause of that grief may be something totally unrelated to Hamlet or to the actor playing Hamlet. The cause is possibly some association that the actress found during rehearsals. Or the final scene of slaughter appears to be a confusion of violence when in fact it is a precision of near misses. As workshop-rehearsals move towards performance, the 'as if' is intentionally sunk out of sight. If the performance is a good one, all the audience sees is the 'is' of the show. Of course, there are variations of this classic scheme. The investigation of the rehearsal process by Stanislavski and Brecht made it possible to play around with the process. Brecht wanted actors to be in character ('is') some of the time and to stand beside their characters ('as if'), questioning these very characters, at other times. Thus Brecht introduced a part of the rehearsal process into public performances. And since Brecht many others have staged rehearsals. But these breaking of frames occur not only in serious drama, but in circus and Broadway musicals as well. There is a scene in *Sugar Babies* where the star, Mickey Rooney, loses his wig. He laughs, his face turns red, he runs to the edge of the stage and shouts something at the audience; he acknowledges that underneath all the puff roles he plays there is the person, the star, Mickey Rooney. Losing the wig looks accidental, but I have confirmed that it happens in each performance in the same scene. Probably Rooney lost his wig 'for real' during one rehearsal, and this nice piece of business was kept. It helps the audience feel good about paying so much money to see the star; for a brief moment they see him as himself, unmasked. Of course this unmasking is a trick, not an unmasking at all. In the 1980 Ringling Brothers Circus a female performer concluding a stunt on the high bar is unable to pull herself up. The orchestra stops, there is silence in the arena. Slowly, inch by precious inch, she hoists herself up until she is able to reach the bar with her hands and regain a safe position. I saw the circus five times and the same 'accident' occurred each time. Paul Bouissac assured me that such tricks are common, especially in acts that need to look more dangerous than they are. I do not criticize the rehearsedness of these scenes. In my own work, whenever I've tried to have 'open rehearsals' where the public was invited to see a work 'in process', or when during finished performances I've tried to include 'raw elements' such as having the green room visible during *Mother Courage*, I learned how quickly the processual or open nature of workshop-rehearsal is lost. The performers in *Mother Courage* soon found a space out of sight of the audience where they went, making that hidden space the genuine green room; what the audience saw was a make-believe green room. The performers even tried to fool me, knowing that I wanted them to 'be really in the green room' in sight of the audience. It was only when I found ashtrays, costumes, and empty soda cans back where the lights were stored did I know what was going on. I shouldn't have been surprised. The 'as if' wants to submerge when the public is present. Only while working with those they can trust, usually a few comrades who have shared a lot of working together, can performers play 'as if' with 'is' material. When working under the eye of a critical public, the performers present only the 'is' of their 'as if'.

The last part of rehearsal is practice. Longer and more complicated units of restored behaviour are organized into the actual performance. Music, costumes, lighting, make-up accumulate. Each of these is blended in with the intention of making an integrated whole. During this final push gestures are edited so that they send the clearest signals, and practised until they become second nature. Pacing, the relation of the rhythm/tempo of each part to that of the whole, becomes all important. This last phase of rehearsal is comparable to the phase of reintegration in a rite of passage. Strangers to the theatre often think only of this last phase when they hear the word 'rehearsal'. But as I have tried to show, reintegration is only the final part of a long process.

Immediately before going on most performers engage in some ritual. The Nō actor contemplates his mask; Jatra performers in Bengal worship the gods of the performance who manifest themselves in the props assembled on the trunks set up backstage; Stanislavski advised 30 seconds of silent concentration. Warm-ups are universal in experimental theatre. These preparations immediately preceding public performance somehow recapitulate the workshop-rehearsal process and concentrate the performer's attention on the task at hand. It's a little like the moment of prayer or the singing of an anthem before a ballgame or prize fight. But these ceremonies are not holy in the religious sense, even when they include religious ritual. I think, rather, the ritual is a way of focusing the work of workshop-rehearsal and bringing this work across a difficult threshold, limen, that separates rehearsal from public performance. Sometimes these preparatory 'moments' are hours long. Tribesmen in Papua–New Guinea, and performers of Yakshagana, Kathakali, and Ramlila in India, spend up to 4 hours putting on make-up and costumes. I always met with The Performance Group 2 hours or more before a performance to give notes, clean up the space, and do warm-ups. The main function of these preparations—even the putting on of effectively transformative costumes, masks, and make-up—is not merely to make the performer 'look' the role, but to set aside time immediately before the performance for the work of training, workshop, and rehearsal to be awakened and take hold. I've seen Guru Sahoo even without the paraphernalia of Chhau, without mask or costume or music, give great performances. But never without a moment of worship.

The three phases—separation, initiation, and reintegration—apply even to performances without audiences such as Grotowski's paratheatre. Participants in Grotowski's experiments leave the city, travel to remote areas, and there perform actions with and under the supervision of Grotowski's people. These actions vary according to who the participants are and the current interests of the Laboratory Theatre. But the actions always involve discovering and revealing hidden personal themes, finding new ways of behaving, sharing in an I–thou relationship. The physical actions—running through the woods at night, sudden immersion in water, circle dances where fire is passed from dancer to dancer, group chanting, singing, and storytelling—are very like those in initiation rites. Maybe these rites served as a model for Grotowski; maybe he came upon these actions independently. When the participants return home after a few days, or weeks, they say that they can't talk about what happened. This isn't due to any vows of secrecy, but to the conviction that words can't do justice to the experience. 'It changed my life' is a frequent summary. So also at the level of action the experience with Grotowski resembles an initiation rite in which a transformation of self, a change of status, is effected. But ex-Grotowski-ites have been mostly unsuccessful in starting their own theatres or feeding what they've done with Grotowski into their own work. They are disabled rather than invigorated. Grotowski has not worked out, nor have his clients been able to supply, phase three of the rehearsal/ritual process: reintegration. There is no reintegration in Grotowski's paratheatre—no way that the participants can bring it home or do it publicly. Thus participants are left hanging: they have been separated, stripped down, made into *tabulae rasae*; they have had deep experiences, been 'written upon', made new; but they have not been enabled to reintegrate this new self into the social world. Not only does Grotowski's theatre no longer perform publicly, he disavows that his work is religious, and so it does not knit in with any existing system.

The absence of a means of reintegration in Grotowski's paratheatre is related to the intentions of Grotowski's experiments. Theatre has but two stances in relationship to society at large: either to be tightly woven into broader social patterns, as rituals are, or else to serve as an analytical instrument for the dialectical critique of the society which is theatre's backdrop and surround, as Brecht's theatre tried to do. Most theatre people are not conscious of these stances, and their work drifts. But Grotowski is among the most conscious individuals I've ever met, and until recently he has avoided taking either of these stances. That's why his work is intentionally incomplete. His newly proposed 'theatre of sources' will culminate in a 'transcultural village' where masters of performance from different non-Western cultures (a performative theme park/theatre zoo) will meet Grotowski's people and selected individuals from Euro-American culture. It is a move towards integrating his work into larger social patterns. It's also very romantic.

The three-phase process is the basic machine for the restoration of behaviour. It's no accident that this process is the same in theatre as it is in ritual. For the basic function of both theatre and ritual is to restore behaviour—to maintain performances of the $1 \rightarrow 5a \rightarrow 5b$ type. The meaning of individual rituals is secondary to this primary function, which is a kind of collective memory-in/or-action. The first phase breaks down the performer's resistance, makes him a *tabula rasa*. To do this most effectively the performer has to be removed from familiar surroundings; hence the need for separation, for 'sacred' or special space, and for a use of time different from that prevailing in the ordinary. The second phase is one of initiation, of developing new or restoring old behaviour. But so-called new behaviour is really the rearrangement of old behaviour, or the enactment of old behaviour in new settings. In the third phase, reintegration, the restored behaviour is practised until it is second nature. The final moment of the third phase is the public performance. Public performances in Euro-American theatre are repeated until there aren't any more customers; theatre 'productions' are treated as commodities. In most cultures performances occur according to schedules that strictly ration their availability. What we call 'new behaviour', as I said, is only short strips of behaviour rearticulated in novel patterns. Experimental theatre thrives on these rearticulations masquerading as novelties. But the ethological repertory of behaviours, even human behaviours, is limited. In rituals, relatively long strips of behaviour are restored, giving the impression of continuity, stasis, tradition: not only the details but the whole thing is recognizable. In creative arts, especially experimental performance, relatively short strips of behaviour are rearranged and the whole thing looks new. Thus the sense of change we get from experiments may be real at the level of recombination but illusory at the basic structural/processual level. Real change is a very slow evolutionary process.

VIII

D. W. Winnicott's ideas add an ontogenetic level and a new set of categories to my description of what the performer does. Winnicott, a British psychoanalyst (now dead), was interested in the mother–baby relationship, particularly how the baby discovers the difference between 'me' and 'not me'. Winnicott proposed a mind/body state between 'me' and 'not me'. This third, intermediate state is a double negative very like Bateson's description of the 'play frame' in his 'Theory of Play and Fantasy'. It also is analogous to Turner's concept of the liminal. Winnicott writes:

> I am here staking a claim for an intermediate state between a baby's inability and his growing ability to recognize and accept reality. I am therefore studying the substance of *illusion*, that which is allowed to the infant, and which in adult life is inherent in art and religion.[40]

> I think there is use for a term for the root of symbolism in time, a term that describes the infant's journey from the purely subjective to objectivity; and it seems that the transitional object (piece of blanket, etc.) is what we see of this journey of progress toward experiencing.[41]

> The transitional object and transitional phenomena start each individual off with what will always be important to them, i.e. a neutral area of experience which will not be challenged.[42]

> The important part of this concept is that whereas inner psychic reality has a kind of location in the mind or in the belly or in the head or somewhere within the bounds of the individual's per-

sonality, and whereas what is called external reality is located outside these bounds, playing and cultural experience can be given a location if one uses the concepts of the potential space between the mother and the baby.[43]

In babies, and in performers (as adults), the movement from 'not me' to 'not not me' is seen in the following objects and situations:

- a security blanket that a child needs to hold in order to feel good
- favourite toys that can't be replaced
- the script—not just words but the whole pattern of words and actions—that during the rehearsal become 'mine'
- necessary props, even some that the audience doesn't see
- the gestures of a role as the role becomes 'mine'
- anything a person acquires, needs, and can't throw away even though a replacement is available and/or the item is of no 'use'

In each of these cases a process occurs in which something that is 'not me' becomes 'mine' in a bodily, deeply felt, ingested way. The thing or action is more than 'mine'—it is 'me'. Or, as I have put it, it is 'not me . . . not not me'. Thus the liminality that Turner identifies at the heart of the ritual process is also an essential part of individual development: at the heart of each person's most private growing. The process is two-directional: some things stop being 'me' and become 'not me':

- mother's breasts
- something deeply 'mine' that I slowly begin to share but never can give away
- 'my' body as it is caressed by a loved one
- a performance I'm in going stale
- any favourite thing once treasured but now no longer 'right'

This constant movement in the liminal space 'not me . . . not not me' is the matrix of performance. Olivier is not Hamlet, but he's also not not Hamlet; and the reverse is also true: Hamlet is not Olivier but he is also not not Olivier. And over the centuries of its performing Hamlet (both play and character) takes on the qualities of those who have entered this dynamic, precarious, playful relationship with it.

But what is 'it'? It is any of those things and situations I just named: security blankets, toys, favourite places, smells, associations, Hamlet, artworks, lovers, situations that feel 'just right', fantasies, routines, 'rituals' if you will. Hierarchies of all kinds—ontological, social, aesthetic—are dissolved, set aside for the 'time being' so that people can 'make believe'. Thus in theatre we get a very powerful kind of subversion/deconstruction followed by a reconstruction of realities according to new, playful possibilities. Winnicott goes on:

> The essential feature in the concept of transitional objects and phenomena . . . is the paradox, and the acceptance of the paradox: the baby [the performer] creates the object but the object was there waiting to be created [actions in the script]. . . . We will never challenge the baby [the performer] to elicit an answer to the question: did you create that or did you find it?[44]

A restatement in psychoanalytic terms of Turner's notion of liminality (= transitional). Also a version of the old saw about 'willing suspension of disbelief', which can be translated into my double negative as 'not agreeing to not believe'. Winnicott is saying the player playing Hamlet is not to be interrupted in the middle of 'To be or not to be' and asked: Did you think up those words? Nor is Othello to be stopped while smothering Desdemona and interrogated about the authenticity of his passion. Or if the performer is stopped—as Brecht might do, or Pirandello—the audience assumes at once that the interruption is itself part of the script. By script I don't mean just the written play, but the whole score of the performance, including what arrangements have been made to deal with hecklers.[45]

Restored behaviour of all kinds—rituals, theatrical performances, restored villages, agnicayana—is 'transitional behaviour'. Elements that are 'not me' move towards becoming 'me', and parts of 'me' move towards becoming 'not me'. The whole process is framed in the negative, the subjunctive, the 'as if'. This is the peculiar but necessary double negativity that characterizes symbolic action in general. Performance is where this double negativity is most visible because in performing, the performer, the 'me', does not disappear as the performance takes shape. A painting may be hung without doing the same to the painter, but a play needs players to be played. More: a performer experiences his own self not directly but through the medium of performance, of what happened during rehearsals, or under the aegis of tradition, of experiencing the Others. While performing, he no longer has a 'me' but a 'not me . . . not not me'. In this way restored behaviour is simultaneously private and social: the performer moves between denying himself in favour of the social reality of the script and denying the social reality of the script in favour of himself. A person performing recovers his own self only by going out of himself, by entering the social field: the 'space between'. A performance 'takes place' in the 'not me . . . not not me' area 'between' performers; 'between' performers and script; 'between' performers, script, and environment; 'between' performers, script, environment, and spectators. The larger the field of the 'not me . . . not not me', the more powerful the performance. It is the ambition of every performance to expand this field until it includes all beings and things and relations. But this field is precarious. The larger it gets, the more doubt and anxiety are aroused. When everything is going well, the 'between' field, the liminal space, is experienced as the 'ensemble feeling' performers enjoy, the sense of being 'touched' or 'moved' spectators talk about: that special absorption the stage engenders in those who enter on it or come close to it.

By integrating the thought of Winnicott, Bateson, and Turner with my own work as a theatre director, I am proposing a theory that includes the ontogenesis of individuals, the social action of ritual, and the symbolic-fictive action of art. Clearly these overlap. That's because their process is identical. It is the process I've called the 'not me . . . not not me'; the restoration of behaviour; the rehearsal process; the deconstruction-reconstruction of experience through workshop-rehearsal-performance; tradition as expressed in ritual; the play frame; the liminal; the transitional.

The field of performance, the liminal time space, is precarious because it rests not on how things are but on how they are not: that is, it rests on mutuality among participants. It's not that the women in Papua–New Guinea don't know who is behind the masks, but that they agree to proclaim that they don't know. As with Londoners enjoying Olivier, these women do not agree to not believe. Why do I insist on a double negative = a positive instead of a simple positive? Because in the direction of negativity lies potentiality. A choice made denies all choices not made; but a choice not made keeps alive every possibility. Thus a double negative has the existential actuality of a doing while maintaining the full potentiality of the suspended choice. The whole performance is 'not real . . . not not real' at the same time/space. Or, to put it another way, the technical mastery of performing is knowing how to do certain things, achieve levels of skills, pull off tricks. But no matter how phony the show, an audience responds to sincerity, and there is as much sincerity involved in tricking as there is in so-called truth-telling. To perform excellently is to master whatever the craft is: telling the truth, telling lies. This amorality is one of the main things that makes theatre dangerous.

In Figure 8 I have tried to portray this system. This figure is a version of $1 \rightarrow 5a \rightarrow 5b$.

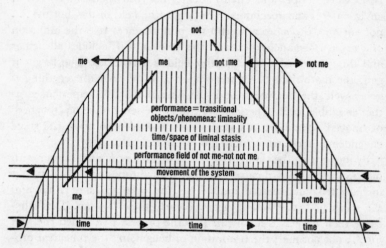

Fig. 8   The me/not me system.

Things, actions, people—whatever is being 'worked on' in the performance (and a shaman will work on different orders of being than a stand-up comic, but the process of their working will, I think, be the same)—move from 'not me' towards 'me' and from 'me' towards 'not me'. This constellation of performative elements passes through the time/space of 'not me . . . not not me'. And in this time/space diachronics are abolished. Actions are thrown forward in time— 'keep that', says the director—to be recovered and used later.[46] A show is assembled out of fragments, rehearsed out of order later to be reintegrated into the order, the 'unity', the audience sees; and many details are repeated over and over again. The French word for rehearsal is *répétition* (repetition), and it's apt. Even where there are no rehearsals in this Western sense—as in Nō drama—the gestures used have been devised over the centuries and practised in the training for years. It's all restored behaviour. Associations from early in life are juxtaposed with spontaneous interactions happening in the here and now of workshop-rehearsals. Or, as in Nō drama and many rituals, in the here and now of performance. The system as a whole moves against the flow of ordinary time. That is, the completed total system is always coming at you from the 'future', where you meet things earlier thrown ahead. During performance, if everything is going well, the experience is of synchronicity, of flow, as ordinary time and performance time eclipse each other.[47] And, as in a solar eclipse, a scintillating corona is briefly visible: a radiance splashing out from the dark core of double negativity. This eclipse/corona is the 'present moment', the 'eternal present', the reactualized *illud tempus*,[48] the ecstasy of trance, liminal stasis, the balancing act of shamans.[49] Great performers are very special because they keep their balance in the presence of onlookers. Not for long.[50]

IX

The theatre of Richard Foreman exemplifies this 'liminal-transitional' process. Much in Foreman's work is interesting, but I'll attend to only one thing: the overall arrangement of space and Foreman's place in it. From 1971 to 1979 he wrote, directed, and designed his own productions in his own theatre—a loft about 100 feet deep and 25 feet wide—on lower Broadway. In terms of control Foreman's work belongs more to painting than to theatre: his struggle is with his material, including people, but not against cocreators who might mess up his vision. The audience of seventy-five sat on steeply rising bleachers facing the long narrow stage area reaching back more than 60 feet. Sometimes this whole tunnel was open to view, and sometimes flats broke or shortened the space (see Figure 9).

Foreman himself was located between the performers and the spectators. To the spectators he was a performer, and to the performers he was a spectator. He was 'not a performer . . . not not a performer', 'not a spectator . . . not not a spectator'. Foreman manipulated all the sound, scenic, and light cues himself, and his voice is the one heard on tape giving directions to the performers and making comments on the action. Foreman not only supervised the performance but indirectly entered it. Yet his position is peculiar and precarious. He was 'in transition' and 'liminal' relative to his own work. His actual presence was made ambivalent by his mediated presence as tape-recording, script, director, technician, and designer. In one of his productions he began to resolve this ambivalence by pointing it up. A Sword of Damocles descended from the ceiling and

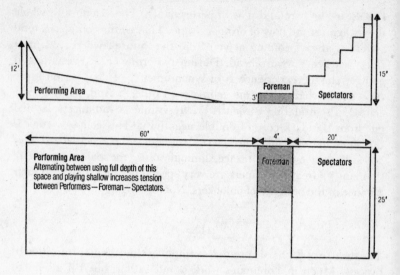

Fig. 9   Performing area in relation to spectators.

hung inches above his balding skull, at once pointing him out to all in the room and threatening him. In the next production he got up from his seat and entered the stage briefly. Shortly thereafter, he sold his theatre.

X

What about Staal and Gardner? They entered Kerala as theatrical producers-directors in the guise of anthropological researchers. Not finding a ritual worthy of being filmed, they arranged for one to be performed. They made sure there was enough lead time to get money to make the film and to import a bevy of important scholars. Their lie, if there is one, comes with the marketing of *Altar of Fire* as a document of an ancient ritual they just happened upon. In the nick of time, too. The film's audience may construe agnicayana as a 'living ritual' when in fact it's a complicated kind of play-acting. But I think I've shown how play-acting itself is a living ritual, though one made reflexive through the use of rehearsals. *Altar of Fire* is not a film of Vedic ritual. The filming itself ritualizes the action of restaging/ restoring the agnicayana. Too bad Staal–Gardner didn't include a reflexive consciousness of this—or at least issue two films, one of the ritual 'in itself' and one of their making of the film about it, a kind of Truffautian film of them filming *Altar of Fire*. The same twist is at the heart of restored villages. They aren't a return to earlier centuries but our own epoch's way of ritualizing our daily lives. And like all rituals a visit to a restored village gives one a sense of tradition, of significance, of continuity. And the ritual includes, of course, packing the family into the car and driving off to the village.

Maybe even today most anthropologists would agree with Turner, who said of his own stay with the Ndembu, 'We never asked for a ritual to be performed solely for our own anthropological benefit; we held no brief for such artificial play-acting.'[51] There are two responses to Turner. First, I think the presence of the field worker is an invitation to play-acting. People want their pictures taken, want books written about them, want to show how they are and what they do. Second, what does he propose relative to traditions that are near extinction? Ought we not recognize that in many societies patronage itself has been traditional and has guaranteed the continuation not only of aesthetic but also of ritual forms? How ought we respond to the dooming of many varieties of ritual theatre by modernization? In Karnataka, South India, not too many miles from where Staal–Gardner filmed, Martha Ashton was studying Yakshagana, a form of dance-drama hardly ever done according to the old ways. Ashton got a company together drawing on several different groups. She hired actors, singers, musicians. She assisted them in recollecting the old stories: in reconstructing the old steps, music, and training. And she filmed the results of their mutual labours. Was she wrong in doing this? Today there are three styles of Yakshagana: the popular version, a style for modern audiences developed by K. S. Karanth, a well-known writer, and the 'classical Yakshagana' reassembled by Ashton's troupe. This last style was the one to tour America. Was it the most or the least Indian?

The position of the purists who won't stage the rituals they are studying and recording is not pure but ambivalent. Their position is analogous to that of Foreman, who, in his theatrical productions, sits between his players and his audience, often running a tape recorder that broadcasts his own voice interpreting and asking questions and giving instructions. To the society the field worker temporarily inhabits he represents his own culture in one of its most inexplicable aspects: why send somebody around the world to observe and record how people live? Why ask all those questions? Why make movies, record songs? What does it mean to embody the contradictory action of a 'participant observer'? But to those who read—or see and hear—the reports of the field worker, he is our big link with both fresh aspects of human nature and the often proposed but never proven thesis that humans comprise one species culturally as well as biologically. As more and more field reports accrue, the exotic annals of human behaviour look less and less exotic: we can detect structural affinities, universal patterns and processes. These are nowhere more apparent than in the arts, which seem to be of a piece from the earliest cave paintings to present-day performances.

The script of the field worker demands a pretended distance, a studied absence: to be present but invisible. Everything is supposed to be as it would if the field worker weren't there. Of course this is a gross fiction, a theatrical convention. The field worker is like the aristocrat preening on the Restoration stage: everyone watches his slightest move, but he's not part of the story. Yes, the field worker's circumstances are theatrical. He exists in a liminal state, a situation in transition. He is not a performer and certainly not a spectator. He's in the middle, like Foreman, between two spheres of actuality, two societies. To each society he represents the other; in each society he is a 'not me . . . not not me'. Foreman put himself precisely where these two actualities press against each other. How can the field worker position himself?

The field worker, like the theatre director, like performers in workshop-rehearsals, goes through the three-phase process Van Gennep mapped out as the preliminal rites of separation, the liminal rites of transition, and the postliminal rites of incorporation.[52] My restatement of this process as it applies to the field worker is:

1 The stripping away of his own culture-habits—a brutal *separation* that is the deepest struggle of fieldwork, which is never completed, learning 'to see with a native eye'. The field worker always lives 'in between'. So does the director who is part of the audience to the performers and part of the performers to the audience.

2 The finding out of what's 'new' in the society he is temporarily a part of, or 'partner of'. This is the field worker's *transition*: his new role, identity, position, status in regard to his adoptive culture. The theatre director works in a similar way to understand and then draw from the performer's 'material'.

3 The task of using field-notes, or whatever, to compose an ac-

Top. Shite performing with mask in Noh drama. Behind are the musicians and the painted ne tree.

Bottom. Village training for Purulia Chhau.

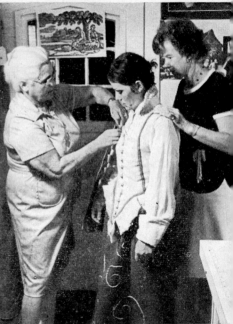

23 TOP LEFT. From *Altar of Fire* : Priests recite mantras over a bundle of some stalks. Photo
Adelaide de Menil.

24 TOP RIGHT. A player getting outfitted in a costume at Plimoth Plantation, a restored villa
Photo by courtesy of Plimoth Plantation.

25 BOTTOM. From *Altar of Fire* : At the end of the ritual—and as the climax—of the film t
ritual enclosures are burnt. After the fire only the eagleshaped altar remains. Photo by Adelai
de Menil.

6 Top. Sheep and townsfolk at Plimoth Plantation. Photo by courtesy of Plimoth Plantation.

7 Bottom. Mudmen of Asaro, Papua-New Guinea. Photo by Joan Macintosh.

28 Top. Richard Foreman's *Une semaine sons l'influence de*, Paris production in 1973. No▮ Foreman's head as he manipulates the control panel in full view of the audience.

29 Bottom. Richard Foreman's *Pandering to the Masses*, produced in New York in 1975. No▮ the great depth of the stage—its tunnel effect. Photo by Babette Mangolte.

ceptable monograph, film, whatever: something that's 'true to' both his adopted people and his home culture. The director must find a way to make a production 'work'. If successful, the field worker becomes a professor, the director is given new works to direct: their *incorporation* is completed.

The field worker is no novelist freely transforming his own actual or fantasy experiences; nor is he a 'hard scientist' building models strictly fenced off from ordinary life.

More and more—especially as films, photographs, and tape cassettes become his tools—the field worker is like the theatre director— the evoker-observer who participates and keeps a distance at the same time; the collector of items to be 'thrown forward' in time and made into a unified construct that 'comes after' but is not necessarily 'true to' its sources: a restorer of behaviour. The field worker, like the director, is present at the mid-phase of making a production but apparently absent at its inception (script making) and conclusion (performance for a public); he does not author the script but somehow guarantees its realization before an audience. The field worker doesn't create the societies he studies, but his presence gives these cultures a special significance, a reverberation felt both among those he studies and back home where his productions find their niche. The field worker, like the director, is the embodiment of linkage, the essence of in between.

Now theatre directors are leaving the shadowy area out of sight off stage. They are entering the stage, as Foreman did, as Tadeusz Kantor, the director of *The Dead Class*, does when all during the show he talks to, manipulates, and coaches the performers: the play is set, rehearsed, but also taking new shapes right before our noses. This doesn't make the director a performer just like the others, just as the field worker isn't a hard scientist or novelist, but a special kind of performer, a master of liminality, a specialist in reflexivity. He is always working the $1 \rightarrow 5_a \rightarrow 5_b$, the 'not me . . . not not me'. Field workers and theatre directors are restorers of behaviour. The time is on us when field workers, like directors, produce for us not only versions of faraway cultures but performative works of our own multiple actualities. In an epoch of hyperconsciousness we are concerned with knowing how we know what we know: restoration of behaviour is the industry of the future. Theatre workers, field workers: we are one with the clowns and jugglers, the double agents and dissimulators, the con men and shamans.

Earlier versions of some parts of this article have appeared in *A Crack in the Mirror: Reflexive Perspectives in Anthropology*, ed. Jay Ruby (University of Pennsylvania Press, 1981).

1. Labanotation, roughly analogous to musical notation, was developed by Rudolf von Laban in 1928. According to an article in *New York Times* (6 May 1979: 'Arts and Leisure', p. 19) by Jack Anderson: 'The system records dance movement by means of symbols on a page that is read from the bottom up. Three basic vertical lines represent the body's centre, right, and left sides. Where the symbols are placed on the lines indicates the direction of the movement, and their length indicates the movement's duration.'

2. Suzanne Youngerman, 'The Translation of a Culture into Choreography', in *Essays in Dance Research*, ed. Dianne L. Woodruff (Dance Research Annual IX, N.Y.: CORD, 1978), p. 95.

3. Edward Deming Andrews, 'The Dance in Shaker Ritual', in *Chronicles of American Dance*, ed. P. D. Magriel (N.Y.: Henry Holt, 1948); *The People Called Shakers* (N.Y.: Dover, 1963); *The Gift to be Simple: Songs, Dances and Rituals of the American Shakers* (N.Y.: Dover, 1967). Andrews had done more research than anyone on the Shaker rituals.

4. Robin Evanchuk, 'Problems in Reconstructing a Shaker Religious Dance Ritual', in *Journal of the Association of Graduate Dance Ethnologists*, 1: Fall–Winter (Los Angeles: UCLA, 1977–78), p. 22.

5. Youngerman, op. cit. p. 106.

6. For my ideas about performances that 'actualize'—and therefore a sense of what I felt eleven years ago about this whole problem—see Schechner, 'Drama, Script, Theatre, and Performance'; and 'Actuals: A Look into Performance Theory', in *Essays on Performance Theory 1970–76* (N.Y.: Drama Book Specialists, 1977).

7. All Emigh citations from a letter he distributed to a few persons concerning his 1975 work in West Irian. Emigh was trying to establish connections relating Balinese performance to West Irian, and other Micronesian performance styles. Most of Emigh's stuff has not yet been published, but I think he is on to establishing a stratum of performance including masks, dance styles, and relationship to sacred geography that was/is present across vast areas of the Pacific. W. H. Rassers, *Panji, The Culture Hero* (The Hague: Martinus Nijhoff, 1959), has shown a definite relationship between Balinese shadow puppetry and Sepik River ceremonies. In performance people tend to be technologically conservative, always maintaining to a degree the ideas that Grotowski gathered under the banner of 'poor theatre'. This keeping out of old ideas of how to do things also preserves, almost in archaeological layers, old belief systems and behaviours too. These are constantly being worn away and then restored.

8. Frits Staal, 'The Meaninglessness of Ritual' (manuscript, 1978). Staal bases much of his argument on the 1975 agnicayana.

9. The shooting script I got when I was in Kerala in 1976. The script gives detailed instructions to camera people, technicians, etc. It also provides drawings of the site, altars, and background material.

10. Robert A. Paul, 'Review of *Altar of Fire*', in *American Anthropologist*, 80 (1978),

pp. 197–9. Frits Staal, 'Response to Robert A. Paul', in *American Anthropologist*, 81 (1979), pp. 346–7.

11. Alan Lomax, 'Cinema, Science, and Cultural Renewal', in *Current Anthropology*, 14:4 (1973), p. 480.

12. Kapila Vatsyayan, *Indian Classical Dance* (New Delhi: Publications Division, 1974), pp. 15–16.

13. Kapila Vatsyayan, *Classical Indian Dance in Literature and the Arts* (New Delhi: Sangeet Natak Akademi, 1968), pp. 325, 365. Vatsyayan's opinion is universally shared by other dance scholars in India.

14. Milton Singer, *When a Great Tradition Modernizes* (London: Pall Mall Press, 1972), p. 172.

15. Asutosh Bhattacharya, *Chhau Dance of Purulia* (Calcutta: Rabindra Bharati University Press, 1972), p. 15.

16. Ibid. p. 23.

17. Ibid. p. 24.

18. Ibid. Introduction.

19. Bhattacharya, 1975 programme used on 22 February, University of Michigan, p. 3.

20. Until John Emigh told me about Mead's account I thought *Trance and Dance* wholly 'authentic'. It proves how easily I can fall into the very trap I'm warning others against. To many American students *Trance and Dance* is the most powerful example of what Balinese trance 'really is'.

21. Maurice J. Moran, Jr., 'Living Museums: Coney Islands of the Mind' (Master's thesis, New York University School of Arts, Department of Drama (now Performance Studies), 1978), p. 25.

22. Ibid. p. 31.

23. Ibid. p. 36.

24. Ibid. pp. 40–1.

25. Ibid. p. 50.

26. Ibid. p. 51.

27. From a three-page mimeograph information paper dated '2/80', sent to me by Ingram, pp. 1–2.

28. From a letter sent by Ingram to Jay Ruby, dated 30 April 1981.

29. From a newspaper article by Tim Miller describing how roles are cast and prepared, in *The Old Colony Memorial* (Plymouth, Massachusetts, 2 April 1981).

30. The repartee between centuries is sometimes seasoned with nice ironies. A visitor at Plimoth apologized for interrupting a craftsperson with questions. 'As many as you like, sir', the performer responded. 'I have a few questions meself about your time period'. For more on restored villages, theme parks, and related entertainment-performance environments see Irwin Haas, *America's Historic Villages and Restorations* (Secaucus: Citadel Press, 1974); Gary Kriazi, *The Great American Amusement Park* (Secaucus: Citadel Press, 1976); and Patricia Mackay, 'Theme Parks', in *Theatre Crafts*, September 1977, pp. 27ff. And James H. Bierman, Department of Theatre Arts, University of California, Santa Cruz, has lots of stuff on the Disney enterprises.

31. Mimeo paper dated 2/80, p. 2.

32. Ingram letter, 1981.

33. See note 29 (Miller).

34. Mimeo paper dated 2/80, p. 3.

35. From a newspaper article by Tom Reilly in the *Sippican Sentinel* (Marion, Massachusetts, 29 April 1981).

36. New York *Times* (Sunday, 5 March 1978).

37. Victor Turner, *The Ritual Process* (Chicago: Aldine, 1969), p. 95.

38. Ibid. p. 103.

39. I use this same figure in another essay where I consider the relationship between 'social drama' and 'aesthetic drama'. There theatrical techniques are the hidden, implicit underbelly of social and political action—the dramatic ordering of events; and conversely, social and political action underlie theatrical works. Thus it is not proper to speak as Aristotle did of 'art imitating life'. But neither is it true that 'all the world's a stage'. Together these statements make up the poles of a dialectical, dynamic process by which artistic action creates possibilities for living and events in ordinary life provide material and models for art. The whole bundle must be looked at as a single system. See my *Essays on Performance Theory 1970–76* (N.Y.: Drama Book Specialists, 1977) for a discussion of the relationship between social and aesthetic drama. The visual pun with infinity was not at first intended when I drew the figure. Later, becoming aware of it, I was not unpleased.

40. W. D. Winnicott, *Playing and Reality* (London: Tavistock, 1971), p. 3.

41. Ibid. p. 6.

42. Ibid. p. 12.

43. Ibid. p. 53.

44. Ibid. p. 89. I thank Cynthia Mintz for pointing out to me the importance of this paradox and how it applies to performing.

45. In 'Drama, Script, Theatre, and Performance', I discuss in detail the relationship among these various magnitudes and dimensions of performance.

46. I discuss the rehearsal process—and compare it to the ritual process as described by Birdwhistel and Lorenz, in 'Towards a Poetics of Performance'.

47. For a detailed discussion of flow, and reports on how it feels to experience flow, see Mihaly Csikszentmihalyi, *Beyond Boredom and Anxiety* (San Francisco: Jossey Bass, 1975). As he says: 'Perhaps the clearest sign of flow is the merging of action and awareness. A person in the flow has no dualistic perspective: he is aware of his actions but not of the awareness itself. . . . Typically, a person can maintain a merged awareness with his or her actions for only short periods' (p. 38).

48. I use the Latin in Mircea Eliade's sense when the mythic or original time is 'reactualized' and made present for the 'time being' of the performance. Among Eliade's many books see especially *Rites and Symbols of Initiation* (N.Y.: Harper, 1965), and *Shamanism: Archaic Techniques of Ecstasy* (Princeton: Princeton University Press, 1970).

49. Barbara Myerhoff, 'Balancing Between Worlds: The Shaman's Calling', in *Parabola*, 1:2 (1976), pp. 6–13.

50. Except for some: At Kumbh mela in Prayag I saw a man who claimed to have stood on one leg for eighteen years. 'The greatest mela of all is the Kumbh mela at Prayag', writes Ved Mehta. This is so because at Prayag (modern Allahabad) the mela takes place at the *sangam* (Sanskrit 'joining'), the place where the sacred river Jamuna meets the sacred river Ganga. There these

rivers are joined by the mythical underground river Saraswati. Kumbh mela at Prayag happens during the dry season, in January, and the rivers are low. A vast city of tents is pitched on the dry river bed. And in 1977, when I was there, between dawn and noon on the most sacred day, some 3 million people bathed from a triangle of sand no larger than a New York City block like the triangle formed at Broadway and 42nd Street, Times Square. Assembled that January, as for every Kumbh mela, were mystics, fakirs, avatars, sadhus, pilgrims, tourists, scholars, performers, merchants, beggars—seekers of every kind. The man standing on one leg was a big draw. Crowds pressed in to see him, his face painted in white and red, his right eye bulging, his whole upper torso twisted to the right, his head askew and looking up over his right shoulder. He supported himself with a staff and leaned against a board. His left leg was tucked behind him, bound to his thigh with cloth. His right leg, from the knee down, and right foot were swollen enormously, the blood and other fluids having drained down to there. The admiring crowd pressed in on him with gazes, small change, and many advanced to offer sweets at his elephant's leg or fed some directly to him as the Hindu gods are offered *prasad*. He talked in a rough voice, coarse and loud, laughed and enjoyed himself. Also he seemed to be in pain. I asked one of his companions-guardians-keepers how he slept, defecated, did the ordinary things of life. 'This way, the way you see him, always, day and night, for so many years, the same.'

51. But now, more than a quarter of a century later, and deep into the practice of what he calls the 'anthropology of experience', Turner himself is helping American students stage some of the rituals he and his wife, Edith Turner, observed among the Ndembu. See Turner, 'Dramatic Ritual/Ritual Drama: Performative and Reflexive Anthropology', in *Kenyon Review*, 1:3 (1979), pp. 80–93.

52. Van Gennep originally published his ideas about liminality in 1908. Particularly through the work of Turner these ideas are still very alive and developing. See Van Gennep, *The Rites of Passage* (Chicago: University of Chicago Press, 1960). Also Turner, *The Ritual Process* (Chicago: Aldine, 1969); *The Ritual Process: Dramas, Fields, and Metaphors* (Ithaca; Cornell University Press, 1974); 'Dramatic Ritual/Ritual Drama: Performative and Reflexive Anthropology', in *Kenyon Review*, 1:3 (1979), pp. 80–93; and forthcoming *From Ritual to Theatre* (working title, N.Y.: Performing Arts Journal Publications).

7

Ramlila of Ramnagar:
An Introduction[1]

Texts, Oppositions, and the Ganga River

The subject of Ramlila, even Ramnagar Ramlila alone, is vast. I
think of the story of Krishna's mouth. I have seen this story danced
in Bharatanatyam. Krishna's mother fears that the little boy has put
some dirt, something dangerous, in his mouth. She asks him to open
his mouth. He refuses. She asks again and again, and finally he opens
his mouth and she looks in. There, in amazement, bewilderment,
even terror, she sees all the worlds. Contained in her baby's mouth is
the unspeakable unmanifest Absolute. Revealed, Krishna closes his
mouth, and with it his mother's memory of what she has experienced.
The dance ends with mother and baby united once more simply as
mother and baby. It is, approximately, something like this with
Ramlila. I look into its mouth and see there all there is to be seen:
but I cannot remember it. And I am not so certain, even though I am
an American, a rationalist, a Jew (talmudic: given to inquiries of all
kinds), that I ought to remember what I have seen.

Vast, I said, is Ramlila. It touches on several texts: *Ramayana* of
Valmiki, never uttered, but present all the same in the very fibre of
Rama's story; Tulsidas' *Ramcaritmanas*, chanted in its entirety from
before the start of the performance of Ramlila to its end. I mean
that the Ramayanis spend ten days before the first *lila* up on the
covered roof of the small 'tiring house–green room next to the square
where on the twenty-ninth day of the performance Bharata Milap
will take place; there on that roof the Ramayanis chant the start of
the *Ramcaritmanas*, from its first word till the granting of Ravana's
boon: 'Hear me, Lord of the world [Brahma]. I would die at the
hand of none save man or monkey.' Shades of Macbeth's meeting
with the witches: 'For none of woman born shall harm Macbeth.'
Ravana, like Macbeth, is too proud.

Nothing of this until the granting of Ravana's boon is heard by
the Maharaja of Benares, or by the faithful daily audience called
nemis, nor by the hundreds of sadhus who stream into Ramnagar for

Ramlila summoned by Rama and by the Maharaja's generosity in offering sadhus dharamsalas for rest and rations for the belly. The 'sadhu rations' are by far the largest single expense in the Ramnagar Ramlila budget—Rs 18,000 in 1976. Only the Ramayanis hear the start of the *Ramcaritmanas*—they and scholars whose job it is to 'do and hear and see everything'. But this, we soon discovered, is impossible: too many things happen simultaneously, scattered out across Ramnagar. While Rama is in Citrakut Bharata sits at Nandigram; when the army of monkeys and bears move towards Rameswaram already Sita, with a band of devoted female spectators, awaits them in the *Asoka* Garden of Lanka; when Lakshmana is wounded by Meghnada's *sakti*, and Rama pitifully mourns his fallen brother, Hanuman is more than a mile away chasing after the herb that will revive Lakshmana. And even when the story itself is over, and Rama coronated, his lesson preached in the marble gazebo of Rambagh, his crown removed for the last time back in the dharamsala near Ayodhya, and the five boys who are the *swarupas* returned to ordinary life, the masks—some of papier mâché, some fashioned from copper and brass—put away for a year, the Ramayanis continue to chant until every last syllable of Tulsidas' text is sounded.

But there is more to the Ramlila texts than the *Ramcaritmanas*. Tulsi's masterpiece is the generating kernel of the performance, but like a tree springing from a great tap root, the branches are spread far and wide. There are the *samvads*, dialogues actually spoken during the 30 or 31 nights (depending on the lunar calendar) of the performance. These *samvads* were assembled and written during the nineteenth century. They are intended to translate the feelings—the *bhavas* and *rasas*, if you will—of the *Ramcaritmanas* into a spoken language that ordinary people can understand. Thus Rama's story is twice told, at least. For each segment of narrative the chant of the Ramayanis alternates with the dialogues of the characters speaking *samvads*. And if the Maharaja is the principal audience for the *Ramcaritmanas*—the 12 Ramayanis always sit close to him—the sadhus and others especially devoted to Rama crowd up near the *swarupas* (who speak most of the *samvads*). In between are vast numbers of spectators —literally people who see more than hear, as the story is acted out. Thus there are three main texts: *Ramcaritmanas*, *samvads*, spectacle.

Consider: the Ramayanis sit in a tightly closed circle, their leader concentrating on the palm-leaf manuscript on which Tulsi's text is written. This text is illuminated at night by burning torches. Far away from the Ramayanis, lit by petromax lantern, and sometimes by blazing flares, are the characters of the Ramlila who utter the *samvads*. There are many such characters, such as Rama, Ravana, Lakshmana, Sita, Hanuman, Angada, Guha, Narada, Bharata, Dasaratha, Sugriva, Siva, Brahma, Indra, Manthara, Kaikeyi, Parasurama, Vasistha, Sumantra, Janaka, Vibhishana. I list them this way, and not according to their ritual importance—the five *swarupas* first—because in Ramlila these gods-characters-beings present themselves to me simultaneously as actors, as performers of a story, as physical theatrical presences. I am not alone in considering them thus. I spoke to a man in the crowd of spectators:

> Everything there [at Ramnagar Ramlila] has a naturality. If they say '*asoka* tree' they have an *asoka* tree, if they say 'jungle' they go to a jungle, if they say 'Ayodhya' they show Ayodhya. Other Ramlilas, it is more drama. There are fancy clothes and loudspeakers and electric lights. Here the Maharaja preserves the spiritual side. He makes certain everything is done right.

So there is, in addition to the literary texts, the performance text: the actual *mise-en-scène*: that which the Maharaja, as *über*-director—the overseer of everything, the director of the *vyases* who do the day-to-day directing and who can always be seen standing onstage, *regiebuchs* in hand, whispering the dialogue into the ears of the role-players, making certain that each *samvad* is correctly spoken, giving signals to the leader of the Ramayanis so that the alternation between *samvads* and *Ramcaritmanas* is correct. Behind this intricate staging is the Maharaja. The performance text he preserves is a nineteenth century one.

Actually, the *mise-en-scène*, and the Ramlila environments—the actual settings for Ayodhya, Janakpur, Citrakut, Pancavati, Lanka, and Rambagh—were mostly constructed in the mid-nineteenth century, when Ramnagar Ramlila most probably originated. Some parts of the environment—the pathways through the back parts of Ramnagar, the countryside setting of Nishada's ashram, the great Durga tank and temple which serve as *kshir sagar*, Rambagh itself (which was once a Maharaja's pleasure garden), the Maharaja's many-chambered Fort (or palace) up against the flowing Ganga: these all pre-exist Ramnagar Ramlila, and have been absorbed into it totally—as Rambagh has, now no longer in use except as a staging place for Ramlila, and as a temporary living quarters for the *swarupas* during some of the Ramlila, and, importantly, as the scene-and-technical shop where Atmaram, a man in the Maharaja's employ for many years, constructs the effigies and props for the entire spectacle. Some environments, like the Durga tank and temple, maintain their own very powerful existence, and merely lend themselves to Ramlila once a year—in much the same way that Siva comes to worship Rama during this season. For Benares is a Saivite city, and the Maharaja is greeted by the crowd with approving chants of 'Hara, Hara, Mahadev!' But Kasi is, as I was told on many occasions, an island of Siva in a sea of Rama. Nowhere, and at no time, is this more clear than during Ramlila season. The most ecstatic crowds, if not the largest, come twice during the month-long performance, when Rama himself performs the *puja* to the Siva *lingam*: once after crossing the make-believe Ganga during his first day of exile; and once the day after Dusserah at make-believe Rameswaram.

I am still talking about the layering of texts: literary and performance texts. Each of these texts may be 'read' independently of the others. They each yield a part of what is in Krishna's mouth.

There is, too, the text of movement. For Ramlila is a performance of movements: pilgrimage, exile, circumambulation, pursuit, kidnapping and running away, processions. All this movement—movement in the story, actual movement through the environments of Ramlila, movement to get to Ramnagar from Varanasi, and back, by crossing the great Ganga—is balanced by the stasis of *arati* at the end of each day's performance. *Arati*, where the *swarupas* freeze and become pure *murtis*: the images of what they are, pictures of action suspended in time, taken out of time, stopped. Thus also a text of complementary oppositions, of which there are many in Ramnagar Ramlila.

Let me name a few as they operate both conceptually and spatially, in both the narrative and the environments of Ramlila. These oppositions are more comprehensible if I summarize them in a chart.

Maharaja and Ramayanis: Siva	vs	Rama, Sita, and other *swarupas* and sadhus: Visnu
Tulsidas, Valmiki, and the Great Tradition	vs	*Samvads, bhajans*, and the Little Traditions[2]
West bank of Ganga, the Varanasi side	vs	East bank of Ganga, the Ramnagar side
Stillness: *murtis, arati,* 'stations'[3]		Movement: processions, pilgrimage, exile, flow

Town space	vs	Theatre space
Present historical time	vs	Time of Ramlila narrative
Mela	vs	*Lila*

These oppositions—and there are more—are not mutually exclusive, or hostile to one another. They complement each other, constructing among themselves a vision of the world that is whole. For example, the Maharaja exists in the field of energy created by Rama; and Rama exists as arranged for by the Maharaja. Not any Rama, but the Rama of Ramnagar Ramlila—a Rama who has auditioned for the Maharaja, who will be paid (a token sum) after the month of performing is over. For his part, the Maharaja is in a way a fictional character. There is no kingdom in secular modern India over which Vibhuti Narain Singh actually rules (as his predecessors and he, himself, until Independence, actually ruled). His existence as Maharaja is confirmed by his function as sponsor-producer of Ramlila. For the month of Ramraj is when the Maharaja of Benares is most visibly and demonstrably a king. It is during this month, more than at any other time, that he rides on his elephant, or in his 1926 Cadillac, is accompanied by troops and a military marching band; that he shows himself again and again as a king to assembled thousands who chant, when they catch sight of him, 'Hara, Hara, Mahadev!'—an homage to the king of the city of Siva that corresponds neatly to the homage this Saivite king gives to Rama, Visnu incarnate. Thus it is that a mediation occurs between Siva and Visnu, between the west bank where Varanasi is and the east bank where Ramnagar is.

Nowhere is this mediating dynamic more clearly operating than in crossing the Ganga herself. The Ganga is no ordinary river; her waters are holy. And to the thousands who cross the Ganga each day to attend Ramlila some special dharma is achieved. That the Maharaja's Fort, or palace, is across the river is a result of the way the British occupied the country in the eighteenth century. But this aspect of military strategy has had more than military consequences: I am of no doubt that Ramnagar Ramlila has gained in importance because it is just near enough to Varanasi to gather audiences from there, and far enough to require crossing the Ganga. A very special balance and tension is thus obtained. So, too, the sharp bend in the Ganga's flow, making it stream from south to north as it passes Varanasi, putting the city on the west (rather than south) bank, has more than geographical consequences. At dawn one can bathe in the

Ganga and witness the sun rising over her vast waters (during flood season). Sometimes, even, the surface of the waters is broken by the surging backs of the population of dolphin who inhabit the river.

To get to Ramnagar Ramlila from Varanasi one must cross the Ganga—travel in the afternoon away from the westward declining sun and towards the brightly illuminated face of the Fort. Each day many thousands cross the river to attend Ramlila. There are several ways of crossing. A large steel bridge spans the river a few miles below Varanasi; a motor ferry leaves from the ghat near Benares Hindu University and docks close to the Fort; many private small rowboats ply the river. It was my impression that most people who attended Ramlila from Varanasi went by boat. Because the ferry operated only during daylight hours a great fleet of rowboats, each seating around thirty persons, assembled each night to take riders back to Varanasi. As a spectator said: 'Each goes to Ramlila as an individual, but returns from it as part of a group.'

What a trip! Leaving amidst the tumult of the after-show surge of people looking for their friends, their pre-arranged boats, the fleet separated on the river as each boat went its own way. On many boats persons sang *bhajans*. By mid-river it was as if the boat I was on, appropriately skippered by an old man, gaunt and beautiful, named Ramdas, was alone on the river. Another opposition: the seething surging crowds of Ramlila versus the ascetic, quiet aloneness of the river. The Ganga is wide enough during flood season so that it was almost as if we were rowing across the sea. Some nights blue lightning flashed, and the wind was fresh: we hastened to avoid storms— storms that could capsize a small boat. Towards the end of Ramlila, as the rainy season gave way to the glorious autumn clear weather, and the moon ran to full, the river sparkled. I experienced the vastness of Ganga, and her intimacy. After about one-half hour of rowing, and being carried by the swift current, the west bank was reached. Different passengers alighted at different ghats. I stepped off at Assi. Others went down towards Dashashwamedha.

At least seventy-five boats worked the river. I realize that this accounts for only 2,250 persons, and sometimes the crowds were closer to 50,000 and even, for Dusserah, 100,000. Clearly many people walked home, and probably, also, my estimate both of the number of small boats, and their capacity, is underestimated. (I never cease to be astounded about the number of people who can crowd onto transport—bus, train, boat—in India.)

Be that as it may, the crossing to and from Ramnagar constitutes a big part of the experience of the *Lila* itself. For the Ganga is no ordinary river. Crossing it puts one in touch with a great life-stream. Songs sung upon returning from Ramlila included, in our boat at least (and many people travelled with the same boatman night after night, year after year), songs that were identified both with Rama and Gandhi:

> King Rama, leader of the Raghu dynasty,
> Born from Shankara's drum,
> Born from the waves of the Ganga,
> Husband of pure Sita.
>
> Born from the mouth of the wise.
> Hail to Sita's Rama,
> And to Hanuman, who relieves us of our burdens,
> And grants us favours.
>
> Hail to Mother Ganga.

This is very close to Gandhi's song (sung to the same tune):

> King Rama, leader of the Raghu dynasty,
> Husband of pure Sita:
> May we worship this Sita-Rama.
>
> He is known as Ishwara or Allah.
> May this God bestow good sense on everyone.

But the crossing of the river is not always peaceful. Sometimes boats overturn and people drown. Always, in the afternoon, on the ferry, there is a great rush and crush.

For example, on 23 September 1978, I noted what it was like to cross the Ganga by ferry:

Boatrush. Pushing down the muddy flood-slicked slope of Somnaghat towards the ferry. People rush furiously to get on the old boat. There used to be two of them, but one is laid up about a half-mile upstream. Who knows why, or when it will return to service. The ferry is free. The private boats can cost a rupee or more. On the ferry people pile up, bikes and all. From the shore to the boat is a narrow gangplank not more than three feet wide. So soon a wild, shoving, shouting bottleneck develops. There is screaming and shouting and jostling. Bikes are handed over the tops of people's heads to friends already aboard. People squirm into the crowd or cling to the handrope and edge along the side of the gangplank. But often everything just stops: things get jammed up. There is a raging crowd on shore, an empty gangplank, a half-empty boat blowing its whistle signalling departure.

Three days ago as we arrived very early for the 3 o'clock boat three women with head-bundles of sticks squatted by the shore. They were the epitome of patience and labour. Their bodies were dark and as thin as the sticks they carried. (Someone told us that these sticks would be made into toothpicks.) It was hot, in the 90s, and humid. After thirty minutes the boat arrived and the ordinary riot occurred. Finally the bikes were loaded, most of the men who wanted to go were on board. Only a few women. The three women with the loads of sticks waited patiently. Occasionally they approached the gangplank, and then they slid back as aggressive men shoved on by. The boat whistled; there was a last minute rush and surge of bikers. Always, here, there's more demand than supply. Over the little mud-hill at the shore more passengers and bikers rushing to the boat. The boat's motor began. More men leaping from shore to ship. A single black bike passed over the heads of some men and thrown on board on top of the other bikes. Shouting. The boat pulls away.

And the three women were as they had been, standing helpless, and then squatting, to wait out the hour till the next boat.

I quote this because there is a tendency, in writing about Ramlila, to be swept up in devotion and admiration; and to forget the ordinary grind and helplessness of lots of people who may never themselves attend Ramlila in Ramnagar but who still, for me at least, comprise part of the Ramlila experience.

So one of the deepest oppositions is between the extraordinary time-space-narrative adventure of Ramlila versus the ordinary grind of daily living in north India. In a real way, Ramlila provides for a number of people a temporary relief from this grind, a festive season, a time out.

Narrative Structures

The narrative structure of Ramlila is very important: it is through the story that much information concerning values, history (both mythic and conceptual), hierarchy, and geography are transmitted. People begin attending Ramlila as children, even babies; much is learned through osmosis. Naturally, the basic story of Ramlila is that of the

Ramayana and the *Ramcaritmanas*: the birth of Rama, his childhood adventures culminating in his breaking of Siva's bow and winning Sita in marriage. Then, just before Rama is to be crowned king in Ayodhya, Kaikeyi—one of old king Dasaratha's wives—insists that Dasaratha pay her two promises he made earlier. 'What do you want?' Dasaratha asks. 'That my son Bharata be made king and that Rama be sent into the forest in exile for fourteen years.' Rama, knowing he is an incarnation of Visnu and that all these troubles are merely parts of Visnu's great *lila* (sport, play, games, illusion, theatre: the way the world operates on the human scale), willingly agrees to go. Along with him goes his brother Lakshmana and his bride Sita. In the jungle live both *rishis* (sages) and *rakshasas* (demons). Rama and his party have many adventures with both.

Rama establishes a kind of royal house in exile at Citrakut. His brother Bharata visits him there and begs him to return to Ayodhya. Rama refuses and moves further into the jungle—further south in India, to Pancavati. Then Surpanakha, sister of the ten-headed demon king of Lanka, Ravana, sees Rama and Lakshmana, is struck by their beauty and tries to seduce first Rama and then his brother. Lakshmana cuts off her nose and ears (a bloody scene in Ramnagar Ramlila). In rage and humiliation Surpanakha flees to her brother Ravana's kingdom. Ravana dispatches an army to avenge her—and the army is slaughtered. Then, using a golden deer as a decoy, Ravana lures Rama and Lakshmana from Sita, kidnaps her, and brings her to Lanka. Ravana installs Sita in an *asoka* garden and courts her. She refuses him. Meanwhile, Rama and Lakshmana gather an army of monkeys and bears (including the great monkey hero, Hanuman) and pursue Ravana the length of India and across the sea separating the mainland from Lanka. In Lanka a great war is fought. Systematically Ravana's armies are destroyed; his family annihilated. Finally, Ravana meets Rama in single combat and is killed. Sita is rescued, her chastity tested in a fire ordeal. Then Rama's whole party begins a slow progressive return to Ayodhya, being greeted by joyous crowds wherever they go—roughly retracing on the homeward journey their outward path. The fourteen years of exile is coming to an end. As they approach Ayodhya, Bharata comes out and meets Rama in the famous Bharata Milap. The kingdom is turned over to Rama who is coronated. The golden age of his rule, Ramraj, begins.

Every Indian knows this story: many believe it to be historical fact. In its details it combines narrative themes from both *Iliad* (the war) and *Odyssey* (the wanderings). There is something deeply Indo-European in the Ramayana. For Indians the Ramayana defines the subcontinent's landscape: Rameswaram where the great bridge from India to Lanka was built is the site of a temple; pilgrims can walk from Ayodhya to Janakpur. A small book by H. D. Sankalia, *Ramayana: Myth or Reality?* (New Delhi: People's Publishing House, 1973), deals effectively (in my opinion) with questions not only of Ramayana's historicity, but of the more interesting problem of its historical presence within the Indian popular consciousness. This presence is renewed, and enhanced, each year by thousands of Ramlilas performed all across northern India. And nowhere is this historical-mythical consciousness more effectively represented than at Ramnagar.

At Ramnagar the whole Ramayana story is told, but with a few emphases and an addition different than what is related in Valmiki or the *Ramcaritmanas*. The classic Rama story has three parts: (1) Initiations, culminating in the breaking of Siva's bow and the marriage of Rama to Sita; (2) exile and growth to maturity through battle and ordeal, culminating in the war against Ravana; (3) Ramraj, which barely begins as the narrative ends. This story is set within various frames, all of which are very interesting from a literary point of view—and for what they tell us about the Indian ways of viewing 'reality', but which are not altogether relevant from a theatrical perspective. That's because in theatre, in Ramlila, the story is shown, acted out, not told. At Ramnagar the story of Rama is divided into five parts: (1) A prelude where Brahma implores Visnu to take the form of a human and rescue the world which is being disturbed by demons; this section is in the *Ramcaritmanas*; (2–3–4) as in the classic versions; and (5) a postlude performed only at Ramnagar where the Maharaja and his family welcome the *swarupas* to the Fort, feed them ceremoniously in front of a huge assembled audience, and honour them publicly. The next day, in private, the Maharaja pays the performers for their services. These two actions—honouring Rama and his party publicly, paying the actors—bring the story of Rama into the field of force controlled by the Maharaja. First as guests and then as employees, first as mythic heroes and then as subjects, the Ramlila characters are adhered to the world, and necessities, of the Maharaja of Benares. This five-part narrative scheme can be outlined as in Fig. 1.

INITIATIONS

Event	PRELUDE		INITIATIONS	
	Gods beg Rama to incarnate himself	Boyhood adventures Killing demons	Contest for Siva's bow. Courtship of Sita. Marriage	Coronation stopped
Day	1	2-5		6-8

RETURN

Event	WAR		RETURN
	Rama pursues Ravana	War in Lanka	Return to Ayodhya Bharat Milap
	17-19	20-26	27-28

WAR / CRISIS / EXILE / MATURITY

Event	MATURITY	EXILE	CRISIS	WAR
	Exile begins	Journey through the forest to Citrakut and Pancavati	Surpanakha appears. Sita kidnapped	Rama pursues Ravana
Day	9	10-15	16	17-19

RAMRAJ / POSTLUDE

Event	RAMRAJ	POSTLUDE	
	Coronation and teaching	Pay	Ceremony at fort
Day	29-30		31-32

Fig. 1

In terms of theatrical time the whole cycle consists of a one day prelude, seven days of initiations, twenty days of exile, two days of Ramraj, and two days of postlude.

This theatrical structure can be represented in another, more revealing, configuration:

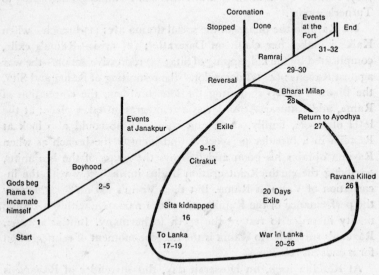

Coronation

Stopped   Done   Events at the Fort   End

Ramraj   31-32

Reversal   29-30

Bharat Milap 28

Events at Janakpur   Exile   Return to Ayodhya 27

9-15 Citrakut

Boyhood   Ravana Killed 26

Gods beg Rama to incarnate himself   2-5   20 Days Exile

1   Sita kidnapped 16

Start   To Lanka 17-19   War in Lanka 20-26

Fig. 2

Without the interruption of Rama's coronation brought about by Kaikeyi's insistence that Dasaratha pay his promises to her, there would be no drama: just a straight line from Rama's birth to his Ramraj. And without the drama there is no exile, no kidnapping of Sita, no war against Ravana. In a word, no point for Visnu to be incarnated as Rama: a kshatriya, a lover, a householder, a protector of brahmins, a sannyasin. The loop from day 9 through day 28 is where most of the adventure takes place. It is, literally, Rama's journey in time and space from the safety of Ayodhya to the adventures that lay in store for him at Citrakut, Pancavati, and Lanka.

Anthropologist Victor Turner has outlined a four-part sequence of what he calls 'social dramas'.[4] These social dramas occur in trials, combats, rivalries, wars. Turner's idea applies very well to Ramlila of Ramnagar—where a great myth has been translated into a religious-aesthetic drama with many overtones of social drama. It is no surprise that Turner's scheme fits Ramlila exactly: Turner constructed his concept of social drama from what he knew of aesthetic drama. What is interesting is how well this model works cross-culturally—in India as well as Africa (where Turner developed it to account for conflicts among the Ndembu) and Euro-America where Shakespeare's plays and the works of other dramatists can be analysed according to Turner's model.

For Ramlila the phases of the social drama are: (1) breach—when Kaikeyi makes her claim on Dasaratha; (2) crisis—Rama's exile, complicated by the kidnapping of Sita; (3) redressive action—the war against Ravana; (4) reintegration—the re-uniting of Rama and Sita, the Bharata Milap re-uniting the four brothers, the coronation of Rama, and Ramraj. At all levels a reintegration takes place: at the level of lovers, family, state, and cosmos. One could also look at Ramlila in a broader perspective and identify the breach as when Ravana obtains his boon and destroys the altars of the brahmins, terrifying the earth. Reintegration begins immediately with the in-carnation of Visnu as Rama. But then Visnu's *lila* makes necessary the performance of the Ramlila story as a narrative within a cosmic reality in order to restore the earth to harmony. In this scheme, Ravana's surrender to Rama is the decisive moment of reintegration for it ends his rebellion.

At Ramlila itself, on Dusserah day, this surrender of Ravana is performed with particular simplicity and beauty. On preceding days there have been great battles involving Lakshmana, Hanuman, Kum-bhakarna, Meghnada, Ravana, and Rama. The victory in these battles go to Rama's side, but not decisively enough to end the war. On Dusserah day the narration of Ramlila itself is interrupted so that the Maharaja can play out his own story—a story that he shares with other Indian kings. On Dusserah there is a special 'weapons puja' in which the Maharaja displays in the courtyard of the Fort a panoply of swords, daggers, guns, and other implements of war. We were not allowed to photograph this display—signalling that in some ways it was a sacred, at least a very special, manifestation.

Then in an extraordinary and magnificently theatrical procession of elephants the Maharaja makes his way amidst immense crowds of more than 100,000 from the Fort, down the main street of Ramnagar, and out to Lanka more than 5 kilometres to the southeast. My notes for Dusserah 1978:

Maharaja enters Lanka on his elephant, followed by the others. They ride straight through the crowd past the battleground, turn and ride up and over the battleground. They leave Lanka the way they came—having stayed less than 10 minutes, never stopping, just passing through and over. What is the meaning of this strange procession that violates the performing space? It is the only time in the Ramlila that the Maharaja literally invades the performing space. Otherwise he remains firmly anchored at the back of the spectators, defining where the audience is. The 'weapons puja' is what's left of a very war-like traditional display of kingly might that used to occupy Maharajas on Dusserah. They would march their armies to the borders of their domain, proclaim the territory as theirs, confront their opposing number across the border and go home. Thus they showed their ability to make war; and they identified themselves, however vaguely, with the ancient horse-sacrifice, which Dasaratha himself performs in the Ramayana. Thus the Maharaja here in Ramlila is staking out his territory, saying in effect that the Ramlila is his. He boldly penetrates the performing space and cuts across the battleground, showing who's boss, who's king, and over what territory. He rides to the very edge of the Ramlila ground, the end of the Ramlila world—and he goes a few hundred feet beyond, then turns his elephants, and returns. This is the furthest out anyone playing a role in Ramnagar Ramlila goes. Then the Maharaja leaves Lanka, he does not see Ravana defeated. 'It is not right', he told me, 'for one king to watch the death of another.'

But this is not all there is to Ravana's death.

Ravana actually doesn't die in battle. Rather, he surrenders. On the afternoon of Dusserah, after the Maharaja has come and gone, Ravana sits in his chariot across the battlefield from Rama. Then, without another arrow being shot, Ravana rises, takes off his ten-headed mask, walks the length of the battlefield—about 150 feet—and touches his head to the feet of Rama. Ravana literally surrenders, gives up, to Rama. The crowd surges to see this surrender; cops wave great sticks threatening the roaring, surging crowd. Then, after surrendering to Rama, Ravana turns and walks off into the crowd. His son carries his mask. Later in that afternoon, after his role in Ramlila is over, Ravana will go to many of the owners of food and tea stalls to collect 'Ravana's rent'. In this way he gets paid for his performance. Those who operate businesses as part of the mela at Lanka pay Ravana for occupying space on his territory. Ravana does not stick around for the end of Ramlila, but returns to his village about 10 miles away. 'I never see the end,' he told me.

Later Dusserah night the giant effigy of Ravana is cremated. Through fire his being is liberated and ascends to Visnu. The war is over.

Environments, Mise-en-Scène, and Directionality

Just as there was a Troy and a Trojan War, so there were occurrences that underly the Ramayana. These events probably took place in north and central India, from Ayodhya on the river Saraju, south to Allahabad (Prayag), west to Citrakut, and southwest to what was a forested area north of the river Narmada. But as the telling of the Ramayana spread southward along with, as part of, Sanskritization, so did its field of geographical references. 'The gradual spread, first of the Mahabharata and then of the Ramayana into the Deccan, Karnataka, and Tamil Nadu, shows the slow absorption by society, high and low, of certain ethical values. [. . .] Simultaneously places all over India came to be associated with episodes in the Ramayana.'[5]

As the Ramayana stories spread—were carried person-to-person south and east—they were identified with local deities and sacred places. Indian culture, like Japanese, does not reject its past when something new comes along. Rather the culture remembers everything and displays it in a palimpsest. Thus in many events, Ramlila among them, one can detect pre-Hindu, Hindu, Muslim, and English elements. Certainly the Hindu colouring is dominant, but it is not alone. The sacred rivers and crossings are surely pre-Hindu; the pomp of the Maharaja, and his very dress, owes as much to Mughal influences as to Hindu ideas of kingship; the Maharaja's marching band, his Cadillac, the petromax lanterns that are 'old-fashioned' in the minds of most spectators, and traditional, are all of Euro-American origins. These are just a few examples of many that could be cited demonstrating the multi-cultural dimensions of Ramlila. But this multi-culturality is natural in India (as elsewhere).

The very geography of Ramlila of Ramnagar echoes with very ancient pre-Hindu and Hindu references. And the geography of Ramlila—its hilltops, rivers and river junctures, cities, temples, caves, trees, wells, and paths—are models of actual places that carry and emit bundles of significance. 'The number of Hindu sanctuaries in India is so large and the practice of pilgrimage so ubiquitous that the whole of India can be regarded as a vast sacred space organized into a

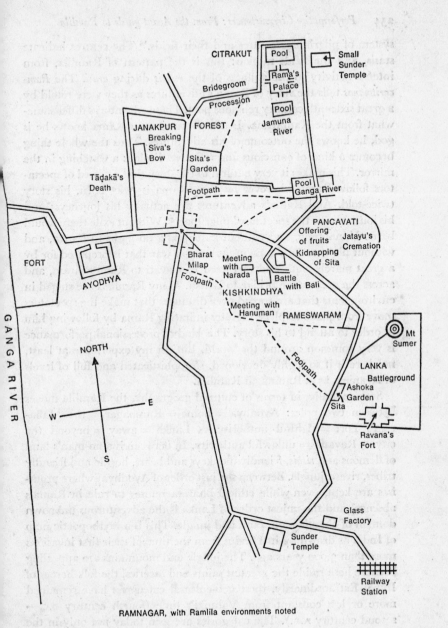

RAMNAGAR, with Ramlila environments noted

Fig. 3

system of pilgrimage centres and their fields.'[6] The centres indicate stasis, and the fields motion: this is the pattern of Ramlila, from intense activity to the stillness of the *murtis* during *arati*. The *Ramcaritmanas* tells the story of Rama's adventures as they were retold by a great sixteenth century religious poet. These adventures differ somewhat from the Ramayana. In the *Ramcaritmanas* Rama knows he is god, he knows the outcome of his adventures. Thus the whole thing becomes a kind of conscious and reflexive display: a watching in the mirror. This makes it very natural to the story that a crowd of spectators follow Rama wherever he goes. Rama is twice-born, his story twice-told. And Rama's adventures are actually his journeys; and his journeys are the spectators' pilgrimages. Without exile there would be no kidnapping, and without kidnapping no flight to Lanka, and without flight to Lanka no great war—a war that is prepared for by a great march south and east from Pancavati to Rameswaram, and across the great stone bridge to Lanka. Many Ramlilas are staged in environments that are spread over distances that make the spectators move from place to place literally imitating Rama by following him in order to attend to his story. This kind of processional performance is very common around the world. But, in my experience at least, nowhere is it so highly developed, so sophisticated and full of levels of meaning, as at Ramnagar Ramlila.

Seen spatially, in terms of cultural geography, the Ramlila moves between two poles: Ayodhya = home = Ramnagar = the Maharaja's Fort = rightful authority vs Lanka = away = beyond the city = Ravana = unlawful authority. In between is a no-man's-land of demons and *rishis*, friendly monkeys and bears, hostile and friendly tribes, rivers, jungle. Between the just order of Ayodhya (where promises are kept, even while ethical Bharata refuses to rule in Rama's absence) and the unjust order of Lanka is the adventurous unknown domain of chaotic mountains and jungle. This is a mythopoetic map of India as drawn by its Hindus from the time of their first invasions more than 3,000 years ago. The jungle and mountains are appealing because here reside the greatest saints and ascetics, the folk-heroes of India. Extraordinarily, these geo-cultural categories have remained more or less constant from Valmiki's time (fourth century B.C.— second century A.D.). The categories are seen today not only in the deep respect for ascetics and renouncers but also in continuing tensions between India's 'scheduled castes and tribes', her 'harijans' (literally, 'children of god', operatively, 'untouchables') and tribal

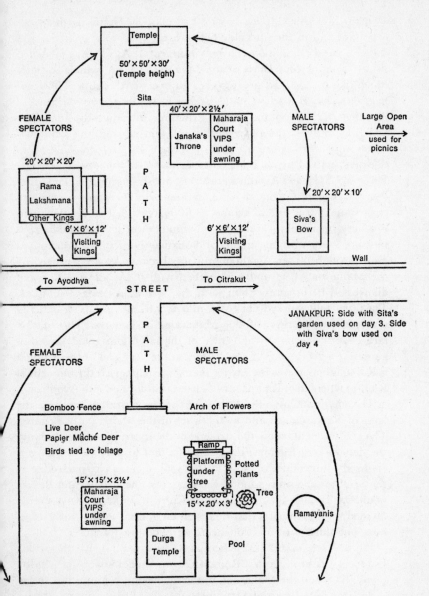

Fig. 4 Environments at Janakpur.

peoples, and other Indians whose ritual-social status is more acceptable; and in the interplay between the relatively few cities and the vast rural population. The environment at Ayodhya is modelled on the interior courtyards of the Maharaja's Fort—which are very much like palaces and great homes all over north India. The great field of Lanka is a self-contained other world far to the southeast of Ayodhya. Lanka contains several structures, including Ravana's Fort which looks like a primitive battlement. Old photographs show that it was once more impressive and even more primitive looking. From one perspective Ravana is a 'great king', from another, he is a savage. Between Lanka and Ayodhya are rivers, forests, hermitages, and other less extravagantly worked-out environments. There are two exceptions. Janakpur is several kilometres to the northeast of Ayodhya, and is a very intricately worked-out environment of several buildings, a pleasure garden, small temple, and auxiliary structures. Janakpur is more developed than Ayodhya probably because Ayodhya is hard-by the Maharaja's Fort and is identified with it. Ayodhya is also not allowed to be in competition with the Maharaja's palace complex. The other fully worked-out environment is Rambagh—once actually the 'pleasure garden' of the Maharajas of Benares. The marble lattice-work gazebo in the centre of the large four-gated walled-in garden is a good piece of work. Only at the very end of the Ramlila is Rambagh used—as the site for Rama's teachings, at the moment of Ramraj when all of Ramnagar has been transformed into Ayodhya.

The environments are at the core of the narrative, both at the level of *Ramcaritmanas* and at the level of the Maharaja of Benares. The environments show the struggle of the incarnated king Rama vs the demon king Ravana; the Maharaja and his city vs the not-yet-civilized countryside; the love for the sophisticated city-palace life vs the need for the simple life of the peasants, the tribals, and the renouncers. In fact, Rama's life as shown in Ramlila is nearly evenly divided into three parts that represent an ancient ideal: one-third as king, one-third as warrior, one-third as renouncer-wanderer.

But why organize the cycle here at Ramnagar on such a vast scale? Induja Awasthi suggests: 'Ramnagar was predominantly a Muslim population, and the Maharaja, in the nineteenth century, in a bid to restore the lost glory to the Hindus and to win them over, might have decided to accord state recognition to the Ramlila.' Maharaja Vibhuti Narain Singh discounts Awasthi's idea saying that his forebears copied the older Krishnalila of Vrindaban, which is staged environmentally. But Hess and I think Awasthi's explanation, though by no means the whole story, has merit. Until Independence the Maharaja was ruler of his realm, and his endorsement of Ramlila, his deployment of its settings across a large territory (larger-seeming in the mid-nineteenth century than now), can be regarded as a political act. Rama is that incarnation of Visnu who rules as a king, who defends his honour as a soldier, who conquers a whole subcontinent. Rama's reign is known as Ramraj, a golden age. The Ramnagar Ramlila developed during the early period of modern Hindu nationalism and is doubtlessly associated with it, a main expression of it.

The audience at Ramlila takes naturally to a performance that includes processions—the crossing by Rama of an imitation Ganga and Jamuna, the long journey of Hanuman from Lanka northward to the Himalayas in search of the herb that will restore Lakshmana after he has been wounded by Meghnada's *sakti* weapon, the magnificently slow two day return journey from Lanka to the boxing-ring-like square where Bharata Milap is staged, the regal procession on elephant from Rambagh to the Fort the night after Rama's coronation when the Maharaja feeds Rama, Sita, and the other *swarupas*. Or, on a more modest scale, the thin line of followers behind Rama and Lakshmana as they wind through the back pathways of Ramnagar on Rama's first adventure—his encounter with the demon Tadaka on his way from Ayodhya to Janakpur.

The Ramnagar Ramlila cycle condenses much of the Indian subcontinent into a comprehensible single sacred space with nine main stations: Ayodhya, Janakpur, Citrakut, Pancavati, Rameswaram, Lanka, Milap Square, Rambagh, and the Fort. Add to these the ponds that serve as the Ganga and Jamuna and you have a map of sacred India according to the *Ramcaritmanas*. Remember that most of the spectators at Ramlila will not travel, even as pilgrims, far from where they were born. Their experience at Ramlila—during a month out from ordinary time—is a very actual moving through of Rama's India. Their experience of following Rama is somewhere between 'going to a play', an entertainment, and some kind of ritual procession through a space that has become what it represents in much the same way as the boys who play *swarupas* have become *murtis*. Without suggesting any disrespect, the feeling is parallel to what happens to Americans when they go to Disneyland and enter the 'magic kingdom' or visit any one of the hundreds of 'restored villages' that mark the American landscape. These places create, or re-create, or actualize, American history and imagination.[7] The stations of Ramlila are anchor points of a very carefully organized system of movements and directional significations.

Ramnagar, of course, literally means 'town of Rama'. I'm not sure whether the town name or the Ramlila performance came first. But like so much that is part of Ramnagar Ramlila the doing of a thing—literally (in the Greek sense) a drama—is tied in with the name of the thing done: thus Ramnagar, the boatman Ramdas, the technical director Atmaram. Others have been absorbed into their roles. Narada is called Narada in his ordinary life where he is the *mahant* of two temples in Mirzapur—his authority and wealth considerably increased because of his reputation as a powerful performer in Ramlila. Brahma was played in 1976 and 1978 by a man who had performed the role for decades, a man now said in 1978 to be 96 years old, and looking it: his feeble voice, gentleness, and very distant-looking eyes becoming, for me at least, an incarnation as well as a representation of the god Brahma. Other performers are more ordinary in their theatrical identities. There is nothing Hanuman-like about the man who plays Hanuman, and a number of other roles too. But then there is 'old Hanuman', now in his eighties with a booming voice but not strong enough to carry both Rama and Lakshmana on his shoulders simultaneously, a requirement of Hanuman. But old Hanuman attends the *swarupas* wherever they are: in their dharamsalas resting, playing, eating, or rehearsing; or on stage where old Hanuman fans them with a fly whisk, holds their feet, and sees to their immediate needs. Thus this person who performed Hanuman in Ramlila for more than 30 years now plays the role's essence as a stage-hand and personal attendant.

As with the characters so with the town of Ramnagar. During the first third of the nineteenth century, under the direct supervision of the Maharajas of that time, numerous stage settings were built throughout the town in order to provide places for the various Ramlila events. Thus the construction of special buildings and areas for Ayodhya, Janakpur, Pancavati, and Lanka. A pleasure garden of the Maharaja's was designated Rambagh and used for Rama's teachings on the next to last, or last day (depending on the lunar cycle) of Ramlila. Next to Rambagh is a very old—some say more than 300 years old—Durga temple with its 1,000 square feet tank. The outer walls of Rambagh are used for the first day's *lila* where Ravana wins his boon and begins to terrorize the earth; next to the tank a great tent is set up to mark Rama's residence-in-exile at Citrakut. And the road to Pancavati leads around the great tank and directly in front of the Durga temple where the procession stops and a scene is played. The Jamuna River is a body of water, analogous to the Durga Tank, on the other side of Rambagh, and the Ganga is a medium-sized lake not far from the Jamuna. (In earlier days, I think the real Ganga was used; at least old photos show Rama emerging by boat from it. But persistent floods and a general, if slow, trend towards modernization has shifted the Ganga scenes to the lake.) Then there is the Maharaja's Fort, certainly not built for Ramlila, but used in it. Finally there are the streets, pathways, and main square of Ramnagar which are used for processions, exile treks, and Milap.

So there are theatrical environments of all types: built from scratch, adapted from what is already in use, and used as it is as 'found space'. This layering of the types of environments employed give Ramnagar Ramlila an impressive reality of its own. It seems to properly belong to and in Ramnagar, and the special environments—Ayodhya, Janakpur, Lanka—emerge naturally from adapted and found spaces.

Once more, and very significantly, the actual orientation of these spaces, as well as their positions relative to each other, is a reasonably accurate model not only of India and Sri Lanka but also of Rama's movements through the countryside. Lanka is far to the southeast of Ayodhya (which is next to the Fort); Janakpur is to the north; Citrakut and Pancavati to the northeast. Rambagh is also to the northeast—and this is where Ramlila begins and where Ramraj is celebrated with Rama's teachings. The northeast, I'm told, is an auspicious direction.

The action of Ramlila is thus both physical and narrative. The actual movements of the characters is itself a decisive part of the story. The first night of the performance, when the gods implore Visnu to incarnate himself and rescue the world, takes place on and around the *kshir sagar* (the tank of the Durga temple), in the good-luck northeast. When Rama goes into exile he crosses make-believe Ganga and Jamuna as he heads from Ayodhya in the northwest back towards the northeast. After Sita is captured, Rama's army moves steadily southeastward. This move is analogous to the historical movement through India of the Sanskritic culture the Aryan invaders of India brought with them. And it's no accident that in parts of the south Ravana is thought of as a hero, for at one level of the Ramayana story he represents the original culture of the area. Among the poems the Aryans brought with them was the Ramayana—or at least an ur-Ramayana. For this story merged with the Dravidian tales, and other native traditions. This merging included absorption of sacred places and routes. And it is this movement and absorption of sacred action and place that the Ramlila re-enacts.

After climactic battles at Lanka, battles that have looked more or less the same for 150 years, Rama victorious and his party are loaded into a great cart, the *puspaka* which flies in *Ramcaritmanas* but is pulled with great vigour through the mud and over the better roads by the people of Ramnagar in Ramlila. The return trip is a recapitulation narratively and spatially of Rama's adventures. As Rama says in the *Ramcaritmanas*:

> 'Sita,' said Raghubir, 'look at the battlefield; that is where Lakshmana slew Indrajit, and those huge demons lying on the field were slain by Hanuman and Angada; and here was killed Kumbhakarna and Ravana, the two brothers who discomfited gods and sages. Here I had the bridge built and set up the image of Siva, abode of bliss.' The gracious lord and Sita did obeisance to Sambhu. Wherever the Lord of grace had encamped or rested in the forest, he pointed out every place to Janaki and told her the name of each.
>
> Swiftly the car travelled on to the most beautiful forest of Dandaka, where dwelt Agastya and many other high sages; and Rama visited the homes of them all. After receiving the blessing of all the seers, the Lord of the world came to Citrakut; there he gladdened the hermits, and the car sped swiftly on. Next, Rama pointed out to Janaki the Jamuna [. . .] then they beheld the holy Ganga. [. . .] 'Next,' he said, 'behold Prayag [. . .] and now behold the city of Ayodhya.'

Interestingly the return trip in Ramlila is much more direct. For theatrical reasons the return trip takes only two days, and there is no retrogressive crossing of rivers, no visit to Prayag or Citrakut. The *puspaka* rests one night near a sacred tree, and another at Nishada's ashram. During the day local children play on it. And on the third night Milap is accomplished in the main Ramnagar city square.

Once Rama enters Ayodhya to be coronated a marvellous conflation of time and space takes place. All the Ramlila places become part of Rama's kingdom, and the whole of Ramnagar becomes Ayodhya. Thus Rama goes to his Rambagh to preach, he travels through the streets of his Ayodhya-Ramnagar on his elephant as a king would proceed through his own capital. And finally he is welcomed by the Maharaja at the Fort: one king receiving another. There, assisted by the royal family, Rama and his family have their feet washed, are garlanded, and fed a sumptuous meal. This feeding takes a very long time, hours, and I mused that the boys who were *swarupas* for the last time during this scene were prolonging it, and deeply enjoying a unique situation where they were being honoured, worshipped and fed by the Maharaja of Benares. Thousands of townspeople crowd into the courtyard of the Fort to watch.

Something very powerful theatrically and religiously takes place, creating a unique social, even political, situation. It climaxes during this evening at the Fort, but it has been present and building throughout the month of Ramlila. In 1949, after India had won its independence after a long and bitter revolutionary struggle, the principalities were abolished. After all, not only were Gandhi's and Nehru's ideals those of democracy, some of India's Maharajas were on the British side, less than lukewarm to Gandhi's populism and Nehru's secularism. A few years after independence the privy purses were discontinued (though the Kasi All India Trust, the Maharaja's foundation, receives money to produce Ramlila). Despite all this, everyone calls Vibhuti Narain Singh 'Maharaja'. And this title is not honorific or nostalgic, though it has elements of both. It is operational: it works in the world of today. Why is this so? The answer, in no small way, is to be found in Ramlila. For the Ramlila season, especially during the performances of the *arati* temple service that concludes each evening's show, the *murtis*—literally 'images' of the gods—the boys playing Rama, Sita, Lakshmana, Bharata, Satrughna—are thought by many in the audience to actually be the gods they otherwise represent. It is a miracle analogous to Catholic transubstantiation.

The presence of the *murtis* bestows on their patron, host and theatrical producer a royalty that might by now be much diminished (as it is with some other former Maharajas). But it's not quite that simple. There is more like a symbiotic, syncretic feedback going on— a circumstance tied up to the whole physical setting of Ramnagar Ramlila, its function as a pilgrimage centre, the particular sanctity of Kasi (ancient name of Varanasi/Benares) and the role in that sacred complex of the Maharaja. For a month, in a whole town, Rama lives and moves throughout the town. The Maharaja of Benares is the only person with enough religious-traditional force to sponsor a great Ramlila—to sponsor it, and participate in it as one of the principal figures or characters. For the Ramlila he sponsors validates his Maharajadom: it gives him a chance to appear on his elephant, displays him before the crowds in a *darsan* of regal splendour; it allows him to manage a great religious and devotional event, confirming in the popular imagination his own authenticity as a ruler-manager. And, through his daily practice of *sandhya puja*—where the performance stops, and everyone but the Maharaja rests, eats, strolls— the Maharaja publicly and yet secretly displays his religiosity. For often a temporary enclosure is set up into which the Maharaja retreats for puja: everyone can see where he is going, and everyone presumes to know what he is doing: yet he does it secretly. Ultimately the climactic visit of mythic-theatrical Rama to the Fort of the actual-mythic-theatrical Maharaja is an intersection of ancient and modern, mythic and theatrical, actual and transformative, extraordinary and ordinary.

The details of the performance of Ramlila also underline the great importance of the environments, of movement, of directionality. More than half of the *lilas* include journeys, processions, or pilgrimages. Movement from place to place is the most salient theatrical action of Ramlila. The permanent environments for Ayodhya, Janakpur, Citrakut, Pancavati, the rivers Ganga and Jamuna, Rameswaram, and Lanka are linked by processions that trace the outline of the story. Instead of ending one day's show in place *A* and beginning the next day in place *B*, often the movement from *A* to *B* is the start of or even most of the performance. A very short scene in one place will begin a *lila*, and then comes a long procession to a new performance area. Some of these processions are great events: the marriage procession of Rama and Sita back from Janakpur to Ayodhya; the start of Rama's exile when many spectators, weeping, follow him into the forest; the procession of elephants on Dusserah day when the Maharaja rides among the 100,000 or more spectators that line the way and follow him the more than 5 kilometres from the Fort to Lanka. Especially tumultuous is the two day return from Lanka of victorious Rama culminating in the Bharata Milap.

For the performances of 1976 these were my notes:

Day 27, 7:30 p.m. After Sita passes her fire ordeal, she takes her place on a huge 20-foot-high cart next to Rama and Lakshmana. Dozens of male spectators tug on the two ropes moving the four-wheeled carriage out of Lanka and down the long road towards Ayodhya. Many in the crowd of 100,000 follow, and many go on ahead: the road is all people. After a few hundred yards the cart stops—it is Bharadwaja's ashrama, where Rama will spend the night. *Arati* is performed. The *lila* is over.

The performers do not actually spend the night on set. They are carried back to their residence near the Fort. But, interestingly enough, partly as a practical consideration, and partly to help the boys who play the *murtis* to experience their roles, their place of residence changes during the Ramlila. They begin living near the Fort; then during the days in Citrakut and Pancavati they live at Rambagh; during the days of war in Lanka they live in Lanka; and during the final days of celebration they live, once more, near the Fort. So the performers, too, make a ritual journey that is a model of the narrative. At the end of each night's performance the *swarupas* are carried back to where they will sleep, eat, and rehearse. On that twenty-seventh day in 1976 I recorded this scene:

> One of the last images of the night: five men trotting down the street with the five boys (*swarupas*) on their shoulders. These actors' feet do not touch the ground while they are in costume, while they wear the crowns that confer on them their status as *swarupas*. But this time as they go by, still in the costumes of their gods-characters, but no longer in the *lila*, there are no shouts of 'jai Ram!' from the crowd: the *swarupas* are noticed but not adored. Like temple ikons they are being put away for the night.

The twenty-eighth day's *lila* begins with several scenes happening simultaneously in different parts of Ramnagar, preparing for the Milap convergence in the town's centre. Near the Fort, Bharata and Satrughna sit under a bower waiting for news that Rama is returning. In the Fort, the Maharaja and his court are mounting elephants for a grand procession to the Milap square. Several kilometres away at Bharadwaja's ashrama, Rama and his court are being very slowly rolled towards Ayodhya. Sitting in their big wagon they look very much like a grand family: Rama, Sita, Lakshmana, Jambavan the bear general, Hanuman, Sugriva and his nephew Angada, the forest chief Guha, the chief *vyas*, several assistant *vyases*, the old *vyas* whose job it is to shout, 'Keep Quiet! Pay Attention!' before each *samvad*—and others who have found their way into the cart. As the wagon rolls over ground covered before, Rama points out the sights to Sita: Here Lakshmana killed Meghnada, here the monkeys built a bridge over the sea . . .

8:30 p.m. Bharata gets the news from Hanuman that Rama is approaching. Bharata and Satrughna set out for the high stage near the arch. Meanwhile the Maharaja and his party on elephants ride out to greet Rama and his party rolling along in their wagon. As the Maharaja passes the great crowd roars, 'Hara, Hara, Mahadev!' ('Siva, Siva, great god!'). As the Maharaja proceeds down the street from the gate of the Fort to the Milap square, flares are lit to illuminate him more brightly. People look up at him from the street, down at him from the roofs. The Maharaja greets Rama, takes *darsan*, and then positions himself at the Milap square to await the reunion of the brothers.

9 p.m. Rama continues his slow advance. It reminds me of a Robert Wilson performance—you know what's going to happen, and can trace out in advance its map; but it takes forever for it to actually physically happen, and in that space of waiting, a certain meditation occurs. At every temple and at many displays of sacred *murtis*, Rama's wagon halts, he gives *darsan*, and the white flare of *arati* is ignited. Much could be made of the continuing importance, from perhaps pre-Vedic days, of fire, the sun, illumination, in Indian worship. Rama himself is scion of the Solar Race, a Sun King, a king of fire.

Up and down the street from the Fort to the arch several blocks beyond Milap square are coloured lights, puppet shows, small temples with groups of people chanting *kirtans*. Walas sell tea, sweets, snacks, temple beads, ochre and yellow powders for making holy marks, betel nuts, cigarettes. The sights, sounds, smells, sense of the whole thing is a perfect mixture, blending, of the sacred and the profane: to such a degree that the distinction is no longer viable. There is the experience. It is whole, total.

Some displays are traditional images rigged with contemporary engineering like the electrically powered figure of Hanuman who opens his own chest to reveal his heart on which is engraved an image of Rama and Sita. Some displays are of old-fashioned painted clay figures.

10:30 p.m. The wagon meets the square stage where the Milap will take place. Rama and Lakshmana step from the wagon onto the stage. Bharata and Satrughna have been standing there for a few minutes. The four boys rush across the stage and embrace; they kiss each other's feet. The flares burn. The crowd roars. The Maharaja watches in what I suppose is full and joyous approval.

But the Maharaja maintains his mask perfectly. It is not possible to get inside or behind that mask. He is what he performs. Once I asked him:

RS: Do you believe that the boys are gods?
MR: If you see a Christian movie, like *The Robe*, what do you feel?
RS: I feel it's a representation, done with devotion maybe, but still a great distance from being god.
MR: The same, I feel the same.

But now, writing this some six years after that interview, and having watched the Maharaja throughout one entire Ramlila (1978), I think he misrepresented his feelings—in so far as those feelings are manifest in his actions. His actions speak devotion—and a seeing through the *swarupas* to whatever it is that he feels is divine. In the Hindu context the divine is not a simple thing to define, nor is it radically separable from ordinary human existence. As with so much else in Indian culture, the divine exists as a palimpsest: it is there in ordinary life, it manifests itself in incarnations and less forceful presences such as *rishis*, sages, sadhus, devout individuals; and it is present in an essential, highly refined, substance as the Ramlila *murtis*, who are and represent what they are presumed to be at the same time.

But not everyone feels—or acts during Ramlila—this way. Many are not watching *arati* but munching snacks; many come for the show alone, or do not attend at all. Even people of great authority. Ramchandra De, longtime personal secretary to the Maharaja, said in 1978 when Hess and I asked him why he didn't attend Ramlila anymore: 'My views on Ramlila have not changed. It is all play acting. Can you take street urchins and make them gods?' De's opinion is definitely in the minority. His characterization of the *swarupas* as 'street urchins' reflects his ironic sense of things. He knows as well as anyone the care with which the boys who perform in Ramlila are selected. The *vyases* search for candidates who must be brahmans, well-behaved, with 'good looks' (itself a complicated criterion) and strong voices. Their families must agree to their participation in Ramlila, which means giving up school for some weeks. Finally, when the number of possible *swarupas* has been reduced to the top candidates the Maharaja himself auditions them. He talks to them, listens to them recite, looks them over. He makes the final selection. They move to a dharamsala near the Fort in July and begin rehearsals. Although it isn't much, they are paid for their work. This payment, and the method of its achievement, signal a return to the non-

Ramlila world after the cycle of performances is ended. The day after Ramlila ends the *swarupas* and major characters come to the Fort where the Maharaja thanks them for their efforts. In 1976 each *swarupa* got Rs 440, a considerable sum, but no fortune—especially considering the work they did over more than three months. Other principal participants—actors, *vyases*, technical director—are paid too. Many confided in us that the pay was inadequate. And the Maharaja complained that the funds available to him for Ramlila were inadequate. Wealth, which used to flow as from a limitless reservoir for a great Maharaja, is increasingly scarce. The Maharaja knows that this lack of funds threatens the Ramlila. He wonders how his 'industries' will do, whether or not his son will be as devoted to Ramlila as he is: what the future of the whole enterprise will be.

There is, on the day before the full payment made in private, a public ritual payment of Re 1 to each *swarupa* during the Kot Viday, or farewell at the Fort. Nowhere is the special place of the Maharaja demonstrated more clearly than on this last day of Ramlila, a cere-mony unique to Ramnagar. Although a portion of the *Ramcaritmanas* remains to be chanted, the events of the 'thirty-first day' are outside the Rama story. Late in the afternoon (or at night, as in 1978, when an eclipse of the moon on the second day of Ramlila skewered the whole schedule), riding two magnificent elephants, the five *swarupas* arrive at the Fort. The Maharaja, dressed simply, barefoot, greets them as if they were visiting royalty. They are seated on a platform, their feet washed by the Maharaja, who also applies *tilak* to their foreheads and garlands them. He performs *arati* to them as if he were a temple priest (he is a Brahmin) and they gods. Then a full meal is served them. While they eat, the final portions of the *Ramcaritmanas* are chanted. As they eat, the Maharaja is handed a Re 1 coin by one of his attendants, and he hands this coin to a *vyas* who gives it to Hanuman: in this way each of the five *swarupas* is paid. Then each of the Ramayanis and the other principal performers take Re 1 from the Maharaja via the *vyas*. I believe this public gesture of paying the performers is an affirmation, at the end of Ramlila, of the order of the non-Ramlila world: it shows who's king. A *nemi* (devout and knowledgeable Ramlila goer) disagrees: 'It is the *dharma* (duty) of a king to give money to the Brahmins.' As with so much in Ramlila the two interpretations do not cancel each other out. After the *swarupas* have eaten—it takes them more than an hour—the Maharaja per-forms *arati* again. Then each of the *swarupas* takes off his garland and

puts it on the Maharaja. This gesture is repeated with members of
the royal family, each of whom gives and receives garlands from the
swarupas. (At this time only are the females of the royal family out
of purdah.) Then elephants arrive taking the *swarupas* back to Ayodhya
where they give *darsan*, and the royal family retires inside the Fort.

The ceremony of the thirty-first day is trivalent: the Maharaja is
paying off his entertainers, welcoming visiting royalty, and worshipping gods. All three events take place simultaneously, being accomplished by the same set of gestures—the meanings radiate outward
through three frames, that of Ramnagar, that of the mythic narrative,
and that of the cosmic-religious Hindu system of reality:

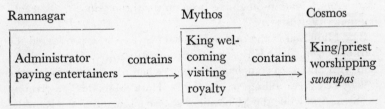

Ramnagar		Mythos		Cosmos
Administrator paying entertainers	contains ⟶	King welcoming visiting royalty	contains ⟶	King/priest worshipping *swarupas*

The largest event cosmically is contained within a mythic event
which in turn is contained within the social order of Ramnagar. And
through this ceremony of multivocal reduction, of the lesser reality
containing the larger, and the private payment that takes place
within the Fort the next day, a month of extraordinary happenings is
ended; things are returned to the ordinary. In Turner's language, a
reintegration has occurred.

Maharaja, Ramayanis, Rama, Sadhus

The Maharaja and Rama are mirror images of each other, the twin
heroes of the Ramnagar Ramlila. The Maharaja is as much a mythic
figure as Rama. His real political power is gone, relegated to history
along with the British raj. But throughout the Ramlila, his Maharaja-
ness is displayed, more so than at any other time of the year. He
appears on his elephant, raised far above the masses of people; or he
rides in his horse-drawn carriage. Occasionally he is seated in the
plush of his elegant 1928 Cadillac. Always he is accompanied by a
dignified elderly man, the Maharaja's companion. 'Someone to talk
to,' the Maharaja told me—though in all the hours of observing them
riding together I have never seen a word pass between them. Also the
Maharaja at Ramlila appears in many different guises—for the wedding of Rama and Sita he is dressed in full turban and glorious silks;

for Dusserah he is similarly dressed but with some royal details added. On other days he may wear plainer clothes. On coronation dawn *arati* he has on a military style overseas cap. Among the people—and we spoke to many all of whom confirmed our observations—the Maharaja is honoured as an upholder of religion, a repository of tradition and authority. His job as sponsor of the Ramlila is recognized as a difficult one. Several people spoke affectionately of the 'poor Maharaja' who was doing his best to keep up the old traditions in the face of myriad difficulties. In Varanasi the Maharaja's reputation is based on something more than nostalgia: the rulers there are known for their support of the arts and learning, as well as for their piety. And Vibhuti Narain Singh has been on the throne since 1936, reaching majority in 1947.

The Maharaja is the representative of Siva, who is considered the lord of ancient, holy Kasi (one of Varanasi's names). The identification with Siva is so complete that everywhere the Maharaja goes he is hailed by great rolling roars of 'Hara, Hara, Mahadev!', a greeting for Siva. And while the Maharaja is cheered as a god in the Ramlila, Rama is cheered as a king. The traditional shout that goes up whenever Rama speaks is 'Bol Ramchandra ki jai!'—'Victory to King Ramchandra.' This inverse link between the two kings/deities is a helix at the heart of Ramnagar Ramlila.

The Maharaja himself recognizes this situation, but denies his personal enhancement of it:

RS: The people call you 'Mahadev'.
MR: It's not personally for me. It is for my whole family. My ancestor who started the dynasty also began a renaissance of Hinduism.
RS: The Ramlila is part of this renaissance?
MR: The Ramlila was started by Tulsidas. My family gave it a push.
RS: For the people, the eternal realm of Rama is mirrored in the role of your family?
MR: Not quite.
RS: But Ramlila is the only drama I know of that can't begin until a certain spectator arrives. What happens if you are sick?
MR: Some member of my family must represent me.
RS: That means?
MR: It is really an administrative aspect. Someone must be in control. From the audience point of view, my presence does

give some prestige. Someone has to take the lead. It is also spiritual: in the Ramayana, Siva tells the story to Parvati. So the representative of Siva must be there.

This last little comment is extremely revealing. In a sense, the whole Ramlila is the Maharaja's–Siva's story: he is telling it, Parvati (in the Maharani's case, a woman still in purdah, often barely visible behind a curtain at the Ramlila grounds) and the great audiences listen.

Usually the Maharaja, positioned on his elephant, with several other elephants bearing various VIPs, forms one of the spatial limits of a scene, with Rama forming the other. Both Maharaja and Rama are elevated, though the Maharaja is usually the higher of the two. The audience is on ground level, except at Ayodhya where women and children sit on the walls and roof of the palace. In some scenes, the gods are represented by large effigies fixed atop very tall bamboo poles, 45 to 50 feet high, overlooking the whole spectacle. These gods are the ultimate spectators.

The Maharaja is often very far from the action. But he is scrupulously aware of the specific gestures necessary for his role:

RS: Sitting so far away on your elephant, you can't see the scene very clearly, or hear.

MR: My father used to use opera glasses. I don't. There is a practical reason for my sitting at the back. My presence establishes control. The crowd is in front of me.

RS: What do people think when you sleep during the performance? (Occasionally I saw the Maharaja doze.)

MR: I don't know what they think. But I am aware of the way I watch. I keep a serenity, a dignity. I don't talk.

The environment of every scene—both processional and fixed—features the Maharaja as strongly as any other character, including Rama. There are scenes where Rama is not present; but the Maharaja is there for the whole Ramlila, except for three scenes:

RS: You leave the Ramlila twice, at Sita's kidnapping and at Ravana's death. Why?

MR: And a third time, too: during the confrontation between Dasaratha and Kaikeyi. My great-grandfather did not leave, but my grandfather did because of the tragic scenes. Dasaratha weeping, the emotional power of that my grandfather didn't like to witness. And also the kidnapping of a queen, the killing of a king, he did not want to see these. But it is only a rule, not a tradition, so I sometimes break the rule.

Part of each day's *lila* is a break of one to three hours while the Maharaja performs his *sandhya puja* (evening prayer). The Maharaja's arrival, his departure for *puja* (sometimes a tent is set up on the spot and the Maharaja withdraws within), and his re-arrival mark out each day's three-part structure. Most days the performance begins at 4:30, while it is still bright day, breaks for *puja* at 6, and resumes at 7:30 as twilight arrives. The *lila* ends by around 9:30 or 10, except on several exceptional nights, and on Coronation Day which goes all night until dawn. During the *sandhya puja* break, which is also the time of twilight, neither day nor night, the strict drama of the Ramlila is relaxed into a *mela*: a great fair mingling the sacred and the secular. The sadhus celebrate wildly, dancing and singing—sometimes even, especially at Citrakut where a large temporary stage has been erected, going onto the stage itself to dance and sing. Performers in costume mingle with spectators: I took tea with Hanuman and chatted about his performing. Families picnic, food stalls do a brisk business, trinkets and powdered colours and toys are sold. There's a festive feeling in the air quite distinct from the more solemn attention paid to the *lila* itself. During the *puja* break, while the Maharaja prays, the people play. All except the *swarupas*, who remain seated in place, their crowns off, but their demeanour serious. Often spectators will come up and touch their feet. A person may enjoy some snack, gossip with a friend, and then change mood and approach the *swarupas* for *darsan*. The *swarupas* sitting for *darsan* during *puja* break give a sense of the timelessness of Ramlila: during the drama they perform the actions of ancient, mythic days; during the *puja* break they are deities present here and now.

The open structure provided by the *sandhya puja* break is not at any time more meaningful than on Dusserah day. The action is set in Lanka, a huge square plain almost a half-mile across in all directions. To the south is Ravana's four-gated Fort and next to it, his throne. To the north, on a hill, is Rama's camp. To the west is the *Asoka* Garden with Sita sitting kidnapped, surrounded by adoring women spectators. In the centre of Lanka the rectangular battle-ground. During the afternoon's *lila* Ravana has surrendered to Rama. A great 75-foot high bamboo-mâché effigy of the demon king is set up atop his Fort. A crowd of nearly 100,000 has gathered. The Maharaja has come and gone. His procession from his Fort has been magnificent: elephant after elephant, each hung with cloaks of purple and gold brocade, adorned with jewels and silver. The Maharaja is in gold himself, like Rama, and he wears a turban with a peacock feather: the symbol of his royal authority. He arrives but does not stay long. After the Maharaja's departure, Ravana surrenders to Rama and disappears amidst the huge crowd (going to collect his 'rent' and return to his village). Then ensues an extra-long *puja* break.

At this climactic moment of the story is a time/space where the many themes of the Ramlila are in suspension: good vs evil, the ever-present vs the evanescent, gods vs demons, people vs superhumans, commoners vs rulers, the outer circle of the *mela* with its commercialism vs the inner circle of the *lila* with its devotion. For a few hours, as it gets dark, all is in balance, the great struggles neutralized, the principles of the cosmos revealed: Ravana = evil, insatiable appetite, is dead but not cremated; Rama and Lakshmana = good, absolute but sportive, sit on their temporary thrones, victorious but still in exile; Sita = mother of the world, sheer devotion, waits patiently under the *asoka* trees. The population of this world, the audience in attendance at Ramlila, circulates among and between these great figures that triangulate Lanka. Of the gods they take *darsan*; but they also peer up at Ravana's giant effigy. The great figures are immobile, but lesser performers, in costume, drink tea, chat: a demon next to a monkey next to a sadhu next to a businessman next to a beggar next to Schechner next to a one-armed wala selling roasted peanuts next to Hess next to a crying child next to a blind man next to a tourist next to an itinerant singer next to a student next to a mother nursing her infant next to three men on solitary camels. 'Where do you come from?' I asked them, imagining a very long, dusty journey from Rajasthan. 'We are the men who come on camels,' one answered. 'Each year we come, for this day only.' That was all they would speak. Nearby sadhus were dancing so energetically that sweat had soaked one's saffron shirt from shoulder to hips. Their drumming and singing pierced the evening air. In no other theatre does the audience as such emerge so clearly as part of the performance. Nowhere else is there time/space allotted for the audience to so clearly, easily, and fully play their various roles. At Ramlila spectators watch, drop out, say their prayers, eat, join small groups singing *kirtans*, sleep, press in close for scenes of high drama—all within the scheme of a performance with a story to tell, a score to follow. Dusserah night at Lanka was one of those great Bruegel paintings with no centre yet full of harmony—thousands of people organized by their interdependent activities. And above them, overlooking it all, the three poles of the world on the last night of their conflict and captivity.

Thinking about this suspension/balance at the climactic moment of the epic cycle, I recognized that Ramnagar Ramlila combines the feel of big events/environments like World's Fairs, Olympic Games, Disneyland, and great religious gatherings and political assemblies with their endorsement of ideology and enactment of patterns of behaviour through audience participation, with relatively tighter dramas such as the processions of the Bread and Puppet Theatre, Robert Wilson's spectacles, Peter Brook's *Orghast*, and Grotowski's paratheatrical experiments. These smaller events have stories and/or themes, but they can't match the scale, both theatrical and conceptual, of Ramnagar Ramlila. They fall within the aesthetic-critical range: they can be 'enjoyed' and 'evaluated'. They need not be 'entered into' as Ramlila demands. Even as Hess and I tried to keep our distance in order to analyse Ramlila we felt ourselves, happily, caught in its cosmic, social, religious, and theatrical web.

Ram Chandra De is not so enmeshed or hopeful:

> Because people have more money, they come to see the show only. Religious belief is fading. The Ramlila hasn't changed because the Maharaja is a conservative. After him? Elsewhere Ramlila has changed. Today people come to see friends, relations, make purchases. Before they had to walk, had no money to waste or spend. Now with good income they travel by train and bus, they visit the city and buy. Some leave before *arati*.

But I'm not certain the deterioration De speaks of is occurring. In India people have the habit of saying that the old times were better—at least in the aspect of religion. I think that Ramlila—like other great gatherings I attended, for example, the Kumbh mela at Prayag in 1977—always combined the sacred and the secular.

The Maharaja is not alone at his end of the playing space. Near him, always, are the Ramayanis—the twelve men who chant the *Ramcaritmanas*. Because the Maharaja is at the back and not in their midst, spectators must turn away from the stage action if they wish to see the Maharaja. Attention is on the Maharaja mostly when he arrives while his elephants or carriage are manoeuvred into place. Then, sitting with the crowd, the closer one is to the stage the less clearly can the *Ramcaritmanas* be heard; conversely, the closer one is to the Maharaja and the Ramayanis the less clearly can one see the stage and hear the *samvads*. Intentionally or not, a situation has been set up that makes spectators choose whether they will gravitate towards the Maharaja or towards Rama.

The Ramayanis focus attention on the Maharaja as well as give him a special experience of the performance. The chanting of the Ramayanis is a counterpoint to the *samvads*. The *Ramcaritmanas* is a sacred text, a beautiful poetic text. The performance of Ramlila alternates between the chanting of that text and the stage action. The Ramayanis form their oval close to the Maharaja: he hears every word of the *Ramcaritmanas* but only some of the *samvads*. When he is separated from Rama by a great distance, and an immense noisy crowd, it is as if there were two performances going on, the link between them stretched almost to the breaking point. At one end of the performance field is the brightly petromax-lit stage, its well-composed arrangements of figures in gaudy costumes; at the other end is the Maharaja, either visible in daylight, or barely visible after dark; and the Ramayanis with their palm-leaf manuscripts of Tulsidas illuminated only by the burning of kerosene-dipped torches. At night especially the performance seems stretched in two directions. The stage is for the eye; the Ramayanis for the ear. And if you turn to follow your ears, you perceive the ever-present Maharaja high on his elephant. On clear nights he sits in an open box; on rainy ones, in a closed cabin strapped to the giant elephant's back, like some weird boat floating atop a sea of people. When the Maharaja moves into the action on the final days of the cycle, the Ramayanis move with him, resolving the duality of the drama into its ultimate unity.

Just as the Maharaja has his Ramayanis, so Rama has his sadhus. These holy men crowd to the front of every scene—they are devotees of Rama and want to get as close to him as they can. They are different than the rest of the audience. Some are naked, many wear only loincloths, most are bare-chested; their bodies are gray-blue with ashes dusted onto their dark-brown skin; their hair is very long, uncut, matted, sometimes wound into high buns or done in braids. They sing, chant, dance, laugh, smoke, shout—sitting or standing in circles of from fifteen to 250. For them the Ramnagar Ramlila is a great annual reunion. In 1976, Rs 18,000 were spent on feeding them. The Maharaja gives them rations and places to sleep. The free food and lodging is one thing that attracts numbers of sadhus to Ramnagar Ramlila. The sadhus attend because they are devoted to Rama; they attend because the Maharaja gives them free food and dharamsalas. Since the sadhus exist mostly by begging, a month's free bed and board is an important part of their year's economy. (In 1976, fewer than usual attended because there were rumours that the Indira

Gandhi government had decreed that men found travelling on trains without tickets would be sterilized—and sadhus routinely travel without tickets. That they are supposed to be celibate did not encourage them to become sterilized. In 1978, the sadhu population at Ramlila had returned to normal, about 200–300.) Among the sadhus are many regulars who have come to Ramlila for as long as people can remember. These sadhus are theatrical characters in their own right. Their presence is expected; their gestures are fixed not by text or through rehearsals but by habit, tradition, and the expectations of the audience.

The sadhus attend to Rama. They lead each other and the crowd in chanting *kirtans*—especially one whose whole text is 'Sita Ram, Sita Ram, Sita Ram Jai!, Sita Ram.' On and on this chant goes, until I found myself singing it too, even in my dreams. The Maharaja and his Ramayanis (their leader is the Maharaja's chief domestic priest) represent formality, order, the formal text; Rama and his sadhus (living Hanumans of our own century) represent ebullient devotion, sacred clowning, the deep informal texts of the oral tradition.

The presence of the Maharaja and the sadhus makes a difference in the kind of performance obtained. Certainly Ramnagar Ramlila is different than others. Hess and I attended the Ramlila that Tulsidas himself began—the one sponsored by the Sankat Mochan temple of Varanasi. This Ramlila is performed over ten days at several sites: near Tulsi's house on the bank of the Ganga; at Sankat Mochan; and in a triangular field called Lanka near the temple. We went to the coronation of Rama in 1976. Here is what I recorded in my notebook:

9:30 p.m. This is like a home movie while the Ramnagar Ramlila is a Hollywood epic. There is authenticity here, a lack of big resources, and therefore the clear impact of modernization: Men and women spectators less rigidly segregated; the stage is an elevated square platform at one end of the space under a *shamiana* with a painted backdrop—just like many other modern Indian folk theatres I've seen (Yakshagana, Raslila, Jatra). The pronunciation of Hindi is not standardized here—it is the way people talk, so I get the feeling of a small town with its own particular dialect. The Ramayanis are very strong, they use a drum and *shenai* which adds to their power. Only one sadhu in attendance— not a naked *baba* but a jolly man in saffron. We don't feel sneaky photographing: we don't feel intrusive, like we're violating anything. This event does not demand, command, and get the kind of attention common at Ramnagar.

The difference is in the attitude of the spectators, and this attitude is controlled by extra-theatrical factors: (1) no Maharaja here; (2) no sadhus; (3) no police with their big sticks beating back the surging crowd; (4) no uniformed guard as the Maharaja has who, along with the police, give Ramnagar Ramlila the feel of an event where an important public person, like a Prime Minister, is making an appearance. At Ramnagar there is both a religious and political presence felt. At Ramnagar the sadhus give the event religious significance, the police and honour guard give it temporal significance, and the Maharaja combines these. Also at Ramnagar the sheer size of the audience is awesome. Here it is small, less than 1,000, and homey. At Ramnagar, when the coronation was over, spectators fought to have *darsan*, and the police with their sticks beat them back to keep order. Here all who want *darsan* can easily get it. The *swarupas* themselves are not so formal or formidable looking. Deities they may be, boys they certainly are.

About 85 per cent of the close-up spectators are children, mostly under ten years of age. They laugh a lot. Their attention wanders. Except for Rama and Sita the *swarupas* here are very casual even during the performance, sometimes snacking and talking.

In Ramnagar a world is created with six circles of attention, drawing people towards a very hot centre; at Tulsi a neighbourhood performs a play with four circles of attention, actually leading away from a cool centre:

Ramnagar: Centripetal	*Tulsi: Centrifugal*
1 Maharaja–Rama	1 Performers
2 Ramayanis–Sadhus	2 Ramayanis
3 Male spectators	3 Children spectators
4 Female and children spectators	4 Other spectators,
5 Fringe spectators	walas, all with
6 Walas, who are kept out	wandering attention
except during *puja* break	

Significantly, the most skilled performers at Tulsi are the Ramayanis, while at Ramnagar, the Maharaja, Rama (and other principals), Ramayanis, sadhus, and *nemis* (attentive spectators), all play their roles beautifully. The absence of Maharaja, sadhus, and attentive male spectators undercuts the effectiveness of the Tulsi Ramlila: there is no model of how to experience the performance.

Performing Styles, Roles, Rehearsals, Directors, Staging, Ikonography

Earlier I quoted a spectator who thought that everything at Ramlila was 'natural'. This just shows what a slippery culture-bound concept 'natural' is. From my Western perspective the acting styles and staging are anything but natural. More: they are not directly analogous to what is current in mainstream American acting or staging. The use of Ramnagar itself—both the constructed environments and the found spaces (streets, forests, streams, fields)—has more in common with American experimental theatre than with anything in the mainstream. Ramlila is like the movies, staged 'on location', using non-actors ikonographically.

The acting is flat for most of the time. Words are spoken, or declaimed in a sing-song fashion and shouted so that the vast crowds can hear. Only rarely—when Rama laments the wounding of Lakshmana, when Parasurama storms in angry that Siva's bow has been broken, when Sita complains of her imprisonment in Lanka, when Angada taunts Ravana in an often humorous dialogue, when Narada sings his haunting song about Pancavati—does the acting carry emotional weight. Much of the dialogue recited by the more than 30 characters of Ramlila is mumbled, inaudible beyond the first few rows. Sometimes the performers actually appear embarrassed by who they are or what they have to say, as when several teen-aged boys enact the young women of Janakpur reciting long speeches in admiration of the beauty of Rama and Lakshmana. (All roles are played by males.)

The gestures of the actors are the same scene after scene, regardless of the situation. The most typical gesture is a sweeping motion of the right arm from the shoulder, with the hand and arm moving away from the chest making a broad semi-circle that sweeps over and includes the audience. The actors look mostly at the audience and not at who they are speaking to.

Many big moments are non-acted. For example, the contest for Sita's hand. Many princes have come to compete for Sita, who will be given to the man who can lift Siva's great bow. Several princes try, all fail. In their attempts no effort is made to indicate how heavy the bow is, how massive its size. Each prince perfunctorily stoops over the bow, pretends to tug at it, and fails. Then Rama steps up and effortlessly, without hesitation or doubt, lifts the bow, snaps his wrists, and breaks the bow in two. Instead of this gesture revealing Rama's incredible strength, it underlines the fact that the bow is made of papier-mâché, designed to break at the slightest touch. As Rama breaks the bow the white *arati* flare burns, a cannon goes off representing the thunder crack as Siva's bow snaps, and the crowd roars. This impressive staging is not matched by the acting, which remains flat. Yet, for me at least, the non-acting fits perfectly with the ikonography and meaning of the scene. Rama's playful, even ironic, omnipotence is shown by the way he not only breaks Siva's bow but exposes it as a stage prop. In Rama's—Visnu's—*lila* the great bow is a toy. Then Parasurama storms into Janakpur yanking the mood back to that of conventional and effective drama. Often these two kinds of style succeed each other giving Ramlila a special tension—a sense of existing in two worlds at once, that of ritual and that of theatre.

The Bharata Milap also conveys several levels and kinds of performance simultaneously. On an elevated square stage, something like a boxing ring, set up in the intersection of two main Ramnagar roads, the brothers enact their reunion after Rama's fourteen year exile. After embracing and then lying prostrate on the ground and kissing each other's feet, the *swarupas* stand up in a straight line and face the crowd eight separate times, slowly rotating clockwise. Each time they face a direction the white flares associated with *arati* are lit and the crowd goes crazy. It is simple, abstract, extended, and moving: a sheer display of the five divine figures united at last showing themselves to all the assembled people. Thus the narrative drama is transformed at this moment into *darsan*.

So it is also, if less spectacularly, at the end of each night's *lila* with the performance of *arati*. Rama and Sita, and often Lakshmana too, are the 'ikons' of the nightly *arati* service. Different characters wave the camphor lamp, Hanuman usually wields the fly whisk. During *arati* first white and then red flares are lit brightly illuminating the scene and flattening the perspective so that it appears that temple *murtis* are there, not living performers. The *swarupas* are carefully instructed in the pose they must maintain, their bodies stiff and still, their faces frozen. Spectators surge forward to take *darsan*. On one occasion, at the start of his exile, after crossing the make-believe

Ganga, Rama performs the temple service to a Siva *lingam*. This service is particularly exciting to the crowd, which mercilessly presses inward to catch a glimpse of the action that brings together these two most powerful gods.

The *samvads* which the characters recite are dialogues in modern (nineteenth century) Hindi, but they are far from colloquial either in tone or meaning. The *samvads* repeat or elaborate what is chanted in the classical Hindi of the *Ramcaritmanas*. Classical Hindi stands in roughly the same relationship to today's Hindi as Chaucer's English does to today's. Thus, as in several Asian traditional theatres, some of the language spoken is not understood by most of the audience. And, as in Nō where the Kyogen tells the story in a more accessible Japanese, the *samvads* in a sense translate the *Ramcaritmanas*. But often the *samvads* do much more than translate: they elaborate. The story of how King Janaka got hold of Siva's bow is not in the *Ramcaritmanas*, but it is in the *samvads*; the episode between Kaikeyi and Manthara is drawn out extensively in the *samvads*.

The *samvads* are rehearsed in two different ways. The *swarupas* change from year to year, though boys are encouraged to stay with the Ramlila for several years and move up the ladder of roles so that frequently enough a boy who plays Satrughna or Bharata one year will 'graduate' to Lakshmana or Rama in a year or two. Still there is much turnover, and extensive rehearsal. Training begins two months before Ramlila for up to ten hours a day (including a two to four hour siesta). For the first month the boys work just on memorizing the dialogue. Then they learn how to speak and move. This practice is sheer imitation. One *vyas* works only with the *swarupas*. He says a line, they repeat; he shows a gesture, they do it exactly the same. Everything is learned by imitating the *vyas*: pronunciation, intonation, projection, rhythm, gestures, movement. During the performance itself the *vyas*, *samvad* book in hand, stands behind the *swarupas* making sure that all the words are said correctly, all the gestures acted precisely. In fact, if one is close enough to the action, you can hear the *vyas* pronounce every word quietly into the *swarupas*' ears: in an actual sense, the dialogues are twice done. Rehearsals are not over when performances begin. Each day the *swarupas* practise for several hours. Then another hour or two is spent in putting on costumes and makeup. All the boys attend all the rehearsals. In 1976 the father of the boy playing Lakshmana died in the middle of Ramlila month. It was not possible for the performer to continue to play Lakshmana

because the death in his family polluted him. The boy playing
Satrughna took over the role. 'I was at all the rehearsals, I knew
what to say.' The training pays off.

Within the conventions of flatness and ikonographic rather than
naturalistic staging, the over-all effect of Ramlila at Ramnagar is very
powerful. I remember from the 1976 Ramlila especially Sita's lament
on day 25. After Rama fails to defeat Ravana, the whole vast crowd
moves to where Sita sits imprisoned under the *asoka* trees. There, in
the clearest voice of the Ramlila, Sita spoke and moaned, a formal-
ized moaning that extended certain final vowels, their sound diminishing slowly, vanishing like smoke in the air. Her voice was clear,
her moans moving without being sentimental. Still, the chief *vyas*
thinks the quality of acting has gone down:

> In the past more rupees were spent. They get the same amount
> now but it buys less. If they do a good job, it is out of faith and
> love, and if that is lacking, the performance gets worse.

Hess and I spoke to the assistant *vyas* who played Sita when he was
young.

RS: When you played Sita were you possessed by her, or was it
'just a role'?
VYAS: I get the feeling in my heart that I am Sita. It is written:
Whoever is a true devotee becomes absorbed in god. When
you're absorbed you behave as that person. If you cry it is a
real crying. When the actor believes 'I am the character', then
he really cries.

This is very much the same kind of reply Jane Belo got when inter-
viewing people in a Balinese village about their experience of being
in a trance and performing various beings (animals, gods, household
things like a broom).[8] We asked the same question of the chief *vyas*
and of the boy playing Rama:

CHIEF VYAS: If in the play it says 'it's raining', and you look into
a clear sky, still it is raining.
RS (To Rama): When people come and touch your feet, what do
you feel?
RAMA: The feeling of god is in me.
RS: Why did you audition for Ramlila?
RAMA: I have the desire, the respect for all the important people
involved, and my faith. If you come from a poor family it is a

good chance; and if you come from a rich family, it gives you a good reputation.

Earlier I asked the Maharaja how the *swarupas* are selected early in July. The chief *vyas*—a temple priest at the Fort—has searched the neighbouring communities for candidates; about fifty boys are invited to the Fort to meet the Maharaja.

> RS: How do you choose the performers?
> MR: Voice, good looks, family bringing up.
> RS: What happens to the boys after their experience in the Ramlila?
> MR: Some become sadhus, one became a *vyas* and gives discourses on the Ramayana. This particular *vyas* played all four roles [except Sita]. For many years his voice didn't change so he could continue to perform.

I suspect there is some romanticizing here in regard to the lives former *swarupas* live. Hess and I tried to track down a few. One man was a journalist and he said that his experience as Lakshmana, his work 'in the theatre', opened up for him the possibility of a career in 'communications'. Another young man had played Rama in the early 70s, and had earned a great reputation for his sincerity in performance. It was said that he shed real tears when Lakshmana was wounded. This boy, very poor, was attending a religious school, though his widowed mother was finding it hard to pay the tuition. His ambition was to be a scholar. Most ex-*swarupas* had vanished into the population.

There are more performers in Ramlila than the *swarupas*. Some roles are hereditary—Ravana has been in the same family since the time of Iswari Prasad Narain Singh who ruled from 1835 to 1889: the time that Ramnagar Ramlila developed its present form. At present Ravana is played by both father and son. The scenes that are not physically demanding are played by the frail father, the rest by his more vigorous son. The son tells how Ravana came to be in his family:

> The story is people were being selected there in Ramnagar [the Ravana family, called 'Ravanraj' by all the neighbours, live in Surauli village about 15 kilometres from Ramnagar]. My *baba* reached there in Iswari Narain Singh's time. His name was Ayodhya Pathak, and the king's minister was Bhau Bhatt. My *baba* reached the place where they were choosing among 18

men. Yes, an open selection. My *baba's* age was 35 to 40 then. So they heard the voices of all 18 men. My grandfather's voice pleased Iswari Narain Singh. He asked Bhau Bhatt, and Bhatt said, 'Your Highness, he is Maharavana [Super Ravana].' The other people around said that for the other candidates you could have hopes—they were all younger and lived nearby. You may hope for them, but this one has fulfilled all hopes. The Maharaja gave the order. That was it. They gave my *baba* the book to study. He memorized it. Since then the part of Ravana has remained in our family. By now it's been about four generations. Ayodhya Pathak, Jogeshwar Pathak, Narayan Pathak— he's the one you see here, and his son, me, Kaushal Prasad Pathak.

RS: So Sri Narayanji has played Ravana for a long time?

NARAYAN: I have said the role for 58 years.

The man playing Parasurama has performed it 34 years. He says the role is already being passed on to his son.

Some people literally grow into their roles so that their physical being appears to be a reflection of their Ramlila identities. The man playing Brahma is 96 years old, with a feeble voice and very delicate gestures. He has played Brahma more years than he can remember. Other performers play several roles. The man who plays Visvamitra also plays Valmiki, Atri Muni, Agastya, Lomas-rishi, and Trijata. Some of the best actors, such as the man who plays Angada, are young—and they came into Ramlila by accident. The family of the *vyas* who rehearses the roles other than the *swarupas*, and who is in charge of all technical arrangements, had come into possession of a number of key roles, including Hanuman, Angada, Sugriva, and others: a total of 11 roles. Then, in 1977, a death occurred in this family during Ramlila season. This meant that a number of key roles had to be replaced immediately, causing a great strain on the performance, and perhaps even a decline in its quality. Through this crisis, the Maharaja recognized that too many roles had been centralized in one family. It was during the rush to find replacements that the man who now plays Angada was brought into the Ramlila. The process of decentralization continues.

In one case at least a Ramlila role has had a deep effect on the performer's non-Ramlila life. The man who plays Narada with great force is the *mahant* of two temples in Mirzapur, about 75 kilometres from Ramnagar. He is a relatively wealthy man. He moved to Mirzapur in 1957. But he was not always a *mahant*. He's been in the

Ramlila for 30 years, since 1948. When he lived in Ramnagar he was 'in the service of the Maharaja'. He did various jobs: 'I used to be the priest of the *saligrama* for the Rani in her palace. I did all kinds of work. I did *puja-path* [a general term for priest's work].' But with Independence 'many people had to be let go, that was in 1952'. I asked Narada—he is known by that name in or out of Ramlila—how he got involved:

> My own story is this. When I was first at the Maharaja's, I was just a child, 13 years old. During the time of Ramlila my job was to stay with Ramji. Every year I was sent there, and since there was never any complaint about me, there was no objection. From 1929 to 1951 I stayed with Ramji for a month, and looked after all the arrangements. I was in charge of all their studying, training, teaching. You know the Ramlila books? Well, besides me you won't find anybody who has them.

RS: You have the whole *samvad*?

NARADA: The whole *samvad*. If you come to my place I can show it all to you, the dialogues of all four *swarupas*. Then from 1951 to 1958 I was the *vyas* for the *swarupas*. There was a *baba* there too, Baba Kamala Saran. He was very old. So I said to him, you just sit there, I'll do all the work, but you'll get the credit, don't worry. He, poor thing, was 80 years old. It was then that the Maharaja gave me a copy of the *samvads*. It took me three years, working an hour every day, to make a copy. I gave the copy to the Maharaja and he showed it to a German lady and she ran away with it. Now I'm helpless. He asks me for another copy. I say, 'Look, I live in Robertsganj. My brother is old and sick. How can he write it?'

RS: After 1958, when Raghunath Datta took over the *vyas* work, what did you do?

NARADA: I became a projectionist in the cinema in Benares. I went to Calcutta to pass an exam to be a projectionist. I was a projectionist for eleven months, and worked in the Ramlila for one.

RS: And since when have you played Naradji?

NARADA: Always, for 30 years.

RS: So you played Narada all the time you were doing these other things?

NARADA: Yes. Narada's part comes only for five or six days. The other days I spent with the *swarupas*.

RS: Who played Narada before you?

NARADA: He also stayed with the Maharaja. When he played I

used to stay near him. Nobody explained anything to me. I just listened to him and did it the way he did it. One day he said to me, 'Listen, you do this work now.' He went to the Maharaja and said, 'I won't do this work now, my body has reached the state, my age, where I can't.' The Maharaja asked who should do it. I was a *vyas* at the time so he said to me, 'You do it.'

RS: We like your acting very much. How do you do it so well?

NARADA: My experience is this. When I put on the crown and before Ramji, then I feel sure that I am really before him, only before him. I don't see him as a man. I see him as a *bhagwan*. At that time, if anybody tries to talk to me, I don't want to talk. At that time, everything appears extraordinary. What people call *tanmaya* [completely merging, losing a sense of the self]. It's like when you're in love. Whatever exists, it's only Ramji, only he.

RS: Could the same feeling come to any good actor playing any role? As a projectionist you've seen lots of actors.

NARADA: No, the same feeling couldn't come. Acting is done for money. When anybody works for money he just says, 'All right, let me do my duty.' But for him who works in a feeling of love, there is no question of money. Didn't I tell you before that the Maharaja can't make me work for money? It is my love, and only because of that, that I've reached this condition. By god's grace I've arrived here.

RS: What do you mean?

NARADA: Imagine. I used to live with the Maharaja like an ordinary man. I got Rs 50 a month. Now I have reached a high position. Everyone in the city respects me. A *mahant* is like a king. I get Rs 1,000 a month.

RS: When did you become *mahant*?

NARADA: In 1970 my *guruji* passed away. And this is 1978. In 1970 it all came into my hands.

RS: Have Narada's words and personality influenced your life and your work as a *mahant*?

NARADA: There is a proverb: 'Whatever anybody does, it's only Rama. Man can do nothing by himself. The doer is only Rama.'

Very few people know Narada by his actual name, Mahant Baba Omkar Das. The role of Narada he has played in Ramlila has come to define his ordinary actuality. And this, I'm sure, is due largely to the quality of his acting—his projection of deep sincerity, his demeanour which is imposing and authoritative, and his gifts as a singer.

Thus in Ramlila we are presented with an incredibly complicated aesthetics. At one extreme is the flat acting, at the other a role so powerfully performed that the player is absorbed into it, his whole present life is defined by it. The ikonography of key scenes, and the nightly *arati*, projects Ramlila into the realm of the Hindu temple service with its manifestation of divine presence. Hereditary actors perform side by side with those who audition for roles on a yearly basis. Certain roles are not hereditary but still are controlled by families. The Maharaja, as producer, oversees the whole thing but it is too vast for him to know everything that's going on. This is in keeping with what seems to me to be perhaps an unconscious but still all-pervasive intention of Ramnagar Ramlila: to be more than any single human being can take in. As I wrote in my notebook after Dusserah 1978:

> No one, not even the most knowledgeable, not even the Maha-raja, the *vyases*, Atmaram the carpenter, the most diligent scholars, the most faithful *nemis* [who attend every performance] —no one knows it all. Even at the basic level of what's being done day by day by everyone involved. No one even knows how many are involved. Where do you stop counting? With the direct participants? With the man who takes a month out every year from his work to fashion with his own hands the garlands that the *swarupas* wear each night for *arati*? With the *nemis* or sadhus who travel great distances to attend? With the spectators who attend irregularly? With the operators of the tea and *chat* [snacks] stalls who never see any *lila* at all, but who keep the *mela* going night after night? No one can see every scene because so many are simultaneous and occur far removed from each other in space.

Thus Ramnagar Ramlila creates its own model of the universe.

The Future of the Ramlila of Ramnagar

There's no doubt that Ramlila will continue to be celebrated in northern India. But about Ramnagar Ramlila there are some problems which I can only touch on here. Money is getting tighter all the time, and tradition is wearing thin. Even given the fact that it is normal for people in India to speak of the 'old days' as having more splendour, more piety, more devotional intensity (paralleling in everyday discourse the devolution outlined in the *yuga*-theory of history), it seems that Ramlila of Ramnagar is less opulent and less lavishly produced than earlier. A large part of this is a question of budget. Subsidy is given to the Maharaja by the Government of Uttar Pradesh, but it is not enough. Since 1949 when the Maharaja's political power was abolished and after the privy purse ended, Uttar Pradesh gave first Rs 100,000 and more recently Rs 115,000 annually to support the Ramlila. This money cannot be simply translated into dollar equivalents to give Americans a sense of its worth. In terms of buying power think of a grant of about $150,000. This is still very little compared to the scope of Ramlila, its grounds, costumes, props, and other items of expense including salaries to performers, *vyases*, Ramayanis, guards, musicians, and so on. A budget accounting from 8 February 1977 showed the following items as major expenses:

Feeding of sadhus	Rs 18,000
Contractor for effigies	3,500
Pay for *swarupas*	2,200
Rental of petromax lamps, payment to their bearers	2,160
General labour (grounds, porters, etc.)	1,700
Arati flares	1,375
Other actors	1,350
Bullock cart rental (to transport *swarupas*)	1,295

Items ranged down to Rs 20 paid for 15 days' service of a washer-woman. Lots of things are not budgeted, but kept from year to year, such as costumes and the basic environments. The costumes are getting threadbare; those at Tulsi, new in 1978 at a cost of more than Rs 20,000, are out of reach for Ramnagar. Other items are collected over the year when they can be gotten most cheaply. For example, bamboo is collected in February. Also many persons on the Maharaja's staff spend much of their time organizing the Ramlila. The four *vyases* are temple priests in Ramnagar. Their budgeted salaries for 85 days' work is a total of Rs 576, but they also receive support from their temples and from the Maharaja's temple trusts. All in all, 231 persons spent 1,441 work days preparing for and per-forming the 1976 Ramlila. A detailed analysis of the budget shows that in 1955 Rs 103,763 was spent on Ramlila; in 1975 it was Rs 125,360. According to information supplied by the Maharaja's staff 'there has not been any change in the amounts paid to performers over the past fifty years or so'. Which means, simply, that the amount has gone down drastically as inflation eats up the value of money.

Make no mistake—Ramlila is a big production by any measurement. In it are employed 95 performers, more than 100 workmen, and 4 persons from the Maharaja's temples. Thirteen temples connected with the Ramlila are maintained by the All-India Kashiraj Trust at a cost, in 1977–8, of Rs 51,262. It is difficult to put all the information together but Hess and I estimate that the total actual cost for each year's Ramlila, as of 1976 or 1978, was about Rs 350,000 —or a buying power equivalent to about $500,000.

The Maharaja is not a poor man, but neither is he in command of fabled wealth, unlimited resources. As Maharaja of Benares he is in a somewhat difficult situation economically speaking. Because of the particular religious significance of his position he cannot turn the Fort into a tourist hotel, or become a full-scale industrialist the way some former Maharajas have done. To do this would be to sacrifice his authority earned by virtue of his apparent 'disinterest' in the economic affairs of this world. The Maharaja exists at least to some degree as a figure of religious mystery. Mystery in the medieval European sense: a person who draws on force that can't be itemized in a budget or reduced to a time-effort flow chart. The Maharaja is the chief causer of the Ramlila and he is chiefly caused, or kept in his special existence, by the Ramlila. The Ramlila and the Maharaja are in a symbiotic relationship.

On the other hand, if some economically productive plan is not developed the sheer production elements of the Ramlila—the effigies, the environments, the costumes, the flares—will get shoddier and shoddier. Looking at old photos and etchings it is apparent that much decay has already occurred. The Maharaja is trapped: he can't be the kind of Maharaja he is and make a lot of money; without a lot of money he can't maintain the Ramlila. The unique situation of Kasi–Ramnagar precludes this double role. Thus the Maharaja faces the contradiction of supporting a ritual superstructure by means of a modern infrastructure that will undermine the very thing it purports to support. I spoke briefly to the Raj Kumar, the heir to the throne. He wants to be an industrialist; he wants to keep up the Ramlila.

The Maharaja of Benares is special because the Ganga and Kasi are special. Even as India has become a modern secular state, or is in the process of becoming such on its own terms, the ritual aspects of its culture, especially in the villages and in the village-like neighbourhoods of many cities, remain resilient, living, very active. The Maharaja of Benares maintains his identity as Maharaja solely on the basis of ritual: tradition, pomp, parades, public religious devotion, Ramlila: theatrical activities.

In Ramnagar Ramlila we have a fundamentally folk art perfected during the colonial phase of India's history, arising in a 'princely state', continuing to exist in the modern era, reflecting the very special qualities of Benares. This theatrical-religious-political-social event is of great interest to me as a theatre person, and I recommend it to Indian theatre workers. If Kathakali, and like forms, have developed meaningful and powerful aesthetics based on classical norms (reinterpreted to be sure), then Ramnagar Ramlila has developed its own aesthetics based on folk norms. These are even more appealing to me than the classical dance and drama. Ramlila uses myth, audience participation, political allusion, constructed and found environments, performers at all levels of skill and involvement, and even the existing socio-political circumstances to develop a performance of great diversity and power. Ramlila cannot be imitated, but it can be learned from.

1. Research on Ramlila was carried out by Linda Hess and me in 1976, 1977, and 1978. Portions of the article here are adapted from our co-authored article, 'The Ramlila of Ramnagar', in *TDR*, 21: 3 (September 1977), pp. 51–82.

2. The distinction between 'Great' and 'Little' traditions was first made, I believe, by anthropologist Robert Redfield. I am using the application and elaboration of that idea as expressed by Milton Singer in his *When A Great Tradition Modernizes* (London: Pall Mall Press, 1972).

3. I am using the term 'stations' as it is applied to 'stations of the Cross', or the stations used during medieval cycle plays in Europe. Christ stopped at 14 stations on his way to the Crucifixion and down from it (carried to his grave). Easter processions frequently move from station to station with stops at each. This pattern of movement and stopping followed by further movement is typical also of Ramlila. I am not suggesting any connection between Ramlila and the Christian celebrations—just a parallel solution to analogous narrative situations.

4. See 'Towards a Poetics of Performance' in Schechner, *Essays on Performance Theory 1970–76* (N.Y.: Drama Book Specialists, 1977). See also Victor Turner, 'Social Dramas and Ritual Metaphors', in *Dramas, Fields, and Metaphors* (Ithaca: Cornell University Press, 1974). Also 'The Anthropology of Performance' in *Process, Performance, and Pilgrimage* (New Delhi: Concept Publishing Company, 1979).

5. H. D. Sankalia, *Ramayana: Myth or Reality?* (New Delhi: People's Publishing House, 1973), p. 55.

6. Surinder Mohan Bhardwaj, *Hindu Places of Pilgrimage in India* (Delhi: Thomson Press Ltd., 1973), p. 7.

7. See earlier in 'Restoration of Behaviour', pp. 194–206, which deals, in part, with restored villages.

8. See 'Trance Experience in Bali' in *Ritual, Play, and Performance*, eds. Richard Schechner and Mady Schuman (New York: Seabury Press, 1976), pp. 150–61. Or: Jane Belo, *Trance in Bali* (New York: Columbia University Press, 1960). As trance-dancer Darja said: 'When I've already gone in trance, my thoughts are delicious, but I do not remember it. [...] I feel just like a puppy, I feel happy to run along the ground. I am very pleased, just like a puppy running on the ground. As long as I can run on the ground, I'm happy.'

8

Performance Spaces:
Ramlila and Yaqui Easter

To speak of performance spaces is also to speak of time and function. Not only what spaces are used, but for how long and in what ways. And it is not always true that space follows function—that a particular arrangement of a performance space is the way it is because of the use to which it will be put. Certain shrines arise around special places: place comes first, and around it gather definite kinds of performances. Nō drama itself may be considered, among other things, a theatre of marking special places. Also to speak of performance spaces is to speak of rhythmicity: the alternation between activity and inactivity, sound and silence, fullness and emptiness. In a chart (Figure 1) comparing a number of performances with regard to genre, space, and time in several cultures I find almost no limits to what a performance may be, where it may take place, how long it takes to complete, what its functions are. There are private performances for no audiences, or audiences of 1; there are performances with a live audience of more than 100,000 and a media audience of many millions. There are performances that take place secretly, in hard-to-get-to places closed off from public view; and there are performances that aggressively try to reach as many persons as possible employing every available means of publicity and broadcasting. There are performances closely identified with specific places—so closely linked that a performance elsewhere is impossible; and there are performances that cannot be said to belong to any place.

The varieties, magnitudes, and functions of performances are so vast that it may not be helpful to generalize, except by providing Figure 1. Instead I will look a little more carefully at a few examples. I will concentrate my remarks on Ramlila of Ramnagar, a 31-day cycle play of north India that tells the story of Rama's great war against the demon king, Ravana. Then I will examine aspects of Yaqui Easter, as celebrated in New Pascua, Arizona. The Yaqui Passion Play begins at Lent and ends Easter Sunday. Holy Week, and especially Wednesday through Saturday, are climactic. Finally I shall survey some experiments with performance space made by American theatre artists in the 60s and 70s. I intend that this intercultural comparison will form the basis for a discussion.

I've described Ramlila in detail elsewhere in this book. Ramlila is a cycle play lasting ten to thirty-one days performed outdoors in the Hindi-speaking region of north India. Its season is around the Dusserah holiday in September–October. Dusserah is Durga Puja in Bengali-speaking India. A very important day. Ramlila is based on Tulsidas' late sixteenth century epic poem, *Ramcaritmanas*, a Hindi version of Valmiki's Sanskrit *Ramayana*. Although thousands of Ramlilas are performed, of varying complexity and duration, I have studied only one carefully: that of Ramnagar, acknowledged throughout India as the fullest, most theatrically sophisticated, and holiest of them all.

Ramnagar is across the Ganga River from Varanasi, also called Benares, one of the most sacred cities in India. Due to the patronage of the Maharaja of Benares, who lives in Ramnagar, this Ramlila draws the largest audiences of any. The whole subject of Ramlila is vast, touching themes of *bhakti* (devotional worship), pilgrimage, reincarnation, nationalism, theatre, relationship between performer and role being performed, kingship, poetry, the secular government, and patronage. Here I will deal only with the space of the performance.

But in Ramlila even space is complicated. To discuss it involves consideration of pilgrimage, processions, the Maharaja as King and as performer, theatrical *mise-en-scène*, ancient and modern Indian history, the relationship between myth, theatrical space, and local geography.

Ramnagar literally means 'town of Rama'. Fittingly named because the town of Ramnagar is the actual setting for the enactment of Rama's deeds. During the first third of the nineteenth century, under the direct supervision of the Maharajas of the time, numerous stage settings were built throughout the town in order to provide places for the various Ramlila performance events. Thus there is Ayodhya, the capital of Rama's kingdom; Janakpur, the home of Sita, his queen; Citrakut, Rama's first residence in exile; Pancavati, the spot where Sita is kidnapped by Ravana, ten-headed demon king of Lanka; and Lanka itself, Ravana's kingdom and site of the great battles between Ravana's and Rama's armies. More than this, there are the pathways and main streets of Ramnagar used for processions;

and the main town square used to depict the reunion of Rama, Sita, and Lakshmana with their brothers when Rama's exile ends. And there is the outside and inside of the Maharaja's Fort, or palace, which becomes part of the drama in its final days.

Importantly, the actual orientation of these spaces, as well as their relative position in Ramnagar, is a more or less accurate model not only of India and Sri Lanka, but also of Rama's movement through the countryside. The Ganga River makes a loop at Benares (also called Varanasi and Kasi) so that the sun rises over the river, with Benares on the west bank, Ramnagar on the east. This helps in orienting the Ramlila environments so that actually Lanka is far to the southeast, Ayodhya to the northwest, Janakpur to far north and Citrakut (also Rambagh: Rama's pleasure garden in the last night's performance) to the northeast, a direction of good luck.

The action of Ramlila is both physical and narrative. That is the actual movement of the characters is itself a decisive part of the story: movement has significance. The first night of the performance, where the gods implore Visnu to incarnate himself as Rama, is performed around the *kshir sagar*, in front of an ancient Durga temple near Citrakut and Rambagh, in the auspicious northeast. When Rama goes into exile he crosses makebelieve Ganga River—the holy river— as he heads from his capital at Ayodhya in the northwest back towards the northeast. When Sita is kidnapped, Rama's army moves steadily to the southeast. This move parallels the actual historical movement through India of the Sanskritic, Vedic culture the Aryan invaders of India brought with them. Among the poems they brought, merging into Dravidian and other native Indian traditions, was the Ramayana. After the climactic battles and cremation of Ravana at Lanka, battles that have looked just about the same for 150 years, Rama victorious and his party are loaded into a great cart hauled by spectators through the streets of Ramnagar first to the reunion with their brothers and later, in a conflation of time and place, to an actual meeting with the existing Maharaja of Benares who, assisted by his family, feeds visiting King Rama a sumptuous meal as thousands of townspeople look on.

At this point something very powerful theatrically and religiously is creating a unique social, even political, situation. Since 1949 when India became an independent, secular state, there has been, officially speaking, no Maharaja of Benares. All principalities were abolished, and a few years later, the privy purses were discontinued. Still every-

one calls Vibhuti Narain Singh 'Maharaja'. Why? The answer in no
small way is to be found in Ramlila. For the Ramlila season, especially
during the performance of the *arati* temple service that concludes each
evening's show, the *murtis*—literally, 'images' of the gods—who are
the boys playing Rama, Sita, Lakshmana, Bharata, and Satrughna—
are thought by many in the audience to actually be the gods they
otherwise represent. It is a miracle parallel to Catholic transubstantiation. Thus the presence of the *murtis* bestows on their patron and host
a royalty that might by now be much diminished (as with some other
Indian former Maharajas). But it's not quite that simple. There is
more like a symbiotic relationship tied up as well to the whole physical
setting of Ramnagar: to the fact that for a month, in a whole town,
Rama lives. The Maharaja of Benares is the only person with enough
religious-traditional force to sponsor a great Ramlila. And the Ramlila
in turn validates the Maharaja's Maharajadom. The climactic visit
of mythic-theatrical Rama to the Fort of the actual-theatrical Maharaja is an intersection of ancient and modern, mythic and theatrical,
extraordinary and ordinary time and space.

In Ramlila there are three kinds of movements in three spatial
spheres—a situation parallel to that of Yaqui Easter. The three movements are those of pilgrimage, those of the nightly performance, and
those existing within a mythic narrative; and the three spatial
spheres are of India, of Varanasi to Ramnagar and back, and of the
Ramlila story. The three spheres are not concentric, nor does one
replace or abolish any of the others. They all exist simultaneously in a
palimpsest.

The most far-flung sphere is that of those in the audience who
consider Ramnagar Ramlila a pilgrimage centre. Many people take
a month out from their lives to attend Ramlila, and some travel from
distances of more than 1,000 miles to get to Ramnagar. More immediately, on a daily basis, many thousands of spectators cross the
Ganga from Varanasi to attend Ramlila in Ramnagar. At the end of
the night's performance they cross back, often singing *bhajans*, devotional songs, in honour of Rama, as they row back across the sacred
river. To immerse oneself in Ganga is itself an act of purification. To
cross the river daily to and from Ramlila is a sacred act. More than
one boat capsizes each year, and some people drown. At one level of
experience this is a bad thing, at another level it is a good thing.

The third sphere of movement, also immediate and actual, are the
processions and shifts of theatrical environment that comprise so

much of Ramlila itself. At Ramnagar there are ten major shifts. And
these movements are precisely analogous to the Ramlila narrative.
To attend Ramlila, therefore, is to participate with Rama in his
adventures. Many thousands of spectators go with Rama into exile,
attend him and his army on their march through India and across
the great bridge of stones into Lanka, and throng around triumphant
Rama and his party as they return to Ayodhya. These movements are
not incidental or cosmetic. They are the core of the performance.

The environments of Ramlila are surprisingly detailed: a correct
model of the mythic narrative—even to being laid out in the correct
directional orientation. Thus the performance, like the narrative,
moves from the northwest to the southeast and back again to the
northwest. Throughout the month of Ramlila each spectator is reminded that Rama's story takes place in an actual and a mythic
India simultaneously—for the places in the narrative, Ayodhya,
Lanka, Janakpur, Citrakut, Pancavati—actually exist. And many
spectators believe that by attending Ramlila they can visit these
sacred places: to perform them in Ramlila is to bring them into
existence for one month, just as the gods themselves, as *murtis*, exist
for this same month. Thus to move through Ramnagar is to move
through India—not the India of today, but the India of Ramraj—
the time when Rama ruled. This is an epoch not like today's debased
Kali Yuga, but of an earlier more perfect time. So the movement in
space is also a movement in time—and many who attend Ramlila feel
they have been literally transported both spatially and temporally.

So do those who perform in Yaqui Easter. The performance I saw
at New Pascua near Tucson, Arizona, though more modest theatrically, is very much like Ramnagar Ramlila in terms of the use of space.
At New Pascua the organization of space contributes greatly to the
bringing into theatrical existence of beings and forces that otherwise
would remain unmanifest. (And this process of making manifest the
unmanifest is, I think, one of the links connecting aesthetic and ritual
theatre. It is also the area—of training and *mise-en-scène*—where
theatre specialists can exchange techniques with ritual specialists.) As
with Ramlila, though not as extensively or with as many people,
Easter is celebrated by Yaqui speaking peoples in the USA and Mexico.
My study of Yaqui Easter has just begun, and I will rely both on my
own observations and the writings of Muriel Thayer Painter (*A
Yaqui Easter*, Tucson: University of Arizona Press, 1971) and Edward
H. Spicer.

The Yaqui situation is complicated by the fact that the ceremonies in New Pascua are versions of earlier observances performed in other places. This is doubly significant because the Yaqui put strong emphasis on place. The 'original' eight Yaqui towns of Rio Yaqui in Mexico date from the early period of contact with the Jesuits in the seventeenth century. These towns, hundreds of miles from the Yaqui settlement in New Pascua, are both actual and mythical. They constitute an arena of Yaqui history as the Yaquis relate their history; they are also the place where Christ walked during the three days between his crucifixion and resurrection. But before the eight towns, and surrounding them, as if they were islands, is the *huya aniya*, the wildlands, home of the deer. As Spicer says:

> The *huya aniya* of the Yaquis is neither wholly separate from the Christian realm nor does it interpenetrate in a way comparable with that in the Christian–Maya synthesis. [. . .] Every ceremony devoted to a Christian supernatural required participation by ceremonialists whose power was associated with the *huya aniya*.[1]

Thus the Easter Passion Play incorporates Deer and Pascola dancing, and a very dense interplay of these with two other kinds of performance figures: masked Chapayekas who pursue and crucify Christ and unmasked beribboned Matachin dancers who celebrate Christ's triumphant resurrection. This resurrection is marked by the throwing of flowers—flowers that actually drive back, disarm, and unmask the Chapayekas who, defeated and transformed, burn their masks on a pyre piled up against one of the main crosses in the village square and then, unmasked, enter the church to gain the blessing of Christ. The symbolism is so dense because it is a dynamic system of conscious and non-conscious oppositions and interpenetrations: countryside vs town, flowers vs masks, masked vs unmasked, Deer vs Pascolas (ritual clowns), Chapayekas vs Matachins, ancient musical instruments vs instruments introduced by the Spaniards, men vs women, adults vs children, pre-Columbian ceremony vs Jesuit-introduced Catholicism. And so on. To list these as oppositions does injustice to the complexity of their inter-relatedness. I do not have time here to even begin to decipher this system. But I need to point out a few more 'movements' of the Yaqui that figure in their Easter performances—for these movements are recapitulated in the *mise-en-scène* itself.

The Jesuits entered Yaqui country in 1617. They were withdrawn in 1767. Much of what is celebrated today by the Yaqui took shape from after the Jesuit withdrawal when contact with Euro-Mexican power was occasional and often bloody. In the early twentieth century a climax was reached in the relationship between Yaquis and Mexicans. The Mexican revolutionaries wanted to bring the Yaqui (and other Indian groups) into the Mexican nation—but on strictly Mexican terms. The struggles that followed, and continue to this day, resulted in at least two major dispersions of Yaqui. Many Yaqui were sent as forced labourers to the Yucatan. Others fled across the Rio Grande to Arizona—and some of these settled near Tucson. Thus if the Jesuits introduced concentration—the establishment of the eight towns—the Mexicans forced diaspora. Most recently, in the 1960s and 70s, as Tucson grew and encircled the Yaqui settlements there, a group of Yaquis led by Anselmo Valencia, who is both their political and religious leader, established New Pascua and won for it status as a Federal Indian Reservation. New Pascua is today the largest single settlement of Yaquis in the USA.

Thus there is a recurrent pattern in post-contact Yaqui history. This pattern is of concentration and dispersion, settlement and diaspora, centre and beyond (*huya aniya*). This pattern comprehends space as something significant in itself, and dynamic. This sense of significant movement is at the heart of Yaqui Easter.

During the performance there are three main spatial spheres. These are concentric; and there is much power in each of them making for a complicated inter-relation between the centre, the mid-space, and the beyond. The Easter ceremonies—though they can be studied from any number of perspectives—are extremely interesting as an unfolding relationship among these three spheres—for this relationship, theatrically speaking, can be discussed as a concrete *mise-en-scène*. The over-all movement of the Easter performance is from the outside in, finally climaxing in the combat and absorption into the centre of formerly disruptive but plainly ancient and native, and therefore necessary, forces.

Figure 2 shows the arrangement of space for Easter in New Pascua. The food stalls are temporary structures. Local people sell various foods and drinks (non-alcoholic). The stalls mark out the difference between the beyond—where the stations of the cross (numbered 1 through 14) are, and beyond them, the outside world of Arizona and *huya aniya*—from the interior outdoor space of the village square. The unnumbered cross immediately in front of the open church door

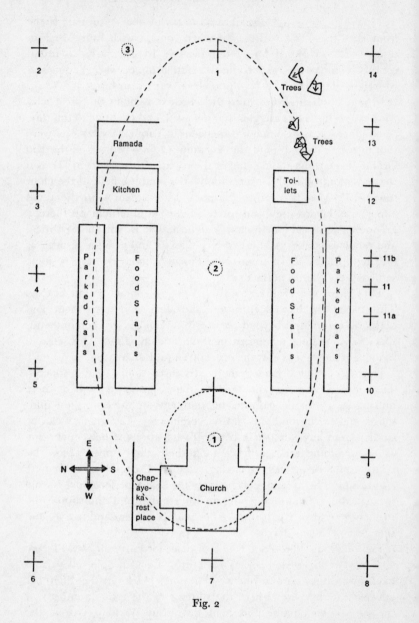

Fig. 2

marks an area that includes the inside of the church. This is the most
central area, the place where the final reconciliation takes place; and
where the Matachins dance their celebratory steps.

There is another 'open door', that of the Ramada in the northeast
of the square. In the Ramada dance the Deer and Pascolas—a kind
of sideshow literally. The significance of the Deer to Yaqui Easter is
explained by Spicer thus:

> The Deer and the Pascola are essentially secular, but I am sure
> that the Deer Dancer has not always been so. Because they are
> not sacred, they may be danced throughout the Lenten period at
> household fiestas. Their meaning, despite being joyous like the
> Matachin dances, does not conflict with the Fariseo ritual mean-
> ings. It is just outside the realm of the sacred, and therefore not
> incompatible with the austerity and discipline of the Fariseo
> ceremonial season.[2]

When the Deer dances publicly, on Holy Saturday night as part of
the Fiesta that celebrates Christ's victory—actually, with the Yaqui,
the victory of the 'little angels', young boys and girls whose thrown
flower petals literally disarm and unmask the Chapayekas, both
defeating and reconciling them—when the Deer dances he does so in
the Ramada: its open door being parallel to, not in conflict with, but,
as Spicer points out, different than, the open door of the Church.
And the Deer brings with him the space of *huya aniya*, and the flower
world: the wild, the beyond.

Of all the spatial manipulations visible in the Yaqui 40-day Passion
Play, let me concentrate on two only: the appearance and actions of
the Chapayekas from Lent through Holy Saturday and the representation of the Crucifixion itself on Good Friday. The first manifestation
of the Chapayekas is the appearance of a single one who emerges
from under the Church altar on the first Friday of Lent.

> Slowly a figure emerges who is obviously out of place in the
> church. It looks around as though in puzzlement, but it is not
> easy to know what it thinks, for it says nothing and seems to be
> expressing uncertainty by knocking two painted sticks together
> tentatively. Moreover no facial expression is visible. The being
> wears a helmet of hide painted black, green, red, and white with
> two large loosely flapping ears and a slender pointed nose. It
> ignores the services in front of the altar where hymns and prayers
> preparatory for going around the Way of the Cross are in progress
> among the assembled townspeople. The Chapayeka goes up to

the prayer leader and insolently cocks its head to look at him better, shuffles among the kneeling people, but when the name of the Blessed Virgin is mentioned begins to shiver and shake and then appears to wipe filth from its thighs with one of its sticks. In the midst of the solemn devotions, the Chapayeka suddenly shakes deer hoof rattles on a belt around his waist, momentarily drowning out the sacred chant. Turning his back on the altar, he trots among the people and out the door of the church.[3]

Then the Chapayeka joins the Soldiers of Rome, whose camp is next to the church (see Figure 2). Accompanying the Soldiers, the Chapayeka goes ahead of the faithful as they make their rounds of the Way of the Cross; the Soldiers surround the faithful. Thus a pattern for Lent is set.

On the following Friday two more Chapayekas enter town, this time from the northwest corner of the square—a direction farthest from Cross 11, the Crucifixion Cross; and a direction not usually used to approach the church whose door opens eastward, towards the rising sun. One of the entering Chapayekas is the being from the previous Friday, and both Chapayekas seem a bit disoriented. At the same time that they appear almost comical they also are sinister and scary. They carry their beating sticks. The sound they make is a leitmotif of Yaqui Easter. It will be heard throughout Lent and mark the marching of the Soldiers of Rome and the Chapayekas. The Crucifixion itself—the hammering of imaginary nails with a wooden hammer into a cross at Station 11—will echo this same sound of wood-on-wood. When the two Chapayekas see the church they become agitated and uncertain. Then from somewhere else in town two more Chapayekas appear. 'Now elaborate gesturing takes place. It becomes evident that these beings communicate by using their sticks, employing various gestures and rhythmic beats.'[4] The Chapayekas 'demonstrate that they have come from somewhere to the north [a direction from which wild things come] and are very reluctant to stay in town and especially to go near the church'.[5] The Soldiers of Rome invite the Chapayekas to join them in their enterprise—the pursuit and crucifixion of Jesus. The Chapayekas express interest mostly in food and fiesta, but agree to join the Soldiers who promise the same. Thus an alliance against Jesus is made. An alliance that is parallel to the alliance Rama makes with Hanuman the monkey general and Jambuvan the bear. The Chapayekas are in some way acculturated by the Soldiers—and even as they join against Jesus they lay the groundwork for their eventual salvation.

But who are these Chapayekas who do not know what's going on? And why was the first one discovered inside the church they so evidently fear and avoid? I am not going to give an anthropological answer—that is, use Spicer's great authority to assert that the Chapayekas are linked to Hopi and Zuni kachinas (which would surely place them to the north). I would rather stick to the theatrical evidence close at hand because I can handle that kind of material more confidently. By not knowing what's happening the Chapayekas demonstrate their origins in a distant place both geographically and conceptually—they are literally out of touch with Jesus. By being discovered first in church—as maybe a stray dog or even wild coyote might wander unknowingly into an improper place—the first Chapayeka demonstrates his innocence—the sophisticated Soldiers of Rome must educate the Chapayekas to their evil purpose. But his discovery in church also foreshadows the resolution of the drama: it is a prediction acted out rather than spoken (as befits the mute Chapayekas): for on two more occasions the Chapayekas will enter the church. First after they capture Jesus from Gethsemane they will guard him in church—taking over that holy space and converting it entirely to their needs. Then on Holy Saturday, the Chapayekas will enter the church again, but this time as supplicants and devotees of Jesus. And, strictly speaking, not as Chapayekas at all because their masks will have been discarded and burnt. So the Chapayekas in church show a definite progression: first as alien, unknowing, confused figures; then as sinister agents of the Soldiers who crucify Jesus; finally as transformed beings—townsmen who have shed their Chapayeka personae to become rededicated to Jesus. The flower-power of the Little Angels literally unmasks and converts the Chapayekas into family men: for even as it is as lone males that they enter the town it is as men-with-their-families, their children and women, that they accept Jesus.

Each Friday during Lent more Chapayekas appear, until they number 35 or 40.

> They are all outfitted according to a similar pattern, although some may wear old overcoats instead of blankets and some are barefooted, while others wear the traditional flat Yaqui sandals. But there is great variety in the masks. Each Chapayeka makes his own mask, and each is different.[6]

In 1982, when I saw the Holy Week part of the Easter performance, I observed masks of many kinds: a goat, a sheep, a penis-nosed racoon, a Moor or Arab, a man in a top hat with a black face smoking a fat cigar, a pink-faced bald man, several 'fantasy figures' of yellow, pink, black, and white, a yellow-faced man with Dracula teeth. All had the characteristic jug ears, and most had pointy thin noses.

> It is apparent that the Chapayekas are under the influence of the Soldiers of Rome, having agreed to help them, and they grow more and more intent on their one purposeful activity of tracking down Jesus. This is apparent with each new Friday procession, as they interfere with, almost jostle the faithful, pushing their sticks in front of them and turning over every tiny stone they come to; circle the processional groups; and silently taunt the Maestros [Yaqui priests] by dangling stuffed badgers and other animals over the prayer books. [. . .] The Chapayekas in fact go all about the town not only on Fridays but other days as well spying on people and trying to catch children. [. . .] People live in fear of possible punishments, and the tensions heighten as the Chapayekas make their presence increasingly felt.[7]

The Chapayekas are something like Namahage of Ota in Japan, or Halloween maskers in Euro-America: comic and sinister at once; originating in some other world (the north, the mountains, the dead) and making themselves visible and active in the world of humans to which they really don't belong. But finally they are unmasked and revealed as loved relations and trusted neighbours: a fact everyone knew but, according to theatrical and religious convention, agreed to ignore. This 'willing suspension of disbelief' is no trivial thing: it is the very key to worlds of subjunctivity, of 'as if', to what Artaud called the 'theatre and its double'.

The processions around the Way of the Cross take Mary and Jesus and the faithful out into spatial sphere 3, away from the church, out of the plaza, out beyond the foodstalls. It is dangerous out there. Going the Way of the Cross means losing sight of the church. The Crucifixion crosses are set behind the stalls, near the toilets, in the far south and east—a direction (from the perspective of Rio Yaqui) from whence came both Jesuits and hated Mexicans; and the direction to which the Yaqui were deported at the end of the nineteenth century. And, importantly, the Yaqui Easter performance is not an uninterrupted tradition dating back centuries. It was stopped during the great diaspora.

For about twenty years, Yaquis did not carry out Easter Ceremonies anywhere. There was a hiatus in their continuity from about 1886 until 1906, when what has become the Old Pascua Ceremony was revived in Arizona. The Easter Ceremonies that we see today in Sonora are also revivals.[8]

Thus when the Yaquis reinstituted their Easter performance they could consciously choose what to include, what to modify. The directional motifs are very particular: written in the geography of the performance is a model of Yaqui experience. Just as directions and movements have deep significance in Ramlila, so they do in Yaqui Easter.

In the interest of brevity (if not wit) I'll skip some important activities of the Chapayekas and get to the Crucifixion. I note only that the Chapayekas capture Jesus in Gethsemane and take him to the church where they guard him throughout Thursday night of Holy Week. For the second time—now with a definite purpose, an evil purpose—the Chapayekas have penetrated the church itself.

There are actually two simultaneous processions around the Way of the Cross on Good Friday. One group, the largest, is led by a man who carries a large cross. This group proceeds in a counterclockwise direction—the 'correct' direction if the Crucifixion is to take place at the 11th cross. The other group, mostly of women, bearing with them the effigies of the Three Marys, move clockwise—but only for five stops, from Cross 1 back to Cross 11. Actually there are three crosses there, for three people are to be crucified: Jesus and the two thieves. The representation of the Crucifixion itself, out of sight of the church, in the south to southeast in relation to the church, is done by having a man hit the wooden cross with a wooden mallet. There is no body, not even an effigy. But the sound of the wooden mallet striking the wooden cross is a version of the Chapayeka wooden stick music.

Once the Crucifixion has happened the Chapayekas 'swarm all through the church and out into the plaza. They uproot every cross of the Way, throwing each in the dust. They then play games and chase each other in a spirit of complete abandonment during the rest of Good Friday.'[9] By contrast the rest of the town, the women especially, are solemn and in mourning for the crucified Jesus.

There is a constant stream of mourners. One household has dedicated itself to provide a flower-bedecked bier in which to place the body of Christ. The decoration is elaborate, the highest effort of a whole large family. The bier is blessed and borne to the church by a contingent of the Soldiers of Rome. The Adora-

tion by the townspeople goes on all day and into the early night
and creates a mood of deep sadness.[10]

The bier is inside the church. And in the bier is a small statue of
Jesus. The feeling I got, in New Pascua 1982, was of a combination
bier-crèche. For the colours of the bier were bright, the effigy small,
the feel of the cloth material within that of a crib.

The action of the Passion Play has now moved to the centre of
sphere 1: inside the church. The next morning, near noon, the
Soldiers of Rome and the Chapayekas storm the church. It is not
clear exactly why: they have already won their victory. But they have
not really occupied the church. Their 'camp' is next to the church,
and they have entered the church on several occasions, but it is still
not their territory. They march in formation, clicking their sticks,
and then they charge the church. But they are driven back by the
Little Angels who throw flowers at them. After three attempts the
Chapayekas are defeated, their masks are taken off and burned, and
they enter the church as supplicants. The Matachin dancers begin
their dancing, as do the Pascolas and Deer. At this point the whole
space of spheres 1 and 2 are operating, and sphere 3—the outer
world, the space of the Way, the route of great agony—is ignored. At
this moment one can sense the theatrical and metaphysical function
of the foodstalls and parked cars: they block out the space of sphere 3
as the whole town celebrates in various ways in spheres 1 and 2: in
the church, the ramada, the plaza: they eat, dance, socialize and
worship. And it is not easy, nor is it necessary, to make sharp distinctions among these activities.

What is clear from even this brief description of Ramlila and the
Yaqui Easter is that these performances knit aesthetic, social, religious,
and mythic themes together; and that the actual physical space and
mise-en-scène of the performances are in important ways meaningful
assertions of these themes. That is to say that although the Ramlila
and Yaqui performances follow certain aesthetic conventions with
regard to dance steps, costumes, dialogue delivery, and so on, in the
matter of over-all scenic arrangement—the use of the town as stage—
a mythic-religious model has been constructed. In this large *mise-en-
scènic* sense aesthetics is less important than to provide an actual geography in which to act out very important material that seems to find
its most powerful form not as literature but as theatre. And it is
precisely this kind of meta-aesthetic sense—an aesthetics that goes
beyond aesthetics—that Western contemporary theatre lacks.

Experimentalists have felt this lack and have, in their own ways, tried to remedy it. Again many of these experiments over the past 30 years have taken the pathway of exploring new kinds of theatrical space. Experiments in environmental theatre, and in audience participation (even to the dissolution of the audience altogether by Grotowski), have been the major avenues of meta-aesthetics in Euro-American theatre. I want now, very briefly, to give a few examples of these experiments concerned with performance space. They are individualistic and modest, but clearly connections can be seen between them and Ramlila and Yaqui Easter.

Of course at least since the Bauhaus designs of 'total theatre' an active campaign has been waged demanding new theatre space—something different than the proscenium. But it was not until the 1950s and 60s that ideas were translated in a large way into theatrical practice. Some of the theoretical basis for this is outlined in my 1968 article, 'Six Axioms for Environmental Theatre.' The first axiom is that 'the theatrical event is a set of related transactions'. This relocates theatre away from the enactment of a set literary text to what goes on in the performance space—between performers and spectators, events and space, production elements and texts (not necessarily written texts). The second axiom is that 'all the space is used for performance; all the space is used for audience'.

> Once one gives up fixed seating and the bifurcation of space, entirely new relationships are possible. Body contact can naturally occur between performers and audience; voice levels and acting intensities can be widely varied; a sense of shared experience can be engendered. Most important each scene can create its own space, either contracting to a central or a remote area expanding to fill all available space. The action 'breathes' and the audience itself becomes a major scenic element.[11]

What we get is a 'global sense' of theatrical space rather than a 'stage sense' of simulated actuality or contrived artificiality. The third axiom said that 'the theatrical event can take place either in a totally transformed space or in "found space"'. Thus Allan Kaprow in 1964 staged *Eat*, an event in cave in the Bronx. And he played with the relationship between time and space by building a large monolith of ice in a hot Los Angeles street in 1967. Artists worked inside galleries not designed as theatres, such as Meredith Monk's *Juice* in 1969 at the Guggenheim Museum in New York, Trisha Brown's outdoor dance with spectators on the roof and dancers crouched behind barriers on the Lower East Side of New York; or more bucolically, on the beaches of California, or on a mountainside near Shiraz, Iran, where Robert Wilson staged his week-long *Ka Mountain* in 1972.

The Living Theatre in 1975 staged an outdoor performance on the campus of the University of Michigan that used the buildings as architectural markers of 'death', 'the state', 'money', 'property', 'war', and 'love'. The work premiered in Pittsburgh—so the job of the Living was to find on the University of Michigan campus, or wherever *Six Public Acts* was performed, the necessary 'houses'. The Living wanted to use architecture, and the uses to which certain buildings were put, in roughly the same way that space is used at Ramlila and Yaqui Easter. They wanted to make geography 'speak' the way it speaks in Ramnagar and New Pascua. I saw the performance. The difficulty with it, as with so much political theatre, was an ambivalence on the part of the audience which reflects an analogous ambivalence among the performers. The Living assumed that the audience shared political values with the theatre. But everyone also knows this is not true. Not only does a distance open between what is performed and the audience, but a definite hostility erupts on both sides. It is precisely this hostility that is missing in Ramlila and Yaqui. There certain figures—demons and Chapayekas—are permitted aggressive, even sacrilegious acts; but these are played out within the context of ultimate reconciliation. Ravana's final surrender to Rama—an exact parallel to Yaqui Easter—is to remove his mask and touch the feet of Rama.

I want to end here, abruptly. That is because I've come to the place where divergent societies, and cultural values, make comparisons difficult. Experimenters in Euro-America, and in modern Japan too, have tried to include their audiences by creating special spaces and ritual-aesthetic actions. Have they succeeded in their primary aim, not of creating beauty or impressive entertainment, but of somehow ending, or at least diminishing, the alienation among audiences, and reducing the distance—actual and psychic and ontological—between the performance, the performers, and the spectators?

1. Edward H. Spicer, *The Yaquis: A Cultural History* (Tucson: University of Arizona Press, 1980), pp. 69–70.
2. Edward H. Spicer, 'The Context of the Yaquis Easter Ceremony', in *CORD Research Annual VI: New Dimensions in Dance Research: Anthropology and Dance—*

The American Indian, ed. Tamara Comstock (N.Y.: Committee on Research in Dance, New York University, 1974), p. 322.
3. Spicer, *The Yaquis*, p. 76.
4. Ibid. p. 77.
5. Ibid.
6. Ibid. p. 78.
7. Ibid.
8. Spicer, 'The Context . . .', p. 313.
9. Spicer, *The Yaquis*, p. 80.
10. Ibid.
11. Richard Schechner, 'Six Axioms for Environmental Theatre', in *TDR*, 12:3 (Spring 1968), p. 49.

9

The Crash of Performative Circumstances: A Modernist Discourse on Postmodernism

I

The Mother of Pondicherry, India, was felt by her followers to be immortal. This very old French woman—wife of Sri Aurobindo— was said to be rebuilding her body cell by cell. 'Come back in ten years and you will see a young woman.' That was in 1972. A few years later The Mother was dead. On the walls of her ashrama south of Madras hung exhortations. One of them has stuck with me: 'The future of the earth depends on a change of consciousness. The only hope for the future is in a change of man's consciousness and the change is bound to come. But it is left to men to decide if they will collaborate for this change or it will have to be enforced on them by the power of crashing circumstances.' I wondered what it meant to 'collaborate for this change', and what the 'crashing circumstances' might be. To collaborate 'for'—if it's not just a grammatical mistake— implies that people must collaborate with each other in order to bring about change. And if they don't, the change will come anyway: some kind of nuclear or ecosystem apocalypse. I thought of Artaud's short definition of his theatre of cruelty: 'We are not free. And the sky can still fall on our heads. And the theatre has been created to teach us that first of all.' All this seems to be saying that the Age of Humanism is finished. Man is no longer the measure of all things. The cosmos is multicentred, which means it is centred nowhere, or everywhere: everything from holism to narcissism is sanctioned.

At The Mother's ashrama I lay my head on that old lady's knee, as was the custom in having *darsan* (literally, a vision) of her. Upon leaving her I wrote in my notebook. 'She looked at me. I left trembling. I am confused, unknowing. Her look penetrated. She did not know, she saw.' Saw what? I ask now ten years later. My notes from that day continue: 'Doubts—fundamental denials, remain, but something has happened, is happening.' And I hear now an old Buffalo

Springfield lyric: 'Something's happening here/what it is ain't exactly clear.'

Yes. We've been told by our visionaries, our demographers, our artists, and our ideologues. Change is upon us.

Our Mothers, Malthuses, Artauds, and Marxes agree on that. Our only liberty in the matter is whether we shall collaborate in effecting this change or be its passive victims/beneficiaries.

Beneficiaries of nuclear holocaust? Of ecological catastrophe?

And will the change be from consciousness or from circumstances?

And what kind of change are these dreamers dreaming of? Does anyone believe in the stateless society of Marx? Or any other paradise?

The Mother tried to demonstrate in her own body how consciousness can triumph over circumstances. She failed. Is her failure definitive?

Marx, the perfect modernist, saw history as man-made, and within our control. Brecht tried to push this idea of humanist responsibility in his plays. But Brecht couldn't even control Mother Courage: she turned tragic right on the Berliner Ensemble stage. And our species collectively—as communities, nations, or associations of nations—has not succeeded in reconstructing human history any more than The Mother succeeded in her own single body.

This kind of thing is giving the future a bad smell.

II

I am a person = a mask, a multiplicity, a process to sound through. I live on and in the limen separating and joining the modern from and to the postmodern. All those linked prepositions seem necessary. Pre/positions: the places I'm in before I'm in place—places that are not simply defined but lead in at least two directions. The attention given by so many to Zen and its insistence on 'present consciousness', the centre, the now, is partly explained by the terrible drag of both past and future. What I mean by 'modern' and 'postmodern' I've tried to explain in another writing, 'The End of Humanism' (*Performing Arts Journal*, no. 10/11 [1979]). But I'll add some more here.

My furious obsession with writing—I've filled sixty-five notebooks with more than 20,000 pages over the past twenty-six years—is a modern obsession with 'getting it all down', of catching the flopping fish of experience. Yet my very existence as a 'theatre person' who 'makes plays'—experiences that can't be kept, that disappear with each performance, not with each production but with each repetition of the actions I so carefully plan with my colleagues, each repetition that is never an exact duplication no matter how closely scored, how frozen by disciplined rehearsals—this very existence in/as theatre is postmodern. For the theatre is a paradigm of 'restored behaviour'— behaviour twice behaved, behaviour never-for-the-first-time—ritualized gestures. And if experience is always in flow, theatre attempts, in Conrad's words, to wrest 'from the remorseless rush of time' precise moments of experience. And the domain of theatre is not, as Stanislavski thought, psychology, but behaviour. Writing, of course, also tries to immobilize experience—but writing translates experience into this system of graphemes you are now reading. And film, a trickster, is another system of writing: a behaviour agreeably locked into a mechanical process where it can be edited on a table. Only theatre— live performance, from dance to circus to rituals to plays to sports— works directly with living persons. In theatre the flux and decay of ongoing living is asked to halt, become conscious of itself, and repeat. A paradox Heraclitus already knew about, and the author(s) of the Sanskrit treatise on performance, *Natyasastra*.

The postmodern is possibly a liminal bridge in history, a period conscious of itself, its past, and its multiple potentials as future. By postmodern I mean:

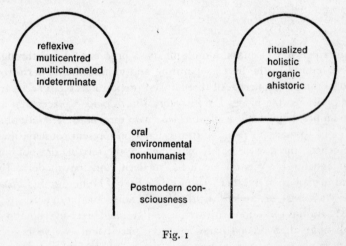

reflexive
multicentred
multichanneled
indeterminate

ritualized
holistic
organic
ahistoric

oral
environmental
nonhumanist

Postmodern con-
sciousness

Fig. 1

These tendencies are not 'resolvable' into a noncontradictory whole. Postmodern holism more than tolerates contradictions. In some of its tendencies we have the hilarious and scary monologues of Spalding Gray and the incredibly energetic performative outflowings of Jeff Weiss, both superbly narcissistic, truly looking deeply into the waters and seeing only themselves worthy of the fullest love. In other manifestations the postmodern births collective works like the Mabou Mines *Dead End Kids* whose range extends from Faustus to J. Robert Oppenheimer, from alchemy to nuclear apocalypse. The postmodern includes both environmentalists helping people gain the consciousness of global ecosystems necessary for survival and one logical outflow of that consciousness in action, an Orwellian world of total information/action control.

Why, you ask, must knowledge of systems lead to tyranny? *Scientia est potentia* is an old saying, still true.

Or to put it another way: Why, I ask, must knowledge of systems lead to paradise?

III

I keep a file of clippings called 'Doomsday'. It's my common book of despair.

Some of the titles: 'Causes of Cancer Called Numerous', '32 Nations Close to Starvation', 'Toxic Trace Elements: Preferential Concentration in Respirable Particles', 'House Report Fears World Starvation', 'Help Is Urged for 36,000 Homeless in [New York] City's Streets', 'Stratospheric Pollution: Multiple Threats to Earth's Ozone'.

The gloomiest of all is the *Global 2000 Report* issued by the Carter Administration in July 1980 and summarized in *Science* (1 August 1980): 'If present trends continue, the world in 2000 will be more crowded, more polluted, less stable ecologically, and more vulnerable to disruption than the world we live in now. . . . Despite greater material output, the world's people will be poorer in many ways than they are today.' The *Global 2000 Report* confirms what we already know, but infrequently stare in the eyeball: that $450 billion a year is spent on arms, against $20 billion on economic aid; that the gap between rich and poor is increasing; that resources are being depleted; that the global environment is losing life-support capabilities. 'By 2000, 40 per cent of the forests still remaining in the less developed countries in 1978 will have been razed. The atmospheric concentration of carbon dioxide will be nearly one-third higher than pre-industrial levels. . . . Desertification (including salinization) may have claimed a significant fraction of the world's rangeland and cropland. Over little more than two decades, 15–20 per cent of the earth's total species of plants and animals will have become extinct—a loss of at least 500,000 species.'

If true, this is a prediction of more than genocide—but of some mean neologism like 'globacide'.

Yet the ecology movement can't get many people out into the streets. There simply isn't any disarmament movement to speak of.

Is it that people don't believe the predictions? That they are too gross to be incorporated into consciousness? That people, fearful, are trying to take care of Number One and letting the rest go rot?

All of the above.

Already in *Tristes Tropiques*, published in 1955, Claude Lévi-Strauss saw what still only a few, relatively speaking, accept:

> Now that the Polynesian islands have been smothered in concrete and turned into aircraft carriers solidly anchored in the southern seas, when the whole of Asia is beginning to look like a dingy suburb, when shanty-towns are spreading across Africa, when civil and military aircraft blight the primeval innocence of the American or Melanesian forests even before destroying their virginity, what else can the so-called escapism of travelling do than confront us with the more unfortunate aspects of our history? Our great Western civilization, which has created the marvels we now enjoy, has only succeeded in producing them at the cost of corresponding ills. The order and harmony of the Western world, its most famous achievement, and a laboratory in which structures of a complexity as yet unknown are being fashioned, demand the elimination of a prodigious mass of noxious by-products which now contaminate the globe. The first thing we see as we travel round the world is our own filth, thrown into the face of mankind. [New York: Atheneum, 1974, p. 38]

Travel around the world? Try any New York street. And yet the rage to clean it all up has fascist harmonies: Mussolini making the trains run on time; Reagan eliminating social programmes and preaching that everyone must sacrifice: as if asking the executive to do with only two cars is equivalent to asking the unemployed to do with only two meals.

Lévi-Strauss's India is not that of Baba Ram Dass, or any of the others who have returned to America saffroned with holiness. No, the French anthropologist looks with earlier, modern, rational eyes, and feels with a heart pumping material blood as he describes conditions:

> ... at Narayanganj, the jute workers earn their living inside a gigantic spider's web formed by whitish fibres hanging from the walls and floating in the air. They then go home to the 'coolie lines', brick troughs with neither light nor flooring, and each occupied by six or eight individuals; they are arranged in rows with surface drains running down the middle, which are flooded thrice daily to clear away the dirt. Social progress is now tending to replace this kind of dwelling by 'workers' quarters', prisons in which two or three workers share a cell three metres by four. There are walls all around, and the entrance gates are guarded by armed policemen. The communal kitchens and eating-quarters are bare cement rooms, which can be swilled out and where each individual lights his fire and squats on the ground to eat in the dark.
>
> Once, during my first teaching post in the Landes area, I had visited poultry yards specially adapted for the cramming of geese: each bird was confined to a narrow box and reduced to the status of a mere digestive tube. In this Indian setting, the situation was the same, apart from two differences: instead of geese, it was men and women I was looking at, and instead of being fattened up, they were, if anything, being slimmed down. But in both instances, the breeder only allowed his charges one form of activity, which was desirable in the case of the geese, and inevitable in the case of the Indians. The dark and airless cubicles were suited neither for rest, leisure nor love. They were mere points of connection with the communal sewer, and they corresponded to a conception of human life as being reducible to the pure exercise of the excretory functions. . . .
>
> ... Nowhere, perhaps, except in concentration camps, have human beings been so completely identified with butcher's meat.
> [Ibid. pp. 128–9]

Nowhere? Try the toilets at Penn Station, Manhattan, two blocks from where I live and write this. Here's a little description from the Sunday *New York Times*, 8 March 1981, describing the nightly rituals of some homeless 'bag ladies':

> At 11 p.m. the attendant goes off duty and women rise from separate niches and head for the bathroom. There they disrobe and wash their clothes and bodies. Depending on the length of the line at the hand dryers, they wait to dry their clothes, put

them in their bags or wear them wet. One woman cleans and wraps her ulcerated legs with paper towels every night.

The most assertive claim toilet cubicles, line them with newspapers for privacy and warmth and sleep curled round the basin. Once they are taken, the rest sleep along the walls, one on a box directly beneath the hand dryer which she pushed for warm air. One of the women regularly cleans the floors, sinks and toilets so that no traces of their uncustomary use remain.

Maybe you're thinking poverty has always been with us—Dickens described scenes that, subtracting their sentimentality, were every bit as dehumanizing and brutish. I look at this same *New York Times* issue and find numerous advertisements on page 2 for diamonds. In fact, newspapers—like TV—are our best evidence of the gap between the experience of the poor, the rich, and the middle classes. The stories focus on what it's like to be poor—to suffer urban life with its violence, filth, insensitivity—while the ads abound with luxury items: furs, perfumes, lingerie, cars, vacations; or with remedies that drug the middle class: sleeping pills, nasal sprays, stomach soothers, bowel movers.

I know I'm 'oversimplifying', but I need to do it. Why? Because a good part of my daily life is spent attempting to negotiate among these 'simple' experiential contradictions.

Not yet have I found the way to include—not negotiate around—these contradictions in my work, in my theatre, my writings, my teaching.

None of the political menus—the Marxists, the capitalists, the democratic socialists, the terrorists, the dropout communalists—is right for me. That is, I don't believe in their programmes, promises, outlooks. And I don't like the people who run their organizations. Ditto for the religious solutions and the solutions of 'consciousness', wherein I get my act together, and you get yours, and yours, and yours . . . until history turns around. I don't buy that approach either.

IV

Frederick Turner, co-editor of the *Kenyon Review*, a poet and author of the science fiction novel about the theatricalized future, *A Double Shadow* (New York: Berkeley Publishing Corporation, 1978), has communicated to me, in a letter, a more hopeful future:

30 RIGHT. Rama worshipping Siva before the Setubandh.

31 BOTTOM. The embrace of the four brothers on Bharata Milap.

32 Left. Ravana's effigy atop Lanka on Dusserah evening.

33 Bottom. An etching from 1829 showing the burning of effigies at a Ramlila near Allahabad.

34 RIGHT. Ravana and Hanuman
grapple in battle.

35 BOTTOM. An old Ramlila scene, *c.* 1920 :
from the Maharaja's private collection.

36 LEFT. Sadhus singing and dancing on Dusserah night.

37 BOTTOM. The scene at Lanka in Ramnagar the day that Kumbhakarna is killed, with Kumbhakarna's effigy in the background.

We are capable of accurate prophecy, subject only to the co-prophecy of other minds and other organized realities; and that prophecy is the same as action. To put it all more simply, it's up to us which alternative will come about. There is no such thing as the future yet and this realization makes us public men, and forces a kind of civic piety upon us. Because if things do go wrong, we are to blame. The plea of powerlessness is no excuse: the power of others is created by our own opinions of it, and nothing more. We can change our opinion, and we do it by making one alternative more beautiful than another.

If we destroy ourselves in a nuclear holocaust or eco-catastrophe, it won't be because of some kind of technological determinism, or innate drive or conspiracy of the powerful or economic forces of history; it will be because we chose to, collectively, and we chose to because we considered that future to be the most beautiful, and we considered it to be the most beautiful because we imaginatively constructed it to be so. Art has the exalted function, the world-saving function, of imaginatively constructing other futures which do not involve the *gotterdammerung* of mass suicide. I don't mean namby-pamby assertions of moral principle or nonviolence. They only increase the desirability of what is forbidden (Blake). Most ecology freaks are imaginatively mass-murderers. They would like to cleanse the filthy, desirous, complicated, upsetting, demanding, loving vermin of humanity from the face of the earth. They're the obverse of the Strangeloves, and less attractive because less straightforward.

The appeal of nuclear holocaust is that it upstages history. Without the expense of imaginative effort it instantly makes our generation more important than Homer's, or Christ's, or Shakespeare's. It's the ultimate oedipal put-down, the final punk concert. If you want my opinion about what I think will happen if we (I mean the artists and imaginative creators in all the fields) do nothing, then I think we will destroy ourselves because we dearly, pruriently want to. It's such a cheap rush.

Feeling is so hard to construct that instead of doing the work of construction we've spent a couple of centuries cracking out the feelings stored in the old sociocultural structures like oilmen pumping steam into old domes to get out the last trickles. . . . We've not much left, we fear. Our image of the universe has been of entropic systems that radiate crude energy by destroying themselves and others. The nuclear holocaust is a perfect picture of our self-excusing version of the universe. If the universe is running down, if there's only so much energy and value to go around, let's use it all up in one go, go out with a bang not a whimper.

Better that than have to invent, think, love, work, take risks. Nuclear holocaust is dead safe. You know exactly where you are with it. It's a future with no variables: the Marxist/Capitalist ideal.

Of course the universe isn't running down, if we realize that it's made of information not of energy. Energy is simply information divided by an unreal measure, space. The world is growing and learning to speak, like a baby, and its information is increasing all the time. We are the chief agents of that increase: in terms of information rather than space, we are the biggest objects in the universe and the galaxies are little specks upon our skins. But the risk is, we could choose to deny our opportunity.

So it's up to us. I predict that we will create subjunctive worlds, not the death-bang. The fact that that prediction is a resolve, an intention, doesn't make it any less of a prediction, but more of one. The road to heaven is paved with good intentions.

Yes, it's the old Protestant Ethic standing on its head. But Turner understands The Mother's 'change of consciousness', and Arthur Clarke's *Childhood's End* too. Turner comprehends that the postmodern epoch is one of information. But, as anthropologist Roy Rappaport reminded me, information and meaning are not the same. An abundance of information uncomprehended, or transformed into ritual formulae, is not meant, but either ignored or felt. I agree with Turner that over the past 200 or so years Western thought has been unbalanced in the direction of rationality: of meaning. The rest of the world is helping us redress that unbalance.

An excess of uncomprehended information over the past 200 years has bred a prodigious science without a comparatively robust religion —or morality, if you will. So here we are, armed to our nuclei, and just about permitted to throw radioactive pies in each other's faces. For farce is what it is: an excess of violence that no one really believes is real. But wait till it explodes. And is Turner right in prescribing 'subjunctive worlds'—a heavy dose of theatre? Is our moral balance to be found among the clowns and acrobats?

Before taking up that one, a caveat about the 'cheap rush' of nuclear holocaust. It won't be so cheap. It won't be a big death bang but a series of painful whimpers. There are films of Hiroshima and Nagasaki —and a little booklet, printed in Japan, entitled *Give Me Water— Testimonies of Hiroshima and Nagasaki*:

What I saw under the bridge was shocking: Hundreds of people were squirming in the stream. I couldn't tell if they were men or women. They looked all alike. Their faces were swollen and gray, their hair was standing up. Holding their hands high, groaning, people were rushing to the river. I felt the same because the pain was all over the body. . . . I was about to jump into the river only to remember that I could not swim.

When I was about to get to our home, a middle-school student in our neighbourhood told me that my son Shiro had been spared. It was almost unbelievable. . . . I examined him and found that his left hand from the elbow to the finger and upper half of his head above his nose were burnt. I too felt that he would be all right soon. I thanked her and carried him on my back to the hospital. . . . My son was only given ointment for his burns. And started a high fever in the morning of August 9. . . . At about 4 in the afternoon, Shiro threw up some stuff which was as dark as coffee several times and passed away in two minutes.

Then I realized for the first time how my mother looked. She had been hit by the blast as she was picking eggplants to feed us at lunch. She was almost naked. Her coat and trousers were burnt and torn to pieces. Her hair had turned to reddish-brown, and was shrunken and torn as if she had had too strong a permanent. She got burnt all over the body. Her skin was red and greasy. The skin of her right shoulder, the portion which bore and lifted the beam, was gone, revealing bare flesh, and scarlet blood which was constantly oozing out. Mother fell exhausted on the ground. . . . Mother began to feel pain. After groaning and struggling, she passed away that night.

On the day of August 6 . . . I was 3 months pregnant. Since I was carrying a baby, my chore was to take care of lunch some distance away from where the bomb hit. That's why I was spared. . . . A week later the often-mentioned atomic disease hit me. All my hair was gone, and I had a rash all over my body. My teeth were shaken up as bloody pus kept coming out from the gums. Because of vomiting blood and bloody excrement I felt so weak that I almost gave up. . . . I may have been lucky. I survived and made a steady recovery. I delivered Yuriko on February 24 next year without much trouble. She was small indeed and the mid-wife told me, 'You really have to take care of this baby.' . . . She was brought up mostly on milk. When her first birthday came, she could not say a word. At the second birthday it was the same except that she could barely manage to crawl. When she was four or five years old I tried hard to teach her to walk and she started walking, but she was lame. . . . She came to school age. But I thought she could not keep up even in kindergarten. . . . We kept our hope every year to no avail. The sixth year came and Yuriko was exempted from schooling. Around that time doctors of the Hiroshima University Medical School came to survey the survivors in the Ohtake area. They examined her and took her picture. She was found to have the small-head syndrome caused by the atomic bombing. Up until recently I thought Yuriko was the only example. . . . Having had no pleasure in her life, she became very fond of movies. . . . She must look strange—standing lame, muttering something to herself in front of a movie poster. People look back at her from curiosity. School-children play lame before her or try to drive her away as if she were a dog. Yuriko herself seems embarrassed to be stared at or have somebody around. Nowadays she tends to stay all day at home and spends the time with TV and radio. That makes her physically weak; she gets easily tired even by just taking a short walk. . . . She is so occupied with movies, TV, and radio all day, from morning till she goes to bed, that she can't make it to the bathroom on time. . . . I have a grandchild who is 3 years old. I think Yuriko is a little bit more immature than him. She is now 20 years old.

Well, there are as many testimonies as casualties, multiplied by the number of people who knew persons who were there. Millions. Thus the inheritance of the twentieth century: the concentration camps of Europe, the atomic bombs of Asia. 'Of' Asia? No, in Asia, but of Euro-America. So, though Turner almost convinces me with his optimism, these daymares return. For the horrors of war are not nighttime things but the outcomes of our most scrupulously rational thinkings, of our most highly exercised cerebral cortexes. More nightmares might be among the remedies recommended for the generals, the Haigs, Weinbergers, and Reagans. I don't exempt the warriors of other nations; I just don't know their names.

The final scene of *Dead End Kids*—the Mabou Mines performance piece that's all about nuclear energy, experimentation, and holocaust —is a parody of a sleazy nightclub act. The comic invites a young woman (a plant) from the audience onto the stage. He makes sex jokes with/against her. He uses as a prop a dead plucked chicken—the kind you get at the supermarket. This prop is naked flesh, dead yet vulnerable, not being used to feed anyone but to stand for the penis, the vagina, the insides of the body, the victims of atomic bombs, the raw meat we are when we are nothing else. And have you ever noticed how chicken skin is the colour of Asians? The audience reacts strongly to this scene. Some offended, some amused, some sickened. This scene—which people advised director JoAnn Akalaitis to drop—is a scary commentary on the current level of consciousness not only about things nuclear but the whole drift of our species towards globacide.

Having lost a sense of the sacred, we also lose awareness of the terrible. So what's so bad about atomic warfare, lead in the air, ozone depletion, extermination of nonhuman species? Everything can be talked about, understood, dealt with, defended against.

I'm not talking about the technological imperative: our almost automatic belief that for every problem there's a solution.

I'm talking about something happening to language, including the languages of art. To 'look something in the face'—to end taboos, to be able to discuss it openly—is believed somehow to be equivalent to solving the problem. But really this openness is a way of deadening.

Again it's an invasion of the rational into spheres of nonrational—what word can I use? certainly not thought—process. The deep process of imagination has been contaminated.

V

Now back to Turner's future of subjunctive worlds, which is a call to re-imagine. Can it be done as efficiently as scarred landscape is reforested, or depleted fisheries farmed? Are we arriving at the paradox in human self-directed evolution when the unconscious, the primary process, is to be directly fertilized? Having spent so much energy in training the cortex to control the rest of the brain, are we now to seek out a limbic resurgence?

There's no way back to a genuine premodernism. Who wants it anyway? Human life then was threatened by the environment. Today human life threatens the environment. What we need is a balance.

In the sixteenth century, after some bloody battles using rifles and cannons, the shogunate in Japan decided that this method of warfare was costing too much. Too many lives were being lost, brute firepower was replacing the more elegant earlier ways of warring. So firearms were banned, and for nearly 300 years Japan went back to its former ways of doing battle.

In today's Papua–New Guinea, warriors arrive by motorbike at the battle grounds. They park their vehicles and fight with bows, arrows, and spears. They know about guns, but know too that their small populations would soon be decimated if guns were used.

Peace loving? No. But there are limits to war. These are very low. War needs to be made a handcraft again.

How can performance art assist in this? And in the other transformations necessary for human social survival.

Experimental theatre in America—and in Europe, too, from what I can gather—is in a bad way. Experiment means, literally, to 'go beyond the boundaries'. There's not much of that going on these days. As things have gotten desperate outside of theatre, they've become more conservative within. The great period of experimentation that began in the fifties ended by the mid-seventies. In my essay 'Decline and Fall of the (American) Avant-garde' (*Performing Arts Journal*, nos. 14 and 15 [1981]) I discuss the history of this period and the reasons for the decline in detail. No need to belabour the story here. What I want to focus on is the phoenix aspect: what's rising from the ashes. For the experimental period has given us the foundation in practice for what Turner calls for in his letter.

This foundation is a performance art based on postmodern consciousness. A consciousness that relies on bundles and networks, on spheres, modes, and relations. It is a performance world reminiscent of medieval totalism, where actions are instantly transformed into relations. This performance world is the source of renewals of religion —and by religion I don't mean only the known creeds, most of which are frozen, nor do I mean theology. I mean sacralizing the relations among people: creating special, sacred, nonordinary—you pick your descriptive adjective—space and time. And enacting within, or in relation to, such space/time events that resonate significance not only to the audience but also to the performers.

Ironically, the modern period, which made 'man the measure of all things', proposed an idea that could not yet operate openly. Forget for now whether this programme was projecting a social order dominated by males at the expense of females, and whether there is enough innate difference in aggressive potential to make the male–female argument worthwhile at the level of 'who rules'. The modernist programme was humanist—extraordinarily noble and optimistic. But it didn't work out so well for whales, forests, and billions of human beings born outside of Europe, North America, Japan, and a few other domiciles of superiority, economically/militarily speaking.

Maybe, if you like Turner's scheme of reality, the humanist world was a subjunctive possibility dreamt in the fifteenth century a few epochs before its time.

The posthumanist, postmodern subjunctivity we are in the first moments of dreaming these days may be better suited to our capabilities. I see ten qualities of this postmodern subjunctively projected future.

1. It is multicentric. Everything, or nothing, is at the centre. Experiences exist without frames, giving time/space a sense of 'insideness', of being-in-it. Experience—flow alternating with reflexivity, an awareness of flow even while not stopping flow—replaces analysis. This multicentricity demands the construction of holistic, global systems. Because there is no centre there must instead be an order of relations, not a hierarchy or a pyramid or a circle with a centre point, but more like what the earth's atmosphere looks like from close space: whorls, and constantly shifting but totally interrelated patterns of movements. Socially, such comprehension of a global ecosystem leads to a feeling of limitedness, of feedback, recycling, inner-focusing. It's not too big a leap from there to ideas of reincarnation, which is a way of saying there is feedback of personal-being-soul-stuff as well as of the more obvious material stuff.

But.

Actually, the concept of multicentricity and holism do not contradict but need each other. Both indicate fully significant worlds, and both indicate the dominance of rhythmicity over all other kinds of space/time orderings. Not lines, which mean single-point perspective, but rhythmical relations, which mean dance.

This danced universe is opposed to the modernist ideal of an ever-expanding—that is, receding—point of origin or frame of reality, and an equally expanding human consciousness that regularly 'breaks through', leading to 'new fields' that sooner or later are 'known'. Clearly, that world is the one from the age of great discoveries by Euro-American navigators and astronomers, the line from da Gama and Galileo to Glenn and *Voyager*.

This line need not end for multicentricity to take over. Multicentricity is just that, multiple.

2. The ability to support, even delight in, contradictory or radically paradoxical propositions simultaneously. From the sound of one hand clapping to a frameless yet limited cosmos. Here's where clowns and shamans come in. And theatricalism as the realm of reality founded on projecting experiences that are true/not-true.

3. The process of knowing that the 'thing' is part of the 'thing and the experiencer of the thing'. All observations are participations. And all participations are creations. The modern ideal:

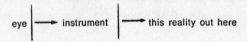

becomes the postmodern:

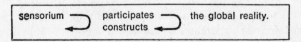

Also reflexivity develops as each global reality is experienced both from within and from without simultaneously. The experiencer is also that which experiences herself experiencing. Dizzying, fun, subjunctive (as if, would, could, should); terrifying, hard to hold onto, uncertain, relative.

4. In the modern period people could correctly speak of absolutes. In the postmodern each set of relationships generates transformations that hold true for this or that operation. As modern seeing becomes postmodern experiencing, postmodern performance leaves the proscenium theatre and takes place in a multiplicity of spaces. The proscenium theatre is known for two qualities: there is a best seat in the house; there are clearly defined areas for different activities— stage, backstage, house, lobby. Half the structure belongs to the performers, half to the spectators. The postmodern performance space is strictly relational: you don't know what it is until you use it for whatever you are doing. Although it seems that now we're in a reactionary period where the proscenium theatre appears to be making a comeback, this is only an illusion. Of course orthodox spaces are being used, but so are countless new spaces that twenty-five years ago weren't. Like galleries, lofts, clubs, courtyards, beaches, roofs, streets. The environmental possibilities of performance have expanded to include dozens of new territories.

Not only space, but time too. I mean time as a when and time as an experience of. Again this emergence of rhythmicity.

5. The use of multiple channels of communication. This goes beyond the human. Everything from genetic codes to lasers to body language to pulsars seems to be 'saying' something. An aspect of the totality of significance. And in performance it is no longer necessary

to put forward the linguistic channel as the dominant one. There is multicentricity of communication as well as of experience and cosmic construction.

This is the operational feature of Turner's subjunctive worlds. As many worlds as can be imagined can be communicated. Or maybe it's more interesting the other way: as many worlds as can be communicated can be imagined.

The artistic mind—the mind that specializes in inventing possible worlds—is emergently important.

How does this jibe with Lévi-Strauss's painful witnessing of humans reduced to meat and excretion? The horrors he writes of are the products of humanism. The delights of the connoisseur and the luxuries of the rich are resting on the backs of the poor. These horrors will not just go away. But I doubt whether revolution as conceived of from the eighteenth through twentieth centuries is the answer either.

How to eliminate or at least reduce these horrors until they are a fraction of the many, is the main thing this writing is playing with.

Playfulness may be part of the answer.

6. The alternation of flow and reflexivity. Sometimes we're in it, sometimes we're out of it. Even when we're out of it, we're in it; and even when we're in it, we're out of it watching ourselves in it.

A very theatrical way of doing things. Rehearsing, stopping, repeating, taking the action up in the middle, playing around with it, making it 'better'.

Also a way of theatre-going, wherein spectators do not agree to disbelieve in what's going on. This disagreement to disbelieve preserves individual experience in a collective act.

The alternation of flow and reflexivity leads to fragmentation as well as holism.

The postmodern transmutation is not of gold but of experiences, not to perfect heavy metals but to offer new ways of being, which are ways of doing, ways of performing.

7. Dreams are not considered only secondary reflections of hidden primary processes. Dreams are not automatically in need of interpretations that strip them of their imagery.

In 1977 I ran a dream workshop at American University. During two hot weeks about a dozen of us shared sleeping space and performance workshop space. We observed each other sleep and dream, and experimented with controlling our dreams and performing dreams immediately upon being awakened from them. Systematically some of the differences between waking and dreaming consciousness were elided. Persons experienced mutual dreaming (where two or more dream the same dreams, or elements of the same dream) and lucid dreaming (a dream where you know you are dreaming—an ultimate in reflexivity). Finally we staged for ourselves a sequence of dreams, and acted out within the Washington area aspects of our dream-lives.

The workshop was scary. But I'd like to resume its experiments.

Also to look more to dreams as Aborigines experience them. As gateways to the first time, as a way of making present that first time.

Interestingly, dreams in several cultures are the sources of dances. Dreamers learn dances while dreaming, and bring the dances back.

Dreams, vision quests, trance.

The nightlife of the brain. What worlds are there waiting to be staged.

But not dreams in their mystical sense. Dreams, rather, as a continuation and elaboration of day-brain activities. In other words, along with the expansion of brain activity to include both noncortical and cortical languages—body languages as well as verbal languages— a parallel integration of the night brain and the day brain. This has been going on a long time. The theories of Freud are based largely on his investigations of dreams. But he attempted to interpret dreams rationally, to see them as texts presented by the unconscious to be sorted out, understood, by the conscious. Such interpretation needed the assistance of another, the analyst. So that, in fact, there were three or four interactants in Freud's scheme: the conscious and unconscious of dreamer and analyst. I don't want to abandon Freud's process, but add to it the ability to apprehend the dreaming directly, without translating it or reducing it.

To a degree, this is what Robert Wilson and Richard Foreman have been doing. Wilson in regard to time, the showing in space of different rhythms of time, different ways of thinking-doing, including the ways of dreaming. And Foreman by his insistence on trying to represent in the theatre as clearly as possible the primary process of his own thinking, unedited. And, as it is becoming increasingly clear, day thinking is like night thinking, if we let it come through unedited. Writers have known this, but it is taking longer to get through to the theatre. Cultures other than Euro-American have also known, and practised, performances based directly on primary process activity.

8. This relates to accepting body thought alongside cerebral cortex

thinking. As the concept of body thought is unpacked, people will discover how many different modes of thought our species can do. We already know that learning and artistic expression can occur autonomously, like dreaming. Again dance is a good model, for much dance learning is at the neuromuscular and subcortical brainstem levels. The development of body thinking is not threatening to cortical thinking, any more than the discovery of left-brain, right-brain tendencies threatens word language. What I am arguing for is the coexistence of many different kinds of thought, and a discriminating use of different kinds of thinking for different kinds of tasks. This means, for me at least, that cortical—rational—thinking is, and remains, very very important. It is the kind of thinking used in making the discriminations necessary to use other kinds of thinking; it is the kind of thinking used in writings like the one you're reading; and it is the kind of thinking used in doing the reading.

It's the same in making theatre. I don't want to throw away words, text, dialogue, narrative, character relationships. I want to use them in a fuller range of theatrical expressions. Certainly, the finest works of postmodern theatre show this wish to include, not exclude, to expand the range of thinking, theatrical technique, language—all kinds of languages.

9. Process itself is performance. Rehearsals can be more informative/ performative than finished work. The whole structure of finishedness is called into question. If the world is unfinished, by what process are the works of people finished? Why should these works be finished? The world is a process we are making and changing as we go along. This is the nub of Turner's optimism. The virtual futures we construct are predictions, some of which are being translated into actualities. And this is what a rehearsal does, how it works.

It is not an excuse for sloppiness, lack of discipline, self-indulgence— any of the errors so often associated with process work. It is not a mask for mysticisim or self-serving obscurantism. It is more like the scientific method, through which every assertion is the basis for further investigation, counterassertion, more experimentation, and/or observation, further work.

Kaprow's pieces and Grotowski's series of explorations—Holiday, the 'active culture' phase, Theatre of Sources—are examples of process performance. This work is always prey to preciousness, indulgence, exploitation. Nothing stinks worse than rancid sincerity. But still, it is worth the mess. Because process work is the true leading edge of knowledge. Not the historical avant garde, which is an art movement along with all the rest, but a way of approaching experience, a method of seeing and dealing with the world.

10. Interculturalism is replacing—ever so tenderly, but not so slowly—internationalism. The nation is the force of modernism; and the cultures—I emphasize the plural—are the force (what word can replace force?) of postmodernism. As a world information order comes into being, human action can be mapped as a relationship among three levels:

PAN-HUMAN, EVEN SUPRA-HUMAN,
COMMUNICATIONS NETWORKS.
information from/to anywhere, anyone

....

CULTURES. CULTURES OF CHOICE.
ethnic, individualistic, local behaviours
people selecting cultures of choice
people performing various subjunctive actualities

....

PAN-HUMAN BODY BEHAVIOURS/DREAM—
ARCHETYPE NETWORKS.
unconscious and ethological basis of
behaviour and cultures

This map may scare you. It sometimes scares me. It can be of a totalitarian society, an Orwellian world. But it can also—depending on what people 'predict' from it—liberate. It depicts three spheres, or levels, or actualities; but the dotted lines say that a lot of sponging up and down—transfers, transformations, links, leaks—joins these realms, making of them one very complicated system. Yes, that's what's most interesting to me: the whole thing is one system. I mean, without the overarching and the underpinning universals there is little chance for the middle—the multiplicity of cultures—ever achieving harmony, ever combining stability with continuously shifting relations among and in the midst of many different items.

Maybe the most exciting aspect of this map is the possibility for people to have 'cultures of choice'.

People are born into a culture. They get that culture, maybe some of it before they are even born. Each culture has its distinct ways of doing things; and these ways as much as anything, from the experience of birth on, form individual human beings. Are infants swathed or allowed to run free? Are they nursed on demand or according to a schedule? Are they born into large families, even extended families, where many different people care for them directly, or into small families, even families of one person only, where there is a single caretaker? And so on, through what kinds of food are eaten, who the playmates are, what are the toys, etc. On through all the experiences of living. I don't think this culturing will change. But I do think that very early on—I mean after two or three years—children can be given the experience of different cultures. Again, like second languages, there can be second cultures. And surely, as children grow to an age where they make choices for themselves—and I don't know how my own sense of what this age is, is actually determined by my own cultural habits, is not something absolute and fixed—as kids become people capable of making choices, one of the things they must be encouraged to do is to go into several cultures other than the one they were born in. This will be the groundwork for cultures of choice.

Our current view, I think, is soaked with a kind of belief in genetic racism, the assumption that only blacks can be African (in the full black African sense) or that kids from Brooklyn can't be Amer-Indians. But as cultures more and more come to be performative actions, and information links among them emerge into view, people will choose cultures the way many of us now choose what foods to eat. I'm aware of the cruel irony here: altogether too many of the world's people not only can't choose what foods to eat, but even whether they can eat or not.

'Cultures of choice' may not be 'of choice' at all but a function of the political and economic turmoil of this century: many millions of people have become refugees and/or immigrants. Wars, famines, need for cheap labour, exploitation, adventurism: there are many reasons why people have moved from one culture to another. These moves, of course, are as old as human history—but I believe they have accelerated greatly over the past 150 years or so. Efficient means of transportation coupled with an ever more integrated world economy, and the particular cruelty and magnitude of this century's wars (not only the wars in/of Europe but wars in Africa, Asia, Latin America, the Middle East: everywhere), have combined to put dozens of millions of people on the road. Many of these people—along with the more fortunate ones, artists especially, who have chosen second cultures (or even third, fourth . . .)—are in a very unusual ontological and social situation. They are no longer part of their cultures of birth nor are they totally part of their cultures of choice. And if they return to their birth cultures—as many artists have done—they find themselves in a situation closely akin to Brecht's *verfremsdungeffekt*: distanced even from the familiar. These people are, in a sense, strangers in whatever culture they are in. Or, conversely, they are 'almost at home' in more than one culture. In either case, these people are in the position of performers: they are always learning 'how to be' in whatever cultural situation they find themselves (by choice, by dint of 'crashing circumstances').

There is some actual culture choosing going on right now. Some of it forced on people. In New York City, at the McBurney Y on 23rd Street—about six blocks from where I live—the Thunderbird American Indian Dancers run powwows on a monthly basis. Powwow is itself a form of pan-Indian gathering that developed in the nineteenth century as the Euro-Americans annihilated the Indians and drove them to reservations where they were regarded not as Sioux or Kiowa or Cherokee but as Indian. As it exists in New York—and I think parallels can be found elsewhere—the powwow combines social dancing, ceremonial dancing, socializing, and the display and auctioning of artifacts. Ann Marie Shea and Atay Citron have been studying the McBurney powwow. They find that it has at its core the question of identity. Who is an Indian, how is this identity discovered, displayed, reinforced? There is a lot of debate among Indians about this. But at McBurney actual Indians, genetically speaking, dance side-by-side with many who are only part Indian and many others— enthusiasts and hobbyists, they are called—who are not Indian at all, but who participate very fully in the Thunderbird's activities. Ann Shea and Citron, in a yet to be published study of the McBurney powwow, write, 'Some organizers and board members are not Indian. ... Yet Marvin ('Standing Bear' according to his Sioux name) is unofficial sergeant at arms for nearly every event; Charlotte appeared in both the January stage show and the fashion show; Arnie is a regular drummer and auctioneer; ... Matt is a fixture of the Fancy Dance competitions.'

It can get complicated. At one McBurney powwow some enthusiasts showed up for the dancing with top hats and tuxedo elements as part of their dancing costumes. These people had carefully researched what Indians wore to the powwows of the 1880s. The attire that included, eclectically, elements of Western clothing were more authentic historically than the 'all natural' feather works worn by many contemporary Indians. But what does authenticity mean? By the 1880s Indians had included in their ceremonial dress many things that weren't originally Indian. People are always doing that. What's different these days—with our ability to preserve on film and in photographs much direct evidence of 'how it was'—is also the ability to ransack different periods and select authenticity according to how the evidence is assembled and performed. The enthusiasts at the McBurney powwow were both more and less authentic than the 'actual' Indians. My point is that this kind of actuality will increasingly become a matter of choice for all of us—and not simply an unhappy residue of genocide.

To a degree I'm taking up Turner's challenge in this writing. I do not endorse in any sense what people have done to people, or what we as a species are doing to the biosphere. But I do think we have to incorporate our histories, our collective experiences, into our ways of being. That is, because genocide was practised against the American Indians is no reason to reject the McBurney powwow. Or even to reject its means of culture of choice. That descendants of the ones who committed the genocide are dancing side-by-side with descendants of the victims . . . well, make of it what you will, I refuse to reject this kind of behaviour out of hand.

I think that the possibilities for the world are actually very grim. The future proposed by *Global 2000 Report* seems to be what most people are dreaming these days. But, Turner says, if we imagine, and work towards incarnating, embodying, making real what we imagine —and this is close to a working definition of what artists do—then we can bring into existence another future, not the one envisioned by *Global 2000*. And that is what I am doing at this moment.

There is a politics of the imagination, as well as a politics of direct action. The politics of direct action is aimed at the injustices of the world. We need that kind of politics. The politics of the imagination is aimed at describing virtual or subjunctive futures, so that these can be steered towards or avoided. The politics of the imagination is real. That is why so much effort is spent by totalitarian regimes, fascist regimes, capitalist industry, and others, to gain thought control and control over human expression. You could almost say these people attempt to control dreaming, the primary process itself. They aim at depriving the people—masses and artists alike—of having imaginative alternatives. Imaginative? Actual alternatives.

For imagination, Turner is saying and I'm agreeing, is an actual alternative: it is the opening to any number of alternatives. Not the idle dreams that go up in smoke, that don't get translated into action, that are cheapened by interpretation after interpretation. But the kind of things I've been talking about: performative acts of great power.

VI

Crashing performative circumstances = emergence of subjunctive processual worlds = changing human consciousness = the inevitable and reflexive awareness of psychophysical evolution = the ability to restore behaviour = cultures of choice = free dreaming = ????

The alternative?

There are billions of alternatives.

Index